PC Video
MADNESS!

PC Video MADNESS!

Ron Wodaski

A Division of Prentice Hall Computer Publishing
11711 North College, Carmel, Indiana 46032 USA

*This book is dedicated to the one person
who did so much to make it possible: my wife,
Donna Brown-Wodaski.*

Overview

Contents

Acknowledgments

I owe the biggest debt of gratitude to my wife, Donna, whose support was essential to completing this book. I've also received outstanding cooperation from numerous companies whose software and hardware is reviewed in this book. It takes a lot of effort to ship dozens and dozens of products in both directions, and I'd like to take this opportunity to publicly thank everyone who helped out in this regard.

A special thanks goes to our two kids, Justen and Chanel, who had to wait sometimes while Daddy finished a chapter.

I also want to tip my hat to all the folks in the various multimedia-realted forums on CompuServe. If you aren't already a member of CompuServe, you're missing out on one of the world's best idea exchanges. I visit the multimedia forums every day, both to answer questions and to learn. Multimedia in general and PC Video in particualr are fast evolving fields. Electronic communication is the most effective way to keep up-to-date.

About the Author

Ron Wodaski currently resides in a small community on Puget Sound, Washinton, where he tries to keep up with the latest advances in multimedia. He started out as a journalist, but caught the computer bug when he bought one of the original Osborne computers as a word processor.

He designed and wrote custom software using BASIC and dBASE II for several years, eventually joining the dBASE team at Ashton-Tate until it was merged with Borland. Somewhere along the line, he graduated to C and then retired to Visual Basic and Toolbook. He has worn a number of different hats in the computer industry, including programming, test management, project management, and product design.

He currently writes books on a variety of computer subjects, creates a monthly multimedia column for *Nautilus* (a CD-ROM magazine), pens the occasional science fiction story, and writes documentation for several software and hardware companies. When no one is looking, he avoids computers entirely.

Introduction

The first time I saw Video for Windows, I was very impressed. The idea of digital video, right there on my computer screen—especially video I can capture myself—excited me. I've been involved with microcomputers almost from the beginning, and I've seen a lot of technology come and go. I had one of the first portable computers, an Osborne Executive. It was a miracle machine, with 128K of memory and CPM (Version 3). Like many miracles that followed, it didn't last very long. I felt very lucky to sell it a year later for about a third of what I payed for it.

That was ten years ago, and I didn't really expect to see something that would get me excited at a visceral level. Video for Windows changed all that. I'm a kid again!

Not everyone is as excited as I am about digital video, however, and I want to take a moment to explain. When Video for Windows first hit the scene, it was like a dancing elephant: it was so unusual that it was wonderful it could be done at all. But when the first excitement faded, everyone noticed a few things:

➤ The size of the video window was very small—160x120 pixels.

➤ The playback rate was slow, 15 frames per second, sometimes even less.

➤ The image quality was limited by the need to compress frames.

➤ The cost of reliable, quality capture hardware was too high.

Granted, these are legitimate complaints. A small window isn't as much fun as a big window. Slow frame rates result in jerky playback. Poor image quality is hard on the eyes. And money is, well, money.

But, after all, the elephant *was* dancing.

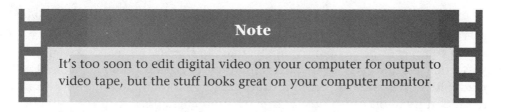

Note

It's too soon to edit digital video on your computer for output to video tape, but the stuff looks great on your computer monitor.

And there are lots of great ways to use digital video on a computer:

➤ Interactive training materials

➤ Sales presentations

➤ Kiosks

➤ Multimedia software

➤ Electronic mail (yes, electronic mail!)

➤ Corporate presentations

➤ Creative multimedia

➤ As an art form

The What of Digital Video

It's important to realize why digital video is hard to do, and why conventional video is easy. This is also a good place to introduce some technical terms that you'll be seeing later in the book.

Digital video is not at all like the video you watch on your TV, or that you get from a video tape, or on cable. All of those video sources are analog. (Analog means "varies continuously.") That means that they all rely on a single signal that varies as the image is traced onto the screen. It's the single signal that makes that easy to do. You might think of it as being as easy as drawing a line with a pencil—it doesn't take long to draw a single line.

Digital video, on the other hand, is, well, *digital*. (Digital means "varies in steps.") A digital image describes each tiny dot in the image (a dot is called a *pixel*). It takes more effort to put a digital image on a screen. Painting a digital image on a screen is like drawing a line using a series of dots—it takes longer that way, but it's very precise.

That precision is the whole reason that digital video is desirable. Have you ever compared a TV screen to a computer screen? The TV screen isn't very precise. If you ever owned a home computer that put characters on a TV screen, you know that putting even 40 characters from left to right was about the limit of readability. A standard computer monitor uses 80 characters, and high-resolution monitors can double or triple that number.

Because a digital image is made up of pixels, it's very easy to make copies of an image. Each pixel is precise. A certain number describes just how bright the pixel is, what color it is, and so on. An analog signal varies continuously, so there is no precise number for each point on the screen. Each copy is a little less precise; if you make a copy of a copy, it gets worse. Figure 0.1 is an origial video image; Figure 0.2 comes from a tape copy of the original; Figure 0.3 is a copy of the copy; and Figure 0.4 is a tenth-generation copy.

You can make as many copies of a digital image as you want to; it never changes because the numbers don't change. This is what makes digital video so desirable: you can modify the image as much as you want without losing clarity in the image. The high-end video equipment in video production studios is all digital for exactly this reason. Those commercials you see with 50 images of the same actor, or characters from old movies, or cars turning into tigers, are only possible with digital video.

But that kind of digital video isn't available on your desktop computer—yet.

Figure 0.1. The original video image.

Figure 0.2. A tape copy of the original.

Figure 0.3. A copy of the copy.

Figure 0.4. A tenth-generation copy.

The Zen of Digital Video

Let's return to the four basic problems of digital video: size, rate, quality, and cost.

It only takes a moment of contemplation to understand that it will not be too difficult to deal with these four problems. In fact, the technology to solve each of these problems is already there, waiting only for predictable advances in hardware and software technology to bring the solutions into the mainstream.

I will cover the details of many of these issues in Chapter 11, *Hardware for Recording*. But you should also know something about the issues behind the technology. Let's examine each obstacle, one at a time.

Small Video Window

Digital video stores a lot of information about each pixel in an image. It takes time to put those pixels on your computer screen. If the image is small, there is enough time to paint each image completely. If the image is large, the entire image

cannot be put on-screen before it's time to start the next one. There are several ways that this can be dealt with. Faster hard disks will make it possible to read the image from the disk faster. Faster video hardware will make it possible to paint the image on the screen faster. It is even possible to build capabilities into the hardware just for faster video playback.

Slow Frame Rates

The issues behind slow frame rates are the same as for the small size of the video window—too many pixels, and not enough time. The frame rate is limited by disk speed and video speed.

There's another consideration as well. One way to move more data around more quickly is to compress the data. There are two ways to compress data—using software, or using hardware. Software compression is slow compared to hardware compression. Software compression relies on a general purpose computer chip, otherwise known as the CPU. The CPU has a lot of other work to do, which slows down the compression/decompression process. Hardware compression is faster because it uses a specialized computer chip, whose only job is to handle the compression and decompression of the video images.

Right now, such chips are very expensive, and there are several of them to choose from. In the not-too-distant future, if it becomes cost effective to put such chips on the motherboard of your computer, high frame rates will become affordable. There are already some hardware compression capture/playback boards at the high end of the comsumer price scale.

Hardware compression will also make it possible to use larger image sizes. For right now, most digital video will involve software compression and decompression. As you will see later on, in Chapter 8, "Digital Video Compression: Tradeoffs You Can Live With," some software compression is definitely better than others.

Low Image Quality

Low image quality results from compression. The kinds of compression used with digital video are called *lossy compression*. The name is accurate: these compression techniques result in loss of detail in an image.

For example, look at Figure 0.5. It shows an original captured digital video image—a single frame. Figure 0.6 shows the same frame after compression. There are a variety of compression techniques, and each results in a different kind of data loss.

Figure 0.5. An original captured digital image.

Figure 0.6. The same digital image after compression.

In an ideal world, you wouldn't have to compress the video at all. But the data rate of full-screen, uncompressed video is astronomical. Consider the arithmetic:

3 bytes per pixel for accurate color
640 bytes wide
480 bytes high
30 frames per second
60 seconds per minute

A little quick multiplication shows that it would take 1,658,880,000 bytes to store one minute of digital video—that's just under 1.6 gigabytes. For one minute of video. That means a half-hour sitcom would require 48 gigabytes (less if you don't include the commercials) of disk storage.

That should make it clear why compression is essential.

By the way, that doesn't include audio data storage. Add another 5.3 to 10.5 megabytes per minute for CD-quality audio (mono or stereo, respectively). Normally, 10 megabytes per minute would seem outrageous, but it looks downright trivial next to 1.6 gigabytes.

Fortunately, all is not lost. Data compression rates from 10:1 to 25:1 provide reasonable image quality. At 25:1 compression, you only need 64 megabytes per minute for full-screen video. If filling just one quarter of the screen meets your needs, and you can live with 16-bit (not 24-bit) color, you can cut that down to just under 11 megabytes per minute. Hey—that's quite reasonable compared to a gigabyte and a half, right?

And if huge hard drives become economical, so much the better.

By the way, there's another advantage to compression: because there's less data to pass around, the bottlenecks—video and the hard disk—are less of a problem.

High Cost

So far, the cost of hardware keeps dropping. Because we are nowhere near the theoretical limits of what can be done in hardware, there's no reason to think that that will change. As prices drop and the performance of what you can afford goes up, digital video becomes more and more practical.

The When of Digital Video

Thus the only important question about digital video is: when? I have spoken with some of the engineers who are working—now, today—on the kinds of solutions I just outlined. I can't reveal any secrets, but it is safe to say that it won't be very long before what you can do on your computer will be as exciting, powerful, and creative as the work being done in the major studios right now.

If you buy the right hardware and software, in fact, you can do a lot of those things already. It's too soon to put the results on video tape for general distribution, but it looks great on your computer monitor right now. If you don't believe me, all you have to do is look at the CD-ROM that comes with this book.

P A R T I

Video for Windows

1

Fun with Video
for Windows

Once upon a time, there were several ways to put video on a computer, but none of them were selling all that well. There was Intel, with its trusty DVI that could capture a video sequence. And then there were all of the capture boards—Video Blaster, Super VideoWindows, Bravado, Snap Plus, and so on—which could capture one frame at a time. Quality was all over the map, from buggy and quixotic to professional, from wiggly to solid as a rock, and from uncertain color to sharp, accurate color.

The market was fragmented, and not going anywhere fast. Then along came Video for Windows.

If you have already seen Video for Windows or own a copy of it, you know that it excels at capturing a live video sequence. By making Video for Windows a natural part of Windows, Microsoft has put video squarely into the mainstream. Now we can all (well, if we have a 386, anyway) play videos on our computers.

First Look: Playback

Several months ago, while I was participating in the beta program for Video for Windows, I was preparing a multimedia presentation. It was for the multimedia magazine *Nautilus*, which is a CD-ROM magazine. (The CD-ROM disc in the back of this book includes a sample issue of the magazine, by the way. I think you'll find it interesting.)

I had just received my first video capture board, a Bravado from Truevision, and I used it to add some video to the presentation—myself talking about multimedia, as a matter of fact. I wanted to make a point: the computers we have now are really *monomedia* computers, and what we are now calling *multimedia* is what computers really ought to be like. It's like stereo versus mono: once we had stereo, mono just disappeared. I hope the same thing happens with multimedia.

I invited my two kids up to the office to look at what I had put together; they are excellent critics. If they fall asleep, or even start talking, I know that the presentation doesn't have enough punch.

They were beginning to fidget when the video part came on. Their jaws literally dropped when they saw the on-screen video. When they had recovered a bit, words such as "neat" and "radical" came out.

That's the "dancing elephant" effect of on-screen video—it's something a lot of folks haven't even heard of before. It's very impressive the first time you see it. If you haven't seen one yourself, now is the perfect time.

The first step is to install the Video for Windows drivers that are included on the floppy disk. If you have not yet installed the drivers, refer to the instructions for installation, located at the end of the Introduction. Once you have them installed, here is all you have to do to start having fun:

1. Open Media Player. (It will be a new version of Media Player that supports OLE for video files.)

2. Select Video for Windows on the Device menu.

3. Select a file with the extension .AVI; this will open the video file.

4. Click the play button at the lower-left of the Media Player window. (This window is shown later in Figure 1.4.)

5. Sit back and enjoy playback!

That's the really neat part about Video for Windows—it's so easy to use. In this chapter, you learn how to fine-tune playback.

What Is Video for Windows, Anyway?

There has been much confusion about just what Video for Windows *is*. That's understandable because there is a lot of high tech behind it. To begin with, Video for Windows is a *standard*. It's not about image size, compression techniques, or other specifics. It is the larger package where all those things are housed.

To give you a better idea of what I mean, look at some other standards. Consider the high-end Windows video standard, 1024x768. It's not limited to just one kind of hardware board. There is a wide variety of video cards that support this standard. All that matters is that the board support that screen size (1024x768). Well, there are some other considerations—8, 16, or 24 bits per pixel, for example—but the point is that as long as you meet the standards set for that screen size, you're OK.

Video for Windows is like that—as long as you have the right hardware and software in your computer, you can play with Video for Windows.

The two parts of the standard are hardware and software.

Hardware Standards

The hardware part of the standard is as flexible as can be. The bottom line is that a wide variety of hardware types can be used successfully with Video for Windows. You will find both inexpensive and expensive boards on the market. The less costly hardware may have certain limitations, whereas the more expensive hardware adds sophisticated features.

For example, the least expensive hardware is usually limited to an image size of 160x120 pixels and to a frame rate of 15 frames per second. For comparison, analog video uses 30 frames per second. (Chapter 5 "Digital Video Recording Secrets and Techniques," covers the hardware issues in detail.) The better hardware adds things such as hardware compression, which optimizes capture and playback so that you can use larger image sizes and faster frame rates.

Software Standards

The software part of the standard is also very flexible. As long as a hardware manufacturer provides a software driver for its capture card, the steps to capture a video sequence are almost exactly the same for each piece of hardware. For playback, as long as you have the matching driver installed, you can play back any Video for Windows sequence.

There is one exception to this. Boards that compress and/or decompress using special hardware (hardware compression) create video sequences that cannot be played back with software alone. To play back such a file, you need the same kind of hardware that was used to capture it.

Fun with Video

You can do a lot of serious things with video in a window. You can dress up a sales presentation, or include action examples of how to assemble a robot in an online instructional manual.

There are many fun things you can do, too. If you have a video capture board, you can put some of your home videos on your computer. I have included some of my own favorite home videos on the CD-ROM disc that comes with this book. One of my personal favorites is racoon.avi; you can find it in the directory \video\animals.

Even if you don't have a video capture card, you can have fun with videos. There is a screen saver on the floppy disk that plays video files, and it is easy to use. Use the copy command to copy the file from the floppy disk that comes with this book to your Windows directory. For example, to copy the screen saver and a sample video to c:\windows from floppy drive a:, type the following two commands:

copy a:\vidsaver\vidsaver.scr c:\windows

copy a:\vidsaver\scr_sav.avi c:\windows

To make this your active screen saver, start the Windows Control Panel by clicking its icon.

You will see a variety of controls, as shown in Figure 1.1.

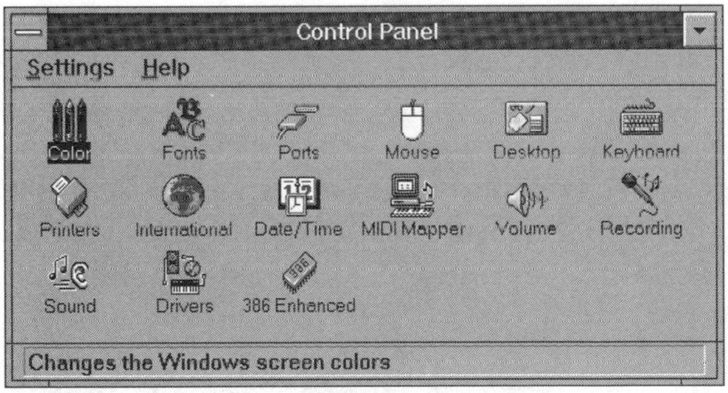

Figure 1.1. A sample Windows Control Panel.

Figure 1.1 shows the controls on my computer; yours may be somewhat different. We're interested in the one called "Desktop." Double-click the Desktop icon.

This opens the Desktop window, shown in Figure 1.2.

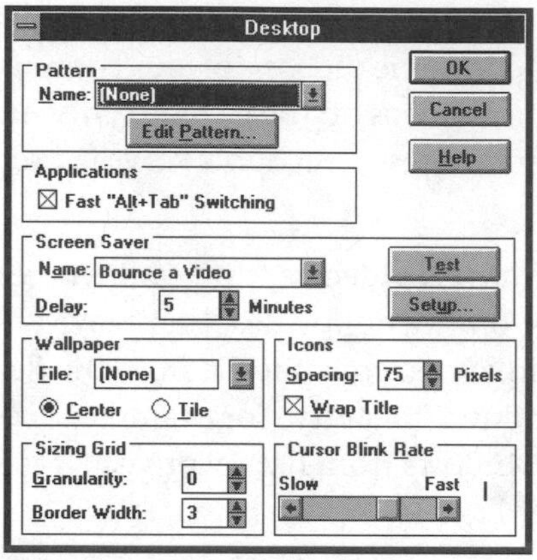

Figure 1.2. The Desktop window.

To add the Video screen saver, you will need to work with the section of the Desktop applet called "Screen Saver." It's located in the middle of the dialog box. Click the arrow at the right of the list box titled "Name," and select the screen saver "Bounce a Video" by clicking it. There may or may not be a version number.

Once you have selected the screen saver, you can set the delay time, or click the setup button to display the configuration dialog box (shown in Figure 1.3). If you do not configure the screen saver, it will play a short video that shows my neighbor's dog, Beauty, hanging by her teeth from a sock. This file was copied to your Windows directory during installation of the screen saver. The filename is scr_sav.avi. If you do choose setup, you will be able to select any .AVI file of your choice for playback.

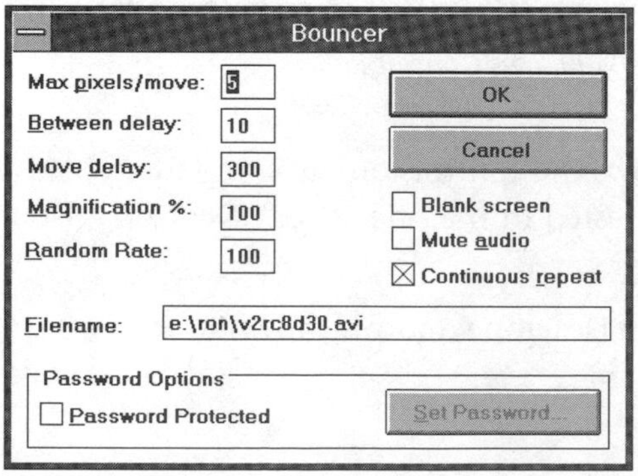

Figure 1.3. Configuration dialog box.

Using the screen saver is easy. To see how it works right away, click the Test button in the Desktop dialog box. Otherwise, wait the amount of time you set for the delay to see the video screen saver in action.

Just Playing Around

There are a surprising number of ways to play a video in Windows. By far the easiest is Media Player. A radically improved version of Media Player comes with the Video for Windows package. It improves on earlier versions in some significant ways. You can also play video files using VidEdit, part of the Video for Windows retail package, and with OLE (Object Linking and Embedding). OLE is a lot of fun because it allows you to incorporate a video into just about any cooperative Windows application. Almost all newer Windows applications work well with OLE, but you may not be so lucky with older versions of many programs.

The new Media Player is included on the floppy disk that comes with the book. If you haven't already installed the stuff on that floppy, you should do it now. You can find the instructions at the end of the introduction. The floppy includes the full runtime version of Video for Windows—everything you need to play the video sequences on the CD-ROM disc that is included with this book.

Media Player

Media Player is easy to use, but it has some hidden tricks that are worth a look, too. Let's start with the easy stuff. This section will explain everything you need to know if you haven't used the new version before, or if you haven't used Media Player at all. Even if you know the basics, you will probably find some tricks worth learning.

Media Player is installed in your Windows directory, usually c:\windows. You can find the icon in your Accessories group.

The dialog box in Figure 1.4 is from the new version of Media Player that was distributed by Microsoft with Video for Windows. If you don't have Video for Windows yet, install the Video for Windows runtime version from the CD-ROM disc included with this book. The new Media Player will be copied to your Windows directory as part of the installation. There are some important features in

the new Media Player. Not only can you use Media Player to simply play something, you can use it to edit your selection, as you'll see shortly.

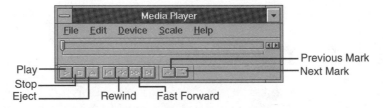

Figure 1.4. The new Media Player.

The simplest thing you can do with Media Player is play a multimedia file. Double-click the Media Player icon in the Accessories group to start the program. Once the program is running, the first thing you'll need to do is select the type of files you want to play. In our case, that's Video for Windows. Make sure the CD-ROM disc from this book is in your CD-ROM drive, and then click Device on the menu bar. You will see a list of the multimedia devices available on your computer. Figure 1.5 shows the list of devices I have available on my computer; Video for Windows is right at the top.

Figure 1.5. Media Player Device menu.

Click the Video for Windows selection; this displays a typical Windows File Open dialog. Pick any Video for Windows file. All Video for Windows files have the extension .avi. (See the sidebar "What Does AVI Mean?" for the origin of this extension.)

What Does AVI Mean?

It's not immediately obvious why Video for Windows files use the letters "AVI" as a file extension. If you think about it, the only thing it might suggest would be a bird, with *avi* being short for *avian*. But that's the wrong road.

AVI is an acronym for "Audio Video Interleaved." Interleaving refers to the mixing of audio and video data in the file. First there is some video data, then some audio data, then more video data, and so on. This kind of file is critical to practical use of digital video on the PC.

Each frame has some video and audio data associated with it. Usually, there's a *lot* of data involved. Unless you have a very fast hard disk, it can be difficult to move all that data from the disk to the screen quickly. Anything that makes it easier and faster to move that data is important.

By putting the video and audio data for each frame next to each other on the disk, it becomes very easy to pull all the information for one frame into memory. The hard disk does not have to waste time getting the video information from one place on the disk and the audio information from another.

This scheme makes it possible to read Video for Windows files from something as slow as a CD-ROM disc. A fast hard disk can move 1.5 megabytes or more of data each second. Most CD-ROM drives can only handle 150 *kilo*bytes per second—just one-tenth of what a hard disk can do. To use such low data rates for video, every single step in the process has to be as direct and uncomplicated as possible. Interleaving video and audio data is just one part of that. You'll look at several more parts of the puzzle in Part III, "Recording."

11

Once you have selected a file to play, the appearance of Media Player changes. Many of the buttons that were grayed out (inactive) are now active. To play the video, just click the Play button at the lower left of the Media Player window. Table 1.1 describes the functions of the Media Player buttons.

The way that the video plays will vary depending on how you have the options for playback set. If the playback doesn't seem suitable, there are two upcoming sections, "OLE" and "Video Playback Tips," that will help you change the options.

At the middle of the Media Player is a horizontal slider. The position marker moves along the slider to tell you approximately where you are in the video file. If it is all the way to the left, you are at the beginning of the file. If it is all the way to the right, you are at the end. Any place in between marks a relative point somewhere between the beginning and the end. You can use the numbers below the slider for reference.

The various buttons at the bottom of the window (see Figure 1.4) can be used to control playback. They are similar to the buttons you might find on a tape recorder or a VCR. Let's look at what each one does.

Table 1.1. Media Player controls.

Control	Description
Play	This is the play button. Click it to begin playing a video sequence. When the sequence starts to play, this button changes appearance, becoming the Pause button.
Pause	The play button turns into the Pause button when you click it. The button does just what you would expect: it pauses playback without changing the current position of the video.
Stop	When you are playing a video sequence, the Stop button is identical to the Pause button. It stops playback without affecting position.
Eject	This button is not active for video files. It has no meaning.

Control	Description
Previous Mark	Marks are explained later, in the section "Video Playback Tips."
Rewind	Moves the position marker back toward the beginning of the file. The move varies with the size of the file. It is larger for big files, and smaller for little ones. Usually, it moves about one-tenth of the total length of the video. For example, for a 20-second video, that would be about 2 seconds.
Fast Forward	Works just like the Rewind button, but it moves you forward instead of backward.
Next Mark	Marks are explained later, in the section "Video Playback Tips."

There are two additional buttons to the right of these buttons; they also have to do with Marks and they are also described in the section "Video Playback Tips."

I have described the buttons in terms of video operations, but most of the buttons are also used with other types of files as well. When used with other file types, the buttons sometimes have different meanings. For example, if you play a music CD-ROM, the Eject button becomes active (only, of course, if your CD-ROM player supports the capability!).

If you haven't used Media Player before, experiment with these buttons to see what they do and how they work. Because it takes a lot of the computer's time and effort to display videos, you may find that the Media Player does not respond to your mouse clicks instantaneously. You may also notice the position marker moving in short jumps—that's so the computer doesn't waste its time on screen updates while it's playing the video.

If you haven't changed any playback options, the position marker will return to the beginning of the file after playback, ready for another go.

VidEdit

VidEdit is an application that is part of Video for Windows. If you don't yet have the full Video for Windows package, you won't be able to experiment with it. I

will only cover the basic playback options of VidEdit right now. For complete information about VidEdit, see Part III of this book.

VidEdit's name describes what it does: it edits video files. It is designed primarily for basic editing tasks, such as cutting and pasting, but it also has a number of video-specific capabilities. Most of these relate to recording and compression, and are covered in Part III.

Figure 1.6 shows the main window of the VidEdit program. The first thing to notice is the set of buttons at the lower left of the window. They look a lot like the buttons in Media Player, and they work just like the buttons in Media Player. The only one missing is the Eject button; it has no meaning for a video file because there's nothing to eject.

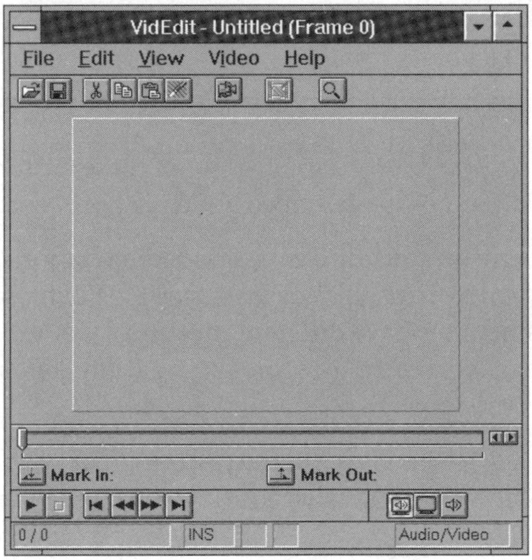

Figure 1.6. VidEdit window.

There is one other small difference. The Play button in Media Player becomes a pause button when a file is playing. The Play button in VidEdit just goes gray while the file is playing; you have to use the Stop button to pause playback.

Both Media Player and the Media Browser (an application that is included in Video for Windows) are much more handy for simple playback. Media Browser works best with CD-ROM discs that include a special index containing information about the video files on the disc. The CD-ROM that comes with Video for

Windows is a good example of this kind of disc. If you load a CD-ROM and Media Browser can't seem to find the video files on it, that disc probably doesn't have such an index.

OLE

OLE stands for *Object Linking* and *Embedding*. Not all Windows applications support OLE, and some support it partially or awkwardly. As time goes by, support is improving.

OLE is an easy way to add multimedia support to applications. If you use Word for Windows as your word processor, you can use OLE to add sounds, images, and videos to your documents. Sounds and videos aren't very useful for printed documents, but can add quite a bit to documents that will be read electronically, such as memos. You can even use OLE in a résumé, perhaps to add a brief video of yourself talking about your experiences.

To use OLE, you can start with an application such as Media Player. The newest version of Media Player has some neat new features that make OLE easier and more flexible than it has been in the past. You'll look closely at OLE in Chapter 3, "The Art of Digital Audio."

The **E**dit menu of the Media Player contains a **C**opy Object selection, as shown in Figure 1.7. When you have a file loaded in Media Player, clicking Copy **O**bject puts a copy of the object on the clipboard. You can then go to an application such as Word for Windows, click **E**dit/**P**aste, and place a copy of the object right into your document. Figure 1.8 shows how a video file looks when it is embedded in a document.

The Grand Tour

One of the favorite projects of many scientists connected with NASA some years ago was the so-called Grand Tour of the Planets. This involved taking advantage of a unique arrangement of many of the planets to send a probe to many different planets without using a lot of fuel. I'd like to take a moment to do the same thing for Video for Windows.

Figure 1.7. The Copy Object command in Media Player.

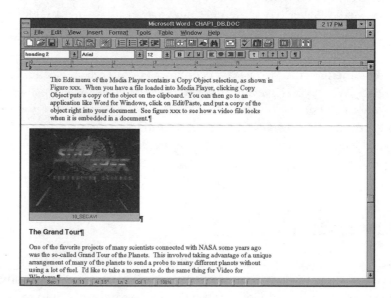

Figure 1.8. An embedded media object.

The tour starts, of course, with a video source. There are a few different possibilities because there are several devices that output suitable signals. You could hook up your family VCR, for example, or a camcorder. A regular TV signal won't work because it isn't encoded in a way that most video capture boards can handle. You could be sneaky, of course, and route the TV signal to your VCR, and then to your computer. The VCR handles the conversion very nicely, thank you.

The next stop is inside the computer, at whatever video capture card you have installed. There is quite a variety of these cards, and the prices range from modest to very high. As you'll see in Chapter 6, "Hardware for Recording," there are good reasons for these differences—different boards can be used to do different tasks. At some level, however, all boards have the same job to do: convert the analog video signal to digital video. The analog signal is made up of changes in voltage, and the digital signal is made up of the usual 1s and 0s of binary notation. How the boards accomplish this, and how well they do it, are part of the reason for differences in price and quality.

Now that we have digital data—the kind that is easily digestible by your computer—we can move the data from the card to other areas of the computer. If you have lots of memory, it might go right into some portion of memory. If your memory is more limited, the data might go right to the hard disk.

This is the sticky part of the tour. Turning that analog signal into digital data creates a huge amount of data. To work on your desktop computer, the data has to be squeezed down—compressed—before it can be handled. The squeezing is a lot of work and takes a lot of time. There are two ways to squeeze it: right on the capture board, using special-purpose chips; or with software that uses the computer's CPU. It's much faster to do it on the capture board, but the chips needed to do it are still very expensive, so most boards don't do this. Most capture cards just relay the raw data to memory or the hard disk until the capture is complete. After the capture, a software program can be run to compress the data. These programs are much slower than the special chips. It can take 15 minutes to compress even a short, 15-second video. Once it is compressed, however, decompression is much, much faster.

One way or the other, then, you wind up with a compressed video sequence on the hard disk, ready for playback. To play the file, use software such as Media Player or Media Browser, which reads the data from the hard disk (or a CD-ROM) one frame at a time. Each frame is decompressed, and the image data is routed to your video display card, which puts it on your screen.

The main reason for taking you on this tour is to make an important point: there's a lot involved in putting video on a computer. A minute of full-screen video, uncompressed, takes up about a gigabyte and a half of hard disk storage.

Add that to all the steps involved, and you can see why inexpensive hardware limits what you can do with video on a computer. The good news is that even inexpensive boards will let you do lots of functional, useful things with video. At the professional level, it takes more hardware to do the job. If you want to edit video for output to tape, well, not yet; it still takes specialized, expensive hardware to handle all that data uncompressed.

But if you want to have fun, or want to add video to a sales presentation, or merely create an interactive multimedia extravaganza, you've come to the right place.

Video Playback Tips

The Grand Tour should also help you see something else about putting video on a computer—underneath the surface, it's complicated. Software such as Media Player makes it trivial to play video files, but there are some not-so-obvious capabilities even in Media Player that you should know about right at the beginning. Knowing where to look for a few key features can save a lot of headaches.

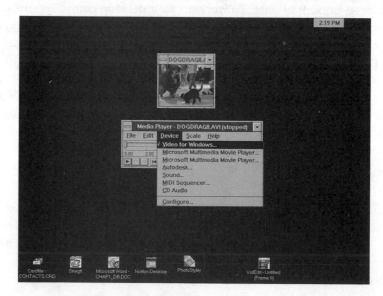

Figure 1.9. Configuring Media Player for video.

The most important thing to know about in Media Player is a menu choice on the **D**evice menu. It's called **C**onfigure, and you can see it in Figure 1.9. Clicking **D**evice|**C**onfigure brings up a dialog box (shown in Figure 1.10).

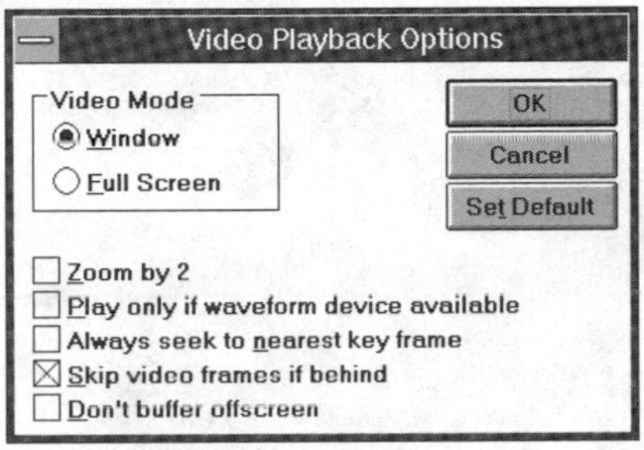

```
┌─────────────────────────────────────────────┐
│ ▭      Video Playback Options                │
├─────────────────────────────────────────────┤
│ ┌─Video Mode─────────┐  ┌──────────────┐     │
│ │ ◉ Window           │  │      OK      │     │
│ │ ○ Full Screen      │  └──────────────┘     │
│ └────────────────────┘  ┌──────────────┐     │
│                         │    Cancel    │     │
│  ☐ Zoom by 2            └──────────────┘     │
│  ☐ Play only if waveform ┌──────────────┐    │
│  ☐ Always seek to nearest│ Set Default  │    │
│  ☒ Skip video frames if b└──────────────┘    │
│  ☐ Don't buffer offscreen                    │
└─────────────────────────────────────────────┘
```

Figure 1.10. Device Configuration dialog box.

Let's look at each checkbox in turn.

Video Mode   There are two video modes: **W**indow, and **F**ull Screen. Most of the time, you'll want to use **W**indow, although some video cards will play better using the full screen. You'll have to experiment to determine which works best for you. When you play a video on the full screen, the video card has to change video modes; this may be distracting. In addition, you won't be able to view anything but the video. This means, for example, that you can't use bitmaps in the background. Depending on the size of your monitor, this may enlarge pixels to the point where the image looks too "digital" for pleasant viewing. There are just too many pixels for an adequate frame rate—many frames will just drop out. Some of the better video cards—especially those that have compression right on the hardware, such as the Intel Action Media cards—will play properly, without skipping large numbers of frames. **F**ull Screen mode uses the standard VGA 256-color screen size of 320x240. The **W**indow mode plays the video in a resizable, movable window. (See Figure 1.11.)

Zoom by 2   If this box is checked, the video will be enlarged by a factor of two. This should be used with some caution. Smaller frame sizes (160x120 or less) look blocky at larger sizes. For example, Figure 1.11 shows a video that is 160 pixels wide by 120 pixels high at normal size. Figure 1.12 shows the same video being played back at a zoom factor of 2. As you can see, the image is obviously blocky in the enlargement. In general, the more severely a video is compressed, the more blocky it will look when enlarged.

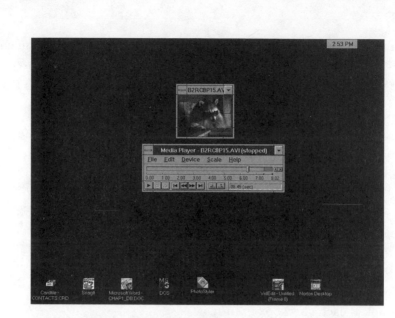

Figure 1.11. Video playing in a sizable, movable window.

Figure 1.12. Playing a video at 2x zoom.

Play only if wave audio device available   The average computer has, at most, one wave audio device. In fact, most of the popular audio devices expect to be the only one in your computer. The problem is that a wave device can play only one audio file at a time. There are two ways for your computer to handle this situation: continue playing the first sound and ignore the second one; or abort the first sound and start the second. (As a matter of fact, every time a sound is played, it must tell the system how to handle any other sounds that come along.) The sound content of a video file is really normal audio data, and is played by the wave audio device. If you play one video file, and then try to play a second one while the first is still running, the wave device is unavailable, and the second audio will not have any sound. To avoid such soundless playback, you can check this box. When it is checked, the system will refuse to play a video file if the audio device is not available.

Always seek to nearest key frame   Many video files are compressed to reduce the disk space they occupy. Most compression methods don't just reduce the size of the image in each frame; they also try more sophisticated tricks as well. One such trick is to store only the differences from one frame to the next. For example, a video of someone speaking has only very small changes from one frame to the next—moving lips, or perhaps a slight movement of the head. The background changes little, if at all. A cartoon image of a character waving one arm would have even fewer changes between frames. It's as if only a few, small portions of the frame were stored, instead of the entire frame. To keep things from getting too far out of hand, key frames—complete frame images—are stored every so often (say, every 8 or 15 frames).

Skip video frames if behind   This is probably one of the most important check boxes in this dialog box. It has the greatest effect on the playback quality of the video. As I described earlier, there are many links in the chain of events involved in playback. If one or more of those links—hard disk or CD-ROM, video display, CPU—can't handle the full frame rate, something has to give. This check box determines what that will be. If the box is checked, video frames will be dropped to allow the audio portion to play normally. That way, a ten-second clip will play for exactly ten seconds; as many frames as necessary will be skipped to allow a normal playback rate. The more frames that are dropped, of course, the jerkier the playback will be. If this box is *not* checked, each frame will be displayed no matter what. The audio will be paused until the video catches up. That means the video will display more slowly, and the audio will play in pieces.

21

Don't buffer offscreen Normally, when preparing to display the next frame of a video sequence, Windows will load the image into a memory buffer. When the time comes to display the image, it is copied to the video buffer. If you need to speed up playback, check this box to eliminate off-screen buffering. This will free the resources involved in buffering, and reduce the overhead for display. This may affect the smoothness of the transition from frame to frame, but it will also allow more frames to display during playback.

There are also three other buttons: OK, Cancel, and Set Default. The Set Default button makes the current settings of the various check boxes the default setting. If you click Set Default, the setting will be used each time a video sequence is played using Media Player or MCI (Media Control Interface) string commands.

There's another dialog box you should know about. You can access it on the **E**dit menu—it's the selection **E**dit|**O**ptions (see Figure 1.13).

Figure 1.13. Video playback Options dialog box.

Most of the options in the Options dialog box apply to OLE objects; the first two at the top—**A**uto Rewind and Auto **R**epeat—also apply to Media Player. The various options are explained in Table 1.2.

Table 1.2. Media Player and OLE Options dialog box settings.

Setting	Description
Auto Rewind	If checked, when playback is complete Media Player will rewind to the beginning of the file.
Auto Repeat	If checked, when playback is complete Media Player will replay the file repeatedly.
Caption	Allows you to define the caption that will appear in the OLE window for the media object.
Border around object	Determines if a border will appear around the media object in the client document.
Play in client document	Determines if the object is playable in the client document.
Control Bar on playback	Determines if a control bar will be present in the client document for controlling playback.
Dither picture to VGA colors	Detetrmines if MCI should dither to the 16 standard VGA colors on playback.

Summary

The programs you learned about in this chapter provide an amazing amount of power for using video in your applications. For many purposes, they provide all of the options and capabilities you will need. In later chapters, you'll learn how to control the finer details of video playback for even more striking video effects than those shown here.

2

OLE: Using Digital Video with Existing Applications

You don't have to dive whole-heartedly into programming to use digital video in your applications. First of all, many applications support MCI directly, allowing you to use MCI commands to control media files; however, there are many applications that don't, and there are many situations where that would be overkill. The solution is OLE, Object Linking and Embedding. It's pronounced "oh-lay," just like the bullfighting exclamation, but without the same gusto.

Take a close look at exactly how you can use OLE with digital video. I will go through the process one step at a time, illustrating exactly how to put a video file into a word processing document. You can use these same techniques to put a digital video file into any document type that supports OLE.

> **Note**
>
> Microsoft has just released a completely new version of OLE to programmers. It's called, simply enough, OLE 2.0. It is intended primarily for programmers who are developing Windows applications, rather than Windows users. OLE 2.0 has advanced linking and embedding features that programmers can use when they write Windows software (such as word processors and spreadsheets). The features of this new version of OLE will start showing up in your Windows programs during 1993. OLE 2.0 offers a whole new level of functionality. This chapter shows you how to work with the current version of OLE; the new features of OLE 2.0 are described in Chapter 14, "OLE Basics: Working with Media Player." Start looking for these features in your favorite Windows applications soon!

Creating a Media Object with Media Player

The Media Player icon is normally found in your Accessories group. Double-click the icon, and then select the **D**evice menu, as shown in Figure 2.1.

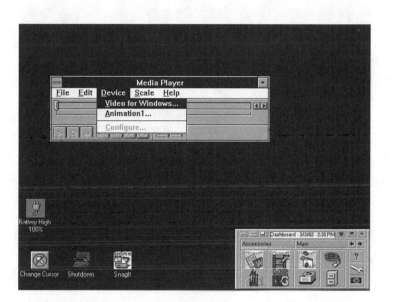

Figure 2.1. Media Player Device menu.

Click **V**ideo for Windows, which will display the Open dialog box (see Figure 2.2).

> ## Note
>
> To run the correct version of Media Player, you must have already installed Video for Windows or the Video for Windows runtime. The examples in this chapter rely on the new version of Media Player, which includes more powerful support of OLE.

Select the .AVI file you want to link by clicking the name in the list of files. You can use the drive and directory lists to navigate around your hard disk to find the file you want to use. Click OK when you have the file you want. The first frame of the file will display in an overlapped window, as shown in Figure 2.3.

Before you copy the video file to the clipboard as a *media object,* you can set various parameters that determine how it will play and display. There is a choice on the **E**dit menu (shown later in Figure 2.7) called Options... that will open the dialog box shown in Figure 2.4. (Refer to Table 1.2 for an explanation of the option settings.)

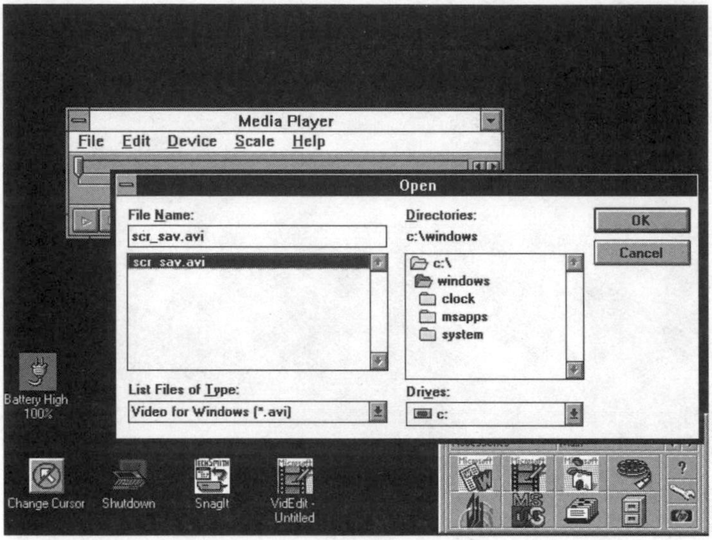

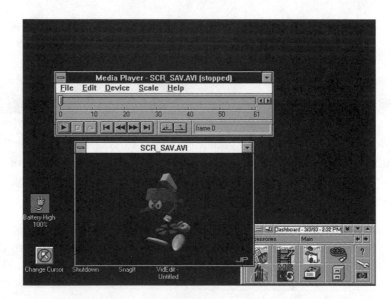

Figure 2.2. The Video for Windows Open dialog box.

Figure 2.3. First frame of a video file displayed in an overlapped window.

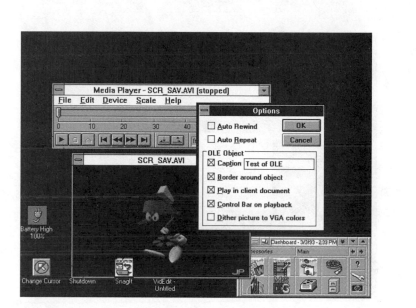

Figure 2.4. Configuration dialog box for video media objects.

While the dialog is open, type in an appropriate caption in the text box labeled Caption; I used "Test of OLE."

Another important item on the **E**dit menu is **S**election (see Figure 2.5). You can select what portion of the video file will actually become part of the media object. For this example, you want to select just the first 30 frames. Set the **F**rom number to zero, and the **T**o number to 30. Click OK when you are done.

The Media Player window now represents the selected portion of the file as a darker band, as shown in Figure 2.6.

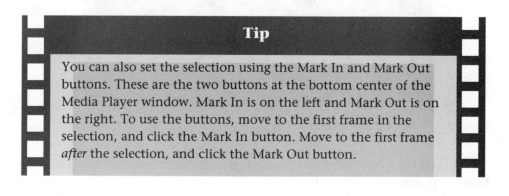

Tip

You can also set the selection using the Mark In and Mark Out buttons. These are the two buttons at the bottom center of the Media Player window. Mark In is on the left and Mark Out is on the right. To use the buttons, move to the first frame in the selection, and click the Mark In button. Move to the first frame *after* the selection, and click the Mark Out button.

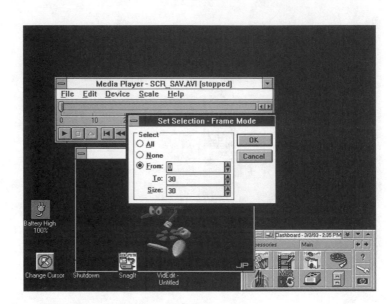

Figure 2.5. Setting the media object selection.

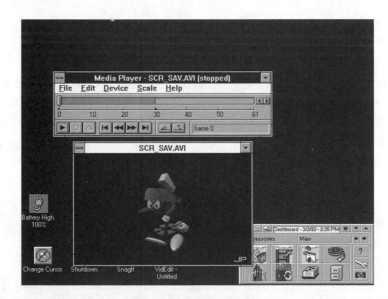

Figure 2.6. A media object selection in the Media Player.

To copy the media object—as you have now defined it—to the clipboard, click
Copy Object on the **E**dit menu, as shown in Figure 2.7.

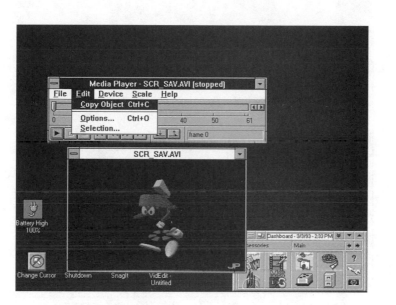

Figure 2.7. The Copy Object menu selection.

Putting a Media Object in a Document

Now choose an application that supports OLE, such as Word for Windows 2.0. Enter some text in a new document, or open an existing document. (See Figure 2.8)

Click Word's **E**dit menu; note that there are two paste selections: **P**aste and Paste **S**pecial, shown in Figure 2.9. Click Paste **S**pecial.

This displays the Paste Special dialog box (see Figure 2.10). Make sure that Media Clip Object is highlighted, and then click OK.

You should now see the first frame of your video file displayed at normal size in the document. (See Figure 2.11.) The caption, located below the image, should be the one you typed into the Options dialog box in the Media Player earlier.

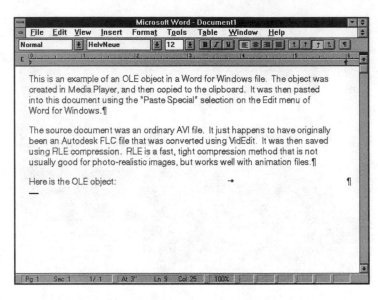

Figure 2.8. A typical word processing document.

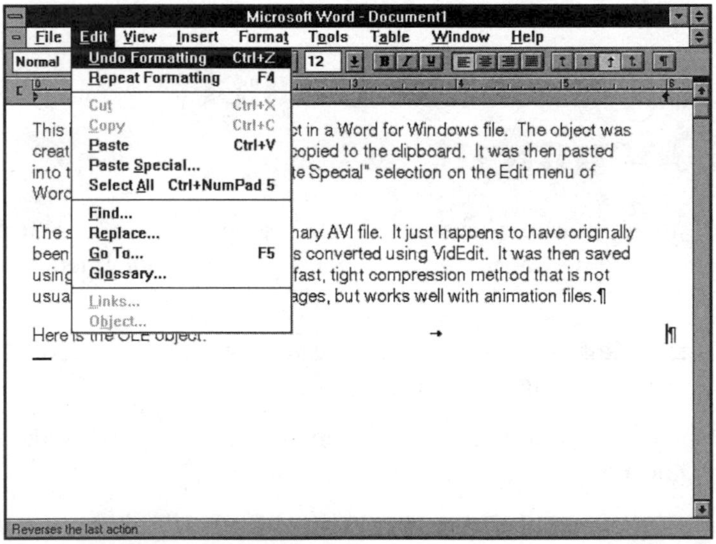

Figure 2.9. The Paste Special menu selection.

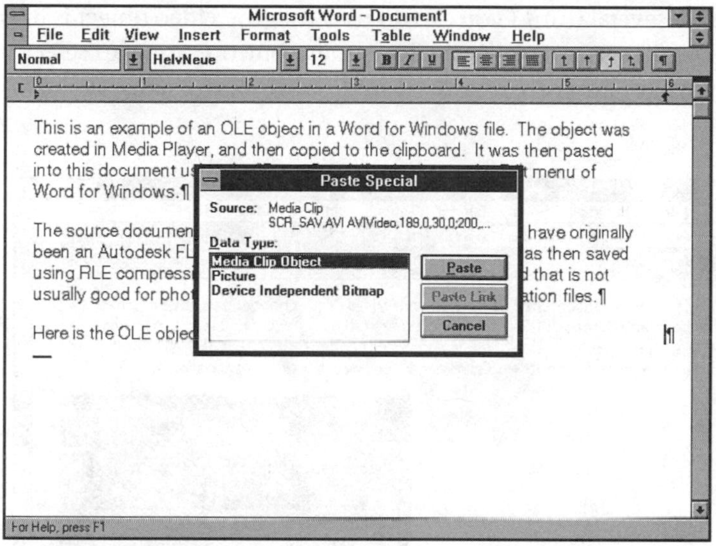

Microsoft Word - Document1

File Edit View Insert Format Tools Table Window Help

Normal HelvNeue 12 B I U

This is an example of an OLE object in a Word for Windows file. The object was
created in Media Player, and then copied to the clipboard. It was then pasted
into this document us [...] t menu of
Word for Windows.¶

Paste Special

Source: Media Clip
SCR_SAV.AVI AVIVideo,189,0,30,0;200,...

Data Type:

Media Clip Object
Picture
Device Independent Bitmap

Paste
Paste Link
Cancel

The source docume [...] have originally
been an Autodesk FL [...] as then saved
using RLE compress [...] d that is not
usually good for pho [...] ation files.¶

Here is the OLE obje[...]

For Help, press F1

Figure 2.10. Paste Special dialog box.

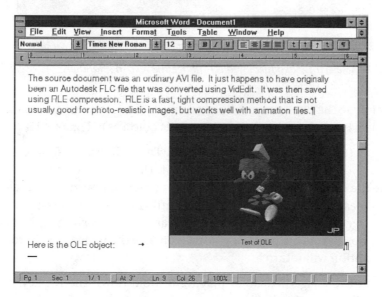

Microsoft Word - Document1

File Edit View Insert Format Tools Table Window Help

Normal Times New Roman 12 B I U

The source document was an ordinary AVI file. It just happens to have originally
been an Autodesk FLC file that was converted using VidEdit. It was then saved
using RLE compression. RLE is a fast, tight compression method that is not
usually good for photo-realistic images, but works well with animation files.¶

Test of OLE

Here is the OLE object: →

Pg 1   Sec 1   1/ 1   At 3"   Ln 9   Col 26   100%

Figure 2.11. A video media object placed in a document via OLE.

There are several things you can do now that the video object is in your document. If you click it once with the left mouse button, you can select it; resizing handles appear at the corners and the mid-points of the sides, as shown in Figure 2.12.

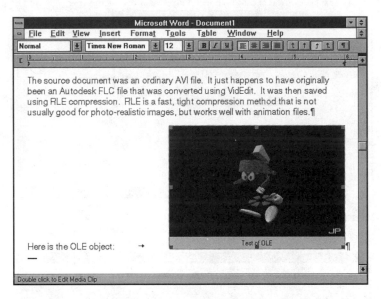

Figure 2.12. A selected video media object; notice the resizing handles.

To change the size or proportions of the object, just select a handle and drag it as needed. Figure 2.13 shows the same media object as in Figure 2.12, but resized.

To play the video object, double-click it. This will display simple controls in place of the caption, as shown in Figure 2.14. Unless you selected automatic repeat, the file will play once, and then the caption will return. If you selected automatic repeat, the file will keep playing until you click the mouse. If you click on the image, the file will pause, and you can resume playing with the control bar at the bottom of the image. If you click outside the image, it will stop playing and the caption will return.

To edit the image instead of playing it, hold down the Alt key while you double-click on the object. This will open Media Player, where you can change the selection or options (**E**dit|**S**election and **E**dit|**O**ptions menu choices).

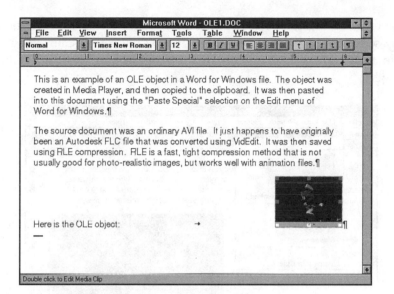

Figure 2.13. A resized media object.

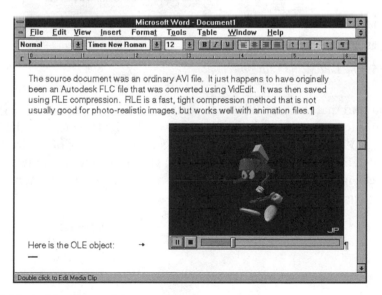

Figure 2.14. A video object with a control bar.

You can also edit the object by clicking the **E**dit menu in Word; note that there is a selection at the bottom of the **E**dit menu called Media Clip O**b**ject, which is shown in Figure 2.15. Click on the video object to select it, then click **E**dit|Media Clip O**b**ject.

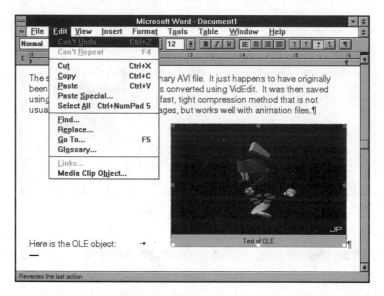

Figure 2.15. The Edit\Media Clip Object option.

If you find that the time it takes to redraw the video image while paging up and down is too long, many software packages will allow you to hide the image. In Word for Windows, click **V**iew|Field Codes to hide display of media objects. Instead of seeing the image, you will see Word's field codes for the object in curly braces. (See Figure 2.16.) **V**iew|Field Codes is a toggle: clicking it again displays all media objects.

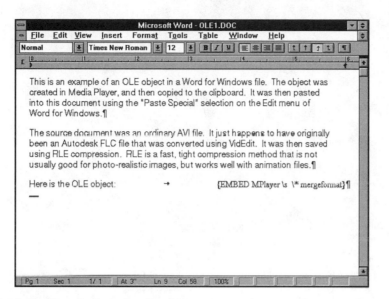

Figure 2.16. Toggling display of media objects.

See Chapter 14 for additional examples of OLE usage.

## PART II

The Technology of Digital Video

3

The Art of Digital Video

Digital video is exciting because, despite all of the high technology involved, it is a medium that both demands and allows for high levels of artistry.

The demands are covered elsewhere—selecting appropriate compression techniques, for example, is described in Chapter 8, "Digital Video Compression: Tradeoffs You Can Live with." In this chapter, we'll stick to just the fun stuff.

The Art of the Camcorder

Because we're talking about video, we need to start where video starts—with the camcorder. Whether you record with a large, VHS machine or a diminutive 8mm unit, whether you use standard or Hi8 tapes, you can never improve upon the original recorded image. The better the image you put on tape, the better the resulting digital video sequence will be.

There are two aspects to consider for the art of the camcorder: general techniques, and specific kinds of recording situations. This chapter covers both.

General Techniques

You might think that there are only so many ways to hold a camcorder, but you would be wrong. There are more ways to hold a camcorder—and more ways to arrange things in front of the camcorder—than are known under heaven and earth.

No matter how many pages I write, no matter how many books you read on the subject, you will always find new techniques and new situations for recording. There will always be new challenges. With that in mind, let's take a look at the fundamentals.

Lighting

Light is the essence of every kind of camera. Without light, there is no image to record. Yet it is easy to overlook the importance of lighting. After all, as long as you're getting an image, you're OK. Right? Wrong.

Here's a simple example. One of the most common shots is of someone's head and shoulders. Figure 3.1 shows a typical head shot without any consideration for lighting (or framing). The background is too bright (there's a window behind the subject, which is me), there is not enough light on the face, and what light there is comes from almost directly above, creating dramatic, useless shadows.

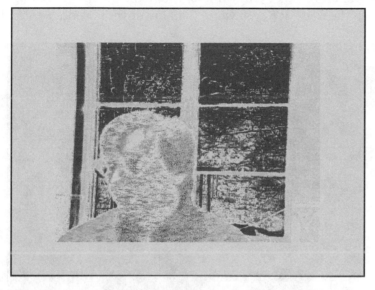

Figure 3.1. Example of a poorly set up head shot.

Too little light is also a serious hazard when using video, as you can see in Figure 3.2.

Figure 3.2. A shot with too little light is not usable.

Another kind of lighting problem occurs when the lighting is fairly even. This creates an overall flatness in the image, as shown in Figure 3.3. The head and the background are not well separated. They are of roughly equal brightness. In fact, of all the pictures I took of myself to illustrate the pitfalls of poor lighting, this one looked the worst; it's even worse than my driver's license photo.

Figure 3.3. Example of problems from even lighting.

This is easy to fix. If the shot is outdoors, you have two choices. You can move the subject into shade, and allow the background to become brighter as you adjust the camera exposure to the face. This gives you a mostly light background, with a normally exposed face. You can also move the subject into bright light, but position him so that an area of shade is behind him. That way, you'll have a normally illuminated face against a dark background.

Both of these are easy because there is plenty of light to go around. On a sunny day, the possibilities of light and shade are numerous. On an overcast day, the choices are not as simple, and you may have to use some of the upcoming tricks for working indoors.

There's usually a lot less light available indoors. Strictly speaking, you can take acceptable videos indoors. However, if you plan to have anyone besides your immediate family look at them, you should think seriously about adding extra lighting. At the least, you should move some of the existing lights around.

There are three basic kinds of lights that you can work with: spot (also called a key), fill, and general.

A spot light is just what it sounds like: a strong, focused light directed at the subject. A fill light is more subtle, adding a medium amount of light to an otherwise dark portion of the subject. A general light is broad illumination of the entire scene, not just the subject. Commonly, it illuminates both the subject and the background.

A sophisticated video shoot might involve a large number of lights of different types, keying, filling, or generally illuminating various parts of the scene. For our purposes, it will be enough to consider how to properly illuminate one or two subjects at a time.

Reflections on Lighting

Lights interact, and if you are using more than two or three sources of light, you will probably need to deal with the interactions. You can, for example, buy "barn doors" that narrow the beam of a light. You can also use reflectors to redirect existing or artificial light where it is needed. Both of these are commonly used by professionals.

For low-budget productions, reflectors are where you find them. A white T-shirt, even while it's on someone's body, can add fill lighting very effectively. A white building is even more effective, although I would suggest moving the subject rather than the building.

As for blocking lights, if you are only using a few lights, your hand, your coat (the thicker and darker the better), or a baseball cap will all do in a pinch. I've even asked perfectly innocent bystanders to help out on occasion.

General Lighting Considerations

Rule number one: make sure there is enough light. Many camcorders will record under low-light conditions, but the resulting video looks like it was boiled in oil. Everything gets fuzzy as the electronics in the camera try to compensate for the lack of light. Not only that, but colors get lost or all blend together.

There are, of course, times when you will want to break this rule. For example, you might have a great idea for a little Halloween video, with just the skeleton's face showing in the scene. At least you might think you're breaking the rule; you're not. Even though the entire scene deliberately has low light, you will discover that you'd better have adequate light on the skeleton! But that's a job for spotlights.

Using Spots

In the case of our skeleton, the spotlight has a simple job to do: light up the face without spilling over into the rest of the scene. That's not really any different from the usual task of a spotlight: to brighten up one item in the scene so that it stands out.

The key (no pun intended) to using spots is to make sure that you expose for the area illuminated by the spotlight. Because it is brighter than the rest of the scene, and because most cameras judge the exposure by the overall brightness of the scene (or, more exactly, a larger portion of the scene than the spotlight illuminates), you may need to use manual exposure to get the best results. The easiest way to calculate the correct exposure is to zoom in on the spotlighted subject, note the exposure, and then zoom back out. Use the noted exposure to film the entire scene.

Using Fills

The two kinds of lighting talked about so far—general lighting and spot lighting—are easy to understand; you encounter them every day. Fill lighting is another story. Although you may encounter it often, you are seldom conscious of its presence. Nonetheless, it plays an important role in how a recorded image will look. It can make the difference between "blah" and "Wow!"

If you have ever studied art, you may be aware of a technique called *chiaroscuro*. It is an Italian word, and it describes the art of secondary illumination—what we're calling a fill. Consider a sphere. If I were to draw a sphere, I would start with a circle, as shown in Figure 3.4.

To suggest the third dimension, I would add shading, as shown in Figure 3.5.

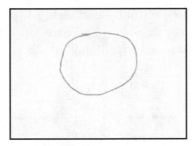

Figure 3.4. A simply drawn circle.

Figure 3.5. Shading turns a circle into a sphere.

So far, the drawing only shows the shadows that result from general light-ing. It is enough to suggest the shape of a sphere, but there is more you can do to make it more lifelike: that's where *chiaroscuro* comes in. You must add a little light to the dark side of the sphere, as shown in Figure 3.6.

Figure 3.6. Chiaroscuro applied to a drawing of a sphere.

This is better, but the eye still balks at seeing a sphere. You need to add an-other detail: a cast shadow, as shown in Figure 3.7. I have also added a simple background, which makes the image stand out sharply.

Figure 3.7. Adding a shadow and some background makes the sphere jump out at you.

You can use the same tricks in a photograph or video. All that is necessary is to consider where the fill lighting might come from. Sometimes, you can use natural sources; sometimes, you must add an artificial light source or use reflec-tors.

Unlike a drawing, where highlights can be added at will, you have to supply the desired lighting while you are shooting a video. There are an infinite number of ways to illuminate a scene, of course, but only some of them are worthwhile. To see the effects of various lighting schemes, I'll light a tennis ball from various angles, and with various numbers of lights. (Why a tennis ball? Because there are so many around the house—my dog loves to catch them, as you can see on the video dogcatch.avi on the CD-ROM disc.)

I'm going to show you more ways to light a tennis ball than you thought were possible, but there is method behind my madness. Although the differences between various lighting methods may seem trivial or subtle, they are often im-portant. Poor or inappropriate lighting can make it difficult for the viewer to follow what is going on.

Figure 3.8 shows a tennis ball in natural room lighting. (All of the tennis ball images were captured with a Canon A-1 camcorder and a ProMotion capture card at 480x320.) In other words, the ball is lit by a light from above, and there is plenty of reflected light to fill in the rest of the ball. (See Figure 3.10 for an example with no reflected light.) The walls are an off-white color, which yields lots of reflected light. If the walls had been wood panelling or otherwise dark, I would get a very different result. The background behind the ball is dark, so the ball stands out well. As you can see, there is a shadow beneath it that helps the eye define the shape—a sphere. Looking at this image, you might even think that I've solved the lighting problem already.

Figure 3.8. A tennis ball in natural room light.

Now look at Figure 3.9. This time, the overhead light is off, and the ball is lit by a single light located slightly below the level of the ball. You can see hardly any background detail at all—there's very little light on the background, and only slightly more on the ball. This lighting has a high contrast—that is, the contrast between darks and lights is extreme. You would rarely use such dramatic lighting for a training application, but it would be fun to use it for more creatively oriented applications.

Figure 3.10 shows a tennis ball lit from above, but this time there is no reflected light to illuminate the background or the bottom half of the tennis ball. The shadow beneath the ball is very pronounced. In general, there is almost no situation where a single light from above will give you a pleasing result.

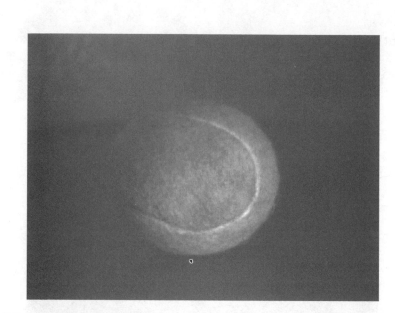

Figure 3.9. A dimly lit tennis ball.

Figure 3.10. A tennis ball lit from above.

Figure 3.11 shows a tennis ball lit strongly from the left side. This lighting casts a long shadow, and partially illuminates the background. It provides good definition of the shape of the ball, but fully half of the ball is hard to make out because it is in complete shadow. I need some light on the off side, just as in the example of chiaroscuro.

Figure 3.11. Tennis ball lit from the left side.

Figure 3.12 has the same light from the left side, but now I have added a light on the front of the ball as well. The shadow on the off side is much less pronounced, and you can now make out details on that side. Overall, however, the illumination is so even that the image has lost most of its contrast. There is too much light here—the whole ball is too white, while the background is lit just right. In this case, I would have been better off to use a manual adjustment of the shutter speed to allow less light into the camera. The background would have been darker, but the ball would have been more pleasing.

Figure 3.13 shows a better approach. This time, the ball is lit from the left side, as before, and from above. This preserves the depth of shadow on the right lower side of the ball. There is still too much light, however; I'm going to have to reduce the amount of light coming in from the left.

Figure 3.12. A tennis ball lit from the side and the front.

Figure 3.13. Tennis ball lit from the side and the top.

In Figure 3.14, I have made several changes to the lighting arrangement. Instead of lighting directly from above, the top light has been moved so that it is located a little behind the ball. This reduces the amount of extra light falling on the front of the ball, but provides a natural highlight at the ten o'clock position. There is still a good shadow on the right side, and the ball is now very well defined and natural looking.

Figure 3.14. Tennis ball lit from the side and from above and behind.

I can add a subtle improvement to what is in Figure 3.14: a fill light, slightly below and to the right of the ball. The result is shown in Figure 3.15. This gives a chiaroscuro effect, and makes the ball the clear focal point of the image. Unfortunately, the addition of the extra light has caused a *hot spot* in the background, just below and to the left of the ball. A hot spot is any bright area of light; often, the details of the subject are said to be "washed out." That is, the light is so bright that you see white instead of surface texture or other details. I would need to fine-tune the light positions to avoid the hot spot, or use a baffle to block the part of the light that is causing the problem. A *baffle* is anything that blocks a portion of the light. Professionals often use something called a *barn door* baffle—it is nothing more than a series of black panels that mounts to a light fixture; the panels swing in the manner of barn doors to block more or less light. You can use anything handy—books, your hand, whatever works.

Figure 3.15. A fill light added to the lighting from Figure 3.14.

Look more closely at one of the lights used in this sequence: the above and behind light. Whenever you are adding an extra light, this should be one of the first ones you think about. It provides a natural-looking accent. As you can see in Figure 3.16, the light should be far enough behind that only a thin crescent of light is visible from the camera position. Note the effect of the light on the horizontal surface below the ball—it adds light to this part of the background. Keep that in mind when you use this kind of lighting.

Such lighting is only part of the picture, however. A modest amount of fill light from anywhere in front of the subject will add detail to the part of the ball in shadow, as shown in Figure 3.17. This is a good two-light arrangement.

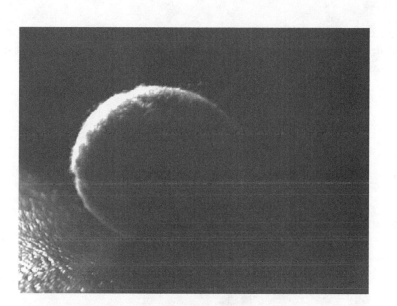

Figure 3.16. A tennis ball illuminated from above and behind.

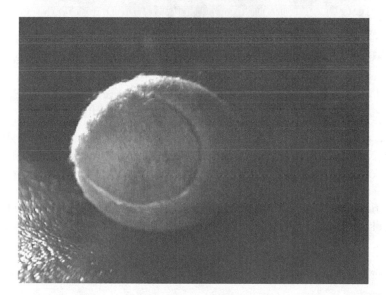

Figure 3.17. Tennis ball with a fill light added to show shadow detail.

You can also directly illuminate the background, as shown in Figure 3.18. Instead of a light-colored tennis ball against a dark background, there is now a bright background and a dark tennis ball. This effect was created using only light;

the tennis ball and the background are the same ones used throughout these examples. This provides a dramatic effect that is more generally pleasing than what was in Figure 3.9.

Figure 3.18. A tennis ball with strong lighting on the background.

The fill light used in Figure 3.18 is essential for good results. In Figure 3.19, only the background is illuminated, with disastrous results.

You can achieve very different results by combining different sources and strengths of illumination. For example, Figure 3.20 shows a combination of an overhead light and a very soft fill light. This is dramatic, with a complex set of relationships. The vertical background is dark, but the horizontal background is very light (except for the full, dramatic shadow beneath the ball). The ball has a strong chiaroscuro effect, revealing much shadow detail without being bright or obvious. If this were a face, the lighting would give it a dark, brooding setting.

Figure 3.19. Illuminated background without any fill light.

Figure 3.20. A soft fill light with strong overhead illumination.

Figure 3.21 shows the same setting, but with additional fill light from the front. The brooding sense is gone, and what is left is an interesting, but less intense feeling.

Figure 3.21. Additional fill light with strong overhead illumination.

Had enough of shining lights on tennis balls? Consider something more in-teresting than my dog's tennis ball. For example, look at the video still in Figure 3.22. It's a simple head shot, taken against a neutral background. It looks pretty flat; the head and the background have similar light and dark values. (OK, so it's a troll doll. Who was going to sit still and have pictures taken of their head?)

Figure 3.22. An evenly lit figure.

In the next example, Figure 3.23, a single light is used to illuminate the sub-ject. The light is coming from the side, which provides good contrast, but the shadow side of the face is too dark—you can't see any details there.

Figure 3.23. A figure lit from one side.

Now look at Figure 3.24; this time a fill light was added, illuminating the shadow side of the face. Notice how the head is more clearly defined against the background? See how the hint of light makes the facial features easier to read?

Figure 3.24. A figure with a fill light added.

Take a moment to visualize how this scene was organized. Figure 3.25 shows the physical placement of the various objects, including not just the subject, but the lights as well. This shows the relationship between the various pieces of the puzzle.

Figure 3.25. The lighting arrangement used for Figure 3.24.

There are many situations where you will encounter the need for a fill light. For example, if you film someone in their office, you will often encounter banks of overhead fluorescent lights. This is not flattering lighting—the illumination is often uneven, leading to the kinds of problems you saw in Figure 3.22. You might want to turn off the overhead fluorescent light to get a more natural look, especially if there is a window nearby. However, all of the light is now coming from one direction—wherever the window is. That's the situation in Figure 3.23, and you solve that by adding a fill light. A fill is never as bright as the other lights; it merely fills in the shadows (which is exactly where the name comes from).

Now apply the last thing learned working with the tennis ball: a highlight for the hair, slightly behind and above the subject. Figure 3.26 shows how this affects the appearance of the subject. Notice how the subject now stands out distinctly from the background. This lighting arrangement is one of the most commonly used in photography. It is relatively simple, and the result is very good looking. The lighting arrangement is shown in Figure 3.27.

Figure 3.26. Adding a key light to the head shot.

Figure 3.27. The lighting arrangementused for Figure 3.26.

You can always create more complex lighting arrangements, of course. For example, you could set up a lighting arrangement like the one in Figure 3.28, still with just one talking head as a subject.

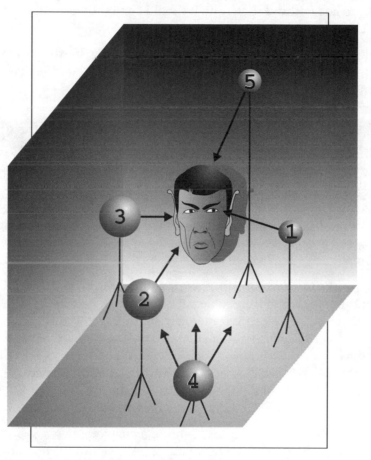

Figure 3.28. A complex lighting arrangement.

The lights in Figure 3.28 are numbered for easy reference:

1. This is a key or spot light, to emphasize the face and cast a shadow on the background. The shadow adds depth.

2. General light to provide even, overall illumination of the scene.

3. A fill light to fill in the shadows on the face.

4. A light to add illumination to the background from below. Usually, light comes from above; this adds a little interest to the scene.

5. A spot light to put a highlight on the subject's hair. This is a common light to add for head shots, and it should be slightly behind the subject for the best effect.

The light to highlight the hair is called backlighting. It exists both naturally and artificially, and it deserves a few words all on its own. (See the sidebar "Backlighting: Friend or Foe?")

Backlighting: Friend or Foe?

Backlighting is any light that is located behind the subject. It can be above and behind, like the light described in Step 5 for Figure 3.28; it can be literally behind the subject, as is the case of a window directly behind the subject. Used correctly, backlighting can add excitement and depth. Used incorrectly, backlighting can render a shoot useless.

When the subject is backlit, there is almost always more light on the scene around the subject than on the subject itself. For example, if the subject is standing in front of a brightly lit window, the camera's automatic exposure will probably expose the scene for the window's brightness, not the subject's. That will give you a perfectly exposed window, with a black silhouette standing in front of it. Or if there is a large region of bright sky, it will force the foreground into dense shadow. (See Figure 3.29.)

On the other hand, if the backlighting merely highlights a portion of the subject, as shown in Figure 3.30, there is no harm done and you might even get a nicer looking picture.

The moral: Backlighting is like salt. A little adds interest, a lot is yucky.

Figure 3.29. Backlighting as foe.

Figure 3.30. Backlighting as friend.

Camera Angle

There is a tendency to ignore camera angle when composing a shot. In fact, if you think about it, the camera is almost always at eye level of a subject. This does not have to be the case.

Recently, I got the idea into my head that I wanted to shoot videos of animals. There are plenty of pets in the neighborhood; I thought I'd practice on them. The hardest was the neighbor's cat. He kept doing cat things, like rubbing up against my leg. I had several minutes of footage that showed little more than the top of his head (see Figure 3.31 where, at the least, he looked up at me). This was not very interesting footage. Then I got an idea: drop down to the cat's level. I was quickly rewarded with much better footage (see Figure 3.32).

Figure 3.31. Stalking the elusive cat: bad camera angle.

This ultra-low camera angle works well with all kinds of subjects, including small animals, babies (especially at the crawling stage, when they are nearly indistinguishable from other small animals), flowers (in the garden, not in a vase!), and so on. There is another fun use for an ultra-low camera angle: humor. Next time you are at a family gathering, try shooting from near the floor to see what the affair looks like to a baby. How you explain it to the members of your family is up to you.

Figure 3.32. Stalking the elusive cat: good camera angle.

A moderately low camera angle can also be useful, but not often for head shots. No one likes to look up into someone else's nose. You also can use a different grip for such shots. You can cradle the camera in both hands, and adjust the eyepiece so that you can see it from above.

Holding the camera at your waist in this manner is less fatiguing than holding it at eye level, and not as obvious to your subjects. I use it frequently when I want to shoot the kids playing. It's not as steady as an eye-level shot, but a wide angle covers that nicely (don't zoom in!). The kids don't notice that I'm videotaping when I use this approach.

There are also many uses for a high-level shot. It's great in crowds, for example; just hold the camera above everyone's head and tape away. It's hard to aim, however; use a wide angle for best results. For digital video, you can easily crop later.

The high-level shot is also sometimes flattering for head shots. It can give a more candid look to the shoot. For example, I will sometimes use a high camera placement, and have the subject look toward the camera before he or she begins to speak. It looks very natural.

Another advantage of high camera placement is that it can make the subject look less threatening. This can be useful for taping an executive who wants to look more relaxed, for example. Have him sit on a couch, but film from eye level.

Focus

What is there to say about focus? You might assume that the camera's autofocus handles all of that, but it has some limitations that are important to know about.

Extreme Zoom

Automatic focus works well in average situations. Zooming in very tight is not an average situation, and many cameras can't handle it well. If you have your camera on a tripod, step out from behind it sometime while it is on, and autofocus is engaged. Set the zoom factor to somewhere in the middle of its range. For example, if your camera can zoom from 1x to 8x, set it at 4x. Watch the lens elements. Are they moving ever so slightly back and forth? Probably not, or, if they are, it is very slight. Even if they are moving, if you look through the eyepiece you will not see any evidence of it.

Now move the zoom factor to maximum, whatever it is for your camera— 8x, 10x, 12x. Do the same test. You will almost surely see the lens mechanism hunting for the best focus. If you look through the eyepiece, you will probably see the image moving in and out of focus.

The reason for this is simple. At average zoom ranges, the camera's optics (the lenses) are not being pushed very hard. At extreme zoom ranges, the optics are working at their limit—they aren't able to provide as clear an image. The autofocus sees that lack of clarity as a lack of focus, and tries to fix it. Well, it can't be fixed by changing the focus!

To deal with this problem, don't zoom too far when autofocus is engaged. Get used to your particular camera's limits. If you do need to use extreme zoom, disengage the automatic focus.

Follow Focus

Following a moving subject can be hard to do, and focusing problems can make it harder. There are two basic situations that you can encounter: movement from side to side, and movement toward or away from you. Various combinations are the most common, of course, but consider the extremes first.

When the subject is moving from one side to the other, focus is not a problem, although moving the camera to follow accurately can be difficult for a very fast-moving subject. Motion toward or away from you is an entirely different matter—focus is everything.

Consider how autofocus works. Most camera lenses are complex, made up of several lenses. Those lenses, although light, do have weight, as does the housing they sit in. The lenses are focused with a small motor. To keep weight to a minimum, it's not a terribly powerful or fast motor. As a result, the speed at which it can change focus is limited. As a result, any subject moving toward or away from the camera at anything faster than a slow walk will probably move faster than autofocus can follow—under certain conditions.

Wide-angle shots are the most forgiving; almost everything in the scene is in focus when the angle is wide. If you are filming a group of children playing, odds are you haven't zoomed in very much. If one of the kids suddenly runs toward you, focus won't be a problem—the zone of focus is large, including both the group in the background and the running child.

If, instead, you have zoomed in tight on just one child, and that child starts to run toward the camera, you have a problem! Try it—you'll see that autofocus is helpless under these conditions. If you want to shoot this kind of movement, you will need to turn off autofocus and adjust focus by hand. That's not as easy to do, but it can be done. It takes some practice, for two reasons. It takes experience to judge the amount of focus change required for a subject moving at various speeds, and it takes a steady hand to handle the focus manually—rotating a lens is not intuitive; it takes time to get used to it.

If you are planning any action taping, I highly recommend taking the camera into the back yard or a playground, and practicing on some running, jumping, unpredictable kids. You'll be an expert in an hour or so.

Wide-Angle Versus Zoom

In the last section, I hinted at the focus differences between wide-angle and zoomed-in images. This difference is called *depth of field*. I'll provide a more technical definition in a moment, but for now you can think of depth of field in these terms: in a wide-angle shot, just about everything, near or far, is in focus. In a zoomed shot, only the subject—perhaps only a portion of the subject—is in focus.

It might seem ideal to use wide-angle shots to make sure that everything is in focus. Sometimes, as in the previous example concerning moving subjects, this can indeed be an advantage. Just as often, however, having everything in focus is not such a good idea. For example, if you are interviewing someone in front of a flower garden, the colors and texture of the background might draw the viewers eye away from the subject. I didn't happen to have a flower garden handy, but I used my brother-in-law's shovel (see Figure 3.33) to illustrate the principle. If this is a photo of a shovel, it would be hard to tell—there are too many other objects cluttering up the scene.

If I move the camera back and then zoom in, the limited depth of field (and the narrower field of view, too) isolates the shovel. (See Figure 3.34.) Notice how much easier it is to focus (pun intended) on the subject in the second example.

Figure 3.33. A distracting background.

You don't need to know why this occurs in order to use it, but I will explain it for those who might be curious. There is a very good reason why this phenomenon is called *depth of field*. Viewed from the correct angle, this is literally what we are talking about.

Consider the situation for both a wide-angle and zoomed-in shot (see Figure 3.35).

Figure 3.34. Using zoom, focus, and narrow field to obscure the background and emphasize the subject.

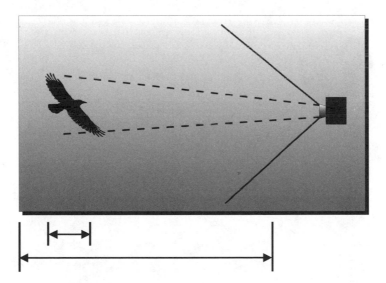

Figure 3.35. Depth of field for different situations.

The vertical bars below the figure mark the portion of the visual field that is in focus for each situation. For a wide-angle shot, the in-focus area starts close to the camera, and extends well beyond the subject. For a zoom shot, the in-focus area starts far from the camera, and ends quickly.

The key difference between the two views, of course, is the angle of view. This change in angle affects something called the *circle of confusion*.

Before I define a circle of confusion, I must define another term: the *focal plane*. Simply put, the focal plane is where the image comes into focus after passing through a lens. In a camera, the idea is to have the film right at the focal plane.

Stay with me on this. I promise it will all make sense. Here's the theory: the wider the angle, the less difference a change in position makes in the focal plane of the resulting image. The smaller the angle, the larger the change in the focal plane that will result from a change of position.

Figure 3.36 and 3.37 show this graphically.

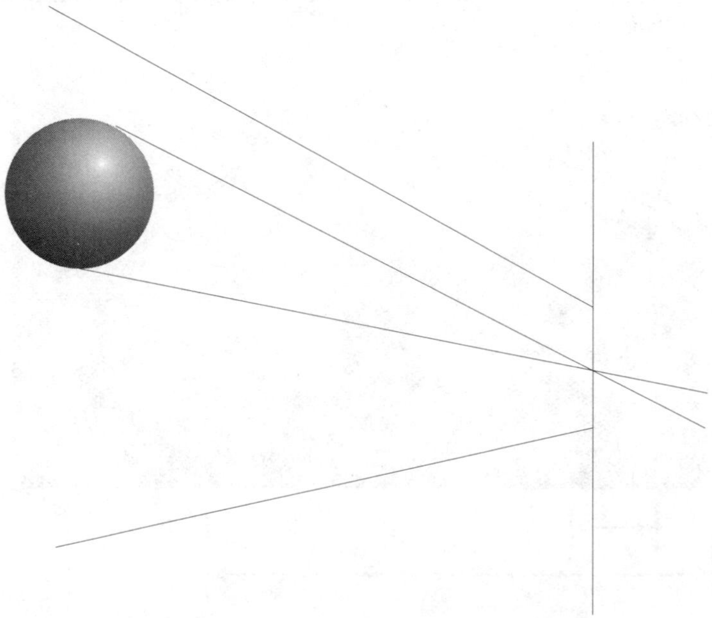

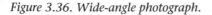

Figure 3.36. Wide-angle photograph.

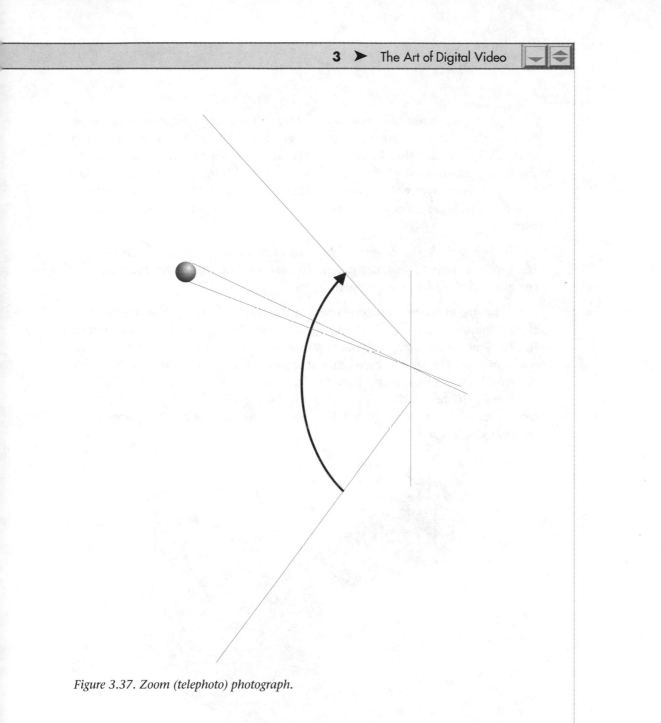

Figure 3.37. Zoom (telephoto) photograph.

Figure 3.38 shows how light moves through the lens for a wide-angle shot. Because the wide angle takes in more image area, the relative size of each object is small. This means that light is reflected from the object into the camera at a small angle. Even large changes in position still result in the image coming to a focus at almost exactly the same plane. The paths that light follows through the lens for objects at various distances all converge at, or very near, the plane of the film.

In Figure 3.38, the case for a zoomed-in shot, an individual object creates (subtends) a larger angle. Small changes in position will change the focus because the angle at the film plane is much wider.

Now, the final step. Imagine yourself standing next to the plane where the film is, looking at an out-of-focus image. Instead of imagining the whole process in two dimensions, imagine it in three dimensions, as shown in Figure 3.39. The paths of the light beams converging at a point form a cone shape. Where that cone meets the film, it forms a circle. That circle is the circle of confusion. The larger it is, the fuzzier the image is to your eye. A wide-angle shot results in very small circles of confusion (Figure 3.39), and a zoomed-in shot results in large circles of confusion (Figure 3.40).

Figure 3.38. Film plane in three dimensions.

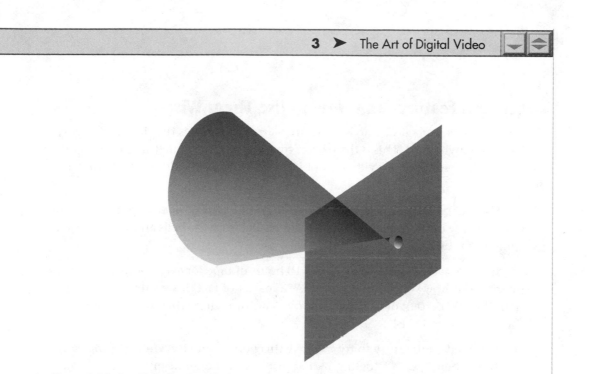

Figure 3.39. Small circle of confusion with a wide-angle shot.

Figure 3.40. Large circle of confusion with telephoto shot.

With any luck, I haven't confused *you* with all of this.

Camera Features and How to Use Them Wisely

Today's video cameras come with such an array of features that it is all too easy to feel overwhelmed. This is the perfect time to point out something that is critical to videotaping. Every video shoot is subject to what I will call the Simplicity Rule.

Simplicity Rule: 90 percent of the effectiveness of any video clip results from what you see in the frame, and 10 percent results from the bells and whistles that come with the camera.

In other words, you should shoot 10 hours of tape for every hour you spend figuring out how your camera works. As a matter of fact, it's even more extreme than that; 90 percent of technique involves nothing more than making sure that the subject is in focus!

I will tell a little story to try to make this point more forcefully. In the early eighties, when I was a fledgling radio journalist, I did all of my work in a very small, simple studio that had the minimum of professional equipment—a couple of tape decks, some microphones, and so on. Anyone could have put together a studio like that for no more than a couple thousand dollars. At that same time, a professional audio studio was a six-figure investment.

I was not the only one using that studio; others did, too, and what has always amazed me is that we succeeded in creating radio news stories that aired on National Public Radio. Lots of stories, in fact, far out of proportion to our tiny little studio. There were no special effects; we had to ask people to be quiet while we recorded; there was no one to start or stop the tape recorder while we interviewed someone; we had to do it all ourselves. There were times when I used my feet to turn things on or off because both hands and my nose were already busy handling other buttons and switches.

Because we did not waste time on bells and whistles, we spent time on the thing that really mattered: the content. Our stories had heart, they had pizzazz, they had substance. A number of the people involved in that little studio (at KBOO-FM, in Portland, Oregon, and also at KLCC in Eugene, Oregon), went on to have careers in radio where they did learn about, and use, the fancier bells and whistles.

This is the long way of saying: don't be intimidated by the doodads on your camera. You don't have to feel that you have to use them just because you paid for them. Ignore them until you're ready, and then you'll have a blast adding neat tricks to your repertoire. You will be able to expand the kinds of shots you can take confidently. For example, my Canon A-1 has the ability to *follow focus* automatically. It can lock onto a moving subject and use that subject as the point of focus, even if the subject moves to the edge of the frame. I had the camera for a year before I ever even tried to use that feature, and it took a while to get used to the sequence for setting the focus on the object. At first, instead of locking onto the moving object, I would often lock onto a stationary object, and the focus would lock onto a chair or a table leg. Messy, to say the least. But now I can use it effectively, and it's great for my son's soccer games.

Tripod Versus Hand-Held

Speaking of taping sports events, let's talk about tripods and inertia.

The heavier a camera is, the steadier it is when held by hand. Conversely, the lighter a camera is, the harder it is to hold it steady. This has to do with inertia. A heavy object has more of it.

Inertia, simply defined, is the tendency of a stationary object to stay still, and of a moving object to keep moving. Something really heavy, such as a grand piano, is hard to get moving, and just as hard to stop once you get it moving. Something really light, such as a feather, is easy to move and easy to stop. Video cameras are no different. If you have a light little hand-held, you may have noticed that taping while you hold it in your hand results in jumpy pictures. No matter how hard you try, you can never quite hold it perfectly still. If you have a large VHS camera, your images are steadier (although there is a limit to just how steady you can be even with these larger cameras).

There are some tricks you can use to steady your hand-held shots. Ultimately, however, you should think very seriously about acquiring a tripod. I'll talk about tripods in a moment; first, some tricks.

The first trick is an easy one, and it comes from still camera photography. It involves using your natural breathing reflexes to your advantage. Once you have a shot composed and are ready to shoot, take a normal breath, let it out, and then hit the start button. You can easily give yourself as much as ten seconds of breathless, steady taping before your urge to breathe in becomes enough of a nuisance to mess up the shot. This is effective, obviously, only for short takes.

The next trick involves using your body to create a three-point anchor for the camera. Normally, you only have two—if that—when you shoot hand-held. One is, of course, the hand doing the holding. The other is your cheek, if you

press the camera against it. This squeeze play isn't as firm as you need, however, because the camera can still rock up and down. The trick is simple—just add your free hand to the setup.

How you add the hand, however, is critical. If you just use it to hold the camera, you will do little more than add one more potential son of vibration to the camera-body system. Think in terms of the bones in your hands and arms. For best support, you want to use them like tripod legs. That means connecting the ends of the bones—elbow and wrist—to solid objects like your shoulder, a wall, or the camera itself. Take a lesson from tennis: bending your wrist backwards makes it stiffer. Test your hold for stiffness before you tape. Adjust as necessary, and adapt to your circumstances. Fence posts, telephone poles, car fenders, and related objects make excellent instant tripods.

As for tripods themselves, the most important consideration is to buy a tripod that was intended for use with a video camera. Such a tripod has features that do not exist on conventional tripods for still cameras. The most important feature is something called a fluid head. A fluid head *dampens* motion in every direction. Damping is the ability to reduce or eliminate small variations in the movement. For example, if you decide to rotate the camera sideways, you want the motion to be steady, not jerky. This is called *panning*.

Pan and Tilt

Panning is one of the most common things you can do with a camera, but without a tripod, panning looks awful. It's the only effective way to include subjects that are significantly wider than they are high, such as a choir or speakers at a conference table. There are just two rules that I suggest for panning:

➤ Pan slowly.

➤ Don't pan too fast.

While you are taping, your mind is undoubtedly racing along at high speed, considering all the variables of the situation—lighting, action, maybe even the next scene. However, when the viewer watches your handiwork, the odds are very high that his mental process is going to be much slower. A pan speed that seems fine at the time it is recorded may be ridiculously fast when you look at it later. Be aware of this tendency ahead of time, and you won't be disappointed.

Tilting is another matter. It is the act of raising or lowering the camera viewing angle. I have only one rule about tilting: don't be like Don Quixote. As you may recall, Don Quixote tilted at windmills while imagining he was in real battle; never tilt in the heat of battle (that is, during taping) because it's very disorienting to the viewer. (Unless, of course, that is your goal!)

Tilt *before* you shoot, not during. Even then, be sure to consider what effect your tilt has on the scene. Avoid sharp tilt angles unless it is for special effect. Of course, you will manage someday to find a situation where you not only must tilt, but where it will be an excellent choice. That's art, not science, and rules only apply to science.

Framing and Composition

Deciding what to put in front of your camera is only the first step. Whether you are taping the next Olympics, or simply want a video clip to play under Windows for fun, how you frame your subject is the most important decision you will make. (If you are curious, the second most important decision you make is when to stop taping. Tape is cheap; tape on!)

The art of framing is just one small part of the art of composition. I could write a book about composition, and so could anyone else who's thought about it. Composition is something an artist considers the way a fisherman considers fly fishing: the nuances are endless. There are more ways to create a successful composition than there are varieties and states of insects over a trout stream on a summer day.

And the hook is just as barbed if you snag yourself. If you do it right, your viewer can be reeled in completely. If you blow it, you'll lose him faster than you can imagine. Nonetheless, good framing and composition cannot be taught, except at the most rudimentary level. For example, consider this simple thought: to frame well, you must look at what is in the frame, and then ask yourself, "What do I see?"

What you see makes all the difference. For example, say there are lots of people in the shot. Here are three things you might see in the frame.

➤ Perhaps you see complete chaos. A disaster! Keep looking.

➤ Perhaps you see the people as a texture. This can work. You can start looking to find a texture that feels right, and then you've got your framing!

➤ Perhaps you see an individual who catches your attention—a face filled with emotion, or a face that is striking. This can work. You can now find a way to frame that face with the other faces, and then frame all of that with the camera.

The way to frame or compose is not to follow rules, but to learn about the things that are there to frame. You cannot compose a proper frame until you are clear about what it is that is inside the frame to compose. When you find that, it will as often as not lead you to the solution.

You see, every artistic success is just that—a solution to a problem. An artist spends his day encountering one problem after another, and each must be solved in its turn. Videotaping is no different in this respect.

Candid Camcorder

I would guess that 99 percent of all videotape shot in the world is candid. That is, the subjects are filmed on an impromptu basis, with no scripting or formal preparation. (I do admit that I am taking the liberty of including taping of one's own children in this figure because they could arguably be categorized as the truest ham actors, not candid subjects at all.) And I would also guess that 99 percent of all candid shots aren't being done right.

The wrong way to do candid videotaping is to simply point the camera and take what you get. This ignores the dilemma of modern photography, both still and video: the camera is no longer an innocent instrument. In this day and age, we all know what the camera is, and how it can embarrass us. There is a tendency for the subject to hold back. I know more about this than you might think because I become horribly self-conscious in front of a camera. I make an irretrievable mess of it unless I pay the strictest attention.

Thus true candid taping is out of the question, unless you are the tricky, practical-joker type who is willing to try taping on the sly. Once, I left the camera on the tripod and turned on during Christmas dinner; I nearly got my head chopped off when we played it back later. I don't know why everyone was so angry at me— I had forgotten that I had done it and wound up the biggest fool all on my own.

The key to good candid taping is to make the camera non-intrusive. If you stick the camera in the subject's face, that's intrusive. Instead, use a modest zoom factor, and keep the camera at a distance. If you keep looking at the camera to make sure it's working OK, that's intrusive. Set it up, check it thoroughly, and then let it operate from a distance using the remote control. If you don't have a remote for the camera, consider just letting it run for long periods of time. When you go back to the camera to adjust it, spend a moment afterwards to get the subject relaxed again and help him or her forget about the camera again. If someone else is working the camera while you interact with the subject, tell them not to speak. If there is a problem, they should step from behind the camera to get your attention.

In other words, do everything you can to avoid making the camera the center of attention.

Even if you are doing a wild, hand-held, candid sequence, if *you* don't pay undo attention to the camera, your subject will likewise ignore it. The less intrusive the camera is, the better your chances for success.

Do's and Don'ts

In addition to everything I've covered here, there are some fundamental guidelines to keep in mind:

➤ Don't pay for features you won't use. This is especially true if you plan to use the camera mostly for digital video—the things you can do on the computer leave most home-style camcorder bells and whistles in the dust.

➤ Buy and use a tripod. A steady image is critical for professional applications.

➤ Don't overuse the zoom. The occasional zoom is fine, but you should use zoom mostly to frame your shots *before* you shoot them.

➤ Timing for digital video is different than for normal videotaping. Digital video eats hard disk space fast—you will sometimes use shorter segments to save space.

➤ Cleanliness is essential—follow the camera manufacturer's instructions for keeping the lens clean. The lens has lots of delicate anti-reflection coatings on it, and you need to use only appropriate cleaning materials. Lint-free cloth is essential. Ask any photo or video retailer if you're not sure what to use.

➤ Camcorder batteries are prone to lose their charge quickly. Always have extra charged batteries around. If you use NiCad batteries, completely discharge them periodically. NiCad (Nickel Cadmium) batteries don't take a full charge if you charge them when they are only partially discharged. This can make an otherwise good battery almost useless. To fully discharge a battery, operate the camera for playback using the battery. That way, there's no harm done when the battery finally gives up its last few electrons.

General Thoughts

There is no end to the subtle and interesting things you can do with a video camera. There is an even greater range of things that people will do in front of it to make the videotaping interesting and worthwhile. The only real limit to what can be done is your own imagination. If you keep reminding yourself that the possibilities are endless, you will find that the challenges you meet will be friends, not enemies. I think of them as provocateurs because they always keep things stirred up. The only bad video is a boring one, you see, and if you can avoid that, you'll have plenty of fun and success in this business. The best way to avoid boring is to think like your eventual viewer: don't tape anything you yourself wouldn't want to see on a screen!

Recording Situations

So far, I've been talking about general video techniques that you can apply almost anywhere, any time. There are certain situations, however, where a video camera is used more commonly than others. This section covers taping scenarios from catalogs to action.

Still Capture for Catalogs, IDs, and so on

With the advent of quality video capture cards, the average video camera has suddenly become a workable input device. The term for this is *still-frame capture*, and it has been around for years. However, the explosion in video cards occurring because of Video for Windows is putting a lot more video capture hardware into computers. Not all of it is going to be used just for video sequences.

On the camera side, capturing still video has several advantages. For one thing, the subject is usually standing still. You can take all the time you need to get the shot done right. The best use of this extra time involves one familiar item—lighting—and one new item—set design.

Big video producers often design and construct their own sets; that's an expensive proposition, however. When you are doing still video, you can usually reuse your "set" for many shots, making it an affordable proposition. If you need to shoot items for a catalog, you might create a simple backdrop to place the objects on. For example, if you were shooting for a catalog of electrical supplies, most of which were metallic, you might create a set that provided a dark background. Conversely, if you were shooting a catalog of lacquered wooden boxes, you might prefer a light-colored, rough-textured background to emphasize the dark woods and polished surfaces.

You could also use a simple set for shooting ID pictures for badges or an image database. A simple curtain or cloth works well, although you may find that a neutral surface outside of the focus area provides a clearer image. Remember that video is not as clear as film for stills, and use every trick to emphasize the subject.

Video stills often demand higher quality video equipment, such as Hi8 or SVHS camcorders. Even so, the limits of camcorder-based still video are noticeable. Figure 3.41 is an image taken from a video tape. I used a Video Spigot and composite input. There are a few noticeable flaws, but there are no scan lines as there would be with cheaper capture cards. (Scan lines are the horizontal lines you notice if you get close to a TV screen.)

Figure 3.42 shows a small portion of the image, blown up to show some of the fault lines more clearly. In particular, note the wavy banisters on the side of the deck—they were actually straight; that was a problem in video alignment. It is minor, and would be completely ignored in a series of moving images. However, as a still, it leaves something to be desired. The worst problems involve straight lines and diagonals.

Figure 3.41. Capture of a single frame with composite input.

  Figure 3.42. The same image blown up to show the fault lines.

Figure 3.43 shows the same frame captured with S-Video output from the camcorder. S-Video uses a higher number of scan lines, and should produce a smoother appearance. In truth, I can't see much difference between the images, and this is typical of the experience I've had with better quality capture boards. Naturally, results vary from one camcorder or capture card to the next.

Figure 3.43. The same shot as before, but this one was done with S-Video output.

Which brings us to some after-the-camera suggestions for working with video still images. Depending on the intended use, you may need to polish up the captured image. If you are outputting to a dot matrix printer, you may be able to use the image as you captured it. If you will be outputting to a laser printer at 300 dpi, you should at least perform some rudimentary cleanup. For example, Photoshop for Windows will remove the characteristic video scan lines (those horizontal lines you see on TV screen). For higher resolution devices, ranging from high-res laser printers to typesetters, still video becomes less and less useful as the resolution goes up. The practical limit usually occurs with 600 dpi printers; printers with a higher resolution than that begin to show the limitations of still video too much.

The best software for massaging still video captures is high-end photo-retouching software such as Adobe PhotoShop or Aldus PhotoStyler. Less costly packages can also be effective, but there is less of a variety of tools.

Here are some tricks I use for getting the best-looking still video images:

➤ Blur the image. Blurring can remove obvious scan lines in the image. You will sacrifice some crispness and clarity, of course, so adjust the amount of blur to balance these factors for your intended use. There are different kinds of blurs you can use. In Aldus PhotoStyler, the blur choices are:

Blur—A minimal blur that is hardly noticeable, but still reduces the extent of scan lines.

Blur more—A more aggressive and more noticeable blur that is very effective in reducing scan lines.

Blur heavily—This blur is usually too much; the resulting image is so lacking in clarity that it's probably not going to be usable.

Gaussian blur—An adjustable blur that uses randomization to achieve its effects. This allows you to adjust the degree of blurring to meet your needs for each image. The nature of the blurring is easier on the eye than standard blurring. However, a Gaussian blur is more time consuming.

Despeckling—Not really a blur; and not very effective with scan lines. More useful for scanned images with dirt or other imperfections. (Also useful when you scan images that have been screened previously; removes Moiré effects.)

➤ Blur and then sharpen the image—In some cases, I find that blurring moderately with a Gaussian blur, and then sharpening the image results in a pleasing compromise between clean-up and a crisp, focused appearance.

➤ Experiment with revising the hues in the image—In some cases, you can compensate for color drift in the image editing software. For example, the images may all have too much red in them. By shifting the hue setting away from red, you can reduce the amount of red in the image and achieve a more natural look. Of course, you can also shift toward a color that *isn't* there if that is the effect you want to achieve.

If your capture software allows, you can also try capturing just one field. Each video frame is made up of two fields. The first field consists of the odd scan lines, and the second field consists of the even scan lines. (Video frames are interlaced—on the first pass, one field is displayed, and on the second pass, the next field is displayed. The eye sees them as one frame. This is similar to monitors that require interlacing of 1024x768 video modes.)

If the two fields are not well aligned, extreme emphasis of scan lines can occur. Capturing just one field reduces this problem, but remember that you are capturing with just half of the resolution you get with both fields.

Talking Head

If you are not familiar yet with the term "talking head," all you need to know is that it is not a reference to a cutting edge rock group with exotic rhythmic undertones. It is what it says it is: one or more heads, talking. You've seen them everywhere you've seen video—newscasts, talk shows, training videos, sales presentations, on and on and on. You would hardly think that talking heads is the most boring possible way to present information, but it is.

Talking heads are also inevitable. When you are working on a budget, it's a lot cheaper to put someone on the screen than to have someone narrate a richly-produced animation or montage. In the world of everyday reality, talking heads will be with us forever. To learn to live with them, you have to understand what's going on.

A talking head is more like a still image than a video. It's nice that we can see the lips move, and it's nice that we can read the expression on someone's face, but you will be a lot more successful with talking heads if you think of them as a photograph that just happens to move a little.

The first thing to consider for a talking head shot is the lighting. Since the subject is most likely static (unless you have the good fortune to be filming someone who can talk and walk at the same time), you can light it once and move on. If you can do it, use the basic lighting arrangement for talking heads: one main light for illumination, one for fill from the shadow side, and a key light above and slightly behind to add a nice highlight to the hair. A weak fill light on the background is nice, but not essential.

Now we can think about that photograph. Here are some examples of things that can go wrong:

➤ Cluttered background.

➤ Getting too close to the subject.

➤ Getting too far away from the subject.

➤ Ridiculous foreign objects near the speaker.

➤ Background objects that jump to the foreground visually, either stealing attention from the subject or making the subject look silly in some unexpected way.

Here are some examples of things that can go right;

➤ Backgrounds that fade into the background.

➤ Finding the right shooting distance.

➤ Appropriate filler objects in the scene.

➤ Well-composed scene for the photograph.

To compose the scene for a head shot, think in terms of your family photo album. All you have to do is arrange the shot so it would look good as a snap-shot.

Once you have the *scene* arranged, you can proceed to arranging the "talent." That's what on-camera personages are called in both the news and entertainment industries. (Don't you find it odd that someone who reads the news is referred to as "talent?" This is a trivial bit of information that I could editorialize about, but won't.) There are two significant levels of talent-arranging, and you should try to be conscious of both. Level one is physical arranging. For example, you can move the talent so he sits at an angle to the camera. This can provide a nice break from the simple, looking-right-into-the-camera style of head shot, which is inescap-ably boring. The talent can sit, the talent can stand, the talent can stand first one way and then another. Whatever you do, no matter how still the talent will be while talking, the basic pose should suggest some kind of action. Shoulders at an angle suggests action—the talent was looking elsewhere, and has now bestowed his attention on us.

Level two of arranging has to do with the inside of the talent's mind. The talent is always, always nervous. It is the nature of the talent to be nervous. No less a talent than Sir Lawrence Olivier acknowledged that he couldn't remember even one time when he had performed without being nervous about it. If you are your own talent, then you already know what I mean.

To get the best results, it is critical that the talent rechannel that nervousness into action. Nervousness inhibits naturalness, and naturalness is critical to effec-tive talking heads. No matter how well you light, frame, and compose the scene, nervous talent will always be the first thing a viewer sees.

Here are some things you can do to redirect that nervous energy into action:

➤ Act confident in the ability of the talent to pull this off. No matter how nervous the talent is, if you convince them you believe in their abilities, they will calm down. I've seen people physically shake from the thought of being on camera. By talking to them calmly, reassuring them about how easy this is going to be, you encourage them to find their own inner resources to make the shot work. In fact, the more nervous someone is, the more energetic the subsequent video can be.

➤ Be specific. If the talent is fiddling with his hair, don't just say, "Sit still." Say something like "OK, your hair is just perfect for the lighting like that. Don't touch it again, OK?" Lots of "OKs" are great with talent. In their heads, they are saying, yes, it's OK. This is a good thing for them to do.

➤ Encourage them to use simple hand and body gestures. Where appropriate, a shrug of the shoulders or a raised hand can achieve two things. One, being physically active helps reduce nervousness. Two, it livens up the video a little, and that's almost always a good thing, too.

➤ Get them to smile. How you do it doesn't matter, but a smile is the most effective way to redirect energy.

➤ Don't be critical. Be positive. Praise the talent for what they do right, and calmly suggest any changes they need to make, building if possible on the things they did right. For example, don't say, "Don't tilt your head like that at the end." Instead say, "Your camera presence was very good. Look right through the camera like you did in the first part, OK?" Keep saying "OK." It's very effective and if you're lucky the talent will remember Joe Pesci in *Lethal Weapon 2*, and smile.

Action Shots

Action shots are the hardest shots in video because there's no time to think; you have to rely on instinct. Unfortunately, instinctive reactions come from years of experience, and it takes several years to get that. What is one to do in the meantime? Until you master them, you stick to the basics. The basics are:

➤ Whenever possible arrange it so the subject is moving across the field of view, not toward you or away from you. This eliminates the need to rapidly change focus, which means you can rely on the autofocus capabilities of your camcorder.

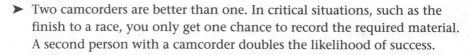

➤ Two camcorders are better than one. In critical situations, such as the finish to a race, you only get one chance to record the required material. A second person with a camcorder doubles the likelihood of success.

➤ Following a moving subject is a lot like hitting a pitched ball or a golf ball. Follow-through is very important. Don't just jerk the camera into motion as the subject enters the field of view, and then stop when it leaves. Anticipate the subject's motion even before you start filming, and go past the point where the action ends, just in case. This gives you almost guaranteed smooth transitions back in the studio when you edit, either to tape or to your hard disk.

➤ If your camera has fast shutter speeds, use them. The standard shutter speed on a camcorder isn't sufficient to freeze action. If you plan to show part of the sequence in slow motion, or to capture single frames for display on a monitor or for printing, you will need fast shutter speeds for clear results. Use 1/1,000th of a second or faster for best results. Keep in mind that the fastest shutter speed you can use will be determined by the available light. You can use a much faster speed on a sunny day, while fast shutter speeds indoors will probably require supplemental lighting.

Business Meetings, Seminars, and Presentations

I may have made a mistake earlier when I said that a talking head was the most boring thing to videotape. Groups of talking heads are even more prone to inciting boredom. With one or two heads, you can still see the facial expressions, which limits the lower level of boredom. With a group, you may not see any expression at all. The boredom level can reach excruciating in no time at all.

What can you do to enliven such video "opportunities?" Well, the optimal budget solution requires two cameras to be effective. One camera takes in the whole scene, varying the actual shot with the following techniques:

➤ Panning from side to side

➤ Occasional zooms

➤ Extended (long-time) full-group shots.

The second camera has a different job. It's like the roaming endzone camera at a football game. Camera number two is responsible for finding where the action is, and zooming in on it. This camera can afford to be wrong, because the first camera is almost guaranteed to capture at least a boring version of the event, even if the roaming camera chooses wrong. When the time comes to record to your hard disk, you can use only the best shots from the roaming camera, and use the main camera for continuity. The second camera can even be a hand-held, adding further variety to the final tape. Be careful with hand-held, of course; if it is too jerky the results will look like one of those Docker's commercials.

Landscape and Scenery

You would think that the easiest subject to tape is an outdoor scene. After all, the subject just sits there, and is probably reasonably good looking, or you wouldn't want to film it. What could go wrong?

To start with, this does not consider a fundamental difference between a camera lens and the human eye. The human eye manages to be a wide-angle and a zoomed-in device all at one time. A camera lens has to choose between these two modes.

When you look at a natural scene, your eye comfortably takes in a very large visual space, extending from directly left to directly right, and almost from straight up to straight down. Our clever brains manage to absorb this vast scene, while paying most of our attention to what's directly forward of us. This gives us the best of both worlds: appreciation for the magnitude and sweep of the scene, and the ability to enjoy the details in any part of the scene.

A camera lens has to choose. It can record the entire scene and lose the detail, or it can focus in on one aspect of the scene. After all, a video screen is much smaller than the full sweep of natural human vision. Actually, it's not that simple. The camera lens can zoom in a lot closer than the eye can, and the eye can take in a much wider view than the average camcorder lens can. This means you will have to pan to show the entire scene, and that is just not as interesting as seeing it all at once, so don't overdo scenic pans. Once, while hiking a small portion of the Pacific Crest Trail with camcorder in tow, I stood at the top of a mountain and slowly panned the camera from one side to the other. The view was, of course, stunning. To make a long story short, when we got home it was all too obvious how poorly my pan captured the sense we had had standing there in person. The scenic pan is informative—it shows what is there—but it is not often vivid enough to make good video. Use it sparingly.

Buildings and Other Tall Objects

Videotaping tall objects introduces a problem that is well-known to still photographers: distortion. For example, the building in Figure 3.44 was filmed from near its base, resulting in a distorted view—the boat looks quite large compared to the house. Stepping back gives a somewhat more natural-looking image, as shown in Figure 3.45. Now you can see the actual size of the boat. Of course, if you wanted to brag about the size of your boat, distortion might be your object.

Figure 3.44. Distortion occurs when a large object is too close to the camera.

Stepping back wasn't the only thing I did to create Figure 3.45; I also zoomed in so that the frame contained approximately the same portion of the scene as is shown in Figure 3.44. Without zooming in, there would be a lot of extraneous stuff in the picture, as shown in Figure 3.46.

In the hustle and bustle of taping, you may not notice that the view of a building is distorted, but the viewer almost certainly will notice. Plant a little program in your mind to be thoughtful of such things, and the next time you're filming someone's corporate headquarters you won't have to go out and redo it when you realize that the building looks more like a pyramid than an office building.

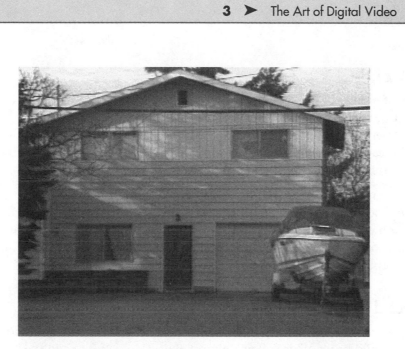

Figure 3.45. Adding distance reduces distortion.

Figure 3.46. The un-zoomed shot corresponding to Figure 3.45.

Low Light

Some of today's cameras offer enhancements that allow you to film in low light conditions. This is great for home videos, where being able to see little Jimmy's Halloween costume at night is a big deal. It's another thing entirely when you have to capture that video to your hard disk at 160x120 pixels and you suddenly find that it looks like garbage.

I mentioned this earlier, but it's worth repeating: adequate light is essential for any video that will be seen in a professional capacity. I can't really think of a situation where low-lighting would be acceptable. That doesn't mean there isn't one, of course, but it does mean you should think twice about where and how you might add light to a underlit scene.

Special Effects

Many cameras come with special effects. I will only say this once: almost all of them should be ignored. You will almost always do better to add special effects after you have the video on your hard disk, and can use editing software for effects. Besides, the effects available in the newest software packages go far beyond anything you can do right on the camera, and you don't have to do the effects live—you can add them later. I am a big fan of focusing my attention on the actual shooting, not on what I consider distractions.

The Art of Animation

If you are asking yourself why there is a section on animation in a book about digital video, pay attention to that word "digital." Boh animation files and video files are digital information, both involve the concept of frames. The only difference is that one comes from live action (most of the time) and one does not.

In fact, the internal file formats of some animation files and AVI files are actually fairly similar.

There are a number of powerful animation tools available for PCs. They range in cost from about $100 to several thousand dollars. In general, you get what you pay for. If you want 3-D animations, for example, you'll need something like Autodesks's 3-D studio, which retails for several thousand dollars but allows you to create photo-realistic animations. I have included several on the CD-ROM, and we'll work with one of them here. If your needs don't involve a third dimension, products such as Autodesk Multimedia Explorer and Gold Disk's Animation Works Interactive offer good solutions at the low end, and Autodesk's Animator Pro offers a high-end solution. We'll look at each of these products in some detail later on. First, let's look at just what animation is, and how that relates to digital video.

Animation Primer

Animation, movies, and video have in common the concept of *frame*. A movie displays 24 frames per second, and we perceive that as motion. Animation movies also use 24 frames per second. Video, on the other hand, uses 30 frames per second. Digital video typically uses anywhere from 10 to 30 frames per second, and animations can use just about any frame rate that your computer can play.

Animation has another concept, the *cel*, which is not as easy to explain as a frame. To start with, a given frame can contain any number of cels. Let's look at an example from real life: Saturday morning cartoons. For our example, let's use something with obvious cels—those cartoons that don't have a lot of animation. They aren't a lot of fun to watch, but they do make the concept of a cel easier to visualize.

For example, if a scene has a painted background, and a single figure in the foreground who is raising his fist to the sky, there would be three animation elements involved:

➤ The background.

➤ A cel with the figure on it.

➤ A cel with the figure's arm on it.

If it takes, say, two seconds for the figure to raise his arm, and there are 24 frames per second, then:

➤ The background image will not change over those 48 frames.

➤ The figure cel will not change over those 48 frames.

➤ The arm cel will change from frame to frame, moving to the appropriate new position in each subsequent frame.

The advantage of using cels is that only a small part of the image needs to be manipulated in each frame. The disadvantage of cels is that large portions of the image remain static. If you aren't careful, all naturalness will disappear from the animation when you use cels.

There are two additional concepts involved in animation on computers that are important to know about. The first is tweening, and the second is morphing. Tweening involves putting a cel in different positions in two different frames, and then having the computer calculate the intervening cel positions for the frames between the two copies of the cel. This allows you to animate a cel very easily. However, if a cel has to change its appearance from frame to frame, tweening won't work. In the example of the moving arm, the cel must change appearance as the arm moves through its arc. Otherwise, the motion would be extremely robotic and unnatural.

Morphing (called polymorphic tweening in Animator) is more complex than simple tweening. You have probably seen sophisticated examples of polymorphic tweening in movies and commercials. For example, in Terminator II, the changing shape of the villain is accomplished with morphing. To morph, you place a cel in one frame, and a different cel in another frame, and then the computer calculates a series of images that metamorphoses one image into the other.

There are many more things that computers add to animation, but they vary from product to product. In the section on Animation Software, we'll look at the key features of several animation packages.

The Relationship Between
Video and Animation

As I mentioned earlier, the relationship between video and animation is very close. Both use frames, and many products allow you to move fluidly from animation file to video file. For example, you can easily import an animation from Animator Pro into a video file. I "write" a monthly column for Nautilus, the CD-ROM magazine (that is, it is distributed on a CD-ROM, not paper) that uses several animations that have been converted to .AVI files. This allows me to add sound to the animations easily.

A Frame is a Frame

The key to using animations in digital video sequences is that both formats are frame-oriented. For best results, *both media should use the same frame rate*. This avoids unforeseen problems when combining material from different source media. For example, if you are capturing a video sequence at 15 frames per second, make sure your animation sequence is also at 15 frames per second. In many cases, you can still work with media of different frame rates, but the results are not as predictable—the transitions between frames become arbitrary as the computer tries to adjust the frame rate. To maintain control over the appearance of your work, keep frame rates the same. It takes time and effort to create a good animation, and even subtle changes can be unpleasant surprises.

Incorporating .FLI and .FLC Files with VidEdit

The most common way to combine animation files and video files is to import an animation into the video file. Most animation file formats do not support sound, while video file formats do. That makes the video file the most logical container for the whole package.

Let's look at how to add an animation to a video sequence, step-by-step.

We'll begin with VidEdit, the video editor that comes with Video for Windows. The opening screen is shown in Figure 3.47.

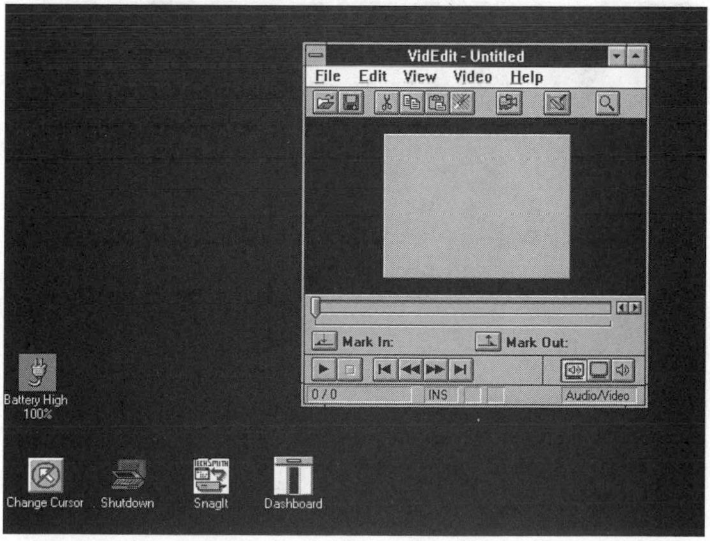

Figure 3.47. Opening screen of VidEdit.

The top part of the window contains the menu and a series of buttons in a toolbar. The most commonly used functions are in the toolbar, and they include access to files, cutting and pasting, and zooming options. The lower part of the window contains controls for moving to specific locations in the file, and for marking selections.

It's easy to import an animation file into VidEdit. The file menu has a selection called Insert that allows you to insert all kinds of files, such as animation and wave (sound) files. It is much easier to insert an animation into a blank file than into an existing file. We need to customize the animation file to match the video file. To determine what changes you need to make, load the video file into VidEdit and use the Video/Information menu selection to determine such things as frame rate and frame size.

We begin customization with resizing. In many cases the animation file size will be different from the video file size. In this case, the animation size is 320x200, and the video file is only 90x120. There are two ways to resize: by cropping the image using the Video/Crop menu selection, or by scaling the image using Video/ Resize. Figure 3.48 shows the Video menu. For this example, we'll use resizing, not cropping, but they are similar techniques. Resizing scales the existing frames to the new size, which can distort the image if the change is not constant between the vertical and horizontal directions. Cropping selects a portion of the frame to fit in the new size.

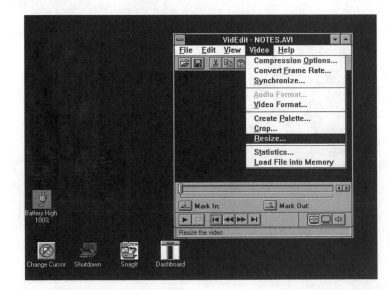

Figure 3.48. VidEdit Video menu.

The Resize selection brings up a small window showing the current size of the video (see Figure 3.49). To resize, we just enter the new width and height.

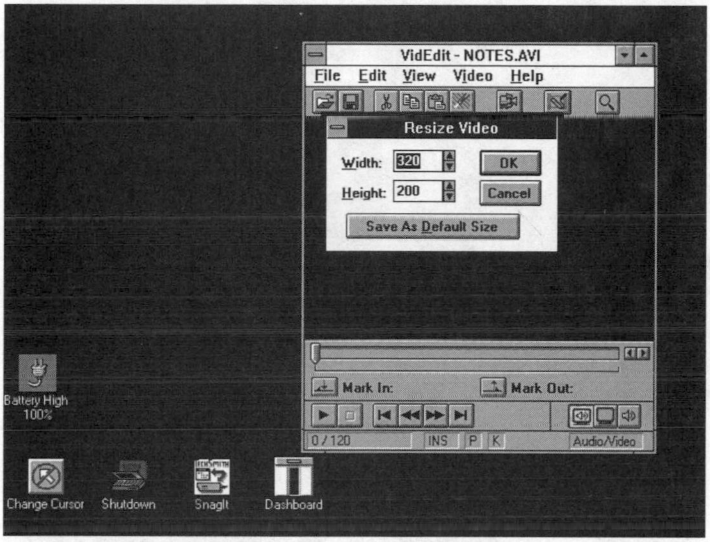

Figure 3.49. Resizing dialog box.

Figure 3.50 shows the original and resized images. The original image, on the left, shows a problem that sometimes occurs when you import an animation into VidEdit: it is stretched horizontally. The resizing, shown on the right of Figure 3.50, yields better proportions.

The frame rate of the animation will not necessarily match the frame rate of the video. In this example, the video frame rate is 8 fps (frames per second) and the animation frame rate is 14. To alter the frame rate of the animation, we use the Video/Convert Frame Rate... menu selection. This displays a dialog box that allows us to enter a new frame rate (see Figure 3.51).

Figure 3.50. Original and resized animation frames in VidEdit.

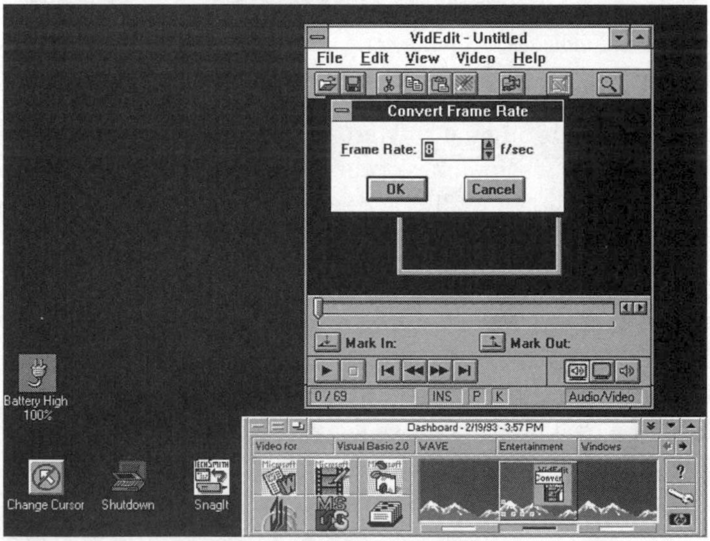

Figure 3.51. Dialog box for changing frame rate.

You can enter a number by typing, or use the arrow icons to change the displayed rate up or down.

The next step shouldn't be necessary, but I have found from experience that it helps to save the animation we just created as a compressed file, using Microsoft Video 1 compression. (If you will be using some other compression algorithm for the video file, use it for the animation file, too.) To save the animation as an AVI file, first use the Video/Compression Options selection to choose Microsoft Video 1 or your favorite compression method.

Advanced tip: if you want the best results with 8-bit palettized files, save the palette from the video file to disk, and then use it as the palette for the animation file. There are two ways to do this: you can import the palette into your animation software, or you can paste the palette using VidEdit. Best results are usually obtained by using the palette in your animation software. Use the Video/Create Palette menu selection to create a palette from your video file, as shown in Figure 3.52.

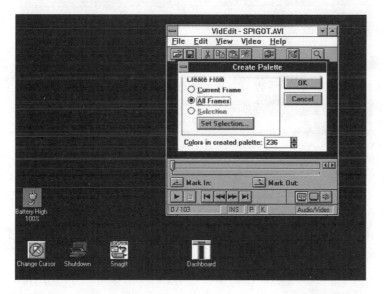

Figure 3.52. Creating a palette from a video file.

You can create a palette from the current frame, all frames, or the currently selected frames. Use the Mark In button to define the beginning frame of a selection, and Mark Out to define the end frame of a selection. Note that the frame that is current when you press the Mark Out button becomes the first frame *after* the selection; it is *not* included in the selection.

Now we have two video files to combine, and that's probably the easiest part of the process. Begin by loading the original video file into VidEdit. Figure 3.53 shows the file I chose for this exercise: President Clinton jamming with the E Street Band at one of the Inaugural Balls.

Figure 3.53. President Clinton jamming with the E Street band.

You can insert the animation file at any point in the file; in this case, we want to insert it at the beginning of the file. If you wanted to insert it at a different point, you only make that frame the current frame.

Use the File/Insert menu selection (see Figure 3.54) to add the converted animation file.

This opens the dialog box shown in Figure 3.55. Note the drop down list box at the lower left corner of the dialog box, labelled "List Files of Type." There are a number of files listed. Note that there is a listing for Autodesk Animation files. I recommend against attempting to add animation files when you already have a video open.

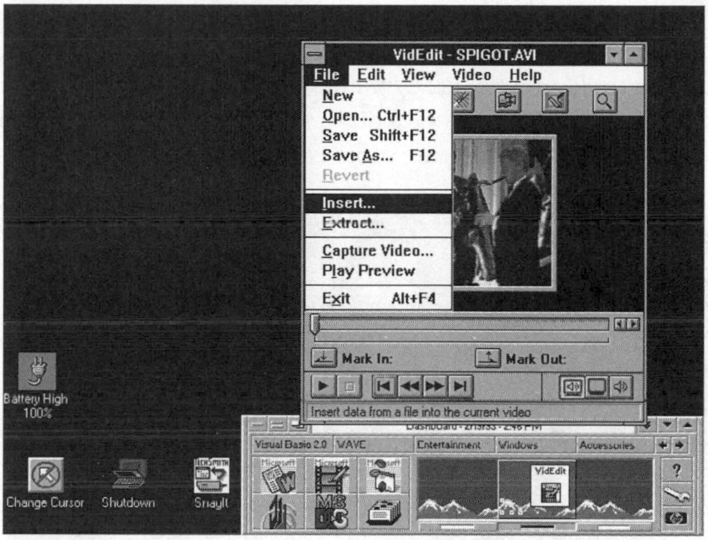

Figure 3.54. VidEdit File menu.

If not already selected, choose files of type Microsoft AVI. Then select the converted filename in the list of files. Click the OK button when you are ready to insert the file. The file will be inserted at the current position; the current frame will become the first frame after the inserted material. Figure 3.55 shows how the insertion affects the appearance of the VidEdit window. The number of fames shown in the status bar has increased (from 103 to 172), the current frame marker has moved from the left of the window to a point closer to the middle, and the length of the file has increased. The frame that was current before the insertion is still the current frame; now it is frame 69 instead of frame 0.

Once the file has been inserted, you can save the combined file to disk, using Microsoft Video or your favorite compression algorithm.

I have not been entirely happy with the current implementation of file insertion in VidEdit, and I caution you to examine the resulting file carefully for flaws. The most common flaw with animation files is improper rendering and playback of non-key frames. When you are selecting a compression method, you can choose how often to have a key frame—the default is one every 15 frames. Key frames are rendered completely, while the intervening frames are stored as a

list of changes to the last key frame. This saves space, but if anything gets out of whack, you'll see bits of colors in the wrong places, or worse. If you get this kind of problem, you could try setting key frames for every frame (that is, enter a 1 for the key frames item). This forces VidEdit to save the file with all key frames. The file will be larger, but the results are more consistent.

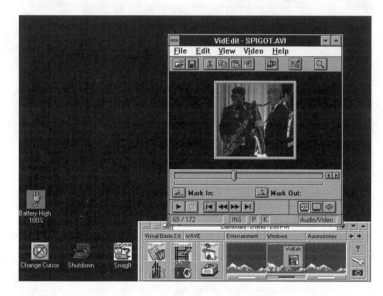

Figure 3.55. VidEdit window after a file has been inserted.

The problem with non-key frames may vary from one computer to the next. This suggests the problem lies in how the bitmap images are being interpreted by the video display driver, so you could also check with the video display board manufacturer to see if there is an updated driver available for your card.

Animation with Your Camera

You may not realize it, but your video camera can be used to create animations. If your camera can play one frame at a time, you can use it to create animations. To see if your camera can do this, check near the VCR controls on the camera; you'll need a control that is marked "Frame advance" or "F. Adv." or something similar.

The process of animating is usually not quite as simple as you might like: you can't just shoot one frame at a time with most camcorders. There are two possibilities:

➤ If your camera supports interval recording (recording a brief segment, pausing, recording a brief segment, pausing, etc.), you can automate the process. My Canon A-1 does interval recording, and I created a sample file that is included on the CD-ROM. The filename is reveng3.avi. I simply set the camera to record .5 second of tape every 10, 30, or 60 seconds—however long it takes to set up for the next frame.

➤ You can also simply shoot as short a sequence as you can manage manually. Position the animation frame, press start, press stop, and arrange the next frame.

In both techniques, you are actually recording more than one frame of animation (actually, 15 or more!), but you can deal with that during digital capture. Instead of just capturing the entire sequence, capture individual frames. If you plan to create a video with 15 frames per second, every 15 frames you capture add up to one second of viewing time. (Keep this in mind as you tape; otherwise, the action may move more or less quickly than you want.) If the animation is short, or if your camera doesn't have a "Frame advance" button, you can capture the entire animation and then delete the extra frames. Either way works well.

The hard part of animation, however, is what you put in front of the camera. If you ever watched the old Monty Python TV show, you may remember some pretty bizarre animations. The only limit is your imagination. Ideas for animation that you can try are listed below.

➤ One of the easiest ways to animate is to simply move ordinary objects around from frame to frame. This can be quite humorous if you give them a little personality. You can create whole new categories of narrative, such as bottle-cap-meets-bottle-opener, instead of the more mundane boy-meets-girl. See the file revng3.avi for an example; a series of sample frames are shown in Figure 3.56a-h.

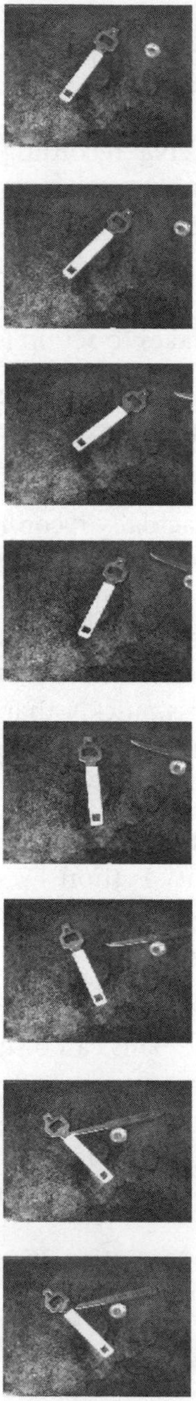

Figure 3.56a-h. Eight frames from a video animation.

➤ In addition to moving ordinary objects, you can move unusual objects, such as bits of paper with illustrations on them. For example, you could take a photograph of a person standing in the street, tear it into pieces, and animate the pieces coming back together to reassemble the photo. You could take a picture of a woman's head and animate it on top of a picture of a man's body.

➤ You can use a variety of plastic materials—clay, play-doh, beeswax, for example—and create original animations. This is not easy, but the effects can be very dramatic if you have an artistic touch. The best known example of this kind of animation is Playmation, originated by Will Vinton.

➤ You can even animate people. If your camera does interval taping, set the interval to its fastest setting (on my camera, that's every ten seconds), and then just assume interesting or appropriate poses for each interval. This can be a lot of fun; I'm not sure it's all that artistic.

➤ And, of course, you can always draw on pieces of paper and animate *that*.

Animation Software

There are a number of animation packages available; they range from simple and fun to complex and fun. The package you select for your needs depends on what you will be doing. Different packages emphasize different aspects of animation. The key tool areas are:

➤ Creating graphics: does the package give you sufficient tools for creating original graphics?

➤ Importing graphics: does the package allow you to import scanned images or images created with other software packages? Does it handle both vector and raster images?

➤ Time painting: can you control how an image is painted into a series of frames?

➤ Special effects: what kinds of special effects are included in the package?

➤ Cel animation: can you animate a cel across a number of frames?

➤ Path animation: can you define a path for an object across a number of frames?

➤ Layering: can you place objects on layers so they appear appropriately in front of and behind other objects, and can you move to a different layer during animation?

➤ Rendering: does the package allow you to create photorealistic images from simple objects, such as wireframe models?

There are three basic kinds of animation; each emphasizes a different set of tools:

➤ **Fun animations.** If you are simply doing animation for your own enjoyment, you will most likely want to go with an animation package that will allow you to express your creativity. You'll need a package that will allow you to import illustrations created with other paint programs, that will allow you to create graphics right in the animation package, and that will include a wide range of "time painting" tools. My favorite package for this use is Multimedia Explorer from Autodesk. Not only is it inexpensive, but it contains a CD with many, many sample animations. The supplied software features Animator, a slightly scaled-down version of Autodesk's Animator Pro. The primary difference is that Animator only works with an image size of 320x200, with 256 colors. Animator Pro works with a wide range of image sizes. Both products share a unique user interface that is powerful but takes some time to learn.

➤ **Business animations.** Ease of use is an overriding concern for most business users, since there is not usually a lot of time available for complex animations. For example, if you are looking to use animations to emphasize the contents of a chart, fancy painting capabilities aren't needed, but the ability to move objects along paths is. Products such as Animation Works Interactive give you the kinds of tools you need, and an easy-to-learn interface.

➤ **Professional animations.** You can create some very sophisticated animations on a PC; the two products that I have found best for complex animations are 3-D Studio and Animator Pro, both from Autodesk. In fact, these two products work well together. 3-D sequences created with 3-D Studio can easily be imported into Animator Pro for enhancement.

In each demonstration that follows, you will learn how to create an animation for which the package is best suited.

Multimedia Explorer

Multimedia Explorer is more of an animation potpourri than a single product. It includes an animation creator, an animation player, and an amazing number of sample animations created with a variety of Autodesk software products. You can have a lot of fun with this package, even if you never use it to create an animation. In fact, for the first few days I had it, I spent most of my time checking out the sample animations; there is a tremendous variety of styles included.

Multimedia Explorer includes a player program which you can use to combine sounds and animations into scripts. A script can play just one animation and one sound, or many, many animations and sounds. You can use the player to control the rate of playback, number of repetitions for any animation, and many other aspects of playback. The opening screen is shown in Figure 3.57. If you already have animation player, your screen may not look exactly like the one shown. New versions are often made available in the Autodesk forum on CompuServe.

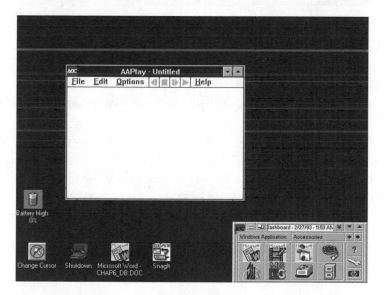

Figure 3.57. The Autodesk Animation Player opening screen.

You cannot create new animations with animation player, but you can create animation scripts. A script can include existing animation files or bitmaps. When you play a script, it will play each animation image. You can alter playback rates, create loops, and add background sounds with the Animation Player. Figure 3.58 shows the Edit Script dialog box.

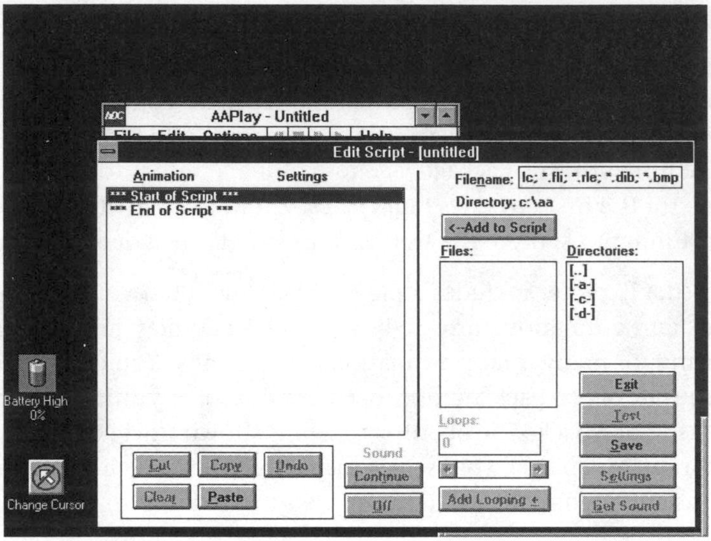

Figure 3.58. Edit Script dialog box for the Animation Player.

As you can see, there are a large number of scripting options available. You can add animation files or images; they are listed in the large list box at the left of the dialog box. Figure 3.59 shows an Edit Scripts dialog box with several bitmap files added.

There are two buttons at the lower right of the Edit Script dialog box that are worth knowing about. Clicking the Get Sound button opens a list of sound files, and clicking the Settings button allows you to change the settings for any one animation or image file. The settings box has a large number of adjustable parameters that allow you to customize the playback script, as show in Figure 3.60.

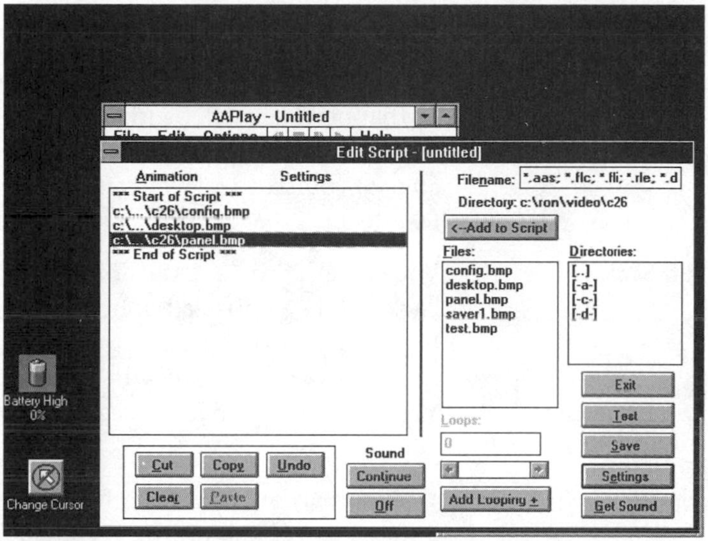

Figure 3.59. An Edit Script dialog with several bitmaps added.

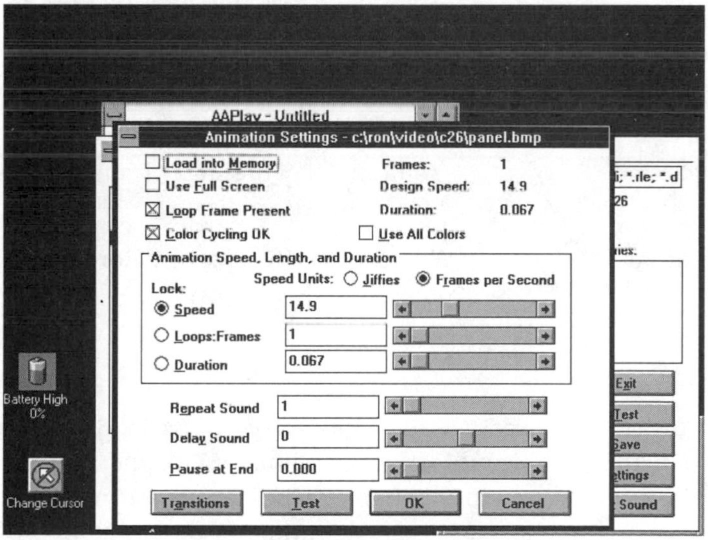

Figure 3.60. Customizable settings for individual files.

Setting	Description
Load into Memory	This loads the animation files into memory so that playback will be instantaneous. You will need to have enough memory available, of course, to take advantage of this feature.
Use Full Screen	You can elect to have the animations play back full screen instead of in a window. I have found that some older video display card drivers don't work with this option. You will need to check to see if your card does.
Lock Speed	You can play an animation file back at a different speed than it was recorded at.
Loops: Frames	This allows you to loop the animation.
Duration	You can change the duration of the animation.
Repeat Sound	You can specify the number of times that the sound is to repeat.
Delay Sound	You can delay the start of sound playback by a specified amount.
Pause at End	You can specify a pause before the next item in the script plays.

Animator

The Multimedia Explorer package also includes a copy of a DOS-based animation package, Animator. While some features of Animator Pro, upon which Animator is based, have been omitted in the junior product, the vast majority of animation tools have been included. This makes Animator the Animation Deal of the Decade. You get a tremendous amount of functionality for a very small price.

The biggest difference between the products is that Animator only supports one image size: 320x200. This can be a disadvantage for professional-level animations, but if your needs aren't that demanding, you'll enjoy working with

Animator. It is geared toward the drawing side of animation. You might say it is a drawing package that let's you cut and paste within slices of time. For example, you can select an area of the screen in one frame, and then paste it in a different position in another frame. Animator will place the selection in intermediate positions in the intervening frames.

As I mentioned earlier, the biggest difference between the products is that Animator only supports one file size: 320x200. This can be a disadvantage for professional-level animations, but if your needs aren't that demanding, you'll enjoy working with Animator.

If you have used conventional drawing or painting packages, you will discover that Animator uses a completely different interface. There are some menus at the top of the screen, but everything else is unique. Dialog boxes aren't transients, like they are in Windows; they hang out on the screen while you work, for example. To get a general idea of how Animator works, refer to the examples of Animator Pro in Chapter 20. The primary difference is the screen resolution—the Animator Pro screen shots were done at 640x480, whereas Animator works only in 320x200.

You won't be able to include video files directly into Animator files, but you can convert AVI files to FLC files using some techniques explained in the section "Hands On with Animator Pro and 3-D Studio."

Animation Works Interactive

If Animator is a great way to work with the drawing side of animation, Animation Works is a great way to work with actors. An actor is a package consisting of one or more cels that can be handled as a single object. Using Animation Works, you could quickly place an animation of a flying bird into your animation, and then fly in some text.

The basics of working with Animation Works are covered in Chapter 16, in the section "Animation Software: Animation Works Interactive."

Animation works allows you to incorporate videos into animations. The support isn't very sophisticated. You cannot, for example, animate a video for playback. You can simply specify the position of the video, and that's where it will play. To place a video, you start with the Event/Video menu selection. This allows you to set the playback parameters for the video. You can enter a filename, determine whether to use the video palette, establish coordinates for the video

numerically or by drawing a box on the screen. The video box is simply a marker; you cannot grab it with the mouse and change its size and position.

There is a check box at the bottom of the Event/Video dialog box called "Kill Video Event." If checked, this will close the file and remove the video image from the screen when it is done playing.

Animation Works also supports direct calls to MCI, but it did not work well with video files. Trying to play movies this way resulted in General Protection Faults, the Windows equivalent of a crash, so I do not recommend it. If you want a button to play a video, you are better off using the "Play Range" command, and jumping to a frame with a Video event.

Despite a relatively weak implementation of video support, Animation Works is an excellent product. However, if you are serious about integrating video into your animations, you may want to wait for a new version that integrates video more tightly.

Hands-On with Animator Pro and 3-D Studio

When pure fun must give way to the need for impressive results, two packages stand out as premiere products: 3-D Studio and Animator Pro, both from Autodesk (the folks who make AutoCAD). Both products can produce stunning results. We'll take a brief look at how they are used.

Animator Pro: Smooth Operator

Like its little brother, Animator Pro offers a lot of tools to work with. It also offers the ability to work with larger screen sizes and more colors, both of which allow you to create dazzling animations. In this example, we'll work at 640x480, and we will animate an imported image and some text.

You can also convert your video files (*.AVI) and work on them with Animator Pro. This allows you to create some interesting effects. In this example, we'll take a video clip of a jet and add some titles. Start by loading the AVI file into VidEdit, and then using the Mark In and Mark Out buttons to select the entire file. Use File/Export to output the selection as a sequence of bitmaps. Make sure that you select DIB Sequence as the file type, and make sure you use a filename of the form "jet00000.bmp" to make sure that a sequence of files is output. This will create a series of bitmap files: jet00000.bmp, jet00001.bmp, jet00002.bmp, etc.

I had to convert the bitmaps to .TIF files before I could load them into Animator Pro; I used ImagePals, a utility included with PhotoStyler, to convert them as a batch. Figure 3.61 shows a typical ImagePals screen with all those .BMP files ready to be converted to .TIF files. I found the ability to operate on many files at one time (141 in this case) to be a great feature, and I recommend ImagePals very highly.

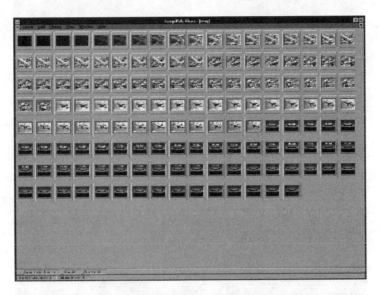

Figure 3.61. ImagePals with 141 image files in an album, ready for conversion.

To import the files into Animator, use the menu choice POCO/Numpics. You will see four choices; pick Load, and then select the first file in the sequence (jet00000.tif) as the filename. Animator Pro will create a frame for each image in the series. Save the file using the FLC menu.

Once you have a FLC file, the fun starts. Figure 3.62 shows a typical Animator Pro screen. It shows frame 14 of the converted AVI file.

The first task is to select the Text tool. (See Figure 3.63.) Use the Swap/Trade menu selection to hide the frame and create a space for us to create some text: "Flying!" would be appropriate. After entering the text, use the Cel/Get menu selection to mark out just the text as a cel. (See Figures 6.64 and 6.65.)

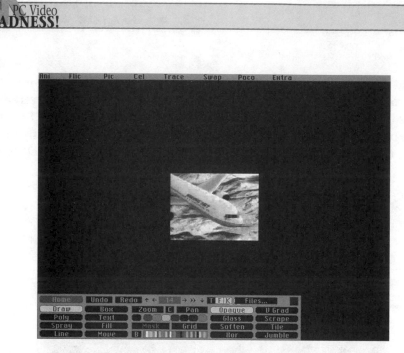

Figure 3.62. Typical Animator Pro screen.

Figure 3.63. Animator Pro's Text tool.

Figure 3.64. Selecting a cel.

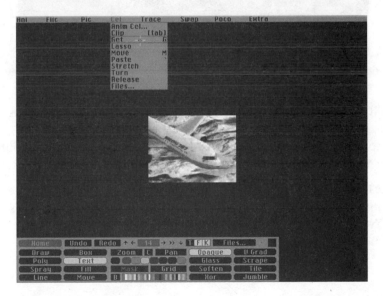

Figure 3.65. Animator Pro Cel menu.

Once the cel is marked, we can use Cel/Move to place it at the bottom of the frame, with the text located outside of the frame. Move to the last frame, and select Cel/Paste. This will highlight the cel in its current location (at the bottom of the frame), as shown in Figure 3.66.

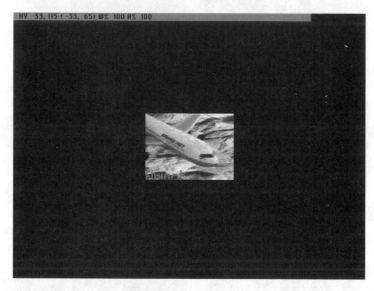

Figure 3.66. Positioning the cel in the frame.

We'll need to use *time pasting* to paste the cel into all of the frames. To turn time pasting on, click the small "T" button in the top row of buttons. Now drag the cel toward the top of the frame while holding down the mouse button; release the mouse button when the cel is where you want it to be.

The Time Select dialog will pop up. Click the Render button to render the new animation, or click the Preview button to check your work. That's all there is to it! Two frames from the animation are shown in Figures 3.68a-b, and the .flc file can be found on the CDROM as jet2.flc.

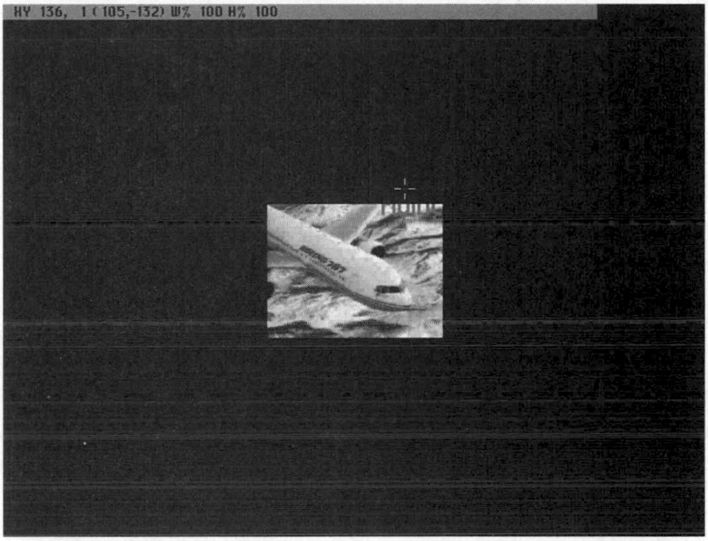

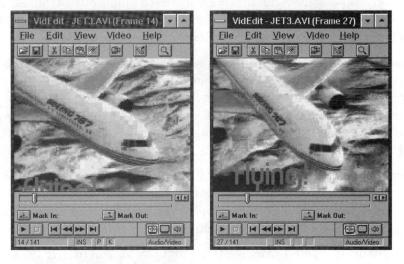

Figure 3.67. Moving a cel.

Figure 3.68a-b. Two frames from an animation with titles.

I have not, unfortunately, had good success loading animation files back into VidEdit that have been created this way. There is a bug that creates a false end of file and makes the inserted animation useless. I have notified both Microsoft and Autodesk of the problem. In the meantime, the best work around is to use the POCO menu selection Numpics to export the animation frames as .TIF files, and then use a utility like ImagePals to convert them into .BMP files. Then you can import them into VidEdit and they'll work fine.

3-D Studio: Master of Animation

The word animation doesn't appear in the product name for 3-D Studio, and you spend a lot of time working with things that have nothing to do with animation when you use it, but it is capable of producing truly stunning animations. It is also very effective in combination with Animator Pro, as we'll see shortly.

3-D Studio is a very powerful and complex product; we can only cover the merest fraction of its capabilities here. My book Multimedia Madness includes some detailed examples that show how to use 3-D Studio for complex animations. The CD-ROM that comes with that book also has a number of 3-D Studio animations on it. You can also find a large number of 3-D Studio animations on the CD-ROM that comes with Multimedia Explorer from Autodesk.

One of the more interesting ways to integrate 3-D Studio with video is to incorporate video into a 3-D Studio animation. For example, we could use 3-D Studio to create a cube. One of the steps in creating 3-D objects to assign a material to each object or surface. Instead of assigning a material (such as brass, blue plastic, leather, and so on), you can assign a bitmap. Even more powerful is the ability to assign a series of bitmaps, or a .FLC/.FLI file, to an object or surface.

For example, we could map the .FLC file of the jet (which we created using Animator Pro) to one side of our cube. As the cube rotates, the various frames of the .FLC file will be put into their proper position and perspective to give the illusion that the animation is playing on the surface of the cube.

Alternatively, if you convert the DIBs output by VidEdit to .TIF, .TGA, or .GIF files, you can list the filenames in a text file with the extension .IFL and use that in place of the .FLC file. This is useful if you don't have Animator Pro, or if you want to load the images directly into 3-D Studio.

For a specific example of working with video in 3-D Studio, see Chapter 20.

The Art of Video Libraries

To paraphrase the Rolling Stones, you can't always shoot what you want, but if you try, sometimes you get what you need. The key is to use libraries of video and other clips.

The use of video libraries is not, however, necessarily an easy thing. There are two kinds of libraries you can use. One is easy, and the other is both hard to use and expensive. The first kind of library consists of video clips that were collected with digital video in mind. These are usually available on a CD-ROM disc, ready for you to use in your productions. The second kind of library is one that stores the video on tape, and that expects its users to also use the clips on tape.

Video Clips: Disc-Based

Companies have just begun to realize that there is a market for video clips on CDs. As I write this book, a number of companies have expressed an interest in creating such CDs, and many others are already at work. The main advantage of using video clips on a CD is that the digitizing has already been done for you; you can just use the clips in your presentations. Be sure to note several factors before you purchase a video clip disc:

➤ What size are the clips? Are they offered at 160x120 as well as at larger sizes, or just at one size?

➤ What playback rate will you be using for the clips? Will they be played back from your hard disk, or will you play them back right from the CD? If you plan to play them back from a hard disk, you can use larger image sizes and faster frame rates than are possible for CDs. Does the CD supply you with the larger sizes and faster frame rates?

➤ What compression techniques, if any, were used on the clips? This will have a very large effect on the appearance of the clips. Or are the clips stored uncompressed, allowing you to decide what level of compression to use, if any?

➤ Is audio included with the clips? What quality is the audio? Will the audio play on the hardware you have available?

➤ What are the distribution rights for the clips? Can you use them anywhere, or are you limited to viewing in the privacy of your own home or office? Are there any licensing fees involved?

Video Clips: Tape-Based

Video libraries that are tape-based are a completely different animal. Not only are the video clips not available in a digital format, the library may not have any policy for digitizing their material—they may flatly deny you access! Where, you ask, are such libraries to be found? They are found anywhere there is tape, most notably at the various news organizations: CNN, and the network news departments. Another source is C-SPAN, the cable-company-sponsored non-profit that tapes government meetings.

Almost all of these organizations expect to get around $30 for each *second* of video they give you. If you have a little ten-second clip you want to use in a presentation, that will be $300, please.

If this price seems outrageous, I agree with you. In most cases, companies that have such tape libraries are used to selling very limited numbers of copies of their video footage. The idea that thousands and thousands of people might want access to it hasn't occurred to them yet. When (and if) it does, perhaps we'll see significantly more reasonable pricing. For now, the only reasonable way for Abigail Average to get her hands on news footage is to wait for someone else to put it out on a CD. If you do need specific video footage and can afford it, you can contact the news departments directly.

Audio Clips

Sometimes, you need a bit of audio to go with your video. Perhaps you have a tape that is so timeless that it needs music, or perhaps the sound quality of an otherwise wonderful video is terrible. In such cases, it's great to be able to turn to a wide variety of sound, including both music and sound effects, that you can add to your video.

The Art of Production

Video production is the process of creating an original video, either on tape or on your hard disk. This includes everything from the initial planning to the recording session. What you do after you have a recording is covered in the following sections "The Art of Editing" and "The Art of Post-Production."

The number of steps involved in creating a video will vary with the scope of the project. Assuming you are thinking of something less than a movie-length production, the most important steps are:

➤ Defining your ideas—It's not enough just to have an idea. To do anything effective with your ideas, you're going to have to play the game of "what if." The larger your production, the more expensive it is, and the more important it is that you consider the ramifications of your ideas early on. If your project is very small—one camera, one director, one actor, and one scene, and all of it handled by you—it's a lot easier. However, having a clear concept of what you plan to do can still be an effective tool, even for a one-person shop. The clearer your ideas, the less time you'll spend doing things over again.

➤ Planning—Once you have a clear idea, you need to plan how to make it a reality. Since you can never plan for every eventuality, don't over plan. Planning involves several key elements:

  ➤ How much money is this project going to require? Or, more commonly, how much money is available, and how are we going to use it?

  ➤ What is the deadline? Is it realistic?

  ➤ What resources will be needed? Are they affordable?

➤ Developing a script—Only the very shortest of videos can be shot without a script. There are, however, a variety of script types. They range from very loose—nothing more than a list of topics to cover—to completely scripted—every word, every movement, is on paper. Prepare the kind of script that will work for the kind of production you are mounting. In general terms, the more people there are, the more exact the script should be. That doesn't mean you can't make changes later; it does mean that everyone involved should sign off on the changes.

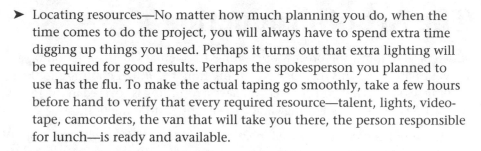
➤ Locating resources—No matter how much planning you do, when the time comes to do the project, you will always have to spend extra time digging up things you need. Perhaps it turns out that extra lighting will be required for good results. Perhaps the spokesperson you planned to use has the flu. To make the actual taping go smoothly, take a few hours before hand to verify that every required resource—talent, lights, videotape, camcorders, the van that will take you there, the person responsible for lunch—is ready and available.

➤ Shooting the video—Whether you are shooting in a studio, an office, or on location, no matter how many or few lights, cameras, actors, and props there are, make sure there is someone with the title Director. The director has the critical task of making sure that there is one person to whom all information flows. Ideally, the director is also in a position to make decisions, but if that is not possible it is still critical that there be one person who is designated to receive all information. It is the director's job, no matter what, to define such things as when recording starts and stops, whether to reshoot, and that the timing, lighting, and context of each scene is acceptable.

Teamwork

The folks working on a video production are commonly referred to as the production team. The analogy to sports is often a good one; there needs to be a leader, and there needs to be a strong sense of commitment to a common goal. An amazingly large number of little things need to go almost exactly right for a good video production; that won't happen unless there's a lot of cooperation. Make sure every member of the team knows what their responsibility is, that they have the resources needed to carry out their responsibility, and that they know where to go if there is a problem.

The more people you have on the team, the harder it is to keep track of everything. At a certain level, you should designate someone to be in charge of continuity. That person must make sure that no piece of the story gets lost or omitted during taping. For example, if a prop is used in scene 1 and you reshoot a part of scene 1, that prop better be there!

Scripting

The script is more important than many video producers and directors realize. Even the barest of scripts gives the people involved in the project a common sense of direction, and allows them to work together more effectively. A script can contain any of the following elements:

➤ Project outline—This is just a simple outline of what the project will include. For example, if you want to shoot a series of videos that show how to disassemble a complex piece of equipment, the script might be nothing more than a list of the steps to be filmed.

➤ Verbatim text for speaking parts—This is what most people think of when they think of a script. It consists of names and text.

➤ Scene descriptions—Even if you have specific, verbatim text in the script, you can also add general directions about a scene. Such descriptions could include things like the general mood for the scene, overall lighting considerations, and so forth.

➤ Prop and scenery descriptions—If there will be any props or scenery in the video, you can describe them in general or specific detail in the script. You can even include drawings, if needed, to show exactly what you want.

➤ Staging directions—This defines how, when, and where the various props and actors move during the scene. It is usually general rather than specific.

➤ Special effects descriptions—If you will need special effects, either audio or video, in a scene, be sure to specify them so they will be on hand for shooting or post-production, as required. Be very specific about what you need.

The Producer

When you watch the credits for a movie, notice where the credits of the producer show up—they are usually one of the first things you'll see when the movie starts. This is no accident—producers like to think they are very important to a movie's success. That's not quite right. A producer is essential to a movie's *existence,* not its *success.*

The job of a producer is to line up resources for a production. On a large film, this means finding the money to make the movie possible. On smaller projects, this means many things, ranging from financing to making sure there's enough tape on hand for shooting. The producer's job is endless and thankless, but it's also essential.

The Director

The movie credits for the director usually are the last ones you'll see before the action starts. I like to think this is because the director is the one person most responsible for the overall greatness or schlockiness of the film; the real "the buck stops here" person.

The list of things about which a director has final say are endless. The director must decide when everything is ready for a shoot; the director must decide when the material on tape is good enough to allow everyone to move on to the next scene. It is the director's job to determine if any words in the script were dropped, and if the drop makes a difference. It is also usually the director's job to tell the talent if they need to change any aspect of their performance.

The Talent

These are the people whose faces and voices you will see and hear in the final tape. Finding good talent is half the battle; motivating the talent is the other half. See "Recording Situations, Talking Head" in the section "The Art of the Camcorder," for a discussion about motivating the talent.

There are a wide variety of things that talent can do; some of them are listed below. These are all tools that you can use when you are creating your script.

➤ Narration—Can be done off-screen or on-screen.

➤ Acting—This is defined as any situation where someone pretends to be something they are not. Paying someone to play the part of a doctor involves acting; getting a doctor to talk on camera is not acting.

➤ Editorializing—This occurs whenever the talent expresses an opinion.

➤ Public speaking—If someone is not acting, and is not editorializing, then you probably have a spokesperson. This is the most neutral role talent can play; it is normally used for dry, but necessary information.

➤ Manipulating—Sometimes, you need extra hands to manipulate objects on camera, but the rest of the person is not seen.

In the Studio

Unless you are a professional, you won't actually find yourself recording in a studio. A studio has the advantage of having all the goodies at hand that you could possibly need for first-class videos. Theoretically, this removes the hassles inherent in video taping, but in reality there will always be something you need that isn't available. However, if you do have the opportunity to shoot in a studio, use it. It will reduce the crisis level significantly. In some cases, you may be able to use a community access studio at your local cable company for certain types of projects that you also plan to digitize.

On Location: The Mean Streets

Shooting on location is a hassle, and there is only one good reason to ever do it: locations are much more interesting than the average studio. Natural locations add force to a video, but be prepared to deal with the hassles of location shooting. Here's a handy list of things to watch out for:

➤ Things you left behind—It is almost inevitable that, in the rush to get out the door and on the way, you will forget at least one essential item. In fact, plan on it. If the project is more than a one-man operation, determine in advance who is most expendable for the inevitable trip back to home base.

➤ Unanticipated eventualities—Murphy's law requires that one or more things will go wrong while you're on location. Again, expect it. Things *will* go wrong. That's why you should have an extra tape or two, a backup lighting system, stand-in talent, extra copies of the script, extra batteries, and so on.

➤ Accidents—You may not be big enough to carry insurance, but if someone gets hurt—either someone in the production, or an innocent bystander—you had better know in advance how you're going to deal with that.

➤ Interference—While on location, someone may take it into his head to make a nuisance of himself, either by talking to your crew, or walking into your scenes. Designate someone to handle these types; the director should not have to do this unless you get a real tough case.

➤ Permission—You may have to get permission to shoot at the desired location. In this day and age, many institutions are surprisingly picky about what you can and cannot do on their property. Check this out far, far in advance of actual shooting.

➤ Craziness—Making videos is an intense undertaking—a lot of things have to happen in a short period of time, and near perfection is required at many steps along the way. Be prepared to deal with any emotions that boil over.

The Art of Editing

Editing is the physical act of separating the scenes that work from the scenes that don't, and arranging those successful scenes in a logical and coherent order. It may be more of an art than anything else in this chapter.

A video normally tells a story. Arranging the pieces that you have taped to tell a story well is not easy. In fact, it takes a lot of attention to detail to make it work right. Things to watch out for include:

➤ Visual alignment—When you join two segments or scenes together, you should observe how they fit together visually. For example, if the narrator is facing left in one scene, and then toward the right in the next scene, the effect of the change can be jarring. You may want to add a brief transition scene, such as a graphic or some text on screen, to smooth the transition from one scene to the next.

➤ Transitions—The method you choose for moving from one scene to the next is also important. You don't want to use a wide variety of techniques in any one video; this annoys the viewer. Often simple wipes and fades are all you need. If you do use fancy transitions, make sure they work perfectly, so the viewer won't be distracted by the special effects.

➤ Continuity—Make sure the edited pieces, when fit together, tell the story in the right order. Look for missing pieces, unexplained concepts, and so on.

➤ Story line—A story normally has a beginning, a middle, and an end. Does your video have all three? Or does it jump right in abruptly, or end without a real conclusion?

➤ Development—A story doesn't just happen by accident; it builds and builds, bit by bit. For example, if you are telling the story of how a particular plastic material is manufactured, you can develop the story chronologically, showing each step in turn. If you are telling the story of how local government works, you might develop the story with separate scenes for each branch of the government.

➤ Conclusion—Every good story has an ending, a point at which the viewer says, "It's over." Do not take it for granted that you have a real conclusion! Many, many videos just fade away, without ever having reached a conclusion. Let's use the two examples mentioned under Development. For the plastics story, you might conclude by showing something made of the material. For the government story, you might show a shot of the borough office, with a voice-over narration tying together the various mini-stories about the branches of government.

Production Versus Editing

Production stops when the tape stops rolling. Editing begins when the various scenes get copied onto a separate tape. There is a very critical step between these two phases of the project. It is called thinking.

One of the great dangers of editing is to start it too soon, before you are really ready. Think about it: before you shoot, you prepare a script. The script focuses your activities. During shooting, the script may be modified. The modified script serves as the input into the edit process. However, you need more than a script to edit well.

The editor should take the script, and view all of the available tape with the script in hand. This will help him find any problems before he gets started—missing parts of the story, problematic transitions, inadequate lighting, and so forth.

The editor should keep a list of these issues, and use them to prepare his own script, specifying what tape will be used where in the final edit. As with shooting, there may be some changes, but having a plan in hand before you start will make the job much more manageable, and the final tape or digital video a lot more successful.

Basic Editing

There are two ways to edit: on tape, or on your hard disk. The first decision to make is which method to use. Each has advantages and disadvantages.

Editing to tape—Generally speaking, you have more options if you edit to tape. In addition to simple editing, you can use any number of sophisticated post-production techniques to dress up the video. Typically, you can supply your tapes and an Edit Decision List (EDL) to specify what goes where. However, the cost of editing to tape at a professional studio can be high. A simpler approach is to acquire a basic editing tape deck, and use it to create a final tape. These are significantly more expensive than regular home decks, ranging from $1,300 to $7,000. Many of these units are *frame accurate,* which means that you can locate specific frames accurately.

Editing on your hard disk—the advantage here is cost—you don't need any extra hardware to edit on your hard disk. If you want even simple transition effects, however, you will need to get software such as ATI's Media Merge. This allows you to perform many of the special effects normally available at fancy post-production houses. In terms of fun quotient, this is Really Neat Stuff. See the chapters on Recording for examples of this software in use.

The Art of the Transition

How you move from one scene to another can either add to, or subtract from, the content of both scenes. A jarring transition can wipe the viewer's mind clean, while a smooth, appropriate transition can add significantly to the value of the video. As a general rule, restraint is usually the best choice. Unless you have a dead certain feeling that a special effect really, really works, keep it simple.

Graphics

You can easily use simple graphics to make a transition from one scene to the next. To make a graphic into a video, just import the bitmap into VidEdit, copy it to the clipboard, and then paste it as many times as necessary to achieve the right timing. Make sure your graphic is the same size as the rest of your video, of course.

Text

Text can also be effective for transition, but be careful not to overdo it. Text can be jarring if it is not intimately related to the flow of the film.

Wipes, Fades, and Other Fascinations

There are four simple transition effects:

➤ Straight—One scene simply ends, and the next one begins.

➤ Wipe—As an imaginary vertical line moves across the frame, the current scene disappears, and the following scene is revealed.

➤ Fade—The current scene fades (usually to black or white), and when the fade is complete, the next scene starts.

➤ Dissolve—The current scene fades out at the same time as the next scene fades in. Halfway through the transition, both scenes are partially visible.

The Art of Publishing and Distribution

It's no good just having a video; people have to see it. There are many ways to publish, some of which we'll examine in detail.

Yes, You Are a Publisher

It is a good idea to think in terms of being a publisher. For one thing, it opens up options for distribution that you might not otherwise think about. For example, you might not think that putting your videos on a CD-ROM is reasonable. However, that may in fact be the most economical way to distribute your video production, even if it doesn't use all of the space on the CD. (A CD can hold about 650 megabytes of data.)

Before You Publish

There are just two things you need to do before you publish:

➤ Make sure your video is totally, completely, absolutely done. The worst thing in the world is to publish and then discover a flaw.

➤ Decide how you are going to publish.

How to Publish

There are a number of different ways to publish your digital video file or files. The one you choose depends on a variety of factors. The most common ways to publish are:

➤ Floppy disk—This is only practical for very simple video files, say under 2.5 megabytes. Any single file that requires two or more floppies can be a problem unless you write your own installation routine.

➤ Electronic mail—Yes, you can email video files, but the large file sizes may annoy some folks, especially network managers facing heavy traffic.

➤ Tape—Single QIC-40 and QIC-80 tapes can hold a very large amount of data, up to 120 and 250 megabytes, respectively. This is more than adequate for most video productions, but the cost of tapes is around $20-30 each.

➤ Hard disk—Yes, sometimes this makes sense. For example, if you are setting up a training session that will involve several machines over which you have control, there's no reason you can't load the video files on each hard disk yourself.

➤ Networking—Most networks will not support the data rates required to play an AVI file, but you can store the files on the network for copying.

➤ One-off CD-ROM—Prices for recording CD-ROM drives are coming down; as we went to press, such drives cost from $6,000 to $8,000. While not cheap, this is much less than they were even a year ago. These drives allow you to create CD-ROM discs one at a time (hence the term "one-off"). If you need less than 30-40 CDs, this may be a cost-effective method of producing them. CDs offer more than 600 megabytes of storage, room for plenty of video footage.

➤ Mass-produced CD-ROM—This involves commercial production of CD discs. If you need more than 30-40 discs, this is the best way to go. In quantities of 10,000 or more, unit costs are less than $2.

Licenses, Royalties, and Rights

One of the hazards of working with the video medium digitally is that you are ahead of most of the planet. The people currently working with video—from CNN to your local television station—mostly don't have a clue about the potential for digital video on the desktop. Unfortunately, this means they will be quite unsympathetic to your needs for their footage. These companies will either sell you video footage at rates around $30 a second (!), or they are unwilling to sell at all. This is typical of how the video industry currently works. If you want to perform a public service, contact companies that sell video footage and let them know that you expect it to be available at a reasonable price!

Art for Art's Sake

In this chapter, I have included a lot of information about a wide variety of the elements that you can use in video productions. A lot of this can be described as technique. But there is a level at which technique fades, and "true art" begins. Exactly where that line exists varies from person to person.

How Wild Can You Get?

The combination of a video camera and a computer is powerful stuff. Add some editing software, and you have a tool whose limits have not nearly been tested. This is the ground floor, the first phase, the Early Days (perhaps someday they'll be called the Golden Days) when the modern equivalents of D. W. Griffith and Charlie Chaplin have yet to be discovered. The possibilities of the medium we call digital video are almost completely hidden—right now. You may be the one who sets new standards, who discovers new ways to fascinate, entertain, and inform.

4

Digital Video
and Multimedia

Digital video has the potential to transform the field of multimedia. However, it's probably going to take a while to happen. The problem? Many of the same problems that delayed the introduction of multimedia on the personal computer also haunt digital video. The most important factors are lack of awareness, inherent cost, and technical stumbling blocks. All of these are changing rapidly. Awareness blossoms the first time you see the impact of digital video on a desktop; cost is falling extremely rapidly; and the technology is advancing with impressive speed.

Why Digital Video Is Important

Before looking into the philosophical, metaphysical, and economic realities of digital video, you need to know why it is so important. You need to look at what digital video *does*.

On the surface, digital video does nothing more than convert a standard, analog video signal into bits and bytes. In the process, it makes it much more technologically challenging to store and play that video. If that was all digital video did, it wouldn't even be a very good toy.

However, once a video is in digital form, you can do things with it that were not possible when it was in analog form. You have given the video a new lease on life. Some of these new things are mechanical, and some have incredible potential.

Here's a brief list of some of the things you can do with a digital video that you can't do with an analog video:

➤ Make endless generations of copies without losing fidelity.

➤ Creatively edit the video in new and different ways—many of the special effects you see on television are actually done using digital video editing. That magnavox commercial with John Cleese appearing in any number of different Magnavox products, for example, uses digital editing.

➤ Create interactive video presentations for training materials with a minimal investment in time and effort.

➤ Incorporate videos into computerized environments.

➤ Use computers to empower and enhance home video editing.

The power of digital video becomes evident when you consider the implications of some of these changes. For example, consider the lowly business presentation. It started out on paper, moved to overhead transparencies and slides, and then migrated to the computer with presentation programs such as Harvard Graphics and Power Point. Some animation capabilities were added (Action!, Animation Works Interactive) eventually. Of course, if one had the money, one could always add video to the presentation, but often at very great expense.

Digital video changes all that. What used to cost $10,000 to $50,000 to do can now be put on a desktop computer for anywhere from $500 to $4,000.

This brings us to the most important fact about digital video. What everyone wants to do on their computer is edit video digitally, and get the same quality images on the desktop that we see on regular TV. That part hasn't happened yet. It's coming, but it isn't here now. To many people that means that digital video on the desktop isn't ready yet. That's incorrect.

Some aspects of digital video *are* on the desktop, *are* ready for Prime Time. In fact, the passive kind of video we see on TV is a poor model for what we'll get from digital video. Because digital video is *active*   *interactive* is the term most often used to describe it—thinking in terms of what we have now will not give us a clear picture of where we are going.

For example, how much impact does a presentation have that combines text and graphics to descibe a new product? And how much impact does it have if it adds a video demonstration of that product in use? I rest my case. To those of you who are saying that the frame sizes are so small—not any more! Just as I sat down to write this chapter I learned that the frame size that can be displayed has doubled; I expect we'll see further advances very soon.

The Introduction of Digital Video

Although digital video was available on desktop computers before either Apple Quicktime or Microsoft's Video for Windows, these two products have moved it from the periphery to the mainstream. The evolution of digital video on the two platforms is very different, however, and it reflects that natural differences between both the hardware and the users of these machines.

Quicktime appeared at the time when Digital Video was very, very new, and as a result it did not generate widespread excitement. In fact, quite a few of my Mac friends simply didn't know it existed. Video for Windows debuted later, with much hoopla and fanfare, no doubt in part to make up for its later entry into the market. One side effect of the publicity has been a stoking of general interest in digital video. I read general mail on the Multimedia forum on Compuserve, and there was a literal explosion of interest when Microsoft announced Video for Windows. Every day there were more and more questions about Video for Windows—how does it work, who is using it, how can I use it, what hardware should I buy, and so on. It was as if digital video hadn't existed before Video for Windows.

In one sense, that was true. Before Video for Windows, the bulk of video on a desktop involved capturing single frames. There were methods for capturing video sequences, but they were either expensive or incompatible, or both.

A Brief History of Digital Video

There are actually several histories of digital video on the PC. At the professional level, there has been a movement of some of the simpler digital capabilties to the desktop, but most of these have been targeted to folks who are acutally creating video tape productions; that's only one small part of digital video. It basically represents the need to accomplish digital editing with the minimum cost in hardware, and has a specialized audience, by and large.

The second history of digital video involves the movement of digital video capabilities into the mainstream of computer use, and that's what we'll look at here.

Digital video goes back a little further than you might expect. There have been a number of advances that predate the appearance of digital video on desktop computers. The reason for that is simple: it takes enormous horsepower to manipulate digital video. The most startling statistic I've heard is that it requires 1.5 gigabytes to store one minute of full-size, full-color digital video. One minute! How big is 1.5 gigabytes? That's 1,500,000,000,000 bytes, allowing for rounding error. If it were a sandwich, and you took one byte each second, it would take you 47,564 years to eat.

The size of hard disk being shipped with "average" desktop computers has grown to several hundred megabytes, but that's obviously inadequate to the task for full-size, full-color digital video. As a result, different aspects of digital video have slowly migrated to the desktop.

The first migration consisted of capturing individual frames. You couldn't watch video on your PC, but you could capture a single frame, store it to a file, and later edit it in a paint program, or incorporate it in a desktop publishing document.

The second migration occurred when it became possible to view video on a computer monitor in real time. (*real time* is one of the great buzzword terms of the digital video world; all it means is not having to wait till later to get digital.) For example, several years ago I used a Digital Eyes/RT (RT standing for, of course, real time) board to watch videos on my PC. It was a delicate operation, sometimes requiring time-consuming adjustments to get a reasonable picture. But, hey, it worked! The video was moving, just like *real* video.

The third migration consisted of the capability to capture video sequences. This meant that the video not only moved, but it could move even if you took away the video source. You could play back the captured sequence from the hard disk any time you wanted to. There were two methods of capture during this stage: software-only, and hardware-assisted. Software compression was cheap, used tiny little windows to display the video, and was available in as many flavors as there were companies manufacturing the hardware and software to do it. Hardware compression was fast, expensive, and could display video in a larger window.

The third migration was still missing a key ingredient: standards. Yes, you could capture a video sequence, but there wasn't any guarantee that you could distribute it and allow someone to play it back. There was one "standard" in the third migration, but it never became popular enough to be a true standard. That was DVI, Digital Video Interactive. DVI used hardware-assisted compression for capture, but it could play back using only software. You didn't need special equipment to *use* it, just to *create* it. It was not marketed aggressively, however, and thus was not widely known or available.

Then came the fourth migration, better known as Quicktime and Video for Windows. These products weren't a major leap in technology; they were a way to standardize how video sequences could be stored in a file. For example, by establishing standards, the AVI (Audio Video Interleaved) file format got everyone on the same track, and digital video could become more than just

a special-purpose tool. It became something you could create or view on any 386 (or better) computer. The key to the success of the fourth migration was the various *codecs* involved.

The word codec is built from the words *co*mpression and *dec*ompression. It is software or firmware (chips) that contain a program for the compression and decompression of video files. This compression makes it possible to store video data on a hard disk. When smaller frame sizes, slower frame rates, and codecs are used, you can store a minute of video in 20 megabytes instead of 1.5 gigabytes; that's a ratio of 1,500:20 (or 75:1) in the amount of space required. Of course, the window the video is displayed in is 160x120 pixels instead of 640x480, and the frame rate is 15fps instead of 30fps, and there are 256 colors instead of 16.7 million, but it works.

One of the smart things about Video for Windows is that it allowed for both existing video techniques (such as the Indeo codec, among others) and future technologies within the AVI file format. This was not complete compatiblity; you couldn't just take, for example, a DVI-format video file and use it. (DVI, short for *D*igital *V*ideo *I*nteractive, is a video file format that was released a few years before Video for Windows, but it never caught on like Video for Windows has.) What Video for Windows supports is a variety of video codecs. Anyone with the technical know-how can add a codec to Video for Windows.

Where is digital video going? The key advances will likely be in two areas: less expensive hardware for hardware-assisted compression in real time, and more efficient codecs for software-only playback.

The Future of Digital Video

The immediate future of digital video is likely to have several identifiable benchmarks. As I write this book, the current standard is capture and playback at 160x120 pixels, 15fps, and 8 bits of color depth. Not only is this close to the maximum amount of data that can be played back at the CD-ROM-dictated data rate of 150k per second, but it is about as much as capture hardware, video displays, CPUs, and hard disks can handle as well. This will change, and it will probably change quickly. How quickly? By the time this book finds its way into bookstores, we will have arrived at the next migration: hardware-assisted compression, and more advanced compression technologies. This should mean the arrival of decent-looking 320x240 images on CD-ROM discs, with 16-bit color and 15 frames per second performance. Capture cards such as the Intel Smart Video Recorder and codecs like Version 2.11 of Indeo and the recently released Cinepak codec already are giving us a taste of this kind of performance.

What will that next step be? Because it will depend on what aspect of technological improvement is winning the race, I will list the various possibilities, and let time be the judge. How will the next migration get started? There are a number of parallel advances in the works right now, and any one of them, or any combination, could jump-start the next generation of affordable video technology:

➤ Cheaper hardware assisted compression

➤ Faster hardware

➤ Asymmetrical codecs

➤ New and better codecs

In addition, there is work going on in totally new areas of technogy. For example, there is a big push in corporate America to develop workable video teleconferencing. Advances in that technology are highly likely to "trickle down" to the desktop.

Let's look at the most likely candidates for pushing video development forward, hardware prices down, and software performance up.

Scenario #1: Better capture technology. There are two aspects of this technology: compression/decompression algorithms and the hardware used on the boards—both for compression/decompression and for anlaog to digital conversion. This is an area in which changes are occurring rapidly, and with intense competition. Look for the following advances:

➤ Cheaper hardware-assisted compression will bring better technology to more and more desktops. Although currently there are splendid solutions for digital video capture (such as VideoLogic's Media Space board), they are very, very expensive—thousands of dollars, in fact. This is not a practical price point, to say the least. Various manufacturers are working to provide hardware-assisted compression for less than $500 retail; perhaps $350 for a street price. With any luck, these boards will be available by the summer of 1993. The main advantage of affordable hardware-assisted compression is that there is no need to post-process the captured video—the compression is done in real time, as the video is captured. For many applications, this will be a significant advantage.

Of course, most hardware-assisted cards have a rather stifling requirement: if you capture with the card present, you must have a card for
playback. The most prominent example of a technology that does *not*
behave this way is Indeo from Intel. Indeo uses the hardware if it is
present, but it will also play back with software-only decompression.
This is probably the best strategy, but it does have drawbacks. Current
versions of Indeo compression don't play back as effectively as some
software-only codecs; Intel is working on a new Indeo algorithm that will
solve this problem when the newer version is released.

➤ Faster hardware digital-to-analog (DA) conversions will improve the
frame rates of captured videos. There is a lot of data to convert to digital;
video uses 30 frames per second, and each frame has two fields (interlaced). Integration of DA conversion and compression will also increase
capabilities.

➤ Asymmetrical codecs are an interesting short-term solution. The term
asymmetrical refers to the fact that compression is very time-consuming
and decompression is very quick. An asymmetrical codec might take an
hour to compress just a few minutes of video, but is able to decompress
and play back larger images at faster frame rates. On a 386/33, a standard
codec might only be able to play a video at 160x120, 8-bit color, at 12 or
15 frames per second. Using an asymmetrical codec, the same machine
could play a 240x180 image with 24-bit color at those same frame rates,
or the same size image at full speed—30fps. The main disadvantage is the
post-processing time for compressing the file. Over the short term,
however, good asymmetrical codecs will be quite useful for distributing
.AVI files on CD-ROM discs because they have such good performance on
machines that do not have hardware-assisted decompression.

➤ Better, faster codecs are also a way to move forward. Even without
hardware assistance or asymmetrical codecs, simply improving the
mathematics used for compression can improve results in two important
ways. One, there will be speed/size improvements. Two, the quality of
the decompressed image will be better. Because most of the computers
already on desktops can't play video effectively with current codecs,
many companies are trying hard to develop codecs that are substantially
more efficient, especially for playback. Fractal technology, for instance, is
just one area of research.

The Costs of Digital Video

The cost of going to digital video varies with the work you expect to do. If you are going to produce commercials and want to use video editing, you'll need some pretty high-end computers and specialized equipment; don't expect to do that on your PC. If you want to use computers to assist you in tape-to-tape editing, the cost ranges from a few hundred dollars (Video Director from Gold Disk) to as much money as you care to spend on such things as frame-accurate VCRs, editing consoles, and specialized software.

Take a look at what it would cost to set up several different digital video operations.

Adding Video to Presentations

Adding video to presentations can be one of the most economical ways to use digital video. All that is needed is a board for capturing the video from your camcorder or VCR. Which board you select, and whether you also purchase software to edit your digital video captures, depends on what types of presentations you want to prepare and who your audience will be.

There are two kinds of video capture cards at the low end: those that only do capture, and do it reasonably well, and those that do both overlay ("Video in a window") and capture, and do both poorly. As you move out of the low end, there is a general trend toward increasing costs as quality increases. The better the results you need, and the easier you want the process to be, the more money you are going to have to spend.

Here are five different situations that explore the types of hardware available and the costs involved for each.

➤ *Just want to capture video occasionally.* If this describes you, and you don't want to spend a lot of money, you should probably look at the least expensive capture cards, such as the Video Blaster or Video Spigot from Creative Labs, or the Pro Movie Spectrum from Media Vision. You will be making some tradeoffs, however, and you need to be aware of them. You may find that the card is difficult to install; you may find it is not compatible with your computer; or you may not be satisfied with the image

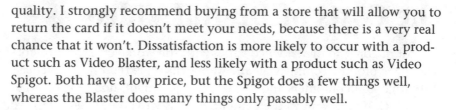
quality. I strongly recommend buying from a store that will allow you to return the card if it doesn't meet your needs, because there is a very real chance that it won't. Dissatisfaction is more likely to occur with a product such as Video Blaster, and less likely with a product such as Video Spigot. Both have a low price, but the Spigot does a few things well, whereas the Blaster does many things only passably well.

➤ *Want to preview video on the computer occasionally.* Strictly speaking, if all you want to do is view video or TV on your computer, you may not need the expense of a capture card at all—you can simply buy one of the cards that allows you to display video in a window. Examples include the Watch It! board from New Media Graphics and IBM's PS/TV card. Quality varies, and you may be limited to viewing video in 640x480 modes (8, 16, or 24 bits of color depth) only. If the idea of capture interests you, you'll need to get a board that handles both capture and overlay. As I mentioned earlier, you will have to choose between cost and quality. A board that captures and overlays costs more.

➤ *Want to capture lots of videos.* If you are going to be capturing a lot of video, your primary goals are quality, efficiency, and (usually) the capability to distribute the results to others. High-volume capture is not possible with the cheapest boards because quality is unpredictable and performance varies from capture to capture. If you do a lot of capturing, and want to spend the least amount of money, the Video Spigot is a good choice. It does a good job at capture, doesn't cost too much, and doesn't waste your money on things you don't require. If you plan to capture and will distribute for both hardware-assisted and software-only decompression, the Bravado 16 from Truevision makes sense. It provides professional results, and has expansion capabilities.

➤ *Need guaranteed professional results.* If you need guaranteed professional results *now,* your choices are limited to those boards that have been around for a while and have proven themselves in actual use. There is really just one board in this category right now: the Bravado 16 from Truevision. It installs easily, has worked on every piece of hardware I've tested it on, and delivers solid image quality. The price is higher than for similar boards, but then so is the quality. If I had to bet my business on a capture card, this would be it. Technical support is excellent and easily available, the engineering is solid, and the results are excellent.

➤ *Minimal needs now, but foresee lots of capture in the future.* This is the toughest situation to be in, because the future will inevitably bring additional advances and make your current purchase problematic. I would recommend purchasing something to meet your present needs. If you buy a cheap board, you can figure on simply replacing it with newer technology later. If you need quality now, the Bravado offers the most extensive upgrade capabilities for later.

VGA Output to Video Monitors

You can output the image from your computer monitor to a video monitor or TV screen. There are two ways to do it. One involves simply putting what you see on your computer screen on a TV screen (NTSC, PAL, or SECAM output), and the other involves combining what you see on your computer with video images from another video source, such as a camcorder or VCR (graphics overlay).

Simple output to a monitor can be done using either a card inside your computer or a box outside the computer. If all you want to do is put your computer display in front of an audience, your choice should be based on convenience and cost. If you'll be travelling, a small box outside the computer might make the most sense; it's easy to carry, can be used on different machines easily, and can be shared. If one computer will be used for output, a card might make more sense. You may some day want to use graphics overlay as well as simple output, in which case an internal card is eventually required.

If graphics overlay is your primary concern, look only at the internal cards. The best I have enountered are the VGA Producer Pro from Magni Systems, and the VideoVGA from Truevision. Whatever product you choose, be sure that it includes *flicker reduction*. This is essential when you try to display computer graphics on a video monitor or TV screen. The reason is simple: a VGA screen has many more lines on it than a video monitor. A line one-pixel thick is thinner than a single scan line on a video monitor, so thin horizontal lines from a computer display tend to get lost on a video monitor. Special circuitry "fattens up" these thin lines so they display with much less flicker. It's not a perfect science, this business of displaying things that would normally fall between the cracks, so flicker will never go away entirely. You can minimize the problem by using fewer thin, horizontal lines.

Digital Editing

Digital editing is at the cutting edge of what you can accomplish with video on a PC or Macintosh. There are two places that digitally edited video can wind up:

➤ In a computer-based application

➤ On video tape

Now, today—maybe even with the hardware you already own—you can do digital editing for computer-based applications. Output to video tape, however, requires more horsepower than even the high-end 486 can provide. You'll need some form of hardware assistance, usually in the form of hardware compression. One example involves the combination of Touchvision's D/Vision software with Intel's Action Media II card. Advances in compression algorithms, lower prices for hardware-assisted compression, and the introduction of the Pentium could change that soon.

If you don't want to actually edit the video images, you might look at the section, "Computer-Assisted Tape-to-Tape Editing for Home," later in this chapter.

On the Macintosh, the most popular digital editor is Premiere Version 2.0, from Adobe Systems. If it is ever ported to the PC, it will be most welcome. On the PC side, the only announced entry is called Media Merge from ATI, the makers of a variety of high-powered video display cards. You can find a detailed exploration of its capabilities in Chapter 12, "Advanced Windows Editing: Media Merge."

Creating Interactive Video Materials

Interactive video materials is, by far, the most exciting aspect of digital video. It involves every aspect of multimedia, including sound, still images, original art, video, interactivity, and hypertext. Some of the most stunning multimedia software, such as Microsoft's Encarta, falls into this category.

But most interactive video materials have more mundane purposes. There are two different kinds: presentations and training.

Interactive Presentations and Video

The interactive presentation has its roots in the world of overheads and slides. Once upon a time, multimedia meant using more than one slide projector, and maybe throwing in a sound track. Adding video to such presentations was a very big deal, and costs thousands and thousands of dollars. Today's video technology enables you to do that on your own computer.

The format of presentations hasn't changed much. Many software packages designed for presentations use the slide metaphor. Examples are Aldus Persuasion, Microsoft Power Point, Action!, and Harvard Graphics. Asymetrix recently introduced a presentation package that was designed from the ground up for multimedia: Compel. See Chapter 13, "Introduction: Programming Options," for an example of working with Compel.

Some multimedia authors have begun to move away from the slide metaphor to achieve a more flexible or dramatic presentation. Products such as Director, Toolbook, Interactive, and Authorware give you the power to create your own look for a presentation, and give you much more flexibility in determining what happens when and how it looks. These products are also often used for interactive training, and they are covered in detail in Chapters 13–19.

Interactive Training and Video

Interactive training materials often require greater flexibility than is required for presentations. Many presentations have a distinct linear flow, so the slide metaphor is effective; as in a slide show, one thing follows another. This is not necessarily the case in training situations, which can be much more complex.

During a training session, for example, questions may come up. The questions may be different for different trainees. An interactive training author needs tools that allow for this. This creates multiple paths through the training session, and that has an impact on the video side. If you use videos in your training materials, you're going to need more video than you would for a presentation. Each alternate path will need its own video sequences.

Video can make a big difference in the effectiveness of a training application. For example, one of my clients designs and manufactures robots. These robots are used to inspect or clean hazardous sites—places where a human being cannot go, such as nuclear waste sites or other planets. Periodically, such robots must be

disassembled and cleaned. They are often very complex, and the instruction manuals are challenging to write. If the manual is not complete, odds are a highly-paid engineer will wind up flying out to help the on-site technicians with disassembly and assembly.

Video offers a good solution for training the field technicians. Instead of struggling with a written manual, they can watch each step of the process in video segments. With careful lighting, and attention to framing, the full process can be accurately demonstrated in a computer-based training session.

Computer-Assisted Tape-to-Tape Editing

You don't have to put video into digital form to get some use out of your computer. With Gold Disk's Video Director, you can use your computer to edit videotapes at home. It's a clever system, involving software, a twin cable which operates your camcorder (video source) and VCR (video destination) connect. It allows many typical camcorders (those that support the Control-L protocol) to be operated from your computer. The Control-L protocol is a simple set of digital commands that can be used to operate the camcorder remotely. These commands include Play, Stop, and so on.

To use Video Director, you must run a simple cable from the camcorder's remote port (usually marked "Remote," "Control-L," or just with the letter "L" in a circle) to your computer. The second part of the Video Director cable terminates in an infrared device. This device uses infrared signals the same way a hand-held remote control does. It sends the appropriate infrared pulses to your VCR for such commands as Start, Stop, Pause, and Record. The ends of both cables connect to a standard serial port.

To use Video Director, you simply use its controls to play the source video on the camcorder. You can create a catalog of video sequences, noting starting and ending times. You can then choose which sequences are to be recorded on the video destination (the VCR). They can be recorded onto tape in any order you specify. When you are ready to record, you just click a button and watch as Video Director controls both source and destination hardware. Each selected video sequence will be copied in the order you specified.

The second cable is a very clever idea. Because it doesn't physically connect to your VCR, but has an infrared generator at the end, just like the infrared generator inside a typical VCR remote control unit, all you have to do is point it at your VCR, and it will be able to start and stop it for recording purposes.

Video Director is easy to set up and use. The most useful function may well be one I did not think of at first. It gives you an easy way to catalog the contents of your video tapes. Once you have been through a tape using Video Director, you will have a log of the starting and ending points of all segments of each tape. This is handy even when you don't use Video Director for making new, edited tapes—using the edit lists, you can find a sequence for showing on your TV very quickly.

Hardware Requirements

To use Video Director, you will need to have equipment that includes two key features:

➤ A camcorder that supports Control-L or any other protocol supported by Video Director.

➤ A VCR that uses a remote control. For best results, you will want a machine with a flying erase head. A flying erase head insures nearly seamless edits.

In general, the higher the quality of your source and destination equipment, the better the results. In particular, using a destination VCR with a flying erase head will yield much better results. A flying erase head allows for nearly instantaneous starts on the record deck. This isn't as good as the results you get from a $2,000 (and up) professional video recording deck, but it's noticably better than a conventional VCR.

The How of Digital Video

There is an old saying: "Any sufficiently advanced technology looks like magic." Digital video is a very advanced technology. No matter how much time and effort I take trying to explain how digital video works, you are going to reach some levels that simply look like magic.

Video as Data

Until recently, video data was always analog data—more voltage or less voltage, just like most other forms of electronic data. In this regard, it was fundamentally similar to audio data; it just required different equipment to decode it.

The nice thing about analog data is that it is an extremely efficient storage medium. However, it has one serious drawback: it is quite inexact. You do not get back out of storage exactly what you put in. This is an inherent fact of analog life—analog data is continuously variable, so no matter how many decimal places of accuracy you guarantee, there are always more decimal places further to the right that are not guaranteed. For example, if your video equipment reproduces video signals with 99.9% accuracy, that also means that there is a 0.1% error rate. This might not seem like much, but if you make a fifth-generation copy, the error rate can be calculated as 99.9*99.9*99.9*99.9*99.9%, or 99.5%. With digital data, values are not continuously variable; they are stepped. If you store digital video data, you get back exactly what you put in, 100% every time.

This digital video data stream, however, is much, much larger than an analog data stream. That's the price you are paying for the last 0.1% of accuracy, and it's the price you pay for the privilige of working with the video data on the computer. How much larger? Well, one way to look at it is this: you can buy a video tape at your local video store for under $5, and you can put an entire movie on it (two, if you are willing to sacrifice some quality and use the EP—extended play—setting on your VCR). Or, you can put the same video on your $2,000 hard disk and use an image size one quarter of standard TV, with degraded image quality as well.

Clearly, raw digital video is not "for the rest of us." Something has to give.

Into the Computer: Make Mine Digital

There is no choice: if you are going to work with video data on a computer—if you are going to do more than just watch TV—it must be converted into some kind of digital format. As you've just seen, it takes enormous amounts of space to store digital video—about a gigabyte and a half per minute, in fact, for full screen video.

Raw Data

This raw data rate is too much for any reasonable or afforable level of equipment. If it were the only way to put digital video on a computer, there would be no need for this book—there would be a handful of technical specialists using digital video, and the rest of us would be far off on the sidelines thinking wishfully.

Even so, there are times when it is desirable to work with raw data. How much raw data you can work with depends on your storage capabilities. If you have a large (gigabyte or more) and very fast (12ms or better access time) hard disk, and are willing to work at less than full-screen sizes, and can settle for short (less than 30 seconds) video clips, and need the best quality visuals, then *maybe* raw video is desirable. For now, this is a distinct minority of video users.

Fortunately, we are about to enter into a new phase of working with digital video that gives us some useful options, and they all have to do with compression.

Compressed Data

Compression of digital video is what is transforming it from a tantalizing and expensive possibility to a practical multimedia tool. There are two kinds of compression: hardware-assisted (convenient) and software-only (not so convenient).

Software Compression

When both Video for Windows and Quicktime for the Mac were introduced, one of the biggest selling points was that you could play the respective video files without having any special hardware in your computer. Although this is nice, it is an oversimplification of the issues surrounding compression.

There are two steps in compression: compression and decompression. The software that does this is called a *codec*, a word made from the initial syllables of *co*mpression and *dec*ompression. A codec is a hard-working piece of software—it can bring all but the fastest hardware to its knees. Depending on what codec you use, software compression can take as much as 45 minutes to compress a single minute of captured video. Ouch!

Of course, not all software compression is quite so time-consuming. There are two kinds of codecs: *symmetrical* and *asymmetrical*. A symmetrical codec takes about the same amount of time to compress or decompress. An asymmetrical compression scheme takes a lot of time to compress, but is very efficient for playback

decompression. Compact Video is an example of an asymmetrical compression scheme. The advantage of asymmetrical codecs is that they play back very efficiently. The disadvantage is that it takes a long time to compress. (Even worse, if you make a mistake, you'll have to start over again.)

Whether or not a codec is asymmetrical, if it is a software codec, capturing with it is likely to be economical—there's no special hardware to buy for compression or decompression. Some such codecs (Indeo, for example) are essentially free. Of course, Intel is giving Indeo away because they hope you'll buy some hardware to run it on—but Indeo works great as a software-only codec. The disadvantage of software-only capture is that you'll need to capture raw video before you compress it—because it takes so long to compress, there is no way to compress the video as it is captured. You'll have to compress after you save the raw data. This is cumbersome—even at an image size of 160x120 pixels, you'll need 20 megabytes or more per minute of video capture, plus space for the compressed version of the file.

Hardware Compression

What if we were to develop special hardware, specifically to handle the compression task? The answer, until very recently, was a mixed one. Hardware compression can be up to 300 times faster than symmetrical compression—so fast, in fact, that it can be done in real time. The bad news is the cost—thousands of dollars for the special hardware required.

There are other advantages to hardware compression. By compressing in real time, there is no need to save the raw video to your hard disk, so you can record a lot more video in the same space.

The cost for hardware-assisted compression is dropping very fast. During the time that I was writing this book, I met with several hardware manufacturers and chip makers. Just about everyone is working on new designs that will use cheaper components and simplified designs that will work specifically with products such as Video for Windows. Costs have already dropped 60% in the last six months, and should be cut in half again within another six months.

There are several things going on to facilitate this. One is simple cleverness. I can draw a parallel to the development of fast video display cards. When SuperVGA cards first appeared, the really fast cards were very expensive, and they used a graphics coprocessor from Texas Instruments. These boards accelerated almost every graphic operation to work their magic.

However, some clever folks noticed that just a few of the common Windows operations were taking up most of the time involved in graphics display. Why not, they reasoned, create special-purpose chips that would accelerate just these Windows-specific operations? The expensive graphics coprocessors could do everything, but Windows didn't need everything. The result was a rapid drop in the cost of graphics boards at the same time that speed and features increased.

The same thing is about to happen with video capture/playback cards. By addressing the real bottlenecks and working closely with the software standards for Windows, it is now possible to greatly accelerate video capture and drop prices at the same time.

Codec Wars

Look more closely at a phrase I just used: "working closely with the software standards for Windows." There are two levels of standards involved, and that makes an important difference. The first standard is the AVI file format. That's more or less cast in stone (soft stone, but stone). But the AVI file format has nothing—absolutely nothing—to do with compression. In fact, manufacturers of video capture cards are free to invent clever compression schemes all night long, and ship them to you for installation in Windows. There's no serious limit to the number of clever and interesting codecs you could install in Windows. After all, codecs are just software.

Unless, of course, the codec is implemented or supported by one of these clever new chips I've just been describing. Putting a codec in hardware makes it very fast, but it casts it in silicon. It is no longer as easy to add codecs!

So look for a mild war of the codecs in the software-only compression field (Microsoft Video 1, Compact Video, for example), and for a knock-down, drag-out war in the hardware-assisted field. Over the long haul, PC digital video will depend on the codec-on-a-chip.

There's another word for that: coprocessor. You would not be far off to think of hardware-assisted compression as similar to putting a coprocessor in a 386. Ideally, of course, the codec would work even if the chip weren't there, just like a numeric coprocessor. In fact, if I were in the codec business, that's what I would do—create a codec that would work whether there was special hardware available or not.

That's where Intel's Indeo codec comes in. Indeo isn't like many other codecs. You can capture raw video, and use software to compress it with the Indeo codec.

You can buy special hardware with built-in support for Indeo, and compress to your hard disk in real time. You can play back Indeo AVI files with or without special hardware. In fact, Indeo is also unconcerned about the color capabilities of your system—it stores data as 24-bit color, but will automatically scale that for 8- or 16-bit color cards.

The first release of Indeo for AVI wasn't, however, efficient enough to be useful on a wide variety of machines. Yes, it ran as software-only decompression, but not well enough for 386 machines. The second release of Indeo, scheduled to appear about the same time as this book arrives in bookstores, is much faster. I saw an early test version, and it plays well on a 386/25 DX machine. This is a significant improvement over the initial release, and Intel is continuing to improve and refine the codec for the future releases.

To make sure you are using the latest version of Indeo, check the version number. To do this, open the Windows Control Panel and click the Drivers applet. Find the Indeo driver listing and double-click it to open a dialog box, which will report the version number. The original Indeo driver that shipped with Video for Windows 1.0 was Version 2.1; the newest driver (as of Spring 1993) is Version 2.11. This and all later versions allow you to use Indeo on 386 computers.

Compression Issues

Until the various codec wars subside, there are going to be a large number of choices for anyone working with digital video. Which you choose depends on your needs.

There are several factors to consider when choosing a codec:

➤ What kind of hardware will be used for playback? If you want your files to play back on limited hardware—a low-end 386, for example—you'll need a codec that delivers the best possible playback performance. That's usually an asymmetrical codec; be prepared to spend lots of time away from your machine while it compresses.

➤ How much time do you have to devote to capture? If you have lots of capture to do, or can't afford to wait for post-capture compression, look at hardware-assisted capture cards such as the Intel Smart Video Recorder, or the Bravado 16 with the hardware-assisted compression option.

➤ What quality level do you need for playback? The higher your quality needs, the more likely you'll want to work with hardware-assisted codecs such as Indeo.

➤ How much storage space can you afford for both capture and playback? If storage is at a premium, hardware-assisted capture can reduce your storage needs.

➤ What hardware will be used for capture? If you can't afford a very fast 486 or better, hardware-assisted capture will be essential.

➤ What licensing requirements exist for the codec, if any? Stay away from codecs that aren't free. There are too many good ones that don't cost a dime. Indeo is free for the download from the Intel CompuServe forum. Microsoft Video 1 comes with Video for Windows 1.0. Check upgrade versions of Video for Windows for the latest and greatest in codecs; an upgrade won't be free, but it will probably buy you significant performance improvements for both compression and decompression.

➤ What are you willing to give up? There are always tradeoffs in digital video—more speed with less quality, better quality with less speed. Find the balance point that works for you and your audience.

Storage of Digital Video

Finding a place to put your digital video files is not a minor consideration. I have two 500-megabyte hard drives, and that's barely enough to create a CD-ROM full of AVI files. You should have access to—or own—a tape backup system, a CD-ROM recorder (such as the Phillips 521), or external banks of hard disks to cope with the large file sizes for a sizable project. If you are looking at digital video as a hobbyist, you'll still need to think about how much storage space you can devote to video.

Playback Issues

Just because you've managed to record a fabulous video file doesn't mean everyone will be able to enjoy it on their hardware. There are so many factors that affect playback:

➤ Speed of video capture hardware

➤ CPU speed

➤ Speed of video display hardware

➤ Bus speed, bus width (16 bit, 32 bit)

➤ Hard disk speed

➤ Data transfer rates (CD-ROM and hard disk)

➤ Overhead for audio data

I strongly suggest getting a clear picture of your audience's hardware capabilities if you plan to publish, and making sure you distribute files that will work for that audience. If you know that everyone you distribute to will have double spin (300k/second) CD-ROM drives, you can safely use those data rates. But most of the time, anything that is not just for your own use will have to respect my least favorite factor: the least common denominator. That may even mean multiple versions of files: a 10 fps 160x120 version for folks with a 386/25, and a 30 fps for folks with a 486/33.

The Why of Digital Video

I may be preaching to the choir here, but why in the world would anyone want to use digital video if it involves complex compression, loss of quality, small image sizes, the cost of capture hardware, and possibly an upgrade to your computer?

There are three reasons to use digital video:

➤ It moves.

➤ It moves.

➤ It moves.

Movement can give an otherwise ordinary computer operation impact. There is a wide variety of areas that will benefit from this impact.

Business Communication

It's the nature of business to seek any advantage over the competition. Since the advent of the computer, this has become more and more true. More often than not, the man or woman who can coax more impact out of a computerized presentation gets the confidence of the client.

The role of the computer in business communication has expanded almost continuously since its introduction. Video should give that process an additional boost. Consider some of the creative ways that companies now (or will shortly) add video to business communication.

Real-Time Video

One of the most exciting applications involves real-time video. This means putting video on or into the computer without any delays or extra steps. No post-capture compression allowed: it all has to happen now.

Video Teleconferencing

Video teleconferencing is a hot buzzword these days. I can recall my visit to the New York World's Fair, where AT&T demonstrated video telephones. We all expected to see them the following year in our homes, but of course that never happened.

The combination of computers and digital video is changing that. Right now, today, you can buy a video teleconferencing network. It's going to cost big bucks, but the point is: it's here. It would be better, of course, if you could put that capability in your desktops.

It won't be long before that happens. I have already seen some impressive technology demonstrations of video teleconferencing. Impressive not because they promise to be affordable, although that is important. Impressive not because they work, although that's clearly important. Impressive not because they use amazingly efficient compression schemes that will work over ISDN lines. No, it was impressive because of the software that built intelligently on top of all of these hardware marvels.

Note

With all the innovations coming from the hardware scene in the past year, it's easy to lose sight of the fundamental guiding principle of computing: select software that will do the job, and then get the hardware you need to use that software. It's easy to get caught up in exciting new hardware, and forget that hardware is only something for software to run on. No matter how good the hardware is, if there isn't adequate or useful software for it, it might as well not even exist. Case in point: CD-ROM drives. CD-ROM drives have been around for more than five years. For most of that time, there wasn't much software that made them useful. Now that the software has finally arrived (Windows 3.1 and multimedia), CD-ROM drives are selling so fast the manufacturers can hardly keep up.

The software that Intel demonstrated early in 1993 included such things as networked white boards and networked presentations with annotations. Although this was a technology demonstration—showing what could, in fact, be done—and may never see the light of day, it did what it was supposed to do: it showed what is possible with digital video in a business environment.

Capture

The nicest thing about real-time video is how easy it makes the capture process. Instead of time-consuming, post-capture compression, when capture is done, compression is done. Very nice!

Non-Real-Time Video

There will also be lots of video that doesn't have to happen in real time. These applications can also make effective use of digital video.

Video Electronic Mail

I don't know about you, but the idea of video e-mail is one that I find very exciting. I am always frustrated by the impersonal nature of standard e-mail. Video e-mail is not as hot as video teleconferencing, but the capability of adding facial expressions and images to e-mail intrigues me. If video compression schemes become efficient enough, the extra data load of video e-mail won't be too much for existing network technology.

Capture

Capture can always be done without real-time compression. It is not as convenient, but it is less expensive. I suspect there will always be a place for non-real-time capture.

Publishing

If you are planning to publish your digital video in any way—on video tape, on a CD-ROM, or via e-mail—you don't have to have real-time compression.

Neat Software

Multimedia has spawned many neat software packages, such as Multimedia Beethoven, Musical Instruments, Composer Quest, Encarta, Grollier's Encyclopedia, and many others. The addition of digital video adds a new dimension to these products: motion. Now, you'll be able to see a bird in flight, or a folk dance in action. This makes such software all the more useful to its audience.

Entertainment

There is a great deal of entertaining video out there, ranging from movies on video tape to sports blooper tapes as a premium for a magazine subscription. At some point, it will become practical to move this kind of material over to digital video.

Training

One of the most significant opportunities for digital video lies in training. The addition of images and motion have a big impact in computer-based training programs. For example, a manufacturer could put assembly instructions in digital video format. Using hypermedia technology, a complete "how to" package could be developed around the digital video portions, allowing a customer or client to easily learn how to use new products or technology.

For example, I once worked with a company that designs and builds robots that are sent to places where no human can go—hazardous waste sites and other planets being two examples. These are complex machines, requiring detailed and sophisticated manuals. With digital video, the manual could be put on a CD-ROM disc, and it could include video of how to disassemble, clean, and reassemble the robot. If there is a problem along the way, a hypertext system could allow the robot operator to quickly locate a video that demonstrates correct procedures.

157

Summary

The bottom line with video is that it moves. It adds action to formerly static computer operations, and it does it easily. All you need is a camcorder, a capture card, and your imagination.

PART **III**

Recording

5

Digital Video
Recording Secrets
and Techniques

In this chapter, you learn about recording from your video source (camcorder, VCR, and so on) to your computer by way of a video capture card. The cards themselves are covered in the next chapter.

If you have decent video sequences that you want to put into digital form—for whatever reason—this is where the bits meet the disk, where the biggest differences depend on what you do. That's the polite way of saying that if things are going to go wrong, this is where they are most likely to go wrong.

Recording to Your Hard Disk

The hard disk was invented before anyone got the idea of putting video data on it. As mentioned over and over, digital video involves huge amounts of data. Full-frame, uncompressed, 30-frames-per-second video assaults your hard disk with bytes at an astonishing rate: 1.5 gigabytes per *minute*. That's 180 gigabytes for your average 2-hour movie. That's also completely unrealistic with the cost of today's technology. Something has to give.

There are several ways to make adjustments:

➤ *Smaller image size.* The number of pixels is related to image area. If you cut the image size in half, the number of pixels involved shrinks to one-quarter of what it was.

➤ *Slower frame rates.* Video uses 30 frames per second. If you can use less for digital video, you cut out a lot of storage requirements.

➤ *Data compression.* You may already be familiar with compression techniques, such as PKZIP or Stacker. Video files use a different form of compression, but the idea is the same: when you aren't using the file, it stays in compressed format.

You'll need to use all three techniques to put video on your hard disk.

Disk Issues

There's more to consider, however. As I said, hard disks came along before anyone had the idea of putting video data on them. Some of the characteristics of hard drives need to be addressed and understood.

Size: the Bigger the Better

It is not possible to have a hard disk that is too big for use with video. If you now have a 100- or 200-megabyte hard disk, yes, you can work with video, but don't expect to work with video clips longer than 5 or 10 seconds. I have a 500-megabyte hard disk, with a 100-megabyte partition mostly for video capture. I can capture up to about 4.5 minutes of video, using small frame sizes and average frame rates. If your needs extend beyond that, a gigabyte drive is a reasonable choice.

Thermal Recalibration

Big drives weren't made for a continuous stream of video data. They make some assumptions about the nature of computer data that are not true for video. For example, many of today's hard drives cleverly compensate for *thermal drift*, the distortion that occurs as a drive heats up and cools down. Every so often (it varies from drive to drive, but the timing is measured in minutes, not seconds), such hard disks recalibrate themselves. It only takes a moment, of course, but if you are shoving huge amounts of data down the drive's throat while recording video, that recalibration could cost you some lost data. (This is also true of audio recording, but audio data rates are even smaller.)

You have two choices: get a drive that doesn't use thermal recalibration, or learn to live with one that uses it. The sad truth: almost all large drives do it. At press time, Maxtor's Panther drives were a prominent exception.

Over the next six months, this is likely to become less of a problem as drive manufacturers and software vendors iron out the problems. Adequate buffering can eliminate the problem for very fast drives (they can catch up after recalibrating), and most drives can delay recalibration while data is coming in if the software asks for it.

Disk Speed

Just as a hard drive cannot be too large for use with video, it cannot be too fast. In a 486 system, the hard disk is likely to be the limiting factor in terms of capture performance. If you want to do a lot of video capture at above-average data rates, don't settle for mediocre hard drive performance. There are two key issues to consider: average seek time and data transfer rate. Seek time is typically measured in milliseconds (ms), and the average seek time is the figure most often quoted. For best results, look for at least 12ms or lower average seek time; 9 or 10ms is better.

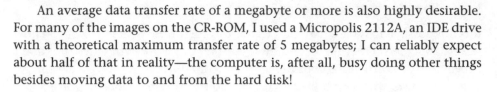

An average data transfer rate of a megabyte or more is also highly desirable. For many of the images on the CR-ROM, I used a Micropolis 2112A, an IDE drive with a theoretical maximum transfer rate of 5 megabytes; I can reliably expect about half of that in reality—the computer is, after all, busy doing other things besides moving data to and from the hard disk!

IDE disk drives, by the way, have a lower maximum data transfer rate than SCSI drives. The cost of a top-notch bus-mastering SCSI card, however, will add to the cost of acquiring your new hard drive. You may want to consider one of the new IDE controllers, such as the ones offered by Ultrastore, which offer increased throughput. See the section, "IDE versus SCSI," later in this chapter for more details.

Also keep in mind that Windows adds a lot of hard drive overhead, which adds fuel to my rule for hard drives: find the fastest hard drive you can afford, then give up popcorn at the movies for a year so that you can afford an even faster one.

Streaming Versus Random Data

Why does video put such a strain on the hard drive? It's more than just the huge data rates. Hard disks were designed for more typical kinds of data, such as you find in accounting, word processing, or graphics. These applications can generate huge, multi-megabyte files, but data access usually involves random access to the hard disk. An incoming video file, on the other hand, might fill half or more of the hard drive in one long, continuous operation. Any flaws, any delays, anything at all that isn't perfect gets in the way.

Living with Your Hard Disk

There are some things you can do to optimize your hard disk's performance with video. The most important thing is to defragment the drive you use for capture. A capture file should always be a single, contiguous file. If the file is in pieces, each piece is in a different place on the hard disk. The time spent moving from place to place limits performance.

There are two techniques you can use for capture, and I'll explain how to use each of them to best advantage.

Technique 1: Maintain a standard capture file.
Technique 2: Capture to a new file each time.

The simplest method is Technique 1. It works whether or not you have a separate drive or partition for capturing video files. (The best course is to have a separate drive; you don't want to have the hard disk interrupting recording to do other business.) Here's how to set up a standard capture file:

1. Defragment the hard disk that will hold the capture file.

2. Make sure you have enough space set aside for capture. If you allow 25 megabytes per minute, you'll be safe. I use a 62-megabyte capture file, which gives me 2.5 to 3 minutes of raw video (depending on frame rate, image size, and so forth). If you are using a card that supports hardware-assisted, real-time compression, you'll get three or more times as much video in the same space.

3. Run the VidCap application. Select File/Set Capture File. Enter a filename in the dialog box. (I use capture.avi to avoid confusion.) Click OK, which displays the dialog box shown in Figure 5.1. Enter the size you want to use for the capture file; the amount of space available is displayed for reference. This file will now be used automatically whenever you capture incoming video.

4. When you have used this file to capture a video sequence, make sure you save the file (with either VidCap or VidEdit) under a different name. This will preserve the contiguous nature of the file you just created.

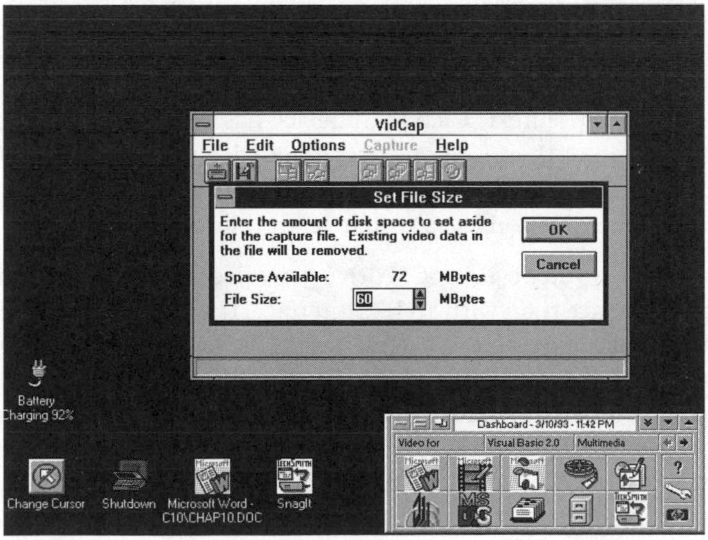

Figure 5.1. Establishing video capture file size in VidCap.

If you don't follow this technique, you will need to make sure that your hard disk is defragmented each time you create a new capture file. If you only capture video sequences occasionally, or do them all in one batch, you might not want to have a large default capture file taking up space on your disk.

IDE Versus SCSI

There are a variety of different drive types available, but two are currently in the forefront of technology: IDE and SCSI. Older drive technologies, such as MLM and RLL, don't have the performance needed for decent video capture. ESDI drives may work, but they are becoming less common and are not being developed for size and speed as aggressively as IDE and SCSI drives.

What do all of these acronyms stand for? IDE stands for *Integrated Drive Electronics*. This refers to the fact that IDE drives have the drive controller right on the drive, instead of using a separate card. You still need an interface to the drive, but it's much simpler than a traditional controller card. IDE drives are both fast and cheap, and extremely common on today's computers. They are also easy to install and use.

SCSI stands for *Small Computer Systems Interface*. It has been around for a number of years, and there is a new version called SCSI-2. SCSI, by whatever name, has a reputation for being difficult to work with. On the one hand, it is a standard. On the other hand, like many so-called "standards," SCSI has been implemented in different ways by different manufacturers. The idea behind SCSI is a good one: it allows multiple devices to share a single card by daisy-chaining the devices from one to the next. Each SCSI device has a unique ID number (theoretically up to seven of them). In practice, not all devices will work with a given SCSI card, and some device manufacturers either design for features on a specific SCSI card or require that you use a completely proprietary SCSI card.

Of course, when you do get a SCSI drive to work correctly, you almost always get better performance than with an IDE interface. For video capture, this advantage may well make it worth your while to get the SCSI drive up and running. Keep in mind that you won't necessarily have problems installing a SCSI drive. There are simply fewer standards, and you may need to do a little work on the phone contacting manufacturers for detailed information before you buy. If you do that, the worst penalty you should face during installation will be a little extra time to sort out the details of setup.

The bottom line with SCSI is this: Buyer beware, but the advantages may well be worth the effort. When buying, keep in mind that:

➤ SCSI-2 devices are more likely to be compatible with a larger number of SCSI cards and other devices.

➤ Make sure you talk with someone who has personal experience with the controller card and drive you plan to use.

➤ Plan to spend some time getting the installation running right. You may not need it, but it helps if you are not counting on instant installation.

I'd also like to add a few words about SCSI cards. There are many different ways of implementing SCSI. Simple SCSI cards do little more than provide a gateway between the bus and the SCSI drive, while bus-mastering SCSI controller cards such as Adaptec's provide buffering, off-loading of the CPU, and faster performance.

MFM (Modified Frequency Modulation) drives are an older standard; if you had a 5- or 10-megabyte drive in your old XT, it probably used MFM or RLL (Run Length Limited) encoding, both of which used the so-called ST-506 interface, an old Seagate Technologies drive designation. ESDI (Enhanced Small Device Interface) was hot for a while, but it has faded because IDE drives are significantly less expensive.

I have used a Fujitsu 500-megabyte and Micropolis 1.05 gigabyte IDE hard drives for capture, and they both did a great job. One caveat: early BIOS revisions on the Fujitsu don't work very well with video capture. Make sure you have revision B or later. This drive has an average seek time of 12ms, and I can capture up to 30 frames per second at 160x120, or 12 fps at 240x180. These figures are for the Video Spigot capture card, at 8 bits of color depth (256 colors). The Micropolis is outstanding; I can capture up to 12 frames per second at 320x240.

Whatever drive you use, keep in mind that the hard disk is the single component most likely to put a lid on video capture performance. If you are serious about video capture, go for all of the speed and capacity you can afford. About the only way to lighten the load on your hard disk is to use a capture card with hardware-assisted compression, such as the Intel Smart Video Recorder.

Too Much Data?

You could make a pretty good case for the argument that today's personal computers really aren't up to handling video—at least not affordable PCs, at any rate. Fortunately, that situation is changing rapidly.

It may seem surprising that you can buy a color TV or VCR for a few hundred dollars that will out-perform thousands of dollars of computer equipment. The difference is in data rates. Analog data is very flexible—you can lose quite a bit of it and still get a usable signal. Digital data is not at all flexible. That's one of the features of digital video: there is no loss of data. The price comes in the form of high data rates.

The key to controlling and managing these high data rates involves chips that will act as the equivalent of *video coprocessors*. Do you remember when the AT computer was introduced? Not only did it use the 80286 processor, but you could also add a numeric coprocessor. The numeric coprocessor off-loaded computational tasks from the CPU, and was designed specifically for number crunching. The CPU was a general-purpose chip; the numeric coprocessor was a special-purpose chip. To get good video performance, we're going to need special-purpose video coprocessors in our computers. See Chapter 8 for more information about compression.

There are several ways that such hardware will find its way into our machines. The most likely path involves adding video coprocessors to video display cards. Such cards will be a lot like the Windows accelerators currently available—the most important part of the video capture/compression process can be built right into the hardware. That will give us the best performance increase for the least cost.

The move toward this kind of solution is already underway. Intel is working on a new generation of chips that will do more but cost less, for example; they are not alone in their pursuit. C-Cube will be offering a low-cost chip for video compression as well.

In the meantime, or if you want to keep the cost of video capture to the absolute minimum, you can achieve acceptable results without a video coprocessor. The key is to understand the limits of frame rate, image size, and compression/decompression capabilities.

Image Sizes

The thing most people notice right away about Video for Windows is that the image size is quite small. The effect is more pronounced if you are working in SuperVGA mode; I recently switched to 1280x1024, and a 160x120 video window is now really tiny! (Fortunately, I'm using an ATI Ultra Pro video display card, and can easily play it at 2x or 3x magnification.)

If image size is a big concern, you want to work with a capture card that has the best performance. The Video Spigot, for example, is extremely efficient at capture, and the image quality is also very good. Video Spigot, however, lacks some features you may want, such as overlay.

You can also learn to work in the smaller sizes effectively. Fill the frame with the subject, and avoid small text elements. You'll also want to look closely at the section on "Compression Techniques" later in this chapter.

Frame Rates

The next thing people notice after small image size is the slower frame rate. However, you don't have to settle for limited frame rates; capture cards are available that will give you the full 30 fps (at least at 160x120). The Video Spigot is a good choice, although many other manufacturers are also reaching better and better capture rates.

There are several things you can do to maximize frame rate. Number one on the list is easy: defragment. A fragmented hard disk has a more detrimental effect on frame rates than almost any other factor. You can also limit the color-depth of capture. 24-bit color uses three times as many pixels as 8-bit color does, for example.

Audio Issues

Many of the issues with putting audio on your hard disk are similar to those for video, but audio adds a few twists of its own. The most important things to keep in mind are synchronization, recording levels, and quality.

Synchronization

Synchronizing video and audio is not, unfortunately, automatic. The basic principle behind AVI files—the interleaving of audio and video data—is not as simple as it might seem. For example, in order to actually synchronize playback, there needs to be a chunk of sound data at the beginning of the file to get things started. Most of the time, this works fine. But if you start editing the file, things can get out of line. Fortunately, VidEdit gives you some simple but powerful tools for getting everything back together again.

Before looking at those tools, however, there's another issue to consider: to properly synchronize audio and video, you will need a very fast computer. The minimum configuration for synchronizing is a 486/33—and a 486/50 or 486/66 is more desirable. The reason for this is simple. If you have a sync problem, you have most likely edited the file in some way. Once you have edited the file, it exists in a noncontiguous stream on the hard disk. This causes delays in reading the data because the read head has to move from one location on the disk to the next. These delays can cause apparent sync problems. When you play the edited file, you will hear and see things at different times. If you save the file and then play it, you may well find that there is no problem at all! The lack of synchronization is coming from the inability of the computer to play the audio and video data streams at the correct rate, not from a problem in the file itself. The faster your computer, the less of a hazard this will be. In general, I save a complete video file to disk before attempting to sync the audio to the video. This practice prevents problems.

Let's look at the tools in VidEdit that you can use to re-synchronize audio and video, or to sync new audio to existing video. Figure 5.2 shows a dialog box that is reached with the Video/Synchronize menu option in VidEdit.

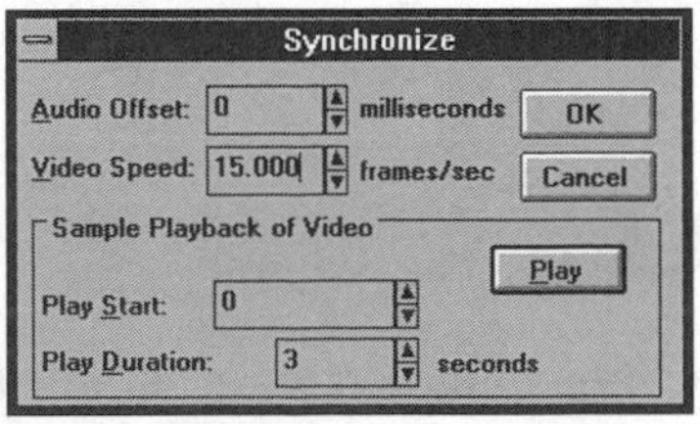

Figure 5.2. Synchronizing audio and video.

This dialog box allows you to adjust two parameters: the audio offset and video speed. The audio offset specifies the number of milliseconds before or after the start of video playback to adjust audio starting time. The video speed is the number of frames to display each second.

> ### Note
>
> There is a related adjustment, Frame Rate, accessible via the Video/Convert Frame Rate menu selection. This is a very different adjustment, and should not be confused with Video Speed. If you change the frame rate, VidEdit will add or remove frames to play at the new frame rate. If you change video speed, VidEdit will change the frame rate without adding or deleting any frames.

Let's look at some real-life examples to see how you might use these controls.

Audio Offset

The most common adjustment involves the Audio Offset, and it occurs when you have added or removed audio data. For example, I recently was editing three "talking head" clips into one longer clip. I had to make a lot of changes to both the audio and video portions, and they got out of sync with each other. The difference was slight, but obvious: the words were sounding after the lip movements. I had to gauge the difference by ear, and I guessed at 300 milliseconds—almost a third of a second. Because the audio was behind the video, I entered a negative number: -300. My guess wasn't quite right, however. I had gone just a little bit too far, and the sound was now *ahead* of the lip movements by a very small amount. Because each audio offset refers to the current audio start position, I re-opened the dialog box and entered 50 milliseconds, for a net change of -250 milliseconds (-300 + 50). That proved to be the correct amount.

Caution

Audio offset adjustments are cumulative—each change builds on the previous change. Don't save over your old file until you know you have it right! You might want to save at intervals, or to a temporary filename, to avoid timing errors that result from file fragmentation.

Video Speed

Changing the video speed setting has a very different effect on the relationship of sound and video.

If a video includes a talking head, increasing the video speed will immediately cause obvious problems. Because each frame displays for less time, and the audio hasn't changed at all, each frame will be that much farther ahead. The longer the clip, the farther out of sync each additional frame will be. Decreasing video speed has the opposite effect: the audio gets more and more ahead of the video.

Talking heads aren't the only kind of video with this problem. Any video that contains obvious visual references for sounds will look wrong if you change the video speed—a hand clap, a hammer strike, or a popping balloon are obvious examples.

If you want to change the video speed, you have two choices: either play the video without any audio, or substitute different audio of your choice. For example, if you want to play a video of a golf swing in slow motion, you might:

➤ Eliminate audio altogether.

➤ Describe the action in hushed tones like a professional golf announcer.

➤ Isolate the sound of the golf ball being hit, and insert that small bit of audio at the appropriate location in the slow-motion video.

➤ Use music timed to the video.

The same is true of speeded-up action—you can't use the audio if it's obviously running at a different speed (unless, of course, you play it for laughs).

I just lied, but not really. What I just said is true, but only if you limit yourself to VidEdit. There is a way you can use audio with altered video speeds, but it has limitations. You could use a program such as Wave for Windows to alter the speed of the audio file. To do this, you will need to specify a percentage change in your audio editing program. For example, if your golf video was originally at 14.96 fps, and you wanted to play it back at 8 frames per second, you would:

➤ Extract the audio portion of the file and save it as a .WAV file.

➤ Load the .WAV file into an audio editing program; I'll use Wave for Windows as the example.

➤ Select Tools/Time Compress/Expand, and enter 187% as the new (expanded) file size.

How did I come up with the number 187%? It is the result of a simple calculation: **<old video speed> / <new video speed>**. The ratio of change in the audio speed must be exactly the same as the ratio of change in the video speed.

There are limits to this kind of change. Wave for Windows will try to reduce the effects of the change—for example, by keeping the pitch constant. But many sounds don't sound the same when they've been stretched or compressed too far. The sound of a golf club hitting the ball, for example, just isn't the same when you stretch it out.

Levels

The most important thing to remember about audio is easy to describe:

Never let your audio level get too high.

There are two important concepts here: *audio levels* and *too high*. I'll try to define both in a useful way. The problem is that the definitions change with the situation.

The audio level is a measure of the strength of the audio signal. Low levels, such as from a microphone, or when you have a tape deck turned down too low, require a lot of boost to play or record properly. High levels, such as from an amplifier or someone screaming into a microphone, can overload equipment. Low levels are a problem, of course, but not as fatal as levels that are too high.

Low levels are said to "raise the noise floor." What this means in plain English is that if the sound level gets too low, it gets hard to tell the difference between the sound and the background noise. If you try to boost the sound, the noise gets boosted at the same time. This is annoying, but not necessarily fatal.

High levels are a different matter. If a sound level is too high, you will encounter "clipping." Clipping means that part of the waveform is gone—vanished forever, and often replaced with a horrid pop or smacking sound that makes your audio useless. Clipping occurs when you run out of *headroom*. Headroom is the difference between the current audio level and the highest possible audio level. An illustration might make this clearer.

Look at Figure 5.3. It shows a waveform with (from left to right) low levels, normal levels, high levels, and clipping. Clipping occurs where the waveform hits the top of the window.

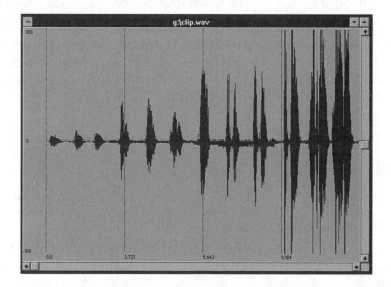

Figure 5.3. Various audio levels, from too low to too high (left to right).

When you are recording live sources, especially voice, constant vigilance is necessary to prevent excessive audio levels. People are prone to moving around, and if someone gets too close to the microphone—or, even worse, drops a book on it—clipping or other distortion can occur. Keeping an ear out for levels is a valuable skill. Until you have it mastered, a set of headphones can prevent many problems.

Quality

The quality of the audio you use with your video images is very important—at least as important as the video quality. Often the audio quality is *more* important than the video, because the video images will be so highly compressed that they need good audio to help carry the message to the viewer.

In fact, a clear audio signal can make a poor video image "look" better. If you plan to distribute your video files in any way, don't overlook the details of the audio portion of your setup. Each link in the chain—microphone, cables, recording medium, sound card, speakers—adds or subtracts audio quality.

Hardware Issues

Digital recording issues don't stop at the software—they reach right down into the hardware you use in your computer. The results you get with the techniques mentioned in this chapter will vary depending on exactly what kind of hardware you are using. In the next chapter, we'll look at exactly how hardware fits into the overall picture of digital video.

6

Hardware for Recording

This is the trickiest chapter in this book, and for two very difficult reasons. One, hardware is constantly changing—in fact, even during the time I researched the field for this book, there have been significant advances in hardware. Two, there are so many issues to consider when you shop for hardware that it's hard to give every one of them the space and time it deserves.

I'll start by defining the important terms you'll need to know about hardware, and then I'll cover the issues that are involved in choosing hardware. At the end of the chapter, I've provided a capsule review of the hardware currently available for you to choose from.

Because hardware is constantly changing, you can check with me on CompuServe, in the Multimedia forum, for the latest information before you buy. You can reach the Multimedia forum with the command **GO MULTIMEDIA**. Video issues are discussed in two sections of that forum: Section 6, *DOS and Windows Multimedia,* and Section 2, *Interactive Video.* You are most likely to find discussions about hardware in Section 6.

If you are not already a member of CompuServe, I strongly suggest that you become a subscriber. I don't receive anything from CompuServe for drumming up new subscribers; CompuServe is just the best way I know to stay up to the minute with multimedia hardware and software issues. You'll find both seasoned professionals and newcomers in the Multimedia forum, so no matter what your level of expertise, you'll be able to find help and information. In addition, you'll be able to find updates to the code samples included with this book, sample AVI files, and code and examples uploaded by numerous other people.

A Dictionary of (Mostly) Hardware Terms

ADC

This stands for *Analog* to *Digital conversion.* It is a very, very important part of the process. The original video signal is an analog signal—that is, it varies continuously. This must be converted to digital data for storage on your hard disk. Overlay video does not require conversion to digital form.

See also: Overlay, DAC

Audio

Many hardware capture cards support audio, but only on a pass-through basis. That is, they have an audio input and an audio output, but all they do is pass the audio from the input to the output—you cannot record the audio to your hard disk with this kind of audio support. The primary advantage of audio pass-through is volume control. Some hardware with audio pass-through allows you to control the output audio volume. To actually record audio, it must be input to a Wave audio device.

See also: Wave Audio

Codec

This is a term made up from the words *co*mpression/*deco*mpression. It refers to the drivers that Windows uses to compress and/or decompress digital video data. There are a number of codecs in wide use, and many more in limited use for special purposes. Video for Windows 1.0 shipped with a handful of codecs, including Microsoft Video 1, Intel Indeo, and RLE. Some hardware capture cards, such as the Video Spigot, come with codecs intended specifically for use with that hardware. There are often speed or other advantages to such proprietary codecs, but keep in mind that you most likely will not be able to redistribute those codecs to anyone who doesn't have the same hardware. Verify that the codec can work with other hardware before you buy!

See also: Compression

Composite Video

There are two kinds of video signals supported by most hardware boards: composite video and S-Video. By far the most common video signal you'll see is composite video. Even the least expensive VCR can output a composite video signal. The composite signal is the standard of the video world. The resolution, however, is inferior to S-Video. S-Video uses additional vertical resolution to present a better-looking image.

You should, however, consider one fact before you go out and invest in an expensive VCR or camcorder that supports S-Video (Hi8 and Super VHS). For the immediate future, the image sizes supported by Video for Windows are quite

small—160 x 120, and maybe as much as 320x240 in special situations. You won't get much improvement, if any, from using an S-Video source at these small image sizes. I've tried some experiments, using the same exact video source (my Canon A1 camcorder) as both a composite and S-Video source. At 320x240, I can't see any difference whatsoever between the two types of input. Of course, if you are buying with an eye to the long view, S-Video makes more sense. It also makes sense if you will be capturing video stills at 640x480.

See also: Hi8; S-Video; SVHS

Compression

The only practical way to work with video in a digital form is to compress the data. Raw, full-size video in full color equals 1.5 gigabytes of data; that's way too much for practical work on a PC.

There are many ways to compress data. The simplest is to look for redundancy, which is the technique used by products such as PKZIP. This method builds a dictionary that contains all unique sequences in the file being compressed. To reconstruct the file, the decompressor pulls each sequence out of the dictionary in the correct order. This method of compression preserves the exact sequence of data in the original. Therefore, it is called *loss-less compression*.

However, this is a very slow way to compress, and you can't compress a whole lot with this technique. Much more serious compression is required for digital video. In fact, the kind of compression used with digital video is called *lossy compression*. That's right: some of the data gets lost in the process. The trick is to lose the kinds of data that matter the least; good compression algorithms do a good job of removing data without affecting the appearance of the image.

The mathematics required to do a good job with lossy compression are very sophisticated. This has one important side-effect as far as the hardware is concerned: if the compression can be done in hardware, it will be about 300 times faster than if the CPU has to do it. This difference is so great that it allows the incoming video data to be compressed in real time, during capture. This means that the load on the hard disk is dramatically lower. Because the hard disk is the limiting factor on a fast 486, this is a significant advantage.

The reason for a 300-fold improvement is simple. Your CPU is a general-purpose processor; it has to be prepared to handle a wide variety of tasks. When you put a compression/decompression coprocessor right on a hardware board, it can be designed to do just one thing and to do it well.

Hardware-assisted compression has a down side, however: cost. This should change very quickly. The obvious advantage of a compression coprocessor is not lost on companies such as Intel; they are working furiously to develop chips and boards that will compete in price with software-only boards. Such boards are expected to hit the market in mid to late 1993. Also keep your eyes peeled for video display cards with support for compression and decompression right on the board. This may well be the most economical way to support high decompression rates.

See also: Codec

DAC

This stands for *D*igital to *A*nalog *c*onversion. This is not a factor in video capture, but it can be a factor in playback with some boards, and may be involved in some boards with overlay capabilities.

In most cases, the digital video data will be displayed as digital data; no conversion to analog is used. With some cards, however, circuitry has been added that will convert the digital data to analog for playback. This tends to make the video look like it does on a regular TV. That is, you cannot see discrete pixels. This may actually be a disadvantage in many situations. Most importantly, DAC hardware must be present to make the conversion. Also a consideration is the appearance of the converted image. A digital image looks very sharp on-screen, and an analog image doesn't. However, an analog image looks a little smoother. Which you prefer depends on personal taste.

See also: ADC

Frame-Accurate Recording

Consumer-level video equipment cannot move to a specific frame number. Professional equipment, on the other hand, is called frame-accurate because it can work with specific frame numbers for both recording and playback. This can be important if you are outputting to tape; you can work with great precision.

VCRs that support frame-accurate access, however, are very expensive—about four times costlier than conventional decks. Unless you are outputting to tape, you won't realize any dramatic advantages. For recording, you can always start the deck a little ahead and pause it a little after the sequence you want to record, and then remove the unwanted frames during editing. Outputting to tape is a different story: what goes on the tape is what goes on the tape; you can't edit it after recording it. In this situation, a frame-accurate recorder such as the Panasonic AG1970 is very valuable.

Framing

One of the most critical things that a video capture card must do is to accurately frame the incoming image. There are three possible situations that you will encounter:

1. The hardware driver allows you to adjust the horizontal and vertical positioning of the image.

2. The hardware attempts to center the video image and succeeds.

3. The hardware attempts to center the video image and fails.

Most cards use option #2: self-centering. This is fine when it works, and miserable when it doesn't because there is no fallback position.

See also: Synchronization

Hi8

Hi8 is one of the S-Video formats. It uses 8mm videotape, which is a very convenient recording format. Originally, there were some problems with the tape used for Hi8, but these have been resolved. At one time, you could expect some dropouts, but tape quality has improved significantly. However, high quality Hi8 tape can be pretty expensive, but the results are great for critical situations where you need high resolution, good color fidelity, and convenience of a small format. I use Hi8 tapes in my Canon A1 camcorder, and the results have been consistently excellent.

See also: Composite Video; S-Video; SVHS

Interrupts

Almost all video capture boards rely on hardware interrupts to signal when one frame ends and the next begins. You must have an available interrupt to do this. Most boards have infrequently used interrupts, but you should pay attention to the interrupts available for the board you choose. This is one aspect of hardware that tends to change over time, so I would recommend you check into this at the time you purchase to make sure you don't have a conflict you can't resolve. Be especially wary of capture cards that use only one interrupt.

See also: Port Addresses

Local Bus

This is a new development in motherboard technology, and it offers some advantages for video capture. Video display cards that take advantage of the local bus, which is 32-bits rather than the usual 16-bits wide, are often extremely fast. ATI in particular has been working to make its local bus video cards work closely with digital video. For example, the latest version of the drivers for the Ultra series of cards includes built-in support for the Indeo and RLE codecs.

Look for more manufacturers to support video data handling in their video display hardware. Faster video has some effect on capture, but it is minimal. The real advantage comes during playback.

Memory Usage

How a capture card uses memory to move video data is one of the most important considerations involved in a purchase decision. For example, a number of capture cards put the memory buffer in the first 16 megabytes of system memory. This means that you can't have more than 14 megabytes installed. If you don't need more than 14 megabytes, this is fine—go ahead and purchase such a board. On the other hand, if you are using large amounts of memory, steer clear of these cards. Some of the finest video capture cards have this limitation, such as the Bravado from Truevision.

NTSC

NTSC (National Television System Commitee) is the video standard for the United States and Canada, as well as many other countries. You don't really need to concern yourself with this issue if you are simply buying a U.S. or Canadian capture card for use in those countries. However, if you'll be buying or using capture hardware elsewhere, you need to pay attention to the video standard that the board supports.

See also: PAL; SECAM

Overlay

Overlay video allows you to watch video in a window. Many overlay devices also support video display outside of Windows, under DOS.

Overlay video is completely different from digital video. You can have a board that supports digital capture, you can have a board that supports video overlay, and you can have one board that supports both.

Overlay is exactly what the name says it is. The video signal is overlaid on the video signal. (It does get pretty confusing that both the video display and video capture both use the word *video*.) A video display card uses completely different display frequencies than the kind of video you see on TV or from your VCR or camcorder. A card that supports overlay is capable of converting the incoming video signal to synchronize it with the computer display frequency.

See also: Video Capture; Synchronization

PAL

PAL (Phase Alternating Line) is the video standard for most of Europe, excluding France.

See also: NTSC; SECAM

Port Addresses

If your card uses a port address, you must be certain that it is either configurable or will not conflict with the port addresses of any of your existing cards. For example, your sound card almost certainly uses a port address.

See also: Interrupt

S-Video

This is a high-resolution video format. You need special, more costly video equipment to record, play, and display S-Video signals. S-Video also uses a special connector.

See also: Composite Video; Hi8; SVHS

SECAM

SECAM (Sequentiel Couleur Avec Memoire) is the video standard for France.

See also: NTSC; PAL

Signal Quality

No matter how good your capture hardware and your recording technique, you can't record an image that is any better than the quality of the incoming video signal.

SVHS

This is another high-resolution video format. It uses full-size tapes, so it is not as convenient as Hi8 and other small formats. VCRs supporting SVHS cost $600 and up.

See also: Hi8; S-Video

Synchronization

Linking accurately to the video signal is one of the hardest jobs that capture hardware has to do. It's also something that you, the operator, have the least control over. If the board does a good job, you're fine. If the board doesn't do a good job, you're not going to be happy. The symptoms of poor synchronization include:

➤ Horizontal bands that are misaligned.

➤ Black space at the top or bottom of the screen.

➤ Missing portions of the video image at the top or bottom of the screen.

If you experience synchronization problems, the cause may not be the capture card at all—it could also be your video source. Try a different video source to see if that has any affect on the problem.

If you do encounter consistent synchronization problems, you should consider it a fundamental problem with your video card, and return it to the manufacturer for service.

Video Capture

Video capture is the process of converting analog video signal to digital data. This process need not involve displaying the incoming video during capture. Cards that support video capture may or may not also support display of incoming video in a window or under DOS.

See also: Overlay

Wave Audio

Video capture hardware does not usually offer support for Wave audio input. In these cases, you'll need to have a separate card to handle wave audio. I recommend the Turtle Beach Multisound when quality is a requirement; it does an outstanding job.

Your video card may support audio input and output, but this almost always is not Wave audio. The software drivers for such boards usually can control the volume of this audio, which is called *pass-through audio*.

Hardware Issues

Buying capture or overlay hardware is the most expensive decision you'll make regarding digital video. At current prices, you can spend from $400 to $15,000 to equip your computer with varying degrees of video hardware. Most of the "good stuff" is available in the $400-$1,500 range. Those numbers will change, of course—and only for the better—over the next 6 to 18 months as new, lower-cost chips are introduced by such chip makers as Intel and C-Cubed.

Cost is only one small part of the overall picture. There are a number of other issues to consider when you are preparing to purchase digital video hardware. These include:

➤ *Maximum frame rate*. The more frames per second, the better.

➤ *Overlay capability*. Do you need live video in a window?

➤ *Image quality*. How good is it, really?

➤ *Design issues*. Is the board well designed?

➤ *Track record*. How well have the company's other products performed?

➤ *Installation*. Is the installation easy, or obscure and difficult?

➤ *Ease of use*. How easy is it to use?

➤ *Documentation*. Is the documentation effective and complete?

➤ *Service capabilities*. Does the company have a reputation for good service?

Maximum Frame Rate

Analog video operates at 30 frames per second, but only a few capture cards can operate at that same rate. The average capture card can handle about 15 frames per second, half of the standard rate. This causes a slight but noticeable jerkiness during playback. However, this also results in smaller file sizes. If you plan to distribute only on CD-ROM, this isn't a problem; the limited transfer rates of CD-ROM (150k/second) require you to make some sacrifices, such as using lower frame rates.

Some boards, such as the Video Spigot, are capable of capturing the full 30 frames per second. The Video Spigot has the advantage of being generally well

designed and easy to use. If maximum frame rate is important, the Spigot is a good choice. However, the Spigot is a capture-only board; it won't do overlay.

If high frame rates are critical, you might also want to consider boards that offer hardware-assisted compression. However, you'll also need such boards for playback unless the codec used by the board also supports software-only playback. The Indeo codec meets this requirement.

Overlay Capability

Overlay enables you to display a live video signal on your computer monitor. This is called overlay because the incoming video signal is overlaid on the normal VGA video signal. VGA is actually an analog signal, so this isn't too hard to do. However, it must be really hard to do right because many boards don't quite get it to work smoothly.

The mechanics of overlay are simple. There must be software to put a magenta box on the screen. The overlay hardware uses this as a mask to tell it where to put the video image. It's a lot like the chroma key process used to put the weatherman in front of the weather map on TV.

The critical link in the process involves converting the scanning frequency of the incoming video with the VGA signal. Matching these two signals must be done accurately to get good results. In practice, different boards vary quite dramatically in their ability to do this well. Symptoms of a poor match include:

➤ Waviness in the VGA image.

➤ Offset of the incoming video image in any direction—up, down, left, right.

➤ Fluttering of certain colors, especially any color close to magenta.

➤ Diagonal shifting of the incoming video image.

If any of these symptoms occur, consider it a fundamental problem with the hardware and contact the manufacturer.

It is highly desirable to have overlay capability in your capture card, but the cost of adding overlay capability makes it tough to have both capture and overlay in one card. In addition, the technical difficulties can be a significant problem unless you get top-quality hardware. There are four kinds of boards that support overlay:

➤ *TV-style boards.* This kind of hardware doesn't do capture; it only does overlay, and is designed specifically for incoming television (Radio Frequency, RF) signals.

➤ *Overlay boards.* These are cards that support overlay only; they generally expect either composite or S-Video signals.

➤ *Overlay and capture boards.*

➤ *Overlay, capture, and VGA boards.* These boards have on-board VGA capabilities as well as capture and overlay capabilities.

Overlay boards that do not have on-board VGA capabilities must interact with the installed VGA card to display the incoming video signal. In many cases, this can be quite problematic. For example, overlay cards may refuse to work with some VGA cards and may work just fine with others. This is a delicate area, and not nearly as reliable as it needs to be. A good example of this kind of board is the Video Blaster. It is inexpensive, but it is almost impossible to predict if it will work in a given computer or with a given VGA card. If you elect to purchase a Video Blaster—and the low price ($499 retail) makes it a very affordable option—make sure you have the opportunity to return it if it won't work with your configuration. You might also think about getting a new VGA card to make it work in your computer.

At the other end of the spectrum is the Bravado 16 from Truevision. The cost ($1,495 retail) is significantly higher than the Video Blaster, but its performance is excellent. If you are looking for a board that does overlay and capture, the Bravado is a very good choice. There are two limitations to be aware of. One, it requires that you have 15 megabytes or less of installed memory. Two, it supports a maximum capture rate of 15 frames per second. However, the image quality is excellent, integration of VGA and Super VGA capabilities is excellent, documentation is very good, and the engineering of the board is well thought out.

Given that I have encountered numerous problems with overlay boards that don't use on-board video, it would be comforting to think that one could expect generally better results with boards that do. However, this is not the case. One capture/overlay/VGA board I received—the SNAPplus from Cardinal—was so poorly documented and so difficult to install that I cannot recommend it at all.

Image Quality

Another area in which there is sadly a large difference between various boards is image quality. Problems to watch out for include:

➤ Washed-out colors.

➤ Streaks, flecks, and splotches in the image.

➤ Yellowish cast to images.

➤ Lack of sharpness.

➤ Incorrect colors.

➤ Image too dark.

The only way to verify image quality is to install a board and see what happens. In some cases, the board may interact with other components in your machine, and that may affect image quality. Boards that support overlay video, and that must interconnect with an existing VGA card, are the most common problem.

Capture cards can exhibit problems, too. If you see the same problem whenever you record, consider it a fundamental problem with the hardware and contact the manufacturer.

Design Issues

Without experience in hardware design, it's hard to simply look at a board and determine how good it is. A good design, however, will show it in ways that you can see. Many of these are little things—are the connectors solidly mounted? Are all necessary cables supplied? Attention to these little details can tell you whether attention was paid to details that you can't see.

Good design will also show up as good image quality. A steady image with clear, accurate colors and no misalignment almost always reflects a careful design.

Track Record

The company that manufactures the card you intend to buy is an important consideration. A company with a history of solid designs, trouble-free products, and excellent technical support is obviously a better choice. In general, you can expect to pay a little more for hardware from such companies, but it may often be worth it in terms of satisfaction and lack of problems.

Creative Labs, which offers the Video Blaster and the Video Spigot, has been a rapidly growing company, and they haven't been able to keep up with the demand for technical support and problem resolution. Keep this in mind if you want to buy one of their products. Also keep in mind, however, that some of the products sold by Creative Labs are only marketed by Creative Labs, and might not have the same kinds of problems. For example, the Video Spigot was actually designed and built by SuperMac, and is marketed exclusively by Creative Labs. SuperMac has a strong track record, and has several technical people available on CompuServe to answer questions and resolve problems. In general, the Video Spigot seldom is a problem, and it's worth serious consideration.

Truevision is a company that specializes in video-related products, and their hardware has been of consistently good quality for a number of years. Their products should always be high on your list of possible choices.

In general, if quality is your primary concern, look for companies that specialize in video, have a good track record with previous products, and that have a reputation for taking the time to support their products.

Installation

Ease of installation varies from simple to impossible. (Yes, I do mean impossible.) I have received video capture cards that I literally was unable to install for one reason or another. Typical problems include missing disks, documentation completely at odds with the hardware and software that was actually in the box, and overly complex setup procedures.

Boards that were easy to install include the Video Spigot and the Pro Movie Spectrum. The SNAPPlus from Cardinal was the one that was impossible to install (the documentation was not consistent with the supplied software). Most other boards fall roughly in the middle of the pack.

Ease of Use

The easiest boards to use are those that support capture only. Installation is usually easy, and operation is limited to Video for Windows VidCap applications. Overlay boards are more complex, and boards that support both overlay and capture are generally the trickiest to master. These are general trends; some boards go out of their way to make themselves hard to use. I had some problems, for example, with the Super VideoWindows card from New Media Graphics. The board itself performed well, but it was a little harder to use than it needed to be.

Documentation

Interestingly, one of the most valuable and unexpected quality predictors has been the size of the documentation for a board. The thicker the documentation, the better the product in many cases. This might seem like a silly way to judge a product, but it does make some sense. One of the worst sets of documentation (for the Cardinal SNAPPlus) was also the thinnest. Some of the best documentation (Bravado 16 and Video Spigot) was also the thickest.

There is a reason for this. Many of the concepts involved in video are new. Manufacturers who take the time—and money—to do a good job at documenting their product are going to have to put a lot of information into the package.

One exception to this was the Pro Movie Spectrum. The documentation was thin, but very clear and easy to read. The board was a good performer.

Service with a Smile?

There are two issues involved in service: which companies make products that are so good they seldom require service, and which companies provide service that is timely and effective.

One of the most problematic companies in the computer hardware business is Creative Labs. They have experienced such outrageous sales growth over the last few years that it has been just about impossible for them to keep up with service. The reason for their growth: offering adequate products at really good prices. If you want the lowest price, be prepared for some service hassles. Creative Labs will not abandon you or anything unethical like that; they simply are overwhelmed with the process of extremely rapid growth. You'll need to be patient if you have a problem. I know some of the folks who work there, and their hearts are in the right places, even if they don't have enough time to deal with everything.

One of the more outstanding video capture boards, the Video Spigot, is marketed and sold by Creative Labs, but was originally designed and built by SuperMac. SuperMac engineers maintain an active presence on CompuServe, and you can get good technical information there. Of course, I've heard of very few problems with the Spigot, so you may not need any help at all to use it.

Truevision is a company that has provided outstanding technical support. The tech support people are very knowledgeable, and were able to help me quickly and correctly whenever I called.

Hardware Reviews

This section puts all the cards on the table. All of the capture cards listed here were tested, tortured, and played with over several days, using a variety of input sources and a variety of image types. I have rated each board in a number of categories:

Maximum frame rate	This is the best frame rate I could get on a 486/66 VESA local bus machine with an ATI Ultra Pro + video card, 8 megabytes of memory, and a 500 megabyte Fujitsu IDE hard drive.
Overlay capability	This will be yes if the board supports overlay.
Image quality	This will be a grade, from **A** to **F**, rating the image quality. The best board gets an **A+**, and all other boards are rated relative to that. A board with an **F** for image quality would not even be usable for playing around.
Design issues	This is also a grade from **A** to **F**. Again, the best board gets an **A+**, and all other boards are rated relative to it.

Track record	This refers to the company's track record with other products. If unknown, then it is so noted.
Installation	This rates the ease of installation on the good old A to F scale. An **F** indicates that you will want to pull out your hair in frustration before you get the board installed.
Ease of use	This rates ease of use after the board has been installed and set up.
Documentation	This rates the documentation for completeness, readability, and accuracy.
Service capabilities	This rates the company's performance in technical support, where that information is available.

The overall price/performance leader is the Video Spigot. If you are on a budget, and need to capture video, this is a good choice. The best choice for a board that supports both capture and overlay is the Bravado from Truevision. Keep in mind, however, that it limits the amount of memory you can install in your machine to less than 16 megabytes.

There are some new boards coming out in mid-to-late 1993 that will merit close attention, particularly some entries from Intel that look interesting. I maintain a presence in the Multimedia Forum on CompuServe, and you can get the latest information about new hardware there by just dropping me a message. My CompuServe number is 75530,3711.

And now, the hardware players in the video capture wars.

Action Media II

Maximum frame rate	30 fps
Overlay capability	Yes
Image quality	A
Design issues	A; uses compression coprocessor.
Track record	A
Installation	B-D (see below for explanation)

Ease of use	C
Documentation	B
Service capabilities	A

This is a high-end board from Intel. Although it does support Video for Windows, it is really intended for very serious video folks. It works well with such high-end software as D/Vision from Touchvision.

A little explanation is in order for the unusual rating for installation. The Action Media II is a complex and sophisticated piece of equipment, and requires some technical knowledge to install. If you have the required knowledge of video and computer hardware, it gets a B rating. If you don't have the knowledge before you start, it will be a real bear to install.

Bravado 16

Maximum frame rate	15 fps
Overlay capability	Yes
Image quality	A
Design issues	B
Track record	A
Installation	B
Ease of use	A
Documentation	A+
Service capabilities	A

The Bravado is a very high quality board. It's also fairly expensive (retail at press time is $1,495), but it does an outstanding job of video capture and overlay. I was even able to do overlay at 800x600 and 1024x768, which many overlay boards cannot do. About the only negative thing was a few problems I experienced during installation. However, I am told that the board now ships with improved installation and utility software that addresses this minor glitch.

The B rating in design issues deserves an explanation. The down-rating comes because the board requires that you have less than 16 megabytes of memory installed in your system. If you don't need 16 or more megabytes, then raise the rating to an A—this board is very, very well thought out. The engineering is excellent.

The Bravado can be used with Windows, Video for Windows, and DOS. You can also easily write programs in C/C++, Visual Basic, Toolbook, and so on to utilize the board via its well written MCI drivers.

At press time, Truevision had announced two important add-on products for the Bravado: a video encoder and a video compression daughter cards. These are modules that snap onto the Bravado's built-in bus. The encoder will output VGA and Super VGS images to a VCR (NTSC or PAL standards, Composite or S-Video) at up to 24-bit color. The unit also incorporates flicker reduction, an essential bit of functionality. The video compression module takes the Bravado signal and uses a hardware chip to compress the incoming data in real time. Maximum image size is 360x240; this limit is based on the ISA bus, not the capabilities of the Bravado card. Prices and shipping dates for these cards were not available at press time.

Intel Video Developer's Kit

Maximum frame rate	30 fps
Overlay capability	Yes
Image quality	B; uses compression coprocessor.
Design issues	A
Track record	A
Installation	B
Ease of use	B
Documentation	B
Service capabilities	A

This board is a scaled-down version of the Action Media II intended specifically for use with Video for Windows. The biggest limitation is that it only does capture at 160x120. The board is being phased out in mid-1993 in favor of the Smart Video Recorder.

Pro Movie Spectrum

Maximum frame rate	24 fps
Overlay capability	No
Image quality	B
Design issues	B
Track record	B
Installation	A
Ease of use	A
Documentation	B+
Service capabilities	B

I had some minor problems with the sample of the Pro Movie Spectrum I received. The image would jump occasionally; this problem persisted even when I switched to a different video source. This is the reason for the B rating in image quality; other than the occasional jump, the image quality was excellent, with rich colors and sharp images. I wouldn't expect to see this defect in all samples, and the high frame rate and good image quality mean you should give this board serious consideration. If you want to feel safe, capture a minute or so of video after you install it to verify that there are no problems.

ProMotion

Maximum frame rate	15 fps
Overlay capability	Unknown
Image quality	D
Design issues	C
Track record	Unknown
Installation	C
Ease of use	B
Documentation	C
Service capabilities	Unknown

I was not impressed with the quality of this card. The image quality was very poor, with washed-out images with little color, and significant streaking in the images.

Smart Video Recorder

Maximum frame rate	30 fps
Overlay capability	Yes
Image quality	Unknown
Design issues	Unknown
Track record	A
Installation	Unknown
Ease of use	Unknown
Documentation	Unknown
Service capabilities	A

This is a new board from Intel, released just as we were going to press. It comes with Version 2.11 of the Indeo codec. The new codec shows a significant improvement in speed and image quality over the version that originally shipped with Video for Windows 1.0.

The primary advantage of the Smart Video Recorder is that it offers real-time compression using the Indeo codec. This means that you don't have to spend time after capture to compress the video sequence. This is a major advantage. The other aspects of the board—documentation, engineering, image quality, and so on—are also well above average. Give this board serious consideration when making a purchase.

The Indeo codec is designed to work on a variety of platforms, so it has some features—and lacks others—that are part of Video for Windows. There is only one such issue that requires any attention on your part. You need to follow these steps to get the best results for capture:

1. Capture to a permanent capture file, using the highest available quality setting for compression, and set key frames to one.

2. Open the capture file in VidEdit, trim leading or trailing frames as needed, and then use File/Save As to save the file under a different name.

   Very important: Make sure you select the correct data rate (such as CD-ROM 150k/sec), set the key frames to 1 again, and make sure that frame padding is turned on for CD-ROM data rates.

   Even more important: Make sure you use "No change" as the compression setting! It will take just a few seconds, and you will get a very compact file at the data rate you want. If you get a message box telling you that the target data rate could not be met, try using more compression (that is, a lower quality setting) or a lower frame rate. As a last resort, recapture the sequence with a lower quality rate. As a last, last resort, you might try using Indeo compression a second time during the Save As, but this might affect image quality more than you'll be willing to tolerate (in particular, bright colors may smear into surrounding pixels).

You should have no problems if you follow these steps. The majority of the video files on the CD-ROM that comes with this book were captured with the Indeo codec and a Smart Video Recorder, so you can judge the results for yourself!

Super VideoWindows

Maximum frame rate	15 fps
Overlay capability	Yes
Image quality	B
Design issues	B
Track record	B
Installation	B
Ease of use	B
Documentation	B
Service capabilities	B

This board was a steady but unimpressive performer.

Targa+

Maximum frame rate	20 fps
Overlay capability	Yes and No
Image quality	A++
Design issues	A+
Track record	A+
Installation	B
Ease of use	B
Documentation	A+
Service capabilities	A+

The Targa, although expensive, is a superb performer in the video arena. Strictly speaking, it's a bit of overkill if all you intend to do is capture video with Video for Windows, but it does a really good job at every aspect of the process and is highly recommended. The Targa's real strengths lie in its analog video capabilities; you can connect a TV monitor to its output as well as its inputs. You can use the Targa+ for sophisticated video production.

Video Blaster

Maximum frame rate	15 fps
Overlay capability	Yes
Image quality	C
Design issues	D

Track record	C
Installation	B
Ease of use	B
Documentation	B
Service capabilities	C

The Video Blaster suffers from two serious problems. First, it will not work in some computers at all, or will distort the performance of the existing video card. Translation: you may not get any results in some computers, and in others you'll have to get a new video display card.

Second, the Video Blaster does not have very good image quality. Many people I spoke with had problems with a yellowish cast in the image that they could not adjust properly.

The main advantage of the Video Blaster is that it gives you overlay capability at a capture-only price. If you are willing to take a chance, or can accept less-than-perfect image quality because of price, then give it a try. Be sure, however, that you buy it with a liberal return policy.

Video Spigot

Maximum frame rate	30 fps
Overlay capability	No
Image quality	A
Design issues	A
Track record	Unknown
Installation	A
Ease of use	A
Documentation	A
Service capabilities	Unknown

This is one of the boards that I recommend highly and frequently. The frame rate is high, it comes with a very good (but proprietary) codec called Cinepak, and the image quality is very good. This board also does not place any restrictions on how much memory you can use. The key to making this board as useful as it should be is free use of the Cinepak codec. If SuperMac, the creators of the codec, ever decide to make it freely distributable, the Video Spigot will be even more impressive than it already is. The Cinepak codec offers significant advantages for CD-ROM distribution, but see Chapter 8 for some important caveats regarding Cinepak before you buy.

Watch It TV

Maximum frame rate	N/A
Overlay capability	Yes
Image quality	B
Design issues	B
Track record	B
Installation	A
Ease of use	A
Documentation	B
Service capabilities	B

This is not a board that supports Video for Windows; it has an on-board TV tuner that allows you to watch TV—even cable TV—in a Window. It's a fun product.

Summary

Video capture and overlay hardware is in the middle of a revolution. For the short term, your best bet is to invest in a card that will do the best job at frame rate and image quality. If you control the machines the video will be played on, and can afford to put hardware-assisted compression cards on all machines, you might want to try one of the current crop of cards with a compression coprocessor.

If you really want to work with standards, however, you are better off post-poning a purchase of a capture card with a compression coprocessor until late 1993 when we should see a whole new—and much cheaper—generation of such cards.

7

Software for Digital Video

There are two sides to recording and working with digital video: the easy side and the hard side. Working with video on a computer is a lot like going swimming in a lake you don't know: the deep places will get you if you aren't careful. If you ever walked in shallow water and suddenly found a drop-off where the water was over your head, you have the basic idea of what it is like to work with digital video. Up to a point, it's actually very easy. Past that point, the degree of difficulty rises quickly.

The line between these two sides, of course, is shifting constantly as both hardware and software get better and cheaper. The goal of this chapter is to show you everything you can do without getting in over your head.

Video for Windows comes with two major tools for working with video: VidCap and VidEdit. VidCap is the simpler of the two; it is used for capturing incoming video to your hard disk. VidEdit has more features, but it's still a simple program. Despite their simplicity, you can do a lot with just these two programs. Once you get your feet wet, of course, you may want to stretch a bit and use software such as Premiere or Media Merge to modify or enhance your videos. You can even use sophisticated software such as 3D Studio to create fancy 3-D effects, but you don't have to do all that to get effective video. Video, by its nature, adds a new dimension to existing material: movement.

This means that even simple video can be very effective. For example, consider a business situation involving a problem finding the right parts to fill an order. No one seems to know what the customer wants, and the boss is in Toledo making another sale. Wouldn't it be great if someone could hold the suspect parts up to a video camera, turning them this way and that, and send it as E-mail to the boss? The problem would get solved in a hurry, and at little cost—and it wouldn't take fancy video to make it happen, either.

VidCap Setup

VidCap is a very simple application. A typical VidCap window is shown in Figure 7.1. Yes, that's Bill Gates in the VidCap window; I used a video of Mr. Gates at the introduction of Video for Windows for the capture and editing examples in this chapter.

Figure 7.1. A typical VidCap screen.

If you haven't already used VidCap to capture videos, you may not realize how easy it is to do. The basic steps are:

1. Defragment the hard disk you plan to capture to.

2. Create a capture file with VidCap (File/Set File Size).

3. Choose audio and video options.

4. Set capture options.

5. Capture the video to disk.

Defragment the Hard Disk

I've said it before, and I'll say it here again because it can't be said too many times: defragment your hard disk before you attempt to capture video. It may seem like a hassle, it may seem like the last thing you want to do when your creative juices start to flow, but if you don't defragment your hard disk you may not get very good results. What will happen if you don't defragment? Your hard disk might be perfectly capable of capturing 30 frames per second at 160x120. If it is seriously fragmented, however, you might drop down to as low as 5 or 10 frames per second!

Fortunately, if you have the space to set up a permanent capture file, you won't have to defragment every time you want to capture video. If you will be capturing 160x120 of raw video with 8-bit color, at 30 frames per second, you can count on needing about 34 megabytes of disk space per minute of video. If your actual capture needs will be different, it's easy to calculate how many bytes of disk space you'll need per minute:

```
width x height x color x fps x 60
```

Width is the width in pixels of the image, and height is also measured in pixels. Color refers to the color depth of the video; 8-bit color has a depth of 1 byte, 16-bit is 2 bytes, and 24-bit is 3 bytes. fps means frames per second, and must correspond to the capture rate you are using. Finally, multiply by 60, the number of seconds in a minute.

If you apply this formula to the numbers I mentioned in the preceding paragraph, you get:

```
160 * 120 * 1 * 30 * 60 = 34,560,000
```

There are 1,048,576 (220) bytes in a megabyte, so that comes out to 33 megabytes. Per minute. If you cut back to 15 frames per second, cut that in half, to 16.5 megabytes per minute. Just for fun, you can apply the formula to full-screen, full-color video:

```
640 * 480 * 3 * 30 * 60 = 1,658,880,000
```

That's 1,582 megabytes—also known as 1.58 gigabytes—of storage space for a single minute of video. Now you know why compression is critical to putting video on a PC, and why digital video isn't as cheap to acquire as good old analog video!

> **Note**
>
> These figures do not include requirements for storing the sound track. The addition of a sound track can add up to 10.5 megabytes per minute for CD-quality stereo sound.

If you are going to create a permanent capture file, plan ahead and reserve all the space you'll need.

Create a Capture File

Actually setting up a permanent capture file is easy; it's finding the space to put it in that's hard. While running VidCap, select File/Set Capture File... from the menu. This will display a dialog box with a button labeled "New Size..." If you click it, you'll see the dialog box shown in Figure 7.2.

Figure 7.2. Setting the capture file size.

As you can see, I was rather generous in allotting space. 60 megabytes gives me almost two minutes of recording time at 30 frames per second and 8 bits of color at 160x120. If I cut back to 15 fps, I get about four minutes of recording.

Most of the time, I record clips in the range of 5 to 20 seconds because longer clips are just too large for general distribution. I only record longer clips when I am going to put the material on a CD-ROM, or for special cases where I can use something such as LapLink to move the file from one computer to another, or when I am sending a tape backup of the files.

Compression will significantly cut these file sizes. If you are fortunate to be using a video capture card that has a compression coprocessor on it, you will be able to use less disk space per minute of recording time. You can cut your file sizes in half, or more, with compression. For example, Figure 7.3 shows an original image I recorded from a video tape Microsoft was kind enough to send me. This is an uncompressed image, and the complete 29.72-second video occupied 11.1 megabytes, including sound. Figure 7.4 shows the same frame from a compressed version of the file, which occupied 4.3 megabytes—39% of the original. I used the Microsoft Video 1 codec, with a quality setting of 85.

There really isn't much difference between the two images; you need to look closely to see how compression altered the image. Figure 7.5a-b shows details from the two images. The uncompressed image is on the left, and the compressed image is on the right.

Figure 7.3. An uncompressed captured video image, original 160x120.

Figure 7.4. A compressed captured video image, original 160x120.

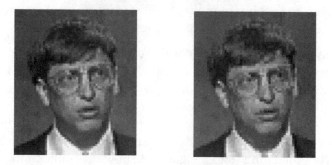

Figure 7.5a-b. Details of original (left) and compressed (right) images.

Enlarged like this, the images show subtle but detectable differences. Look at the subjects mouth, for example—in the original, the open mouth consists of a range of shades, while the compressed image uses just one color for this area. You'll find similar compression effects in various parts of the image, but they are subtle. At a quality factor of 85, you can usually expect to see a relatively faithful image with Microsoft Video 1 compression. At 75, the default, you will see some blockiness in the image, and at lower quality settings, the image will be seriously compromised. Figure 7.6 shows the same frame at a quality setting of 75, and Figure 7.7 shows it at a quality setting of 50. Blockiness is evident in the frame at 75, particularly in the background to the left of the face, but the key features are still OK. The frame at a quality setting of 50 is useless.

Note

Because blockiness first shows up in the background of most images, you can compress without losing key details. However, the blocks seem to jump when the video is played. In some situations, this may make the video unusable because of the distraction.

Figure 7.6. A 160x120 video image compressed with a quality setting of 75.

Figure 7.7. A 160x120 video image compressed with a quality setting of 50.

Audio Format

VidCap gives you access to the complete capabilities of all standard sound cards. You can set audio parameters using the dialog box shown in Figure 7.8.

Figure 7.8. Setting audio parameters in VidCap.

You need to give more than passing attention to how you record the audio portion of your capture. In some cases, you won't be using the audio at all, and you should be sure to turn off audio capture so that the CPU doesn't waste precious resources on data you don't intend to use. In fact, if you are having minor problems capturing video at a certain rate, you might try capturing the video and audio separately, and then joining them later—the extra processing capability that comes from not capturing audio can increase the amount of video you can capture.

There are three parameters that you can set for audio:

➤ *Sample size.* There are two choices possible, although your sound card may only support one: 8- and 16-bit sampling. 16-bit sampling isn't merely twice as good as 8-bit, but it does take twice as many bytes for storage. 8 bits means one byte per sample, which means that each sample can have one of 256 possible values. 16 bits means two bytes per sample, and each sample can have one of more than 65,000 values. Obviously, 16-bit sampling is much more precise. You will definitely hear better results with 16-bit sampling, but if you plan to distribute your videos, you may want to stick with 8-bit samples anyway—most installed sound cards don't support 16 bits. You may also find that the data load of 16-bit samples interferes with efficient video capture on some machines and with some sound cards. You'll need to experiment to determine your hardware's capabilities.

➤ *Channels.* You can record in mono or in stereo. As with 8- and 16-bit sampling, you will find that most installed sound cards don't support stereo; if you plan to distribute your videos, mono may have to be your choice. And, as with other parameters, watch those extra bytes: stereo instantly doubles the amount of data you're working with for sound.

➤ *Frequency.* There are three choices for sampling frequency: 11, 22, and 44 kHz. It breaks down like this: 11kHz is OK for voice, but not OK for music. 22kHz does a very good job with voice, and an acceptable job with music. 44kHz is CD-quality sound. Not many installed sound cards, however, support 44kHz samples. Each doubling of the frequency doubles the amount of sound data. 44kHz is wasted on 8-bit sound in any case.

At the high end—16 bits, 44kHz stereo—you're talking about 10.5 megabytes of sound data per minute. At the low end—8 bits, 11kHz mono—you only have to cope with 0.6 megabytes per minute. (That's one byte per sample, and 11,000 samples per second.) For general distribution, I recommend using 8 bits, 22kHz, and mono sound, which is a load of 1.2 megabytes per minute for sound.

Refer back to Figure 7.8 for a moment. See that little button marked "Level..."? Clicking it displays the dialog box shown in Figure 7.9.

Figure 7.9. Checking audio levels in VidCap.

The horizontal box acts like a traditional recording level meter—it measures the incoming sound level, and moves the black line farther to the right as the sound gets louder; peak sounds are marked by a thin red vertical line. It's a good habit to check audio levels before recording—overloading the audio levels can cause severe noise problems, and can easily make the audio portion of the recording useless.

Video Format

Before recording video, you'll need to set up a few parameters, as shown in Figure 7.10.

Figure 7.10. Setting the video format in VidCap.

The actual contents of this dialog box will change, depending on which hardware capture card you have installed in your computer. VidCap queries the hardware driver to see exactly what video formats are available, and lists them here. For example, some capture cards support a larger number of image dimensions, while other cards have a limited selection. Some cards support only the standard image formats—8-bit palettized, 16-bit, and 24-bit—while others add proprietary image formats. For example, the Video Spigot adds 8-bit dithered and a proprietary format that relies on YUV instead of RGB.

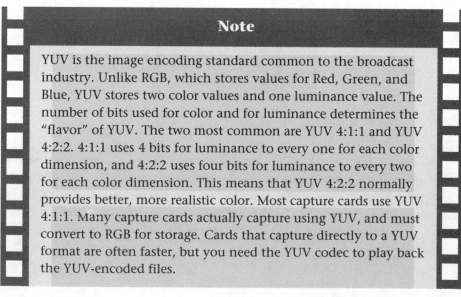

Note

YUV is the image encoding standard common to the broadcast industry. Unlike RGB, which stores values for Red, Green, and Blue, YUV stores two color values and one luminance value. The number of bits used for color and for luminance determines the "flavor" of YUV. The two most common are YUV 4:1:1 and YUV 4:2:2. 4:1:1 uses 4 bits for luminance to every one for each color dimension, and 4:2:2 uses four bits for luminance to every two for each color dimension. This means that YUV 4:2:2 normally provides better, more realistic color. Most capture cards use YUV 4:1:1. Many capture cards actually capture using YUV, and must convert to RGB for storage. Cards that capture directly to a YUV format are often faster, but you need the YUV codec to play back the YUV-encoded files.

You may also be able to set other video parameters, depending on what hardware you have installed. Figure 7.11 shows the Video Source dialog box for the Pro Movie Spectrum.

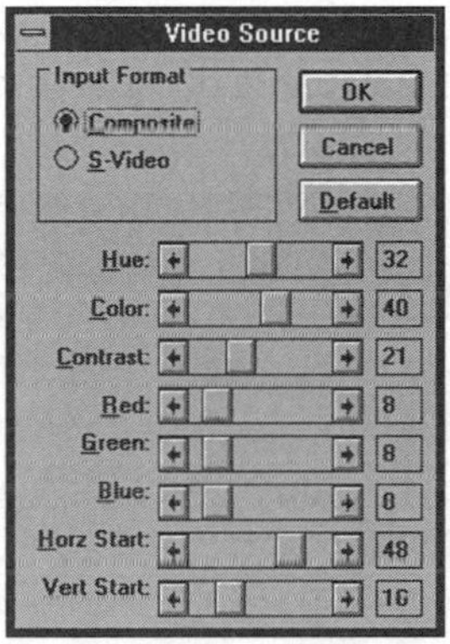

Figure 7.11. Setting the video source options for the Pro Movie Spectrum.

The Pro Movie Spectrum supports both composite and S-Video inputs, and you can select either input using this dialog box. If you have both composite and S-Video sources, this is convenient because you can leave both of them connected, and choose the one you want to use. Some hardware automatically detects which is available, and you sometimes cannot keep both connected.

Note

Composite video is the kind you deal with most often. If you have a standard VCR (including both mono and stereo), you probably have a composite video source. A composite source uses RCA-pin connectors; they are the kind of connectors you use on a typical home stereo system. S-Video is less widely available; you probably only have it if you bought a premium VCR or camcorder. For example, a camcorder that uses Hi8 tapes can output an S-Video signal. S-Video has a higher resolution than standard video. I recommend using S-Video equipment if you can justify the extra cost—the higher resolution yields a distinctly better quality result.

The parameters in the dialog box shown in Figure 7.11 are actually standard TV controls. Unless you have an older TV, or are old enough to have used one, you may be spoiled by today's auto-adjusting TV sets. Table 7.1 describes the uses for these controls. Keep in mind that the controls that are actually available will vary from one capture card to the next. The available selections will also vary if the video capture card is also capable of video overlay.

> **Note**
>
> A video overlay board does exactly what its name suggests: it overlays a video image on the digital video signal. This is quite different from what is required for video capture. Video capture must use a digitized video signal. An overlay image is actually an analog image—because the card puts the video on top of the video display, there's no need to convert it to digital data. The overlay card simply performs a conversion that matches the *scan rate* of the incoming video with the computer video. The scan rate is the frequency at which the image is painted on the screen.

Table 7.1. Video Source options for the Pro Movie Spectrum.

Option	Description
Hue	Moving this slider changes the color balance. If the incoming image is consistently too blue, for example, you can move the slider to add more red to the image.
Color	This slider determines how much color is used. If the image is consistently too washed out, add more color. If the colors are too intense, reduce the color level.
Contrast	Contrast is tricky to describe, but if you have too much or too little, it will ruin the video image. High contrast occurs when the image is mostly made up of very bright and very dark areas; there are few grays. If contrast is too high, colors will bleed into adjoining areas. Red, especially, will bleed easily, and white may wash out adjoining image areas. If contrast is too low, the image will be mostly gray, and lacking in blacks and whites. Colors will look thin.

Option	Description
Red	Controls the amount of red in the image.
Green	Controls the amount of green in the image.
Blue	Controls the amount of blue in the image.
Horiz Start	Change this setting if the part of the image is lost at the top or bottom of the window.
Vert Start	Change this setting if the part of the image is lost at the sides of the window.

Capturing Video

There are four different ways to capture video with VidCap:

➤ Single frames

➤ Multiple frames, one at a time

➤ Real-time video

➤ Palette capture

Single-Frame Capture

Single-frame capture is useful in a variety of situations. You can use it to evaluate image quality, to collect images for a database, or to use your video camera as a kind of scanner for image acquisition.

You can access single frame capture (and all other forms of capture) from either the menu or the toolbar.

Single-frame capture is simple. For example, if you click the appropriate icon on the toolbar or select single-frame capture from the Capture menu, the image in the VidCap window freezes, and you can then use the File menu to Save Single Frame. A number of the illustrations, such as the lighting figures in Chapter 3, were captured this way using live sources.

> **Note**
>
> You will almost always get a better image using a live video source. The process of storing the video image on tape degrades the image, even for high-quality tape formats such as Hi8. Whenever you want the highest quality results, record from live, not tape.

Multiple-Frame Capture

Multiple-frame capture involves manually capturing individual frames. The principal difference from single-frame capture is that the captured frames are loaded into a video sequence, rather than saved as still images. You can use this technique to collect a sequence of images that you plan to later save as individual bitmap files, or you can build a video sequence from still images. For example, you might want to capture a large-format video, such as 320x240, but your hardware might not support real-time capture in that format. If your video source can provide high-quality still images, you can capture your large-format video one frame at a time. This takes patience; there are, after all, 30 frames in a single second of video. Even if you capture every other frame—15 per second—it is still exacting work. The biggest problem is often the video source itself; few camcorders or VCRs can actually hold a stable single image.

> **Note**
>
> The primary difference between consumer and professional video equipment is that professional equipment is usually *frame accurate*. This means that the player can move accurately to specific frames, and hold the frame steady for you. You can also use frame-accurate recording to splice tightly onto tape from another video source.

The multiple-frame capture dialog box is shown in Figure 7.12.

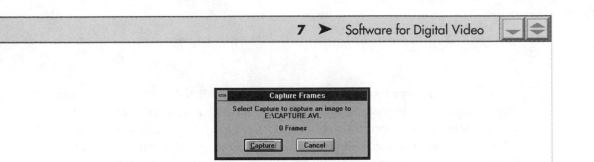

Figure 7.12. Multiple-frame capture dialog box.

The dialog box keeps track of the number of frames you capture, and using it is simplicity itself. When you have an image you want to capture, just click the Capture button. The images are accumulated in the current capture file. If you want to save them as separate bitmaps, use the File/Extract menu selection and select DIB Sequence as the save option.

Real-Time Capture

Most of the time, I use VidCap for real-time capture. But that's because I'm interested mostly in motion video. If you are creating a catalog, and using a video camera to digitize product images, real-time capture is a waste of hard disk space—use multiple-frame capture instead. But if you want to show people or objects in motion, real-time capture is the method of choice.

Figure 7.13 shows the dialog box for capturing a video sequence. You use this dialog box to set parameters for the capture, and you can also get quick access to the Audio Format and Video Format dialog boxes. This gives you an easy way to make changes for particular needs.

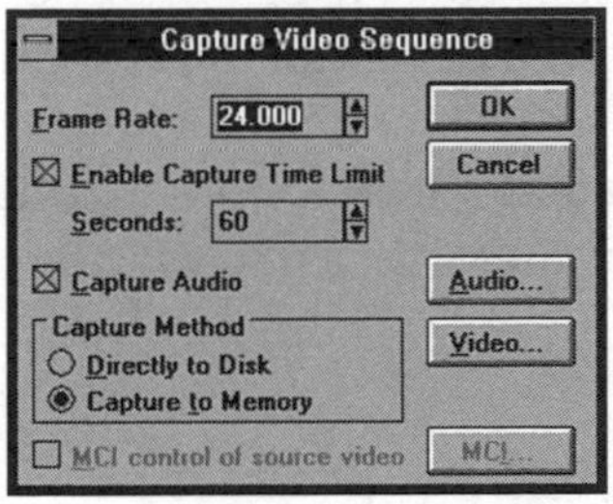

Figure 7.13. The Capture Video Sequence dialog box.

Let's take a closer look at each of the parameters listed in the real-time capture dialog box. At the top, there's a box for the frame rate. This determines how many frames will be captured each second. The highest frame rate you would use is 30; that's the same number of frames as are in the original video signal. VidCap will let you set a higher number, but a situation requiring more than 30 frames per second would be very unusual.

The frame rate you can use will be determined by a large number of factors. If you want other people to play your video on a wide range of hardware, you'll probably want to use either 12 or 15 frames per second. A fast 386 can handle 15 frames per second for playback, and 12 fps is OK on most 386/20 or better computers. If you want the best possible recording rate, you'll have to experiment. The following factors will influence your ability to get high frame rates:

➤ CPU speed

➤ Hard disk speed

➤ Video display speed

➤ Capture card capabilities

➤ Video capture driver capabilities

➤ Image size

CPU Speed

For capture, anything less than an 80486 CPU is asking for trouble. You can do capture with, say, a 386/33, but you will most likely find that you can't capture at the rates the capture card is capable of—the CPU speed will be the limiting factor. Expect capture rates of 8 to 12 frames per second on most 386 machines. A very fast 386 will be able to do 15 frames per second, but the results might not be reliable. Also, you'll need absolutely top-notch hard disk and video display subsystems to achieve high rates with a 386 CPU.

Hard Disk Speed

There is no such thing as a hard disk that is too fast for video capture. If you have a high-end computer, the hard disk is most likely to be the component that limits what you can do with video capture and playback.

I recommend using a hard disk with average access times in the range of 12 to 15 ms. If you can fit one into your budget, a hard disk with average access times of 9 or 10 ms will do even better. In general, I've seen more success with IDE drives rather than SCSI drives. Theoretically, a SCSI drive should be easier and faster in many situations, but the realities of drivers, installation hassles, deviations from standards, and so on, make SCSI a less certain proposition than IDE drives. If you already are very knowledgeable about SCSI technology, you probably can find a path through the thicket of drives, controllers, and driver software. Otherwise, stick with IDE drives.

You will also get better results from newer drives. Older drives were designed before video capture became common, and the drive design or drive BIOS may not do a good job of supporting the high, continuous transfer rates required for video capture. For example, I have two versions of Fujitsu's 500 megabyte 3.5" drive. The one with the later BIOS does a much better job of coping with video capture—the older drive sometimes stumbles in unexplainable ways and corrupts the video capture file. I suspect that the more recent drive has a more sophisticated way of handling thermal recalibration.

Note

Thermal recalibration is probably the biggest hassle for video capture with older large drives . Older drives are more or less leisurely about the process of rechecking themselves for changes because of heat variations. This can cause glitches in recording.

Video Display Speed

Your video display adapter is part of the chain of events involved in video capture. It has a more important role in playback, of course, but it plays at least a small part in the capture process. The capture software will try to display incoming images, if possible; a slow card can interfere just enough to be a minor hassle. As with a hard drive, it is not possible to have a video card that is too fast for video capture or playback.

Capture Card Capabilities

The capture card itself may have limitations that make it impossible to improve performance beyond a certain point. For example, many boards manufactured before the second quarter of 1993 that used RGB for capture (most use a particular chipset from Chips and Technologies) can't do better than 15 fps under any circumstances.

> ### Note
>
> The Chips and Technologies chipset has another issue for you to think about as well. This chipset requires that you have no more than 14 megabytes of system memory because the chipset uses part of your system memory as a frame buffer for the video images. When you are selecting capture hardware, make sure you check into this if you have, or expect to have, 16 megabytes or more of system memory.

To determine the capabilities of your card, you'll need to set up for capture using a minimum of other resources. That means capturing with an image size of 160x120, at 8-bit color. You'll also need a very fast computer to test the card's capabilities; if the hard disk or the CPU limit is reached, the card won't be pushed to its limits.

There is an extremely wide range of capabilities in all price ranges. For example, the Video Spigot is very fast—I easily get 30 frames per second capture with 160x120 images. But the Spigot is one of the most affordable capture cards, and the image quality is very good. On the other hand, you won't get much more than 18 or 20 fps out of a Targa+ card. Of course, the Targa can do a lot more than just Video for Windows, and the image quality is more than excellent—it's among the best I've seen, period.

Video Capture Driver Capabilities

The capture driver also determines how much performance you're going to get from your setup. If the manufacturer hasn't done a very good job with the capture driver, you won't get all of the performance your capture card is capable of. The type of capture driver may also determine performance limits. For example, the Truevision Bravado originally shipped with drivers that saved incoming data as RGB data. By switching to a proprietary YUV format, the Bravado can extend its capture rates.

Image Size

The size of the image you capture has everything to do with the frame rate you'll be able to use. Briefly stated, it works like this: the larger the image, the slower the frame rate. In fact, many capture cards can't even capture one frame per second at large sizes. Only a few cards, for example, can record 320x240 images at reasonable (greater than 10 fps) frame rates. The Video Spigot is one of the better known cards in this category. If image size is important, you will need the fastest possible component in each subsystem of your computer, and you'll need to shop carefully for your capture card to make sure it works well with your other hardware. If you want to capture large image sizes, you'll be pushing the outer envelope of what is possible with video, so be prepared to tweak, twiddle, and cajole performance out of your system.

Palette Capture

Ah, palettes. If there is one thing that is simultaneously a great boon and a big hassle, it's palettes. To explain both sides of the palette issue, I'll need to fill in a few details first.

First of all, palettes only apply when you are working with 8-bit color mode. Although you are limited to just 256 colors, you can pick which 256 colors are used at any one time from a list of more than 16 million colors. It works like this: there is a table with 256 entries in it. This table is loaded with the specifications for the 256 colors that will be used. To refer to a color in the table, software uses the entry number: color 1, color 2, and so on, up to color 256. The good part of all this is that you can change the contents of the palette to display different images. Thus, you only have 256 colors, but you have a lot of flexibility, too.

This works fine until the colors in the palette are changed. If you change the colors in the palette in preparation for displaying a new image, each color in the palette is now a different color. For example, if color 1 was a light blue, it might now be a dark green. If another image is still on the screen when you change the palette to display a new image, the colors of the old image will change with the palette. If the changes are major, the original image might not even be recognizable. This is the down side to using palettes—unless images share the same palette, chaos reigns.

Another problem with palettes is that it takes time to switch them. Not only will your other images get weird under a new palette; you'll have to wait agonizing fractions of a second while Windows flashes from one palette to the next. To see this effect for yourself, just open multiple copies of Media Player and open a different video file with each copy. Then click on each copy in turn to make it active. Watch as the colors gyrate and change for each image. Note also that images in the background have their colors more or less seriously mangled.

That's the background on palettes; now look at how to use them in VidCap. If you are capturing in 8-bit mode, you'll note that the default palette is nothing but grays. There will be no color in the image when you first select 8-bit palettized capture. If you want to capture with a gray palette; you're all set. If you want realistic colors, you have to capture a palette from the incoming video before you capture.

You can click on the little palette icon on the toolbar, or select Capture/Palette... from the menu. In either case, you'll see the dialog box shown in Figure 7.14.

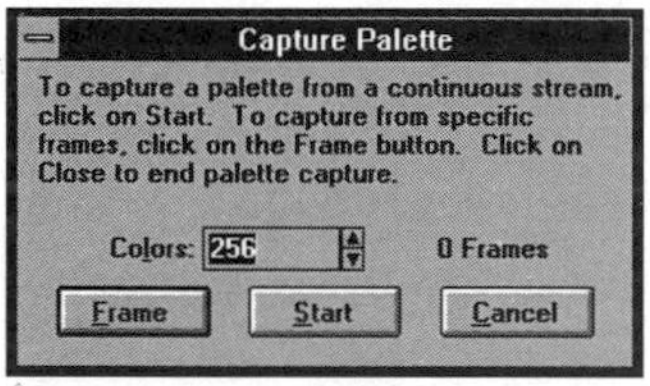

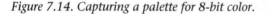

Capture Palette

To capture a palette from a continuous stream, click on Start. To capture from specific frames, click on the Frame button. Click on Close to end palette capture.

Colors: 256   0 Frames

Frame   Start   Cancel

Figure 7.14. Capturing a palette for 8-bit color.

There are two ways to capture a palette: one frame at a time, or a sequence of frames. To capture the palette of a single frame, click the Frame button. To begin capturing the palette for a series of frames, click the Start button.

Important: I want to discourage you from accepting the default value for the number of colors in this dialog box. The default value is 256, the total number of colors available in the palette. Windows likes to reserve 20 entries in the palette for its own use, for things such as menu bars, the desktop, window borders, and so forth. If you take these entries for your video, you may disrupt the appearance of Windows when the video is played back. A single click on the down arrow to the right of the numeric entry will move you to 236 as the number of colors; this is what you should do every time you capture a palette.

To capture a palette, then, simply select the number of colors you want in the palette (usually 236) and then click either the Frame or Start button. When you are done, click the Close button. VidCap will calculate an optimal palette and paste it into the file. From that point on, images will appear in color instead of shades of gray.

> ### Note
>
> If you are adventurous, you can use BitEdit and PalEdit—two utility programs that ship with Video for Windows—to modify palettes by hand. This is not a trivial task, but it can help when you are having problems with competing palettes. You can also save palettes to disk. This allows you to create a common palette for a series of videos and/or still images, which will eliminate the need for palette changes and the resulting distortion of background colors.

Some video capture cards, such as the Video Spigot, come with 8-bit capture cards that will use the standard palette for capture and playback. These codecs use dithering to simulate correct colors from the current palette. This works well for some images, and poorly for others. If you have an image that uses many shades of a single color, dithering won't work well. Similarly, if you have an image that is mostly gray, dithering won't work well. You might think that having only a few colors would make dithering a good option, but because only a few colors will be used, they tend to stand out if they are not perfect.

After capture (and sometimes during, if you have a fast machine), VidCap will report on the capture process. (See Figure 7.15.)

Figure 7.15. Results of a capture.

If more than 10% of the frames were dropped (not captured), VidCap will display a dialog box bringing this to your attention. Otherwise, you'll get a report on the status bar listing the length of the capture in seconds, the number of frames captured, the number of frames dropped, the net frame rate, and the size of the audio data.

Digital Video Compression: Tradeoffs You Can Live With

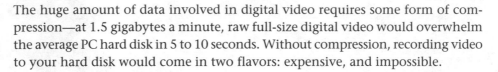
The huge amount of data involved in digital video requires some form of compression—at 1.5 gigabytes a minute, raw full-size digital video would overwhelm the average PC hard disk in 5 to 10 seconds. Without compression, recording video to your hard disk would come in two flavors: expensive, and impossible.

The compression techniques used for digital video are often extremely sophisticated, involving complex higher mathematics. It takes a lot of calculation to do the compression, so this puts a heavy load on the CPU. Video comes in at 30 frames per second, but it takes a 486/66 CPU from .25 to 3 seconds to compress just one frame. Clearly, video cannot be compressed in real time if you rely on the CPU.

The solution is a compression coprocessor. With hardware assistance, a computer can compress as much as 300 times faster. That means you can compress the video as it comes in, and avoid a time-consuming compression step afterwards. Until recently, a card with such hardware-assisted compression cost upwards of $2,000. Prices are now under $1,000, and falling rapidly. By the time you read this, you'll be able to get hardware-assisted compression for less than $500.

The problem with hardware-assisted compression is that you also need the same kind of hardware to decompress and display the video sequence. Until recently, there were no widely accepted standards for hardware-assisted video files. There were a number of cards, but each one had its own way of handling data, and you couldn't mix them. Intel is introducing some low-cost video compression chips during 1993 that are expected to change this. With inexpensive compression chips available, computer makers and video display vendors can start to add hardware compression directly to their products. It's a chicken and egg situation: no one wants to spend money on hardware-assisted compression until there is wide acceptance, and there won't be wide acceptance until there's a lot of hardware compression in computers.

Compression Techniques

Straight out of the box, Video for Windows comes with a variety of different compression *codecs*. This term is short for *co*mpression and *dec*ompression, and it describes the software that is used to compress and expand video files. Compression is probably the least understood, but far and away the most important aspect of digital video.

The most important point about compression is this: if you compress a file using a certain codec, the person who views the file *must* have that same codec installed on their machine. If you plan to publish or distribute your work, this is a very important consideration. If you are working with video on a strictly local basis, you are free to use or experiment with any of the available codecs.

What's Going on Here?

The type of compression used for video files is called *lossy compression*. The key is the word *lossy*. It means that you are willing to lose something in return for really large amounts of compression. The kind of compression you may already be familiar with doesn't lose anything at all, so this may be a new idea. How can lossy compression work?

The key lies in the way that we see. In effect, most images have more detail than the eye can see. For example, there may be subtle differences of color present that mean little or nothing to the eye; those can be removed—lost—without much penalty. By knowing what kinds of data the eye is least concerned with, programmers can design lossy compression intelligently.

Of course, that only buys you so much. At a certain point, you can increase the compression, but the lost material can clearly be seen. Some of this distortion is acceptable; too much, and the image becomes objectionably distorted.

Most compression methods allow you to choose the degree of compression that will be used. Typically, there is some kind of quality setting available. Low quality translates into heavy compression and heavy losses. High quality comes with light compression and minimal loss of data. Many codecs measure quality on a scale from 1 to 100, with 100 being minimal loss and 1 being extreme loss. In practice, you will find that distortion becomes unbearable with quality levels much below 75. Some codecs do not use this scale, but offer their own.

The best way to learn what various codecs mean for your video images is to work with them. In this section, you'll look at how various codecs compress and decompress an image. The reference image is shown in Figure 8.1. This image was not compressed in any way, and is a single frame from a typical video sequence.

Figure 8.1. Reference image, uncompressed.

RLE Stands for "Really Limited, but Efficient"

The simplest compression scheme, RLE, is also the least effective. RLE is an acronym for *Run Length Encoded*. To compress a file, it looks for horizontal bands of the same or similar colors. Instead of storing each pixel of color, RLE stores the color and the length of the color band—hence the name. This is not a very subtle compression scheme; the banding effects are sometimes very noticeable—it's sometimes hard to predict in advance when RLE will result in banding, and when it won't. RLE usually works best with images that have large areas of constant color, such as animation files. (See Figure 8.2.) Cartoonish images compress best with RLE.

Figure 8.2. RLE works best with animation images.

RLE is limited to images with 8 bits of color depth. In the right situation, RLE can be quite pleasing to the eye (see Figure 8.3). However, because RLE isn't a very efficient codec, the resulting file sizes and data rates can easily wind up too high for your system.

Figure 8.3. Image compressed with RLE codec.

Microsoft Video 1

As soon as we leave RLE behind, we also leave behind any possibility of a simple explanation for how compression schemes work. The mathematics behind most compression schemes is very complex, and beyond the scope of this book. Microsoft's Video 1 codec is no exception.

By default, this has become one of the most popular codecs for use with Video for Windows. This may change as more sophisticated codecs become available. The principle advantage of Video 1 is that it is distributed by Microsoft with Video for Windows. This ensures that it will be available if someone wants to play a file compressed with this codec.

The image quality of the Microsoft Video 1 codec is good. At high quality levels (90 to 100), the compression does not distort images badly. At a quality level of 75, image distortion is very noticeable, but acceptable for some uses. Speed of compression is good, and speed of decompression for playback is also good. This codec is only found as a software codec; there are no boards available that provide a compression/decompression coprocessor.

Microsoft Video 1 offers a variety of data formats, including 8-, 16-, and 24-bit color.

Figure 8.4 shows an image compressed with Microsoft Video 1 at a quality setting of 100, and Figure 8.5 shows the same image, but with a quality setting of 75.

Figure 8.4. Image compressed with Microsoft Video 1, quality level 100.

Figure 8.5. Image compressed with Microsoft Video 1, quality level 75.

Indeo

The Indeo codec has many visual advantages, and many practical advantages as well. However, it also involves some tradeoffs that are very important to be aware of.

Indeo's primary advantage is that it stores all images with 24-bit color data. At playback, the codec scales the color to what is available on the playback platform. In other words, if you capture a file in true color (24-bit) and save it with Indeo compression, it can be played back on a 256-color system. This is accomplished through color dithering—the colors available on the 256-color system are mixed to imitate the original colors. This gives Indeo files a characteristic appearance. You may find that the dithered images are not as appealing as images compressed with other codecs, at least for 256-color systems. Image quality on 16- or 24-bit systems is very good. Compare the images in Figure 8.6 and 8.7 to the reference, uncompressed image in Figure 8.1.

Figure 8.6. Image compressed with Indeo, quality level 100.

Figure 8.7. Image compressed with Indeo, quality level 75.

In addition to scaling color, Indeo also is a hardware and/or software codec. That is, you can use special hardware that will speed up compression and decompression hundreds of times over what can be done with software alone. During capture, compression is so fast that it is done in real time. This means that there is no need to apply compression after capture, saving a great deal of time on larger projects. Indeo is also available for a variety of platforms, including PCs, Macs, and UNIX. If wide distribution is a goal, or if you want the advantages of real-time compression, Indeo is worthy of very serious consideration.

The biggest drawback to Indeo involves software-only decompression. Indeo playback performance lags behind other codecs by a significant factor. For example, a 24-bit Cinepak file that will play back at 30 frames per second on a 486/66 will only play at 20 fps with Indeo compression.

Important note: Intel was working on a revised Indeo codec at press time, but copies were not yet available. I did see a demonstration that showed significantly improved performance. Intel expects to release the new version of the codec in mid-1993. This new version may significantly alter the relationships among codecs.

Cinepak/Compact Video

Cinepak (formerly known as Compact Video on the Mac) is representative of a different kind of codec than we have looked at so far. It is called an *asymmetrical* codec. The asymmetry occurs between the time for compression and the time for decompression. Compact Video takes quite a bit longer to compress, but decompression is fast and efficient. For example, it might take 30 to 45 minutes to compress a single minute of video—but playback rates are very, very good. For example, I have seen files compressed with Compact Video that played at CD-ROM data rates (150k/second) with 320x240 size images at 15 frames per second. This is at least double what most codecs can do; most codecs can only use 160x120 images at those rates.

Image quality is good—better than Microsoft Video 1, and similar to Indeo. Depending on the image, Cinepak or Indeo could give you better visual results. Like Indeo, Cinepak is a 24-bit codec, so there is more data to handle. However, it is a very efficient codec, and can compress to high compression ratios effectively. These high compression ratios, however, do not degrade image quality as much as Microsoft Video 1. Refer to Figures 8.7 and 8.8 for image samples at quality levels of 100 and 75, respectively.

Figure 8.8. Image compressed with Cinepak, quality level 100.

Figure 8.9. Image compressed with Cinepak, quality level 75.

The major drawback to the Compact Video codec is the time it takes to compress. If you are capturing a large amount of video, the extra time for compression can be a real struggle if you only have one machine.

The Rest of the Pack

New codecs are appearing just as soon as someone comes up with a new idea for compression trickery. Because the current size and quality of video images is limited primarily by the high data rates involved, the promises of more effective compression is driving a lot of development in this area. The primary advantage of new codecs is the speed and capability they add to your video capture and playback processes. The primary disadvantage is the lack of distribution of such new codecs. Unless you can count on distributing the codec with your images, think twice about relying on it.

There is one class of new codecs, however, that bears close attention. These are the codecs that are based on two important new video compression standards: JPEG and MPEG. JPEG stands for *Joint Photographic Experts Group* and MPEG stands for *Motion Picture Experts Group*. These codecs are currently being defined, redefined, and standardized. Hardware codecs based on the JPEG standard are already available (if somewhat expensive), and will likely be followed in 1994 by MPEG products. These are both extremely sophisticated compression technologies. JPEG (officially, it's *motion JPEG*) focuses on applying lossy compression to individual frames, whereas MPEG applies complex algorithms to determine precise differences, forward and backward, between frames. In technospeak, JPEG involves spatial compression, whereas MPEG utilizes the time dimension as well; you can visualize it as a four-dimensional compression technology.

JPEG and MPEG will almost certainly show up in affordable commercial products that use hardware acceleration of compression and decompression. To get to full-motion, full-frame video, you simply have to have hardware acceleration of these codecs. The exact form the hardware will take is open to question at this point. It might show up on video display cards, for example, or even on the motherboard itself. Without doubt, new high-bandwidth busses, such as the VESA local bus, will be useful pathways for this new technology.

On the further horizon is a recently proposed MPEG II standard. With MPEG II, you can compress a full-length movie onto a compact disc.

The Bottom Line on Codecs

Which codec you use, and when, will vary with your needs. Deciding which codec is best for any situation is not always a clear decision. To help you narrow down the possibilities, I have included a list of the most popular codecs in Table 8.1.

Table 8.1. Common Video Codecs.

Codec	Good stuff	Bad stuff	Comments
RLE	Fast compression times	Compression ratio not very favorable. Only works with 8-bit images.	Most useful for images with broad areas of constant color.
Indeo	Hardware coprocessor available to real-time compression. Scalable architecture Better image quality, especially at 16/24 bits.	Higher overhead for software-only playback. A faster version is under development at Intel.	Scalable architecture makes it well suited for multi-platform use.

continues

233

Table 8.1. continued

Codec	Good stuff	Bad stuff	Comments
Video 1	Provides good image quality and good file size; a good compromise codec.	Image looks blocky if you compress too far.	Good general purpose codec, but no longer leading technology.
Cinepak	High compression ratio while still maintaining good image quality	Asymmetrical compression scheme takes much longer for compression step.	Asymmetrical, so does a good job of compression for distribution via CD-ROM discs.
Spigot dithered	Does not require palette changes at playback— dithers using current palette.	Some images will not look right with dithering, particularly images with a large number of different colors, or images with a variety of similar colors.	This is an example of a codec that comes shipped with a compression board.
Spigot Compression	Optimized for the internal architecture of the Video Spigot	As of press time, codec is not freely distributable	Ditto.

Another issue to consider is how much each form of compression actually compresses the data. Sometimes, a smaller file size is the most important consideration. Table 8.2 shows comparative file sizes for a single frame of video using various codecs and quality levels.

Table 8.2. Compressed file sizes for various codecs.

Codec	Quality	File size	Compression
Original 8-bit image:	<na>	62,568	1.0
RLE	<na>	24,028	0.38
MS Video 1	100	16,320	0.26
MS Video 1	75	11,114	0.18
MS Video 1	60	7,682	0.12
MS Video 1	40	6,862	0.11
Indeo	100	11,200	0.18
Indeo	75	11,148	0.18
Indeo	60	10,004	0.16
Indeo	40	8,988	0.14
Cinepak	100	10846	0.17
Cinepak	75	10558	0.17
Cinepak	60	9956	0.16
Cinepak	40	9136	0.15

Table 8.2 reveals some interesting facts about the nature of the various codecs listed. The first thing that stands out is that RLE compression isn't nearly as effective as MS Video 1 or Indeo—it only reduces the file size to 38% of the original. This is expected; RLE compression is not very sophisticated.

There's another interesting fact revealed by Table 8.2—the relationship between quality level and compression ratio varies from one codec to the next. For Microsoft Video 1, small changes in quality level have a major impact on file size. Indeo and Cinepak, on the other hand, result in smaller file size changes when the quality level changes.

This means that comparing quality settings is a lot like comparing apples and oranges. For example, Figure 8.10 shows an image compressed at a quality setting of 40 with Microsoft Video 1. This is an extreme amount of compression, and the loss of quality is evident as you can see in the figure. The image, however, has been compressed to just 11% of its former size.

Figure 8.10. Highly compressed image.

Now look at Figure 8.12, which shows the same image compressed with Indeo at a quality setting of 40. The image is much better looking, but less data has been removed from the file (14% of former size), so we might expect it to look better on that count alone. Finally, Figure 8.12 shows an image compressed with Cinepak with a quality setting of 40. The Cinepak image was compressed to 15% of its former size.

Figure 8.11. Highly compressed image (Indeo).

Figure 8.12. Highly compressed image (Cinepak).

To really and truly compare these codecs, you should choose quality settings that result in the same relative amount of compression. Indeo shows approximately the same amount of compression with quality settings of 100 and 75—the resulting image is 18% of its original size. A quality setting of 75 provides approximately the same compression for Microsoft Video 1. At 100, Cinepak reduces the file to 17% of original size, which doesn't match up exactly.

There's something else going on here that also affects image quality. Indeo and Cinepak store "true color" information—if you have a 24-bit video card, they will display 24-bit color. For other color depths—specifically, 8 and 16—these two codecs must dither the 24-bit image to create the lower-resolution image. So what you see with Indeo and Cinepak depends on your hardware capabilities. The images you've seen so far are ideal images—what you'll see under ideal conditions without dithering, such as with a 24-bit color adapter.

Indeo and Cinepak do not do their dithering the same way, however, and the results are very different. The dithering is more obvious with Indeo in most cases.

Most machines use 8-bit color for Windows multimedia, and this gives 256 colors. Dithering 16.7 million colors down to 256 takes a bit of time, and this tends to slow Indeo down a little. In addition, it affects the appearance of the image. The kind of "instant dithering" that can be done under such short time constraints—a tiny faction of a second for each image—is limited. For example, look at Figure 8.13. It shows an Indeo image dithered to display for 8-bit color.

Figure 8.13. A dithered Indeo image.

If you were to convert that image to 8-bit color using a radically longer time—something on the order of a second or so—you can do a much better job at it, as shown in Figure 8.14.

Figure 8.14. Image of Figure 8.13 dithered more accurately.

The bottom line is this: Indeo does, indeed, pound for pound, yield better image compression. However, current versions of Indeo don't always show up in their Sunday best on 8-bit color displays. Keep in mind, however, that Intel is working on newer versions of Indeo, which will improve both performance and dithering quality.

How good is Indeo compression? Look at Figure 8.15, which shows an image compressed to 14% of its original size (top) compared to the original image (bottom).

Figure 8.15. An Indeo image (top) and the original image (bottom).

As you can see, the Indeo image doesn't have the contrast or detail of the original, yet the losses are not dramatic. Compare Figure 8.16, which shows an image compressed with Microsoft Video 1 to 12% of original size.

Figure 8.16. An image compressed with Microsoft Video 1 to 12% of its original size.

The characteristic blocking of Microsoft Video 1 is quite noticeable in this example.

Choosing a Codec

If you are wondering which codec(s) I use, well, most of the time I use the Microsoft Video 1 codec—it is the one codec I know other people will have available. The images sometimes look blocky at CD-ROM data rates (that's for 160x120 at 15 fps), but I've learned to live with it. When I need to distribute on CD-ROM, I prefer to use an asymmetrical codec—the compression times are a significant annoyance, but the results are the best for CD-ROM playback.

If this were the best of all possible worlds, every video display adapter would come with decompression acceleration built right into the hardware. Fortunately, that's the direction the industry seems to be going, but it will be six months to a year before you see such products really taking off.

There are some early achievers, however; if you are in the market for a new video card for Windows, you might want to try something like the ATI Graphics Ultra Pro. It comes with a series of special drivers that enhance a number of the graphics operations specific to playing digital video files. I have one in my computer, and I regularly get outstanding performance.

## PART IV

Editing
Digital Video

9

Basic Sound
Track Editing
(Wave for Windows)

There is an entire universe of equipment and techniques for recording sound. It is a separate world from video recording, and yet it is also an essential part of video. Studies show that a video accompanied by good sound is almost always judged to be of better quality—even if the video is no different! Getting the best possible sound is a key element of the process, especially if you want to involve your audience. After all, the current state of digital video produces smaller and coarser pictures than the average TV set. Good sound can offset that handicap.

Creating Digital Sound

Digital sound is different from the sound that surrounds us every day. However, it is still subject to many of the same problems and limitations. Until you record sound, you don't realize how many and how varied the sources of sound are. Most of the sound you hear every day is actually noise. Noise may be OK out on the street where you expect it, but it is a most unwelcome guest during recording.

Where Does Sound Come from?

Almost anything that moves creates sound. A car's tires generate a very loud sound, for example, cruising across the pavement. You probably never noticed, but before you speak, you breathe in—a sound that will be quite noticeable when you record someone speaking. Footsteps, the opening and closing of doors, someone talking down the hall—all of these can get in the way of clean recording.

Sound consists of vibrations. When those vibrations reach the brain by way of the ear, you hear them as sounds. The rate of vibration determines the pitch of a sound. Large things vibrate slowly, and small things vibrate quickly. Thus, a cello has a lower sound than a violin because the cello's strings are longer, and vibrate at a slower rate. The rate of vibration is called the sound's *frequency*.

Analog to Digital

Digital signals, of course, do not vibrate: they are just numbers. Before you can use sound on a computer, it must be converted to digital data. The digital representation is only an approximation of the analog data, however. By breaking the analog signal into small enough pieces, the approximation can be made very, very close. There are some standards for analog to digital conversion (ADC).

Sampling

One standard involves how often the analog sound is *sampled*. Each sample tests the loudness (amplitude) and frequency of the sound at a point in time. As a general rule, the sampling frequency should be at least double the highest frequency you want to record. The approximate limit of human hearing is 20,000 cycles per second. This is usually written as 20kHz, an abbreviation for 20 kiloHerz. A Herz is simply one cycle per second, and a kiloHerz is 1,000 cycles per second. Thus, you would need to sample at least 40,000 times per second to accurately record everything the human ear is capable of hearing. As a matter of fact, CDs are sampled at 44.1kHz.

Other common sampling frequencies used in the digital world are 8, 11, and 22 kHz. As you might guess, the lower the sample frequency, the worse the sound quality. If you only need to record speech, which has an upper frequency limit of about 6kHz, 11k is acceptable. Why use a lower sample frequency? Each sample takes up space. At 44.1kHz stereo, you'll need 10.5 megabytes of disk space for each minute you record.

Bits of Resolution

The next standard involves how much data to store in each sample. The amount of data you can store is determined by the number of bits you use for each sample. The two most common bit rates are 8 and 16. Using 8 bits of resolution, you can store 256 different values. Using 16 bits, you can store more than 65,000 different values. The more bits you use to store each sample, the more accurate the results. Unfortunately, doubling the number of bits to 16 also doubles the size of the recording. In addition, you'll need more expensive sound cards to play 16-bit sounds. Most cards that support 8-bit resolution simply will not play 16-bit sound.

Stereo and Mono

Another choice you'll have to make is whether to record in stereo or mono. Mono is safer if you plan to distribute your work—all sound cards support mono recordings. Mono also takes up half the space of a stereo recording.

Digital to Analog

Digital to analog conversion (DAC) is simply the reverse of ADC. The numbers are converted back into analog data. Specifically, to an electrical signal that varies in proportion to the original vibrations. How closely the reproduced signal matches the original depends on the three topics we just discussed—the sampling frequency, the bit resolution, and whether you used stereo or mono for recording.

The key issue for DAC is the capability of the equipment the sounds will be played on. If you are publishing for a general audience, you'll probably be stuck recording at 11 or 22kHz, using 8 bits and mono sound. If you know that your audience will have better equipment, you can use better recording values. You may also want to create two separate versions of your production, one with average sound and one with better sound.

But there is another issue that you will have to consider when you are using sound with video. Video data is huge. It can push computer hardware to its limits or beyond. Adding a large amount of sound data to the video data can put you over the limit of what your, or your audiences', hardware can handle. So even if your audience has the capability to handle 44.1kHz, 16-bit, stereo sound on their sound cards, the combined video/audio data rate may be too much for the rest of their computer.

The key is to get the best out of what you are able to use. In the rest of this chapter, we'll look at some software and hardware products that you can use to get the best results with the least data rates.

Wave for Windows

My favorite sound editing (and recording) program is Wave for Windows. It has some features that are invaluable when you find yourself with sound that isn't quite right and has to be corrected. It has a feature set oriented toward professional work, but is easy to use. The current documentation is a little weak (it doesn't explain some important concepts), but Turtle Beach is working on new, expanded documentation that should be available by the time you read this. A typical Wave for Windows screen is shown in Figure 9.1.

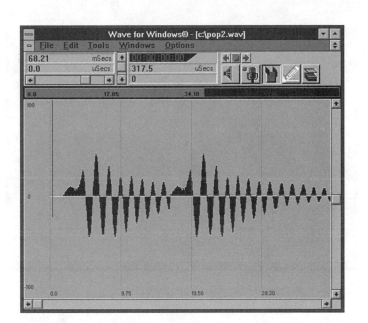

Figure 9.1. A typical Wave for Windows screen.

The sound waves shown in Figure 9.1 is a simple, and very short, "pop" sound. I chose it because you can see the actual sound waves. Where the wave peaks are taller, the sound is louder, and where they are smaller, the sound is quieter. The closer the peaks are to each other, the higher the frequency.

Using Wave

Figure 9.2 shows a frequency analysis of the sound. This allows you to see how the sound's frequencies change over time. This is a useful way to spot problems. In this case, the biggest frequency peak is around 500 to 800 Hz, and it occurs from 14.06 to about 35 milliseconds into the sound.

Wave also allows you to examine the frequencies at specific time points in the sound, as shown in Figure 9.3. It shows a peak centered at about 500 Hz.

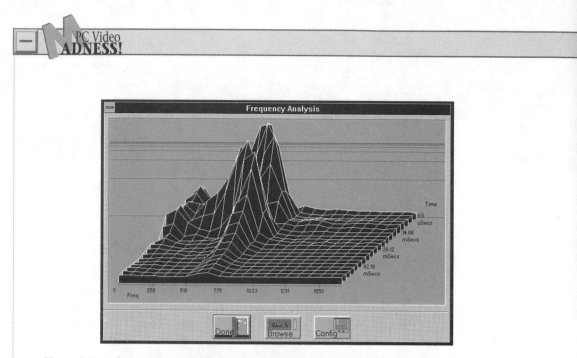

Figure 9.2. A frequency analysis chart in Wave for Windows.

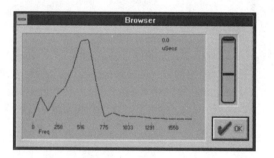

Figure 9.3. Frequency analysis at 0.0 milliseconds.

If a sound was recorded at too low a level, you can use Wave to boost the amplitude. This process is called gain adjustment, and is easy to do (see Figure 9.4). You can adjust the start gain, the end gain, and gain can be a positive or negative number.

You can also adjust *equalization*. This involves making the various frequencies more equal in level. For example, Figure 9.5 shows the Wave for Windows Equalization dialog. There is a set of sliders at the top left which you use to adjust the frequencies you want to cut or boost. The graph to the right shows the effect of the slider settings. If a loop drops downward, those frequencies will be cut. If a loop bends upward, those frequencies will be boosted.

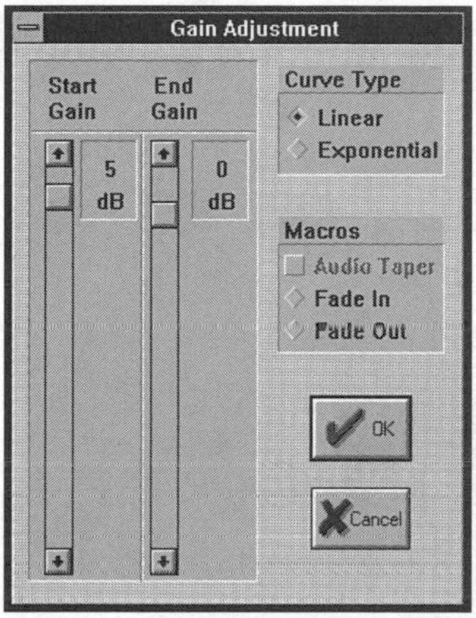

Figure 9.4. Gain Adjustment with Wave for Windows.

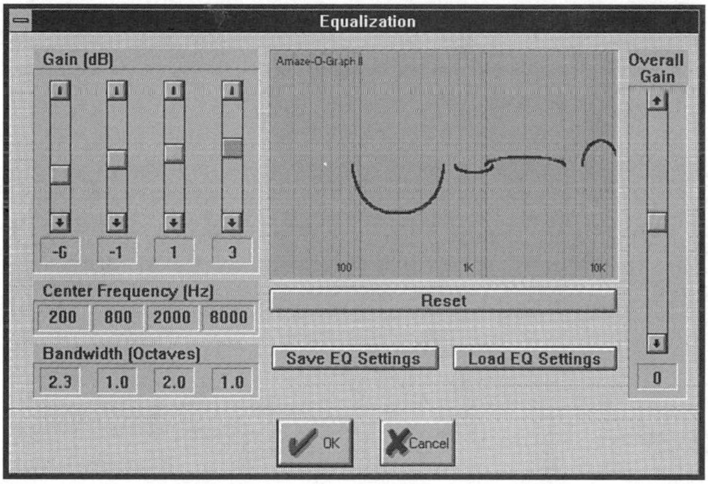

Figure 9.5. Equalizing a sound with Wave for Windows.

The effects of these various adjustments are reflected in the shape of the wave-form in the Wave window. Compare the wave peaks in Figure 9.6 to those in Figure 9.1. In Figure 9.6, the wave peaks are significantly higher. This is the result of the gain adjustment in Figure 9.4.

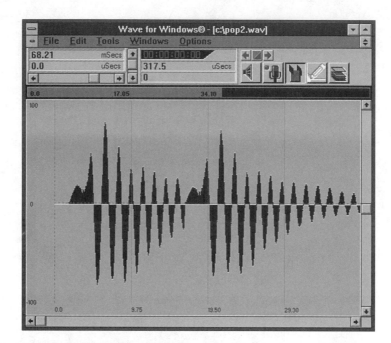

Figure 9.6. Result of gain adjustment.

We can also use Wave to examine the micro structure of the waveform, as shown in Figure 9.7. This figure shows about a 4 millisecond slice of the sound file. Note that there is some noise in the left half of the window—the waveform is irregular. We can smooth this out using the pencil tool; the result is shown in Figure 9.8.

Features of Wave for Windows

There are two kinds of features to look for in sound editing programs. So far, you won't find any one program that does everything. Just as a graphic designer typically has several different programs for dealing with different situations, you'll probably want to select sound editing software to suit your own needs. The two feature sets are:

➤ *Digital enhancements.* These include such things as reverb and echo at the low end, and the ability to mimic specific settings at the high end.

Specific settings include such things as churches, auditoriums, and small rooms, as well as more sophisticated techniques like flanging and phase changes.

➤ *Traditional tools*. These are digital tools that mimic traditional sound editing techniques. Equalization and gain adjustment are two such tools.

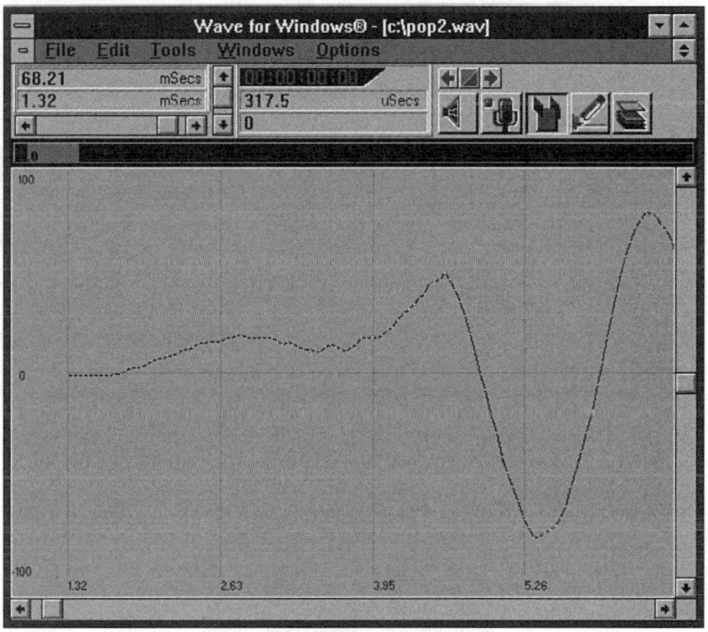

Figure 9.7. A very small time slice in the sound file.

Wave for Windows Version 1.x focuses primarily on traditional tools. Version 2.0, which should be available by the time you read this, will add more fanciful and creative tools.

The current feature set of Wave for Windows is best seen in the Tools menu (see Figure 9.9).

The capabilities of these tools are described in Table 9.1.

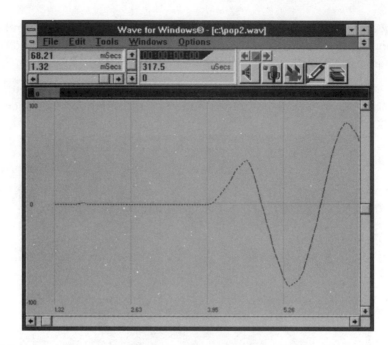

Figure 9.8. A corrected waveform.

Figure 9.9. Tools menu of Wave for Windows.

Table 9.1. Wave for Windows Tools.

Tool	Description
Gain Adjust	Allows you to increase or decrease the volume of all or any portion of the file. You can also fade in and fade out.
Mute	Silence part or all of a sound file.
Equalize	Adjust amplitude of various frequencies in the file.
Frequency Analysis	Display the amplitude of various frequencies. Display range and display parameters user adjustable.
Mix	Combine sounds from multiple files into one output file.
Crossfire	Combine sounds so that one fades out while the other fades in.
Reverse	Reverse the data in a sound file so it plays backward.
Invert	Invert values in the sound file.
DC Offset	Change all values to positive values.
Time Compress/Expand	Remove data to make the sound play faster without changing frequencies. Has user-adjustable parameters.

Wave for Windows also has a strong contingent of editing capabilities, as shown in Figure 9.10. Wave edits directly on your hard disk, using the hard disk the way a traditional tape recorder uses tape. However, all changes are made to a backup of the original file. The key editing features of Wave are listed in Table 9.2.

Table 9.2. Wave for Windows Editing Capabilities.

Capability	Description
Paste Insert	Inserts sound data from the clipboard without removing any existing data.
Paste Over	Sound data from the clipboard replaces existing data.
Paste Fill	Sound data from the clipboard is used to fill the current selection.
Mix Paste	The pasted material is mixed with the existing material. This is a very powerful feature.
Mute	Silences the selected portion of the file.
Delete	Removes selected material without placing it on the clipboard.
Audition Cut Buffer	Plays the sound data on the clipboard.
Sound File Info	Provides information about the format of the sound file.

Figure 9.10. Wave for Windows Edit menu.

Uses for Sound Editors

The most important time to have a good sound editor at hand is when you come back from the field and discover that there are problems with the sound you recorded—too quiet, a mechanical hum in the background, long pauses, etc. But there are many situations that aren't so obvious. Good uses for a sound editor include:

➤ Enhancing the quality of a weak voice

➤ Boosting bass response for more impact

➤ Compensating for cheap microphones or tape

➤ Mixing voice and music into a single file

➤ Removing annoying pops and clicks, or even microphone handling noise

➤ Giving two sounds equal loudness levels

➤ Changing the sampling rate or other digital parameters to match your needs

➤ Special effects for fun and profit.

Sound Editing Techniques

If you have any previous experience with either analog or digital sound editing, you'll be able to pick up techniques on the computer more easily. If you don't have such experience, you will probably discover that there are so many techniques available that it will take some time to learn how to use them well. As with many creative efforts, sound editing has subtleties that take time to learn. In addition, you can assume that less is best. If you are unsure about applying a technique or a special effect, let it be. Over-editing is far worse-sounding than under editing.

On the other hand, the only way to learn the subtleties is to jump in and do it. However, you are usually better off practicing on files that don't matter. This may seem obvious, but if you find yourself on deadline trying to learn a new skill, you'll realize it's not as obvious as it seems. Before you are under pressure to produce some Really Great Sound, play around and get familiar with the tools at your disposal.

One key skill involves learning to read the visual information of the wave-form. The first time I tried to find a simple click in a sound file, I was very frus-trated—I couldn't find it! I expected the click to be a spike in the waveform, but I couldn't find any. It turned out that I was looking at too much data—I had no idea how to find the spike! Spikes occur in a matter of a few milliseconds, and that's a very small part of a file. You'll need to stretch out the data (almost all sound editors give you this capability) until pops and clicks become visible.

There are also some useful hints I can pass along for editing voice recordings. There are certain characteristics of the human voice that you should be careful not to disturb when you edit. For example, you might be tempted to remove a sharp intake of breath; with some microphones, this can be overemphasized. Don't simply cut out the offending sound; either mute it to silence, or reduce the gain so it is not so sharp and noticeable. Pauses are a natural and important part of speech; removing them can make the recording sound unnatural or weird.

You may also run into problems when you try to mix and match speech. For example, your announcer may have stumbled in one place in one shoot, and in another place in another take. You might be tempted to combine the good por-tions into one correct recording. Beware! Inflection, volume levels, and breath-ing patterns change from one take to another, and combining may not be easy. Inflection is the editor's worst nightmare, followed closely by speakers who merge their words together and make it impossible to separate them for editing.

The key to good sound editing is patience. The computer gives you a lot of power, but it takes practice to learn how to control and apply it.

Recording Basics

Getting a good recording can be as simple or as complex as you care to make it. You can use multiple microphones, multiple recording media, filters, mixing consoles, and so on, or you can just use the built-in microphone on your camcorder. More than anything, budget dictates how good your results will be. However, there are some tricks to be aware of to get the most out of whatever equipment you have available.

Sound Recording Fundamentals

There are some basic rules that always apply to sound recording. If you do nothing more than follow these rules, you'll get decent results.

➤ Keep the microphone as close as possible to the sound source. Not too close, of course; that will overload the microphone.

➤ Use quality recording media. That applies to cassette tapes and video tape.

➤ Use an appropriate microphone. That sounds vague, of course, but I'll go into more detail shortly.

➤ Pay close attention to recording levels. Sound levels that are either too high or too low can be a major pain.

➤ Eliminate noise wherever and whenever possible.

Sound Sources

"Consider the source" is one of the cardinal axioms of sound recording. Major recording studios have dozens of different microphones, and many different ways of using each one, for recording different musical instruments. Most of us can't afford even a fraction of that degree of specialization, however, so compromise is the order of the day.

By far the most common sound source is the human voice. If we apply the rules I listed above to just that one sound source, you'll get a good idea of how to follow the rules.

Keep the microphone close. If you are recording sound without video, the best place for the microphone is within 4-8" of the subject's mouth, and slightly below the bottom lip. When there is a lot of ambient noise, and if you are using a quality omnidirectional microphone, you can even lay the microphone against the chin. This might overload a cheap microphone, however. When I call a microphone a "quality" mike, I'm referring to units in the $100 and up range. If you are using a unidirectional (also called *cardiod*) mike, you can be a little further away. Lapel mikes (also called *lavalieres*) are a good choice when you are videotaping at a distance. The microphone is close to the subject, but unobtrusive.

Use quality recording media. There is no substitute for good tape. You cannot re-create an image that is lost, fuzzy, or the wrong color when you get back to the studio.

Use an appropriate microphone. Not every microphone is suitable for voice recording. In some cases, a cheap microphone might deliver better results than an expensive one! A microphone intended for the full range of musical instruments might reproduce sounds that you don't want, such as breathiness or mouth clicks, at higher levels than are acceptable. A cheap microphone misses such things entirely, but it also drops out some of the subtleties and warmth of the voice. If you will be using coarse reproduction—8-bit sound, or 11kHz sampling, for example—a cheap microphone is all you will need.

Recording levels. I can't overemphasize this with voice recording: pay constant attention to recording levels. If the subject moves closer to the microphone, it could overload and distort the signal. Even if the microphone isn't overloaded, the recording medium could be (that's called clipping). A sound that is too low is equally problematic—if you try to boost the sound, you'll also boost both ambient and media noises.

Eliminate noise. Speaking of noise, eliminate it! Noise has many sources. The recording medium has noise; cheap tape has more noise than expensive tape, for example. Your subject makes noise—hand movements, accidental contact with the microphone, rustling of clothing, and so on. Listen, listen, listen! Noise is subtle because we tend to tune it out. However, tape isn't quite as clever and records everything.

Recording for Video

There are some considerations for sound recording that are especially important when you are working with video. There are two kinds of situations you will run into: recording directly to video tape while you record visuals, and recording separately, to either tape or your hard disk. Separate recording involves only one issue: synchronizing with the video. There are a multitude of issues to consider when you are recording sound directly to video tape.

Synchronization is challenging. The most convenient way to synchronize a voice-over is to watch the video while you speak. If you only have one computer, however, playing the video uses so much CPU power that there's not really enough for good recording. You'll need a second computer for sound if you record directly to the hard disk, or you can use a tape recorder and then record digitally. You'll need a good quality tape deck, not a cheap or Walkman style deck, if you need good quality recordings. otherwise, it will have to be a second computer for recording sound. If you do record sound separately, the VidEdit File menu has an Insert selection that will allow you to insert new audio into the video file. See the section *Merging and Extracting Sound Tracks* for more details on synchronization.

If you plan to record live sound while you shoot your video tape, a few suggestions might help. Here's the first one: the built-in microphone on your camcorder is almost certainly not adequate for most of your recording needs. Fortunately, most camcorders allow you to attach a separate microphone.

Microphones

There are three kinds of microphones in general use:

➤ Hand-held microphones

➤ Lapel (lavaliere) microphones

➤ Remote microphones

Hand-held microphones, the kind used by most news professionals in radio and on TV, are rarely used in a produced video. They do have certain advantages, mostly because they are large. Their large size means there is no need to make compromises for miniaturization. They are relatively inexpensive, except for models designed for special recording purposes. You can easily find a good hand-held for about $100. The best cost $1,000 and up.

Lapel microphones, on the other hand, are very miniaturized and tend to cost more than hand-held microphones for the same level of performance. I have always been a big fan of the Sony lapel microphones, although they tend to cost more than their competitors. The Sony models, however, have seen broad use in the broadcasting industry, and are proven technology. Cost is $200 and up. One model is so small you can actually use it *inside* clothing, making it invisible to the camera. I haven't used it, but it would surprise me if there weren't some loss of quality used that way.

Remote microphones are available both as hand-helds (you'll see them on TV) and lapels or clip-ons. Radio Shack sells one for camcorders that's about $50, but it sounds worse than a typical telephone—not suitable for any kind of professional work. Look for prices of $250 and up for remote microphones with acceptable sound quality.

259

There are also a large number of special-purpose microphones. If you plan to buy a used microphone, watch out: it may not be suitable for your needs. Most of the better microphones have been around for a while, and you should be able to get information on specific models from local sound specialists. For voice, I prefer electret condenser microphones to other kinds; they use a battery, but they offer excellent response to the human voice range in most cases. For example, all of the Sony lapel microphones are electret condenser models.

Mixers

If you haven't worked with sound professionally, you may not be familiar with the capabilities of sound mixers. They do just what their name describes: they mix sound from multiple input sources into one (or two, in the case of stereo) output. For most of my work, I use a very simple 4-input, stereo-output mixer. This gives me two inputs for stereo sound (such as from a tape or a CD), and two mono or one stereo microphone input(s). Depending on your needs, you will be able to have 10, 20, 32, 64 or even more inputs on a mixing console. Each input can have a variety of controls to tailor the sound. The most common and important are:

➤ Bass response

➤ Midrange response

➤ Treble response

➤ Left/right pan control

➤ Input level control

Bass, midrange, and treble controls allow you to vary the sound "color" either to your tastes, or to compensate for minor problems in the sound source. My simple mixer does not have any of these controls; I make all such changes digitally on the computer. It can be handy, however, to have such capabilities in your hardware if you do a lot of sound work.

A pan control allows you to "place" the sound where you want it in the stereo image. An input level control allows you to adjust gain to suit a source. For example, a microphone has a much lower input level than something like a CD. In fact, there are names for these two kinds of input levels: mike level, and line level. Some mixers will have different physical inputs for microphones and line-level devices; some will allow you to adjust the input level with a switch or a *pot.* (See sidebar, *What's a Pot?*)

What's a Pot?

If you want to sound like an old pro at sound recording, there's one term you need to know: the *pot.* A pot is not something that musicians use when they're really "cookin'." But it is an integral part of the sound scene, and it's a word with deep historical roots in electronics.

Pot is short for **potentiometer,** and it refers to any control that continuously adjusts a signal. You've seen many "pots" in your time: every volume control knob or slider is a pot.

Technically speaking, almost all of the controls on a mixing console are pots. However, in normal usage, the term usually refers to the one that controls the input level.

Now you know everything there is to know about sound recording, right?

Recording Media

And now, a word or two about recording media. There are three you are likely to run into: cassette tapes, video tapes, and your computer's hard disk. The hard disk can record with superb quality, but it's not always the right solution. You can't, for example, take the average desktop computer to a client site very easily.

Cassette tapes are probably the best-understood medium; if you stick to Chrome (Type II) tapes, you'll do fine. Type I (normal) tapes are acceptable for voice-only recording, but not recommended.

Video tape is another story. Depending on which video format you use, sound will be recorded in different ways. The most common technique is used by, for example, VHS recorders. This lays down an audio track along the length of the tape, just as would be done with a cassette tape. The quality of this technique is, well, adequate at best and unusable at worst. Hi8 camcorders, on the other hand,

record audio using the same techniques as are used with video: in a helical path along the tape. There is a spinning head inside a camcorder, and it multiplies the tape speed to get better results. Why does faster tape speed yield better sound? The faster the tape moves, the more "spread out" the data is along the tape. The more there is for the data, the more accurately it can be recorded, and you can also record more data. This is a very simple relationship:

More data = better sound

This works for both analog and digital data. That's why 16 bits are better than 8 bits for sound sampling, and why Hi8 can deliver near-CD quality sound on tape.

Merging and Extracting Sound Tracks

Much of what we have discussed in this chapter involves collecting good, clean sound. Once you have that, it's time to do something with it. Using some simple techniques, you can combine and extract sounds and merge them with your video files in new ways.

Once you have clean sound, the emphasis changes. The most critical factor becomes **timing.** If you can get the sound right on the mark, it can add real punch to the video. If it is even a little bit off, it will fall flat. Ideally, you need a comedian's sense of timing.

Synchronization

The first step in the timing process is mechanical: making sure that sound and video are in step. Even if you do nothing fancy with the sound, even if you simply record audio from the videotape during capture to the hard disk, always verify synchronization. Video for Windows VidEdit program makes synchronization easy. Of course, it would be even easier if it were automatic and guaranteed, but maybe in the next version.

If, after making some edits, you find that the sound and video are not synchronized properly, select Synchronize on the Video menu in VidEdit. You will see an item in the dialog box called "Audio offset." You can specify the offset of the start of audio playback in milliseconds, positive or negative. Here's something that may not be obvious: each time you click on the OK button, the audio offset is physically changed. If you change it again, you are making the new change on top of the old change. In other words, if you offset the audio by 500 milliseconds, and then offset it again by –100 milliseconds, the resulting offset is 400 milliseconds—not –100 milliseconds.

Beyond Synchronization: Techniques

Merely synchronizing audio and video, however, adds nothing to anything. It's merely the beginning. Possible next steps include extracting the audio for enhancement or modification, inserting modified or completely new audio, and merging audio tracks.

Extracting Audio

It's very easy to extract all or a portion of the audio track from an AVI file with VidEdit. It's as easy as selecting the portion of the file you want to extract, then choosing Extract from the File menu. There is a list box with a list of choices; pick Waveform Audio, choose a filename, and you've got a Wave file you can edit with Wave for Windows. If you want to edit the video portion of the file by adding or subtracting sequences, make sure you don't do that while the audio portion is elsewhere!

Creative Modifications: Layering

My favorite easy modification involves layering sounds. For example, for a recent project, I needed a funny video sequence to make a point. I had one, but it wasn't as funny as it needed to be. It was composed of three pieces of video, not really connected very well—the change from one sequence to another was very abrupt. It was looking like I might not be able to use it, when inspiration struck. I had some odd sounds laying around, including a great "Boing!" sound. I extracted the audio, used Wave for Windows to add "Boing!" sounds at each of the transitions, and wound up with a perfect funny video.

Here's quick tip: if you are adding sound effects, in many cases they'll work better if they occur a couple of frames before the transition they are associated with. The sound alerts the brain to the upcoming transition. Play with this effect until you are satisfied you understand how far ahead the sound should be for the right effect. Usually, just a fraction of a second is all you'll need.

Inserting Audio

Putting the audio back in is also easy; it's nearly the exact opposite of extracting. Select the portion of the file where you want the sound file to be inserted (if there is already audio there, select all of the audio you want to replace). Choose Insert from the File menu, pick Waveform audio, and select the file to insert.

10

Basic Video Editing

In this chapter, you'll be taking a look at the heart of the Video for Windows package: VidEdit. It's not a very sophisticated video editor, but what it does, it does well. It contains all the key technical features you will need to clean up and edit your captured video.

There are three major processes involved in editing a video sequence:

➤ *Sequence editing*—Adding, moving, and removing sound and video to get just the right portion of the clip ready for saving.

➤ *Parameter adjustments*—These include such things as synchronization and frame rate.

➤ *Saving the file*—Selecting a compression method, and saving the file.

The documentation for Video for Windows does a good job of explaining how the individual pieces of the program work and how to use them, but it's also important to know how the pieces work together and what the implications of various choices are. In this chapter, I'll point out the best ways to use the various tools at your disposal. I'll also warn you of problems that can occur if you aren't careful.

Sequence Editing

Figure 10.1 shows the opening screen of VidEdit, with a video file loaded and ready for editing. This particular clip is from a video tape I obtained from Microsoft; it contains footage from the introduction of Video for Windows in late 1992. That's Bill Gates in the image window, describing the future of digital video. The complete clip is available on the CD-ROM; check the CD-ROM table of contents to find out where it is on the disc.

The key features of the VidEdit window are shown in Figure 10.1. There is a toolbar at the top, which gives you quick access to the most-used features of the program. A slider just under the image area marks the current position in the file, and there is a row of buttons at the lower-left that mimic the controls of a VCR. You can use these controls to move around in the video sequence.

Between the slider and the VCR controls are two buttons that you can use to mark the beginning and end points of a selection. You can cut, copy, paste, or delete a selection. The three buttons at the lower-right allow you to choose what you are editing: video and audio, video only, and audio only. The bottom of the window is a status bar that provides important information about the current frame.

Figure 10.1. The opening screen of VidEdit, featuring Mr. William Gates.

Figure 10.2 shows the dialog box for setting VidEdit preferences. Almost all of these settings are cosmetic, affecting only the appearance of the program window. Two items will affect your use of the program: Overwrite Mode, and Memory for caching images.

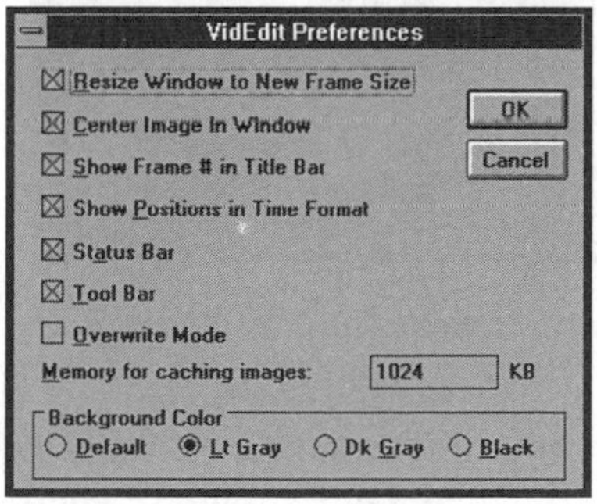

Figure 10.2. VidEdit preferences dialog box.

Overwrite mode works just like it does in a word processor: new material automatically overwrites old material. Memory caching allows you to fine-tune the amount of memory used for caching previously displayed frames. If you'll be stepping forward and back quite a bit, extra cache will speed up operations.

The most common action in VidEdit is creating a selection. You can then copy the selection to the clipboard, cut it, delete it, or export it as a video file or as a sequence of bitmaps. There are two ways to set the selection: visually, and numerically. To set the selection visually:

1. Move to the first frame that you want in the selection.

2. Click the Mark In button.

3. Move to the last frame for the selection.

4. Click the Mark Out button.

The selected area will be marked in gray on the slider, as shown in Figure 10.3.

Figure 10.3. The selection area is marked in gray on the slider.

To set the selection by frame number, click the Edit/Set Selection... menu choice. This will display the dialog box shown in Figure 10.4.

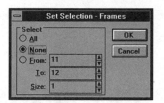

Figure 10.4. The Set Selection - Frames dialog box.

This dialog box enables you to set the current selection to all frames, no frames, or a specified series of frames. To set a selection to a series of frames, you can enter the From number, and then either the To number or the Size number. If you enter a To number, VidEdit calculates the size; if you enter a Size number, VidEdit calculates the To frame. (If all those prepositions—To number, From number, and so on—have you confused, it's a lot easier to do than it is to describe.)

To adjust the size or appearance of the image area, you can use the View menu, shown in Figure 10.5.

Figure 10.5. The View menu of VidEdit.

The difference between Full Frame Update and Fast Frame Update will be particularly noticeable if you are using an unaccelerated video display card. For best performance, use Fast Frame Update. If this results in incorrect images, you'll have to use Full Frame Update instead. To redraw a full frame at any time, click the Draw Full Frame selection, or press F5.

You can zoom to any one of four different magnifications, as shown in Figure 10.5. The available choices are 0.5x, 1x, 2x (the one I use most often), and 4x.

Parameter Adjustments

Once you have decided exactly which portions of the video sequence go where, you must set the parameters for the file. The most important menu in VidEdit is the Video menu, shown in Figure 10.6. All of the parameters adjustments are found here. Table 10.1 lists the available selections on the Video menu.

Figure 10.6. VidEdit Video menu.

Table 10.1. VidEdit Video menu selections.

Selection	Description
Compression Options	Select codec, quality level, and other compression options.
Convert Frame Rate	Change to a new frame rate. Frames will be added or deleted to make the change.

Selection	Description
Synchronize	Allows you to adjust the starting time of the audio portion to match the video portion. Also use to change the rate at which the video frames display.
Audio Format	Adjust audio settings, such as sample rate.
Video Format	Adjust video settings, such as color depth.
Create Palette	Create a palette for 256-color images.
Crop	Select a portion of the frame to create new image borders.
Resize	Change the size of the entire frame.
Statistics	Display important information about the file, including estimates of size.
Load File into Memory	Load the entire file into available memory, if possible.

The compression options, shown in Figure 10.7, are a critical component of VidEdit. They have a tremendous impact on the image quality of the file when it is saved.

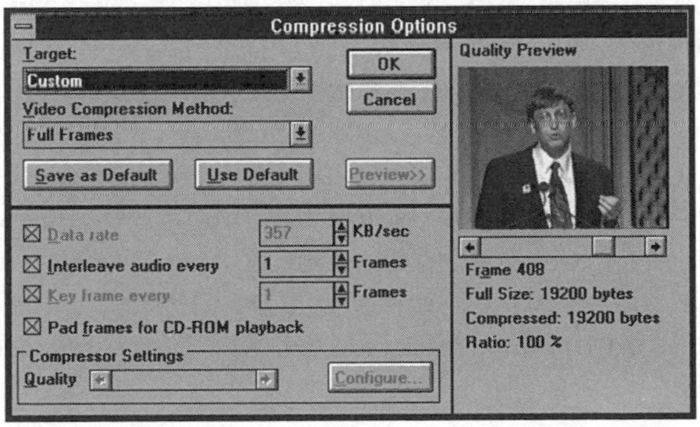

Figure 10.7. Setting the Compression Options in VidEdit.

Compression Options

Look at the Compression Options dialog box one section at a time. There are three sections: Target and Method (at upper left), Save settings (at lower left), and Preview (at the right).

Target and Method Selections

The following targets are available in the Compression Options dialog box:

Hard Disk
Hard Disk (Interleaved)
Hard Disk (300K/Sec)
Hard Disk (150 K/Sec)
Hard Disk (100 K/Sec)
CD-ROM (150 K/Sec)
CD-ROM (80 K/Sec)
Custom

Selecting any of the Hard Disk or CD-ROM choices will automatically adjust the save settings. If you choose Custom, it is up to you to set the correct save settings. Even if you do choose Hard Disk or CD-ROM at any data rate, you can still change individual save settings.

The idea behind selecting a target is to make sure that the video file can be played properly on the intended target. For example, if you will be distributing your video files on CD-ROM, and you expect all of your users to be able to handle a data rate of 150K/second, then you would select CD-ROM (150 K/Sec) as your target. If the desired data rate, 150K/second, cannot be met, you'll be warned by VidEdit, and you'll have a choice to continue anyway or abort the save. You can use the Preview section of the dialog box to estimate whether you can meet a given data rate, as explained in the section "Compression Preview," later in this chapter. It's generally a good idea to click one of the CD-ROM presets if you intend to have your videos played from CD-ROM discs. Clicking these settings automatically turns on the data rate padding, which ensures smooth playback from the CD-ROM.

The following Video Compression Methods are available in the Compression Options dialog box:

No Change
Microsoft RLE
Microsoft Video 1
Full Frames
Cinepak Codec by SuperMatch
Intel Indeo (TM) Video

Most of these methods represent installed codecs. No Change is only available if you have loaded an existing video file and have not made any changes to the video portion of the file. Full Frames enables you to save the raw video as it was converted from the analog signal to digital data. Which codec you choose depends on your needs. See Chapter 8 for detailed information about choosing a codec.

Settings

Table 10.2 lists the available save settings.

Table 10.2. Save settings for VidEdit.

Setting	Description
Data rate	This is the highest data rate you want to save at. You only need to set this if you have a need for a specific data rate. If you select a target with a specified data rate, that data rate will automatically be entered here. If the specified data rate cannot be met, you will see a warning message.
Interleave audio	AVI files allow you to interleave audio and video data for better performance. You can specify the number of video frames to put between the audio data here. In almost all cases, use 1. For CD-ROM, it is critical to use a setting of 1 frame—this allows the most efficient possible playback.
Key frame	Saving a complete frame for every frame in the video is usually not necessary. Most codecs, in fact, use special handling for all non-key frames—they save only the portion of the frame that changes

continues

273

Table 10.2. continued

Setting	Description
	from one frame to the next. A key frame is a frame that is saved in its (compressed) entirety no matter what. It's a good idea to have a key frame about every 15 frames or so to make sure that the image does not get corrupted during playback. If a video sequence has only minor frame-to-frame changes, you can go more than 15 frames without a key frame. If a video has extensive changes from one frame to the next, you might go so far as to make every frame a key frame.
Pad frames	A CD-ROM drive operates most efficiently when it is reading data at a steady rate. It is as bad for a CD-ROM to get ahead as it is to fall behind. Some frames will compress to a smaller size than 150K/second, and this will actually cause problems when you try to read from the CD-ROM. During the time the frame is displayed, the CD-ROM will spin past the beginning of the next frame, and will have to go around an extra time to get to the data. Padding frames ensures that the CD-ROM gets neither ahead nor behind the display.
Quality	This determines how heavily the images will be compressed. Different codecs respond differently to differing quality settings. For example, quality settings of less than 75 with the Microsoft Video 1 codec result in seriously distorted images. Indeo or Cinepak, on the other hand, can use even lower quality settings. Lower quality settings result in smaller file sizes and less image fidelity, while higher quality settings result in larger file sizes and better image fidelity.

I almost always check the Preview after I have set the Save settings to make sure that I haven't messed up the image quality.

Quality Preview

In this section the Compression Options dialog box shows you the results of your settings. A single image from the video sequence is displayed using the selected compression method, using the quality setting in the Save settings area of the dialog box. You can use the slider below the image to select any frame in the sequence. You can check the compressed file size for individual images to get an idea of whether or not the codec and quality setting you chose meets the required data rate.

For example, if you captured a video at 15 fps, and have a CD-ROM at 150K/second as your target, each frame can contain up to 10K of data, compressed. Keep in mind that the codec will actually be storing frame differences (also called frame delta), rather then entire frames, for all non-key frames. This means that the average frame can be more than 10K in size and you may still meet the target data rate. Don't forget to include the audio data in your calculation.

If you want to avoid the calculation, try saving the file; if you don't get a warning message, then the data rate was achieved.

> ### Warning
>
> Asymmetrical codecs, such as Cinepak, can take a very long time to compress a single frame. Changing to a new frame in the Quality Preview could take as much as several minutes while the codec calculates the compressed image.

Convert Frame Rate

If you have audio associated with a video file, you probably don't want to convert the frame rate—the audio and video will be totally out of sync if you convert the video frame rate. The dialog box for converting the frame rate is shown in Figure 10.8.

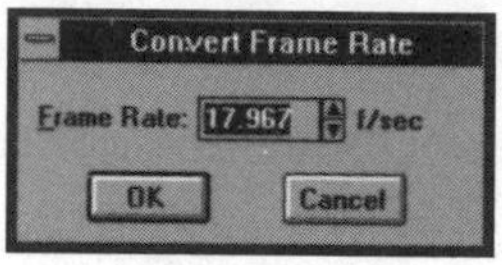

Figure 10.8. Converting the frame rate.

To convert the frame rate, VidEdit will remove or duplicate frames as necessary. You may find that certain frame rate conversions cannot be handled directly. For example, if your video file is at 15 fps, you probably won't be able to convert to 10 fps, but you can convert to 8 fps. This is the result of the calculations required for converting frames rates; VidEdit will not do a conversion if it would result in major timing problems.

Synchronize

There are two reasons to use this menu selection: to synchronize audio and video, and to change the video frame rate. The dialog box for making these changes is shown in Figure 10.9.

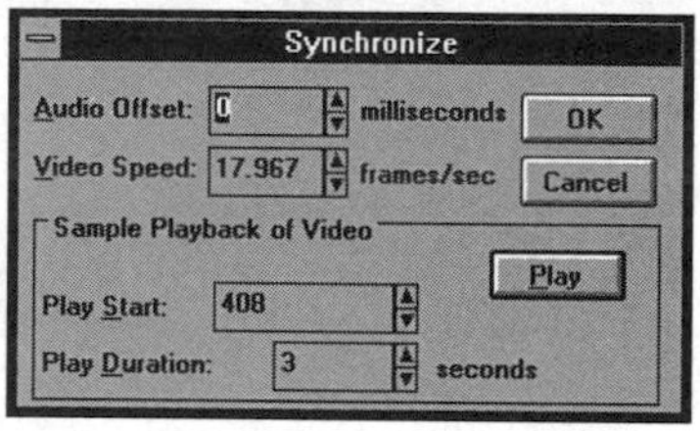

Figure 10.9. Synchronizing audio and video.

The two key items in this dialog box are the Audio Offset and the Video Speed. Use the Audio Offset to change the starting time of the audio portion of the file. You may find that the audio gets out of whack if you make major edits to the video file; this may or may not be an actual synchronization problem. As you cut, paste, and delete segments, the working file gets fragmented, and may not play back accurately. If the audio and video appear to be out of sync, try saving with Full Frames as the "Compression" option, and the reload the file and test it. If it is still out of sync, you have a real problem and need to adjust the starting time of the audio. Each change you make to the Audio Offset is cumulative. In other words, if you change the audio offset by 250 milliseconds, and then change it by −30 milliseconds, the net change is 220 milliseconds.

Changing the video speed is very different from converting the frame rate. Changing the video speed simply changes the rate at which the existing frames are played. Converting the frame rate duplicates or removes frames to create a new frame rate. You can tweak the video speed to correct minor synchronization problems. If there is no audio track, you can speed up or slow down a video sequence.

Keep in mind that changing the video speed has a major effect on the data rate. If you take a 15 fps file, and change the video speed to 30 fps, you have doubled the data rate. The file may no longer, for example, be able to be saved for playback from a CD-ROM drive.

The lower half of this dialog box enables you to play a sample selection of the video to verify correct synchronization of video and audio.

Audio Format

The audio format you selected for capture does not have to be the audio format you save to. For example, you might capture audio at 16 bits of resolution, and then save two versions of the file—one with 16 bits of resolution, and another at 8 bits of resolution. You could then put both versions on a CD-ROM, and users could choose the one that fits their system's capabilities. You can change the number of channels (stereo or mono), the sample size (8 or 16 bits), and the frequency (11, 22, and 44 kHz). See Figure 10.10.

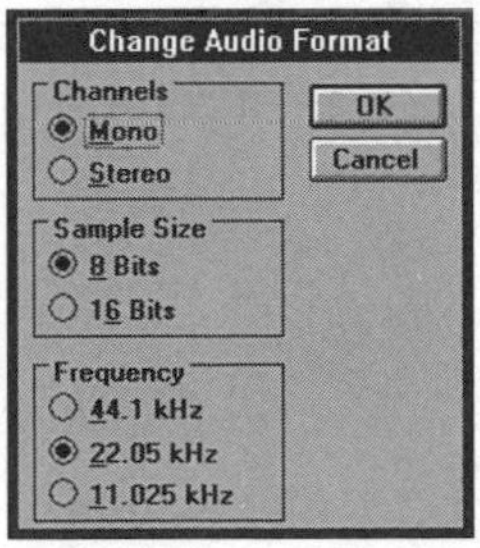

Figure 10.10. Changing the audio format.

Video Format

You can also change one aspect of the video format, the color depth, using the dialog box shown in Figure 10.11.

```
┌──────────────────────────┐
│ ─  Video Format          │
├──────────────────────────┤
│ Set the bit depth that all│
│ frames in this movie will │
│ be converted to.         │
│                          │
│ ● 8 bit       ┌────────┐ │
│               │   OK   │ │
│ ○ 16 bit      └────────┘ │
│               ┌────────┐ │
│ ○ 24 bit      │ Cancel │ │
│               └────────┘ │
└──────────────────────────┘
```

Figure 10.11. Changing the video format.

Changing the number of bits used to represent color will have a major impact on file size, and may also have an impact on the appearance of the image. A file that uses 16 bits for color will be twice the size of one that uses 8 bits, and a 24-bit file will be three times as large. Compression may alter these relationships somewhat, but not a lot.

If you are using a codec that automatically uses 24-bit color, such as Cinepak or Indeo, you won't see any changes. Image quality may or may not be changed when you reduce the number of color bits; some files may be little affected, whereas others will be dramatically different—it depends on the content rather than any formula. In addition, the fact that the frames simulate motion makes the eye more forgiving of faults.

Increasing the color depth, such as from 8 to 24 bits, adds no new color information and does not improve the appearance of the image, but it will increase the file size. You may need to make such a conversion when you want to insert a 24-bit sequence into a file that uses 8-bit color. You could also, of course, convert the 24-bit file to 8 bits.

Create Palette

This applies primarily to 8-bit color files, which use a palette of 256 colors to display an image. You can use the menu selection to capture a palette from the current frames, and then apply that selection to any number of frames. (See Figure 10.12.)

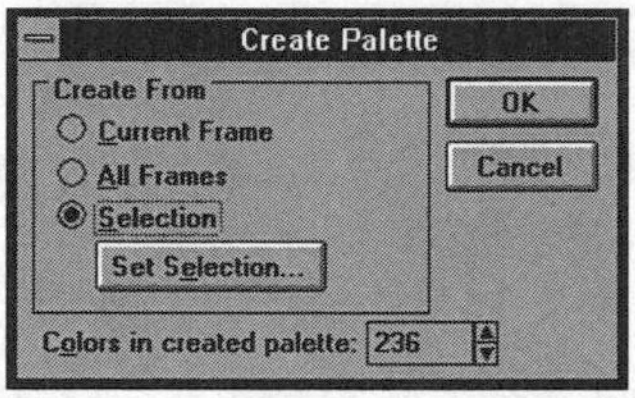

Figure 10.12. Creating a palette.

I have found that the current release of AVI will sometimes cause problems if there are palette changes in the video file, so use palette changes with care, and watch for problems. The problems I had involved the palette getting "lost." That is, if I paused playback of a file with multiple palettes, switched to a different window, the palette would not be restored correctly when I returned.

Crop Video

Cropping enables you to remove unwanted portions of the video frame. If you crop, the same crop will apply to all frames, so make sure that it works before you save the file; material outside the crop will be lost. To crop a video, use the Video/ Crop menu selection, which displays the dialog box shown in Figure 10.13.

Figure 10.13. Cropping a video.

Needless to say, cropping would be tedious indeed if you had to do it by the numbers, as the dialog box seems to suggest. If you move the dialog box out of the way, however, and click and drag in the image area of VidEdit, you can crop visually, as shown in Figure 10.14.

Figure 10.14. Cropping a video.

Resize Video

Resizing, on the other hand, will scale the entire video frame to a new size. The Resize dialog box, shown in Figure 10.15, allows you to set a new width and/or height for the video frame.

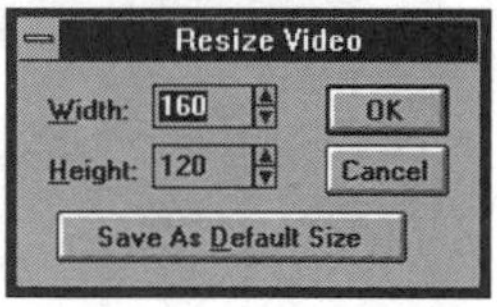

Figure 10.15. Resizing a video.

Because this is a scaling operation, you must change the width in the same proportion as the height to avoid distorting the shape of objects. For example, if you have a 160x120 video, and you resize the width from 160 to 200, the new size is 25% greater than the old size (160 + [160*.25] = 200). You need to apply the same formula to the height: 120 + [120*.25] = 150. The new video size should be 200x150 if you want to avoid distortion.

Statistics

This menu choice displays a variety of statistics for the currently loaded file, as shown in Figure 10.16.

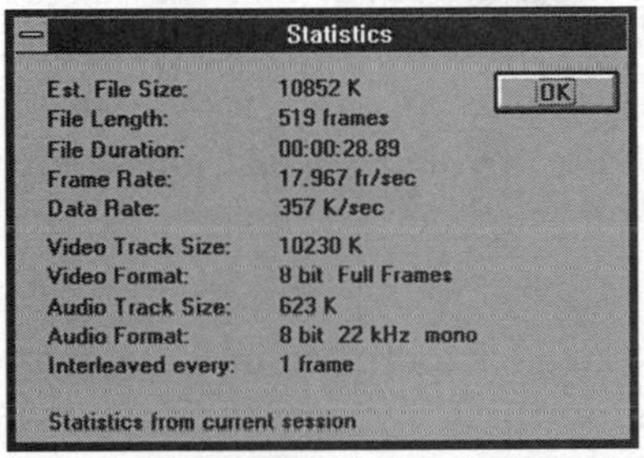

Statistics	
Est. File Size:	10852 K
File Length:	519 frames
File Duration:	00:00:28.89
Frame Rate:	17.967 fr/sec
Data Rate:	357 K/sec
Video Track Size:	10230 K
Video Format:	8 bit Full Frames
Audio Track Size:	623 K
Audio Format:	8 bit 22 kHz mono
Interleaved every:	1 frame

Statistics from current session

Figure 10.16. Statistics for a typical video file.

Note that the file size is actually an *estimated* file size; the actual size of the file may differ significantly from this figure, so use it only as a guide. One of the most important uses of the statistics display is to check the data rate. For example, if you are trying to save the file with a CD-ROM as a target, and you get a warning telling you the target rate could not be reached, you find out what the actual data rate is by using this display. If you missed the target by a little, you can change the quality setting to a few numbers lower; if you missed by a lot, you may have to do something drastic like convert the frame rate to fewer frames per second, such as dropping it from 18 to 15, or from 15 to 12.

Load File into Memory

This menu choice allows you to attempt to load the entire video file into memory for fast frame access and playback. Keep in mind that memory includes such things as virtual memory, which is actually on the hard disk. Unless you know you have enough real memory to hold the file, don't select this option—you could wind up waiting for a very long time just to get a message telling you the entire file could not be loaded into memory.

Saving the File

Saving a file might take a long time, depending on what codec you are using. Saving full frames is relatively fast, whereas using an asymmetrical codec such as Cinepak could take quite a while, especially for large image sizes (such as 320x240). You can try to do other work while saving, but I have found that saving uses up so many CPU cycles that it's not worth the effort. So just sit back and find something else to do. A full minute of video can take anywhere from a minute or two, to an hour. It all depends on the codec, the image size, and the number of frames per second.

Before you save, you can click on the Compression Options button to check or revise the compression settings. I suggest making it a habit to confirm the compression settings before every save; if things aren't what you want them to be, it can be a long time until the save is over. The Save dialog box does report some of the compression settings, but not enough to make me feel safe. If you aren't sure of the settings, you can cancel during a save.

After saving the file, you should defragment and test playback to make sure everything is correct, and that the compression did not mess up your images. I usually defragment after saving a batch of files.

If you plan to do any extensive editing, I suggest saving a "Full Frames" version of the file first. It shouldn't happen, but I often encounter problems when I try to work with compressed images after exporting them to other programs. The best-looking images will always result if you compress as your absolute last step in the process. Because these compression techniques are lossy, each time you compress you lose a little more image quality. Compressing as a last step ensures that you will have the best possible image at playback.

Importing and Exporting with VidEdit

VidEdit supports a large number of import and export formats. This gives you a lot of flexibility in working with images and sequences from a variety of sources. For example, you can incorporate animations in your video sequences, export video still images to a variety of applications and platforms, or export video for inclusion in an animation sequence.

Many of these formats have specific limitations or requirements, which are covered in detail in this chapter. The available import formats (accessible via the File/Insert selection) are listed in Table 11.1, and the available export formats (accessible via the File/extract selection) are listed in Table 11.2.

Table 11.1. Supported VidEdit import formats.

Format	Extension	Comments
Microsoft AVI	.AVI	Standard video file
DIB Sequence	.DIB, .BMP	Must have numbers in filename
Autodesk Animation	.FLC, .FLI	Ignores sound data
Microsoft Waveform	.WAV	Sound only
Apple AIFF		Sound only
Microsoft PCM Waveform	.WAV	Sound only
AVI Waveform	.AVI	Sound only
Windows Metafile	.WMF	Single image as one frame
DrawPerfect	.WPG	Single image as one frame
Micrographix Designer/Draw	.DRW	Single image as one frame
AutoCAD format 2-D	.DXF	Single image as one frame
HP Graphic Language	.HGL	Single image as one frame
Computer Graphics Metafile	.CGM	Single image as one frame
Encapsulated PostScript	.EPS	Single image as one frame
Tagged Image Format	.TIF	Single image as one frame
Lotus 1-2-3 format	.PIC	Single image as one frame

Format	Extension	Comments
AutoCAD plot file	.PLT	Single image as one frame
Microsoft Windows DIB	.DIB,.BMP	Single image as one frame
Microsoft RIFF DIB	.RDI	Single image as one frame
PC Paintbrush	.PCX	Single image as one frame
CompuServe GIF	.GIF	Single image as one frame
Apple Macintosh PICT		Single image as one frame
Truevision Targa	.TGA	Single image as one frame
AVI (First frame)	.AVI	Single image as one frame

Table 11.2. Supported VidEdit export formats.

Format	Extension	Comments
Microsoft AVI	.AVI	Standard video file
DIB Sequence	.DIB	Auto-increments filename
Microsoft Windows DIB	.DIB, .BMP	One frame as single image
Microsoft RIFF DIB	.RDI	One frame as single image
PC Paintbrush	.PCX	One frame as single image
Apple Macintosh PICT		One frame as single image
Truevision Targa	.TGA	One frame as single image
Microsoft RLE DIB	.DIB	One frame as single image
Microsoft RIFF RLE DIB	.RDI	One frame as single image

One of the most powerful uses for import and export involves combining animation and video. See Chapter 20, "Integrating Video with Other Media."

Import Formats

To import images or sounds, you use the File/Insert selection in VidEdit. (See Figure 11.1.) This gives you access to a wide variety of file formats, each of which may have different needs, limitations, or requirements.

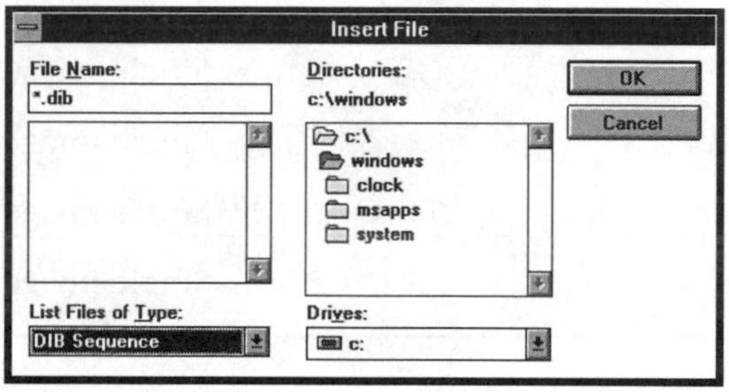

Insert File	
File Name:	**Directories:**	**OK**
*.dib	c:\windows	**Cancel**
	c:\	
	windows	
	clock	
	msapps	
	system	
List Files of Type:	**Drives:**	
DIB Sequence	c:	

Figure 11.1. Importing with VidEdit.

In this section, you look at each file type that you can import in some detail. Some file types are simple to use, whereas others require more detailed handling for good results.

Microsoft AVI

The capability to import .AVI files enables you to construct video sequences easily. You can edit small, individual clips and then load them into a separate file in the correct order. This is the simplest way to create a multi-part video sequence.

DIB Sequence

This is one of the niftiest import features. Even if you don't have a video camera, you can create a series of still images and import them into VidEdit. The key to using this technique is the filenames you use. The filenames must be a numbered sequence of files. Filenames can have up to eight characters; I usually use four characters for a name, and four characters for the numeric sequence. For example, I recently used this technique for a series of pictures of a great blue heron. I used filenames starting at **hern0000.bmp**, and continuing with **hern0001.bmp**, **hern0002.bmp**, and so on, all the way up to **hern0141.bmp**. You do not have to follow this convention; I've also used names such as **animat1.bmp**, **animat2.bmp**, and so forth. The only requirement is that all files have exactly the same non-numeric part of the filename.

There are any number of ways to create a series of still images for import. I'll list a few that I have tried successfully.

➤ *Output from an animation package.* Animator Pro, for example, allows you to output an animation as a series of stills. You can convert the resulting .TIF files to .DIB or .BMP files, and then insert them into a new or existing .AVI file.

➤ *A series of images you create by modifying a single source image.* I once took a single image and applied a 2-D effect (a whirlpool) to it. I created 59 copies of the image, and applied different percentages of the effect to each copy—5 degrees of whirlpool to the first copy, 10 degrees to the next, and so on. I numbered the files as required for a DIB sequence, and then used File/Insert to load them. The result was an apparent moving whirlpool effect on the underlying image. With a total of 60 images (the original plus 59 copies), this yielded 4 seconds of video at 15 frames per second. You could also use this technique to create transitions in your videos. Export the last frame of a sequence, and then use it as an original image that you modify.

➤ *Create original sequences using a drawing package.* Even if you don't own an animation package, you can use many drawing packages to create a series of images. Some drawing packages allow you to use layers; you can put the previous frame's image on a layer, and then draw the next frame on top of it.

➤ *Create sequences using sequences of images.* You can use this technique to create a dazzling potpourri of wildly different images, or you can display a series of images at a rate of .25 frames per second (one frame every four seconds) with a recorded audio track with narration, like a slide show.

Autodesk Animation

This is an import format that should be used with caution. I have found that some animation files do not look right after import. The usual symptoms are mangling of the on-screen image, failure to update a frame completely, or leftover bits of color in the wrong places. If you encounter this problem, you will probably need to use a product like Animator Pro (presuming you have it available) to export the animation as a series of single images. If your version of Animator Pro won't export to bitmaps, you'll need a program such as Image Pals to do batch format conversions (in this case, from .TIF to .BMP).

When it works, however, this is an extremely convenient way to convert animations to video files; it is almost instantaneous. In general, I have had better luck with .FLI files than with .FLC files.

There is one thing to be aware of when you are importing animation files. Animator Pro, the usual source for .FLC files, adjusts the aspect ratio of an animation before saving it to a file. When you import the resulting file into VidEdit, you may find that circles and squares are no longer circular or square. If this happens, you can use VidEdit to resize the image to correct for this.

To resize the image, use the Video/Resize menu selection. This brings up the dialog box shown in Figure 11.2.

Figure 11.2. Resizing a video sequence.

The most common resizing involves images that were saved as 320x200, 256-color animations in Animator (not Animator Pro). You may need to experiment to find the size that looks best in VidEdit. I find that a 320x200 sequence usually looks best resized to 320x240. For example, Figure 11.3 shows an image from a .FLC file that was imported at its default size, 320x200. Figure 11.4 shows the same image resized to 320x240. Note that the head looks more nearly spherical, which is the intended shape.

Figure 11.3. Imported FLC image at default 320x200 size.

Figure 11.4. Imported FLC image resized to 320x240.

Microsoft Waveform

This option allows you to easily add to or replace any existing audio in your .AVI file. I often export the audio track from a video, sweeten it with software such as Wave for Windows, and then import it back into the video file. For example, I might mix some music under a narration, or I might add sound effects, or even something as simple as making the sound a little louder.

There are some hazards to be aware of. The most important thing is to make sure that you edit the audio and video together, especially if there is any need at all to synchronize them. In other words, either make all of your video edits before you export the sound for sweetening, or hold video edits until you have imported the sweetened sound track.

Even so, you could still run into synchronization problems if you edit extensively. You can use Video/Synchronize to re-sync the video and audio tracks.

See also: Microsoft PCM Waveform.

Apple AIFF

This is a type of sound file from the Apple Macintosh. This allows you to use the Macintosh to create sound files that you can port over to your .AVI files.

Microsoft PCM Waveform

PCM stands for *Pulse Code Modulation*, and it is a compressed form of audio that was recently added to Windows. It still uses the .WAV extension, and the only time you need to worry about what kinds of Wave file you have is if you get an error message. In that case, just try a different Wave file format for importing.

See also: Microsoft Waveform.

AVI Waveform

This will import only the audio portion of an AVI file. Use it just like you would any other sound file source.

Single-Frame File Formats

VidEdit allows you to import a relatively large number of file formats as single video frames. If you have a large number of such files, you might want to convert them to DIB files using software that converts a batch of files, such as Image Pals from U-Lead. With Image Pals, I can load even hundreds of single images and convert them all in one step. This is a great convenience when working with the large numbers of images involved in video sequences.

This next section lists and describes the file formats VidEdit will import.

Windows Metafile (*.wmf)

This is a format you might not have used before, but almost all Windows applications support it. The word *metafile* refers to the capability to include both raster and vector formats in a single file. A *raster image* is one that is composed of pixels, such as a photo-realistic image. A *vector image* is one that is composed of lines and fills stored as mathematical expression, such as an encapsulated PostScript (EPS) file.

DrawPerfect (*.wpg)

DrawPerfect is a drawing program frequently used with WordPerfect. In fact, the filename extension, .WPG, stands for *WordPerfect Graphic*.

Micrographix Designer/Draw (*.drw)

These are very sophisticated drawing packages, often used for complex, detailed illustrations.

AutoCAD Format 2-D (*.dxf)

AutoCAD is an engineering/architectural software package.

HP Graphic Language (*.hgl)

This was originally a file format for plotters, but it is also widely supported as an import/export format by many drawing packages.

Computer Graphics Metafile (*.cgm)

When it was originally introduced, this format was intended to be a standard file format supported by a large number of software products. However, it ran into the same stumbling block that most would-be standards run into: different vendors implemented it differently. Each vendor that supports CGM files does it in

a different way, so you may find some problems importing some CGM files. Data may turn up missing, or the file simply may not import. If this occurs, try a different file format if at all possible, or use a conversion program such as Hijak to convert the file to a different file format.

Encapsulated PostScript (*.eps)

This is a vector format common to many high-end drawing programs, including CorelDRAW!, Freehand, and Illustrator. You will almost always find EPS as an export option, rather than a Save As option.

You may have noticed that PostScript printer output can be routed to a file using Print Setup, and that the resulting file is referred to as an encapsulated PostScript file. This is not accurate—if you try to use such a file as an EPS file, you won't succeed. Printing to a file results in a PostScript file, not an encapsulated PostScript file. An encapsulated file has special codes that allow it to be imported into a drawing program.

You may find that you don't get the results you want when importing an EPS file. If possible, try a raster format such as .TIF or .PCX or .BMP instead. Many drawing packages now support such conversions. For example, I often export .TIF files from CorelDRAW! when I intend to use the image in VidEdit.

Tagged Image File Format (*.tif)

This is one of the workhorse file formats; it is extremely common. There are a number of flavors, or different variations, of TIFF files. Unlike .CGM files, however, most TIFF flavors are supported by most programs. The one time you may find problems with TIFF files is when compression is used. Different kinds of compression can be used in different flavors.

If you encounter problems importing a TIFF file, try returning to the source program and saving it without compression, if that option is available. Most of the time, this will solve the problem.

Lotus 1-2-3 Format (*.pic)

This is the file format that 1-2-3 uses for saving charts.

AutoCAD Plot File (*.plt)

Like HGL, this is a file format intended for plotter output.

Microsoft Windows DIB

This is becoming the most common file format for images for Windows programs. In most cases, you can use this option to import .BMP files; you can either re-name them as .DIB files, or type *.BMP in place of *.DIB in the filename portion of the dialog box.

Microsoft RIFF DIB

The RIFF file format, established by Microsoft, can contain a variety of different kinds of data, from sounds to image to video. This option allows you to extract a DIB that is stored in this format.

PC Paintbrush (*.pcx)

This file format has been around a long time—almost as long as personal computers have been around. It is still commonly supported.

CompuServe GIF

This is a compressed image file format originated for use on the CompuServe Information Services. If you are a member of CompuServe, and you have down-loaded images, you have probably already worked with this image format. Many shareware programs have supported the .GIF format for years, but it has only recently been supported more widely by mainstream image editing packages.

Apple Macintosh PICT

This is a common Macintosh image file format.

Truevision Targa (*.tga)

Originally developed as a 24-bit image format by Truevision to support their Targa video hardware, the Targa format is now more widely supported. Many video capture cards, in addition to working with VidCap for capture of sequences, can also capture 16- or 24-bit Targa still images using proprietary Windows or DOS software.

AVI (First Frame)

This option allows you to insert just the first frame of any AVI file.

Export Formats

VidEdit does not support as many export formats as it does import formats. In particular, it does not support many single-frame formats. This is not a serious handicap; you can easily use other software to convert to almost any image file format you need.

In this section, you'll look at each file type that you can export to. As with import, some file types are simple to use, whereas others require more detailed handling for good results.

Microsoft AVI

At first glance, it might seem odd to have the .AVI file type as an export option, but there is a good reason for it—you can use it to save a portion of the currently loaded .AVI file, which you can then import into a different file. This allows you to assemble video sequences relatively easily. This output option uses the current compression settings.

DIB Sequence

Just as you can import a series of DIBs and create a video sequence, you can export a series of DIBs. This is very useful for adding video sequences to animations, or for modifying individual images in creative ways. For example, you can export a series of images, and then apply the same special effect to each image—redden the image to suggest a sunset, for example—in an image editing package. You can then import the DIB sequence and convert it back into a video.

Single-Frame File Formats

You can export single frames to a number of different file formats. The list of supported formats is much shorter than for import, but you can convert as needed.

All of these formats are available as import formats; see that section of this chapter for detailed information about each format. The supported formats are:

Microsoft Windows DIB
Microsoft RIFF DIB
PC Paintbrush
Apple Macintosh PICT
Truevision Targa
Microsoft RLE DIB
Microsoft RIFF RLE DIB

Even if you select a range of images before selecting one of these file formats, only the first image will actually be saved to disk. The only kind of image sequence you can save is a DIB sequence.

Import/Export Tips

VidEdit is a simple program, but the import/export options give you a way to be more creative with video sequences. In most cases, it's going to take a lot of time to work this way; most image editing packages don't allow you to transform more than one image at a time. If you want to perform complex or 3-D transformations, however, this may be the only choice you have—at least right now.

No matter what file format you are importing or exporting, the following tips will help you avoid problems.

➤ *Compress after, not before.* If you compress an image before you export it, you may find that you have some problems, either in the package you will be editing in, or when you re-import to VidEdit. For example, exporting a series of DIBs to 3D Studio will not work right if the images have been compressed—palette mappings tend to get out of whack, and you could wind up with blank spots or incorrect colors when the image is mapped to a 3-D object. In addition, if you compress as the final step, you will retain as much as possible of the original clarity of the captured image.

➤ *Invest in a batch conversion program.* I use Image Pals from U-Lead, and it saves me a lot of headaches. I can't imagine converting a few hundred DIBs to TIFs without it.

➤ *Plan your file format conversions ahead of time.* Make sure you have everything you need for each format conversion from beginning to end of your process.

➤ *Beware of vector formats.* Video images are all raster images; moving to and from vector formats such as .EPS can be problematic. Usually, the best place to perform this conversion is in the program that you used to create the image in the first place. That program probably is the best equipped to handle the nuances of its own file structure.

➤ *Be prepared for problems.* If one method doesn't give good results, be prepared to try an end run using a different file format. Don't lock yourself into one method for any import/export operation, since unforeseen problems could upset your plans at any time.

Most of all, be patient. There are a lot of single frames in a video file, and it can take a long time to do even some simple thing to all of those frames.

12

Advanced Windows Editing: Media Merge

I was fortunate to obtain a pre-beta copy of a fascinating new program for working with video files: Media Merge, from ATI Technologies. This program was going into beta just at the time the book was going to press, and the folks at ATI were extremely cooperative about rushing a working version of their program to me so coverage of it could be included in the book.

Media Merge allows you to edit combinations of video files. You can create fancy transitions from one file to another, and you can layer files on top of one another. You can create moving text, and you can overlap only portions of files. These tools enable you to create digital video effects that add a substantial amount of impact and interest to your video presentations.

Prior to working with Media Merge, I had worked with Premiere 2.0 on the Macintosh. Premiere is more sophisticated, having been through a complete version upgrade, but Media Merge has some significant advantages as well. The Windows version of Premiere was not yet available prior to press time, but based on my conversations with the development team at Adobe, Premiere for Windows will offer substantially the same feature set as Premiere for the Macintosh. Based on this information, it is clear that these products are really intended for two different audiences.

Media Merge is the easier of the two to use. The interface is intuitive and straightforward, and it's easy to create a multiclip video sequence. Premiere, on the other hand, is more sophisticated, but harder to understand and use. Media Merge should appeal to a broader range of users, especially business users who want to start editing and combining video files right away. Premiere will appeal to the user who wants to manipulate video files in more complex ways.

Media Merge consists of several different modules. The two most interesting are the Storyboard and the Scene Editor. Media Merge also includes an Audio Editor with a number of interesting special effects built right in.

The Storyboard

Figure 12.1 shows the opening window of the Media Merge Storyboard. In addition to the usual menu and tool bar, there is a large work area with two kinds of shapes: small rectangles, and larger rectangles. The small rectangles are used for adding and editing transitions, and the large rectangles are used for adding and editing video clips. The time sequence moves from left to right, with clips and transitions alternating.

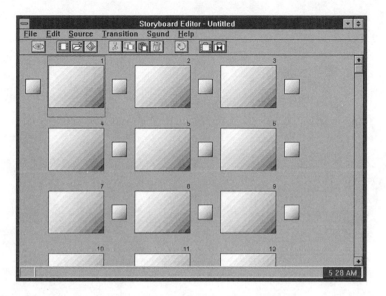

Figure 12.1. The opening window of the Media Merge Storyboard.

For example, you might start with a transition—a fade from black into the first video clip. Then the first video clip plays, and then another transition: perhaps a wipe from left to right, with the second video clip replacing the first one during the wipe. You can specify all kinds of details for the transitions—how long they last, which direction the transition moves, and so on.

Take a look at how this all fits together in the Storyboard. Figure 12.2 shows the Storyboard work area after adding the first video file. The first of the large rectangles has a thumbnail image of the first frame of the video clip displayed in it.

Next, I add a transition to the beginning of the video clip. Double-clicking on the small rectangle immediately left of the first video clip opens the Transition Browser, as shown in Figure 12.3.

There are nine possible transitions shown, including such standard transitions as dissolve, wipe, clock wipe, and sliding bands. I can't show you here in the book, but each transition is animated, so it is immediately clear how each one works.

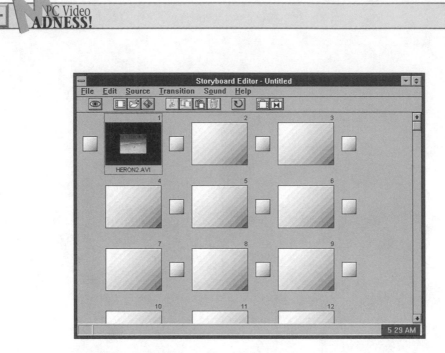

Figure 12.2. A video clip has been added to the Storyboard.

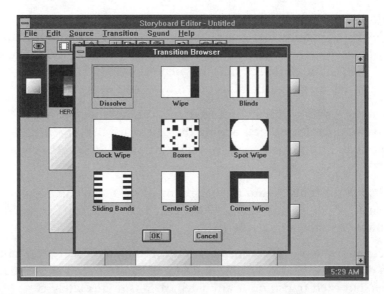

Figure 12.3. The Media Merge Transition Browser.

Part of each image is white, and part is black. To imagine what a transition will look like, imagine one color standing for the **previous** video clip, and the other color standing for the **next** video clip. (The first video is a special case; the **previous** clip is usually a solid color instead of an actual video clip.)

I use the Spot Wipe for this example. Selecting a specific transition opens a transition editor, as shown in Figure 12.4.

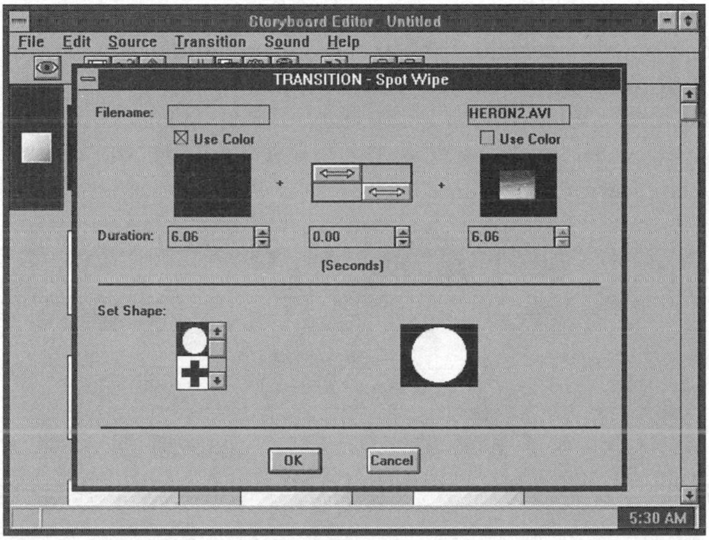

Figure 12.4. Editing a transition.

The transition editor is divided into two parts. The top half is used to set the timing values for the transition, and the bottom half is used to set parameters appropriate for each transition. In the case of the Spot Wipe, you can select from a number of shapes for the spot.

The upper half of the transition editor requires some explanation, but it is easy to use once you know the basic concepts. It is divided into three areas. The first and last areas have a space for a filename at the top, and all areas have an image in the middle and a duration at the bottom.

The area on the left is the previous clip. The middle area is the transition itself, and the area on the right is the next clip. In this case, there is no previous clip, so the little box called Use Color is checked. Black is the color being used. The default duration is the length of the clip heron2.avi, 6.06 seconds.

The middle area shows two arrows of equal size, which do not overlap. This indicates that the transition will be abrupt, with no overlapping between the 6 seconds of black and the 6 seconds of the first video clip. That's not very attractive, so I'll make some changes.

Figure 12.5 shows a revised transition editor. The duration of the black color is now 1.5 seconds (note the shorter arrow in the middle area), and the duration of the transition is 1.5 seconds. The arrows in the middle area graphically show the new relationships. The black color and the first video clip will start at the same time, and over the course of 1.5 seconds the video clip heron2.avi will be revealed by the Spot Wipe. Figure 12.6 shows the first few frames, and you can see how the spot enlarges with each frame.

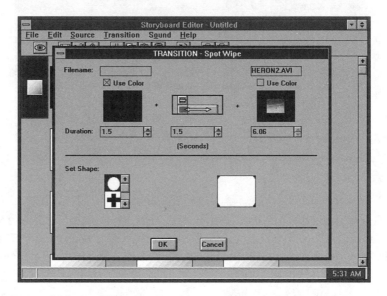

Figure 12.5. A revised transition editor.

Once you understand the fundamental concept behind a transition, and how to work the relationships, it's easy to create and edit transitions.

Figure 12.7 shows another transition being edited. I have added a second clip, face15k1.avi, and this transition is called a Corner Wipe. Note that this transition has completely different parameters than the Spot Wipe. In this case, the wipe will pull the video of the second clip in over the first clip. The transition will apply to the tail end of the first clip, and just the very beginning of the second clip. The arrows in the middle area show the relationship of the two video clips to the transition.

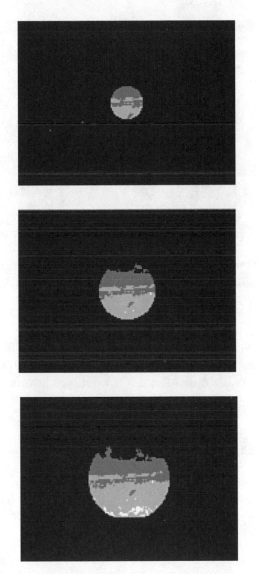

Figure 12.6. Frames from a video with a Spot Wipe.

Figure 12.8 shows several frames to give you an idea of how the Corner Wipe works.

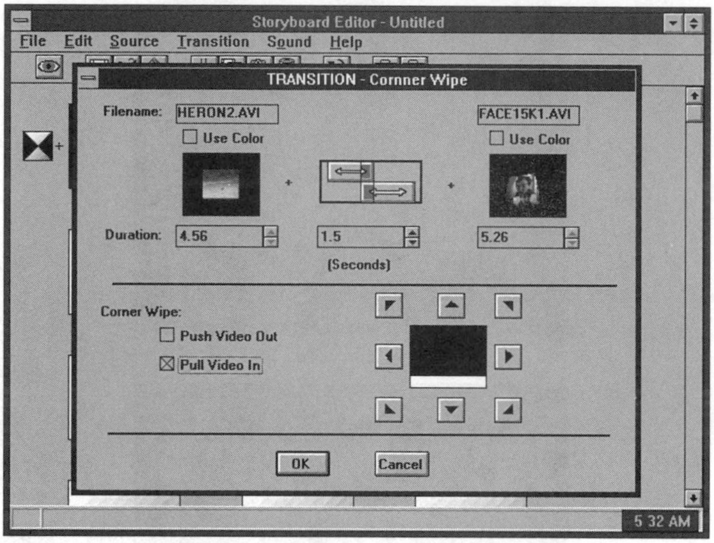

Figure 12.7. Editing a Corner Wipe transition.

To continue developing a complex video sequence, you just keep adding video clips and transitions. Figure 12.9 shows the Storyboard with two video clips and two transitions. To edit a transition, simply double-click its box.

The Scene Editor

The Scene Editor is as easy to use as the Storyboard, but it looks at the process of combining videos in a completely different way. The combination of the Storyboard and the Scene Editor gives you a lot of power. The opening window of the Scene Editor is shown in Figure 12.10.

With the Scene Editor, you can work with video clips in a linear, time-based fashion. Each horizontal band can hold one video clip, including its audio stream if present. A band also can hold just an audio clip, in the form of a Wave file. There is a timeline above the bands; in Figure 12.10, the timeline is marked in single frames, the default.

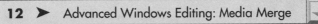

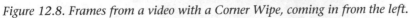

Figure 12.8. Frames from a video with a Corner Wipe, coming in from the left.

305

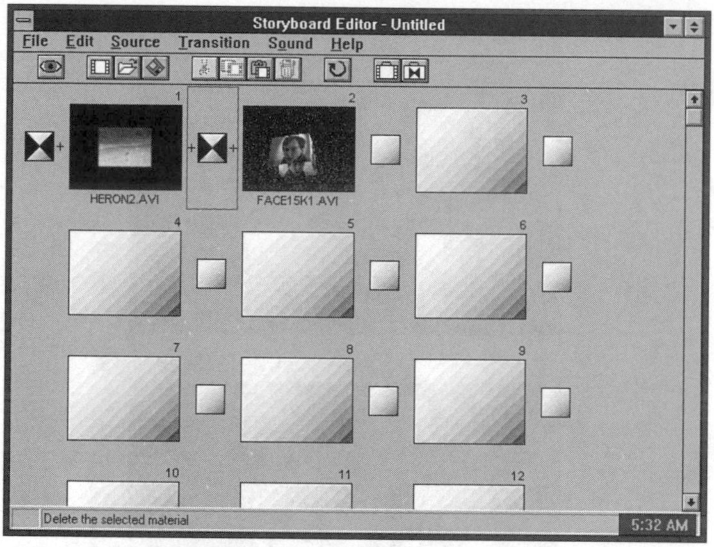

Figure 12.9. The Storyboard with two video clips and two transitions.

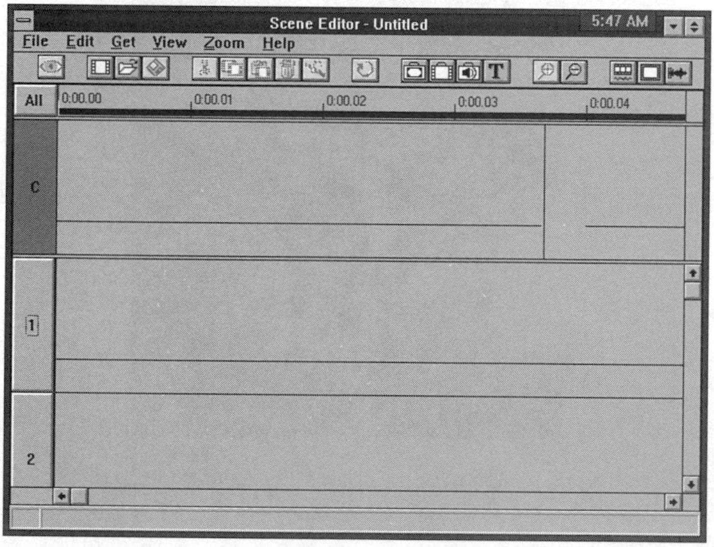

Figure 12.10. The opening window of the Media Merge Scene Editor.

The uppermost band, marked with a **C** at the left of the window, is the composite band. It shows the cumulative image based on all of the bands combined.

The really nifty thing about the Scene Editor is that it allows you to build up a scene in layers. The first step in building a scene is to load a video clip into one of the horizontal bands, as shown in Figure 12.11. That figure also shows the zoom menu, which allows you to select the number of frames that make up a single unit along the timeline. By selecting larger units, you can see more of the video clip at one time. Figure 12.11 shows a VGA screen, which is 640x480 pixels. Larger screen sizes, such as 1024x768 and 1280x1024, make it much easier to work with the Scene Editor because they allow you to view more bands and a larger section of the video clip at one time.

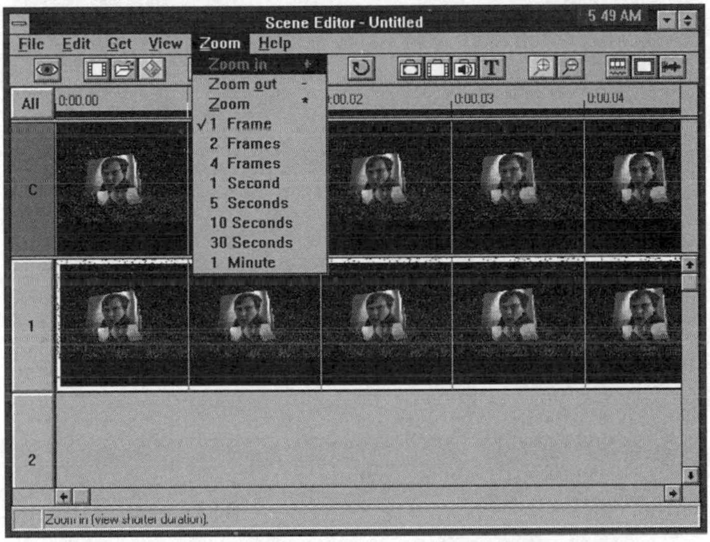

Figure 12.11. A video clip loaded into the Scene Editor, showing the Zoom menu.

Note that the video clip appears to be duplicated. It shows up once on band 1 and once in the composite band. Figure 12.12 shows the same video clip, but with a zoom factor applied. Each segment along the timeline now represents one second of video.

It takes time to draw each of the individual images in each band, which can slow down operations quite a bit if you don't have a very fast computer. There are two good design choices in the software that help with this. First, you do not have to wait while the screen redraws completely; you can select menu choices, move scroll bars, and so on while a redraw is in progress. Second, you can avoid

bitmap displays entirely, as shown in Figure 12.13. This figure shows that a second file has been loaded, and its start point is offset three seconds from the first clip, as shown by the timeline above the bands.

Figure 12.12. A zoomed Scene Editor window.

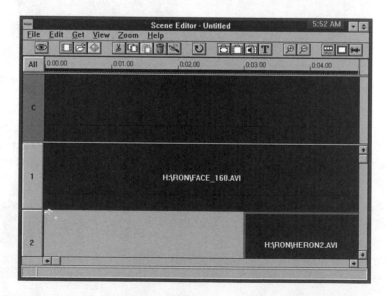

Figure 12.13. Using the alternative screen display, which only shows filenames.

You can adjust the properties of a clip by double-clicking it, using the dialog box shown in Figure 12.14. This allows you to use just the video or audio portions of a clip, or to select only a portion of the clip for the scene.

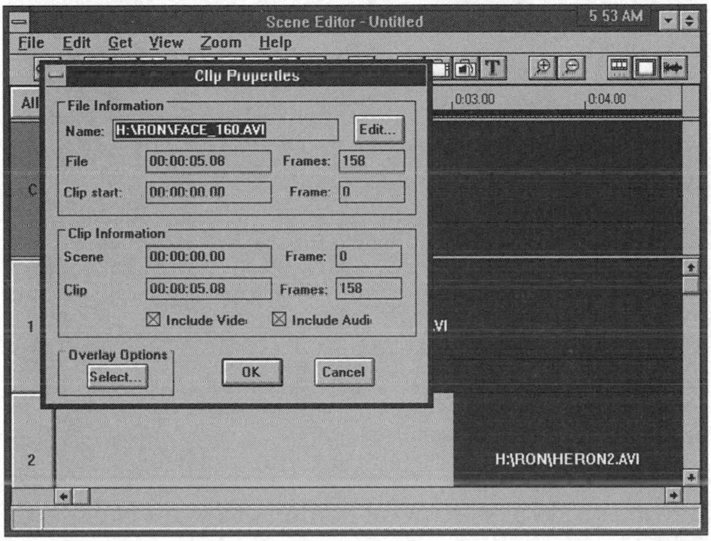

Figure 12.14. Setting clip properties.

There is a button at the lower-left, in the section of the dialog box called Overlay Options, that opens the dialog box shown in Figure 12.15.

By now everyone is familiar with the weatherman who appears to be standing in front of a weather map on television. If you saw the film, *Groundhog Day*—or just happen to know such things—you know that this bit of trickery is achieved by having the weatherman stand in front of a blue backdrop. When the image of the weatherman is joined with the weather map image, the parts of the weatherman image that are blue are simply dropped. This is called an overlay—the non-blue parts of the image are overlaid on the weather map.

This same technique is yours to use in the Scene Editor. The top-left portion of the dialog box in Figure 12.15 allows you to define a key color. In this example, the key color is black. The sample frame at the right has marked all of the black areas with magenta (which of course you cannot see in a black-and-white illustration!). This allows you to easily see which parts of your image contain the key color, and which will therefore drop out of sight when you combine clips with the Scene Editor. This is called Chroma Key.

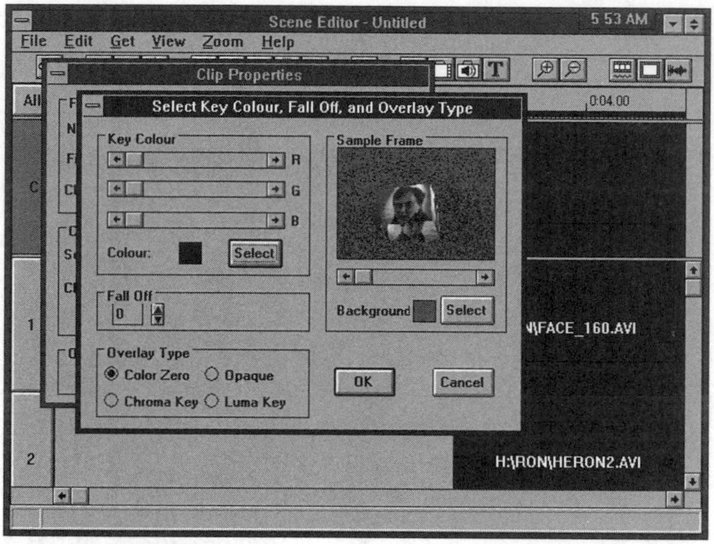

Figure 12.15. Adjusting overlay options.

There are other ways to select what portion of a video clip overlays another clip. For example, you can use brightness, which is called Luma Key.

The color you select for the Chroma Key, black in this case, should be the color you want to drop out. In Figure 12.16, the video in band 2 has a black background that drops out, as you can see in the composite track at the top of the Scene Editor. Note also that the second video clip's start point is offset from the first clip by four seconds.

This overlay capability allows you to create very sophisticated video presentations. With appropriate backdrops, you can add a video of anything to another video. You can also easily incorporate animations created with many of the popular animation packages that export bitmaps. Figure 12.17 shows a series of three frames from the completed scene, with one video overlaying another.

Figure 12.16. A second video clip added to the Scene Editor, using Chroma Key for overlay.

The Scene Editor also allows you to create moving text objects, using the 3 Stage Text Effect dialog box, shown in Figure 12.18.

You can set the color for the text and the background, and you can control the duration and direction of entry, the duration and position of a pause, and the duration and direction of exit. Figure 12.19 shows some text ready to be added, with entry, hold, and exit settings configured.

Figure 12.20 shows the Scene Editor with the text added; you can see how the text changes from frame to frame.

Figure 12.17. A series of frames showing video overlay.

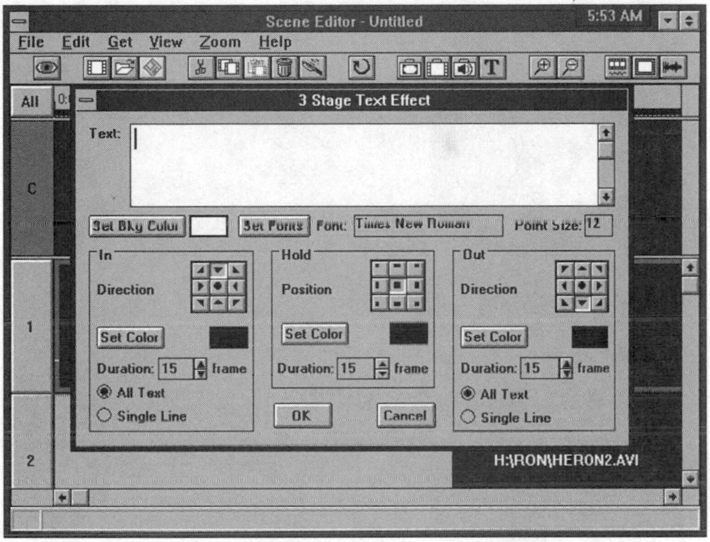

Figure 12.18. The 3 Stage Text Effect dialog.

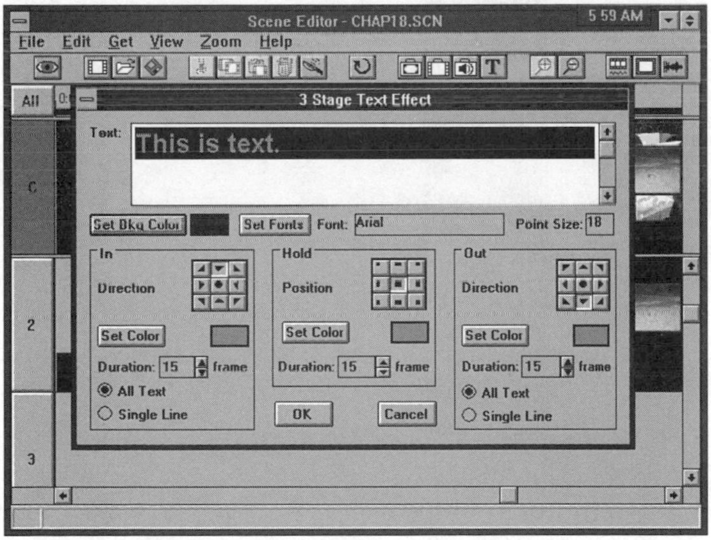

Figure 12.19. Text ready to be added to the Scene Editor.

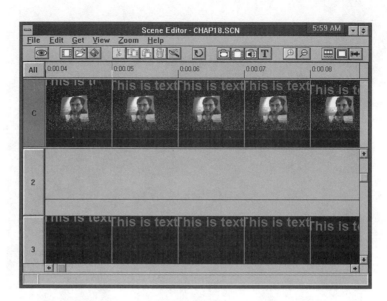

Figure 12.20. A frame sequence with moving text.

## PART V

Advanced Applications with Video for Windows

13

Introduction:
Programming
Options

I've been a programmer for more than ten years, and I have written code in a wide variety of languages. Some of it I enjoyed, and some of it was awful. None of it was as interesting as programming for and with multimedia.

There are several programming options for multimedia. You can get down and dirty with C/C++, or you can use a high-level authoring package. You can incorporate all kinds of media, but digital video is certainly one of the most exciting. If I had to hazard a guess, I would say that digital video will have more impact on the way we use computers than any other medium.

Authoring Versus Programming

There are many levels at which you can program for multimedia, and deciding which level is best is not necessarily a simple task. In general, there is a tradeoff between ease of use on the one hand, and power and flexibility on the other. The choice has to be made on almost every multimedia project.

The language you already know is probably a good place to get started, but there are limits or problems with almost any approach you take. You may find that you are better off selecting a development environment based on the needs of the project, rather than your existing skill set. The time it takes to learn a new system will often be less than the time it takes to force your current development environment to handle multimedia.

Generally, one can divide the available resources into two camps: authoring packages, and programming languages. Some, such as Toolbook, fall into both camps depending on how you use them. Each has advantages and disadvantages.

The Advantages of Programming

The primary advantage of programming is the raw power it gives you over the details of your application. Using a language such as C or C++, you can control every single detail, making everything look and behave exactly the way you want it to. Even a higher-level language like Visual Basic gives you a great deal of control. In the case of Visual Basic, you have a simple, visual design interface and complete access to the Window and multimedia APIs.

Programming also allows you to customize your efforts. You can develop a look that you like, and incorporate it into your applications. If it is important to have a unique interface or text retrieval mechanism, using a programming language to develop your multimedia application makes a lot of sense.

If you are already familiar with a programming language, you may also be able to save some of the time it would take to learn a new, multimedia-specific development system. This should be balanced against the time saved by using a higher-level tool, however.

The Disadvantages of Programming

The biggest disadvantage of programming is the time it takes to do it. The price you pay for control over details is the cost of your time and attention to those details. It can take a long time to develop a multimedia application using conventional methods.

On the other hand, if the scale of a project is large enough, it can still make sense to develop with conventional languages. A large project might justify the costs.

The Advantages of Authoring

The primary advantage of authoring is simplicity. The process of developing a multimedia application is easier in an authoring environment. There is less programming—writing of code—and more WYSIWYG (What You See Is What You Get). Instead of writing a complex code sequence to initialize, place, and play a video, you can do it with one or a few commands. It might even be as easy as placing the playback window where you want the video to play, and specifying what file to play.

Authoring packages also make it easy to standardize. Many authoring packages include a defined interface that will be consistent from one application to the next. A good example of this is Viewer, from Microsoft. The text search and retrieval interface will be the same in all of your applications, making it easier for users to learn how to use a new application.

The Disadvantages of Authoring

Authoring reduces your options. Because authoring is done at a relatively high level, at a distance from the details of the program, you must give up some control over the appearance and function of your application. For example, if you are using Interactive to develop your application, you will find that it has limited text capabilities. If you started using it because of the easy interface, and later move to applications that make heavier use of text, you will either need to wait for a new version that enhances text support, or switch to a different system.

Choosing the Right Development System

Choosing between programming and authoring—and which specific tool you use in either camp—has as much to do with your own experience and capabilities as it does with the strengths and weaknesses of programming and authoring. If you have programming experience, you might be able to accomplish more with something like Toolbook, which has some of the ease of an authoring tool and some of the power of a programming language. If you haven't had a lot of programming experience, your learning curve on Toolbook will be longer; you need to consider carefully whether its power will be worth the effort involved.

About that learning curve

If that reference to a long learning curve seemed out of place, consider this: The learning curve metaphor is one of those metaphors that has gotten completely confused in common usage. If you plot learning versus time, with time at the bottom (a convention, that), a steep learning curve actually means you learn a lot in a short period of time. However, *steep* is commonly used to mean that it's difficult to learn something. I suspect the connection comes from folks imagining a steep mountain to climb, or something like that. Thus, if the learning curve stretches out over time (is "long"), you're spending a lot more time and effort to get your reward.

At least now I've done my part to tidy up my own small corner of the English language.

On the other hand, the task itself may dictate the development tools you use. If you need specific, detailed control over the manner and method of presentation, programming will be required. If you just want to present information in an organized way, authoring is more appropriate.

MCI (Media Control Interface)

The key to programming or authoring for multimedia is the MCI (Media Control Interface) built into Windows. It gives you relatively easy access to a lot of multimedia power. The programming and authoring examples in this book use it heavily to accomplish a wide variety of things.

MCI is easy to access because almost all of the capabilities can be accessed using just a few functions. These functions serve as a gateway to multimedia.

High-Level Functions

Here's the short list of what you can do with just a handful of functions.

sndPlaySound	A quick and easy way to play wave files. There is an example of its use in the code for the Video Screen Saver in Chapter 19.
mciExecute	A simple way to send commands to MCI; MCI will even handle the errors and error messages for you. It is used extensively in the Visual Basic examples in Chapter 16.
mciSendString	A more powerful way to communicate in both directions with MCI. You can issue commands and receive information from MCI about devices, status, and so on. You'll find examples in Chapter 19 for C, and in Chapter 18 for Toolbook.
mciSendCommand	The most powerful, and least easy to use, method for working with MCI. You communicate with MCI via messages/commands and structures instead of the plain-language string commands you use with mciExecute and mciSendString.

There are several different ways to work with digital video using MCI. The two most common are handling overlay video, and video playback.

Video overlay consists of displaying a live video signal, usually in a window. This signal is usually an analog, not a digital, signal. That is, it is suitable only for display; it cannot be saved to your hard disk. You'll look at how to control an overlay device, the Bravado 16, in the next section.

Command Strings

Command strings are the key to easy access of MCI. They are plain-language commands that you can use to control MCI devices. For example, to play track 2 on a CD, you need only say:

```
play cdaudio from 2 to 2
```

It's that easy, if you don't count the necessity of somehow getting the command string to MCI. You use the functions `mciExecute` and `mciSendString` to do this; there are lots of examples in the programming chapters, but the best is probably the Visual Basic example in Chapter 16. As a matter of fact, I use that application to show how to access an overlay video device.

If you haven't already installed the application for Chapter 16, here's how to do it. You can find it on the floppy or the CDROM in the directory **\mcitst**. The filename is **mcitst.exe**. It is a self-extracting archive. To extract the file you need, do the following:

➤ Change to or create a destination directory on your hard drive. I suggest **\mcitest**.

➤ If you just want to extract the executable file, type **<drive>:\mcitst\mcitst mcitest.exe**. This will extract just the program we'll be working with, **mcitest.exe**. If you want the source as well, type **<drive>:\mcitst\mcitst**.

If you do not have the DLL for Visual Basic 2.0, you'll need to copy that to your Windows system directory (usually **c:\windows\system**). You'll find it as a self-extracting archive in the directory **<drive>:\utils**. The filename is **vbrun2.exe**. To extract it, change to the Windows system directory, and type **<drive>:\utils\vbrun2**.

Using mcitest.exe

To follow along with this example, you need a video board capable of displaying video overlay. I specifically used the Bravado 16 from Truevision, but boards such as the Video Blaster and Super VideoWindows will work if you have MCI drivers installed for them. Some of the commands may be specific to the Bravado; I'll try to point those out.

The MCI test program is shown in Figure 13.1.

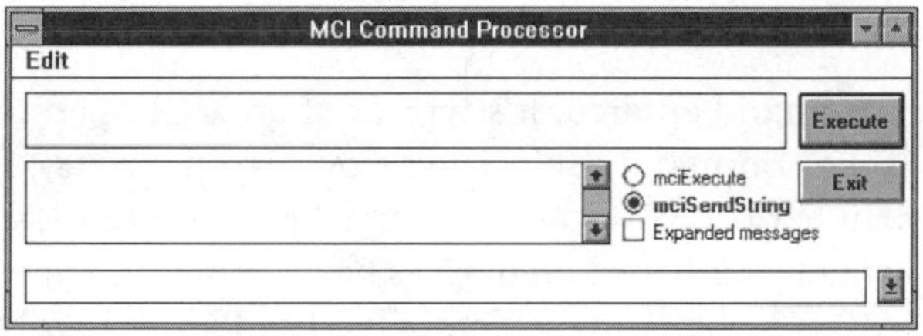

Figure 13.1. MCI Command Processor mcitest.exe.

To use the program, type a command string in the text box at the top of the window, then click the Execute button and the command will be carried out. The results of the command, if any, will be displayed in the middle text box. Each command you enter is stored, and may be viewed, edited, and/or re-executed. To recall a previous command, use the list box at the bottom of the window to view it, and then click on it to place it in the top text box. You can edit it, or execute it by clicking the Execute button.

An example will make this clearer. To open the overlay device (again, this is assuming you have one installed), type in:

```
open overlay style popup alias ovr
```

and click the Execute button. Nothing much happens. All you will see is the return value "1" in the middle text box, as shown in Figure 13.2. The command you typed appears in the list box at the bottom of the window. The list box serves as a collector for your commands. If you want the responses from MCI to be collected as well, check the Expanded messages box.

If you do not have an overlay device installed, or if you do not have an MCI driver for it installed, you'll see an error message instead: **Error: The specified device is not open or is not recognized by MCI**.

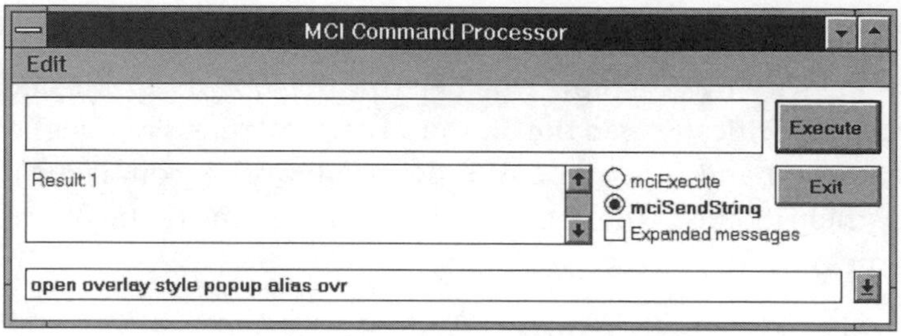

Figure 13.2. Return value from executing MCI open command.

Look at the command entered; it's typical of an MCI open command. The first word, `open` is the command itself. The second word, `overlay`, is the name of the device you want to open. You can also open device elements, such as files, by specifying the filename. Only certain devices have elements. For example, if you want to play an AVI file, that's an element. Overlay doesn't involve files, so you use the device name instead of an element name.

`Style popup` defines the kind of window that MCI will use. A popup window has a single-pixel line around it. The default window is an overlapped window, which has all of the usual window controls, such as minimize, maximize, and it is sizable. I also declared an alias, `ovr`, which will be simpler to type that `overlay` for the remaining commands.

Once the overlay device is open, you can do some fun stuff.

The first order of business is to display the video source in a window:

```
window ovr state show
```

This causes the video input to appear in a window. I can't show you a screen capture of this because of the way that overlay works. The video overlay hardware literally overlays the video image onto the normal VGA or SuperVGA image created by the video display hardware. The MCI driver simply puts a solid rectangle on the screen where the overlay will be, as shown in Figure 13.3. This figure shows an overlapped window to which a title has been added.

If the image were reproduced in color, you would see that the rectangle is magenta. Figure 13.4 shows the image that was displayed in the rectangle—I simply started up the video camera, connected it to the Bravado, and pointed it at myself.

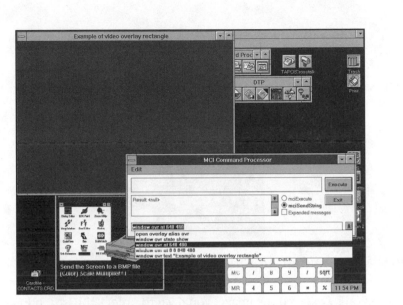

Figure 13.3. Overlay rectangle for a popup window.

Figure 13.4. Sample video image.

You can also freeze the image, locking in a single video frame. The command is simple:

```
freeze ovr
```

You can then save the frozen frame to disk with the save command:

```
save ovr test.tga format tga24
```

The save command uses parameters that are unique to the Bravado 16 overlay card. The resulting image is shown in Figure 13.5.

Figure 13.5. Sample video image saved with MCI command string.

Once you have saved the image, you need to unlock the frozen image if you want to see live video again:

```
unfreeze ovr
```

You've done quite a bit already—you've got live video in a window and saved an image to disk. It was pretty easy to do, too. Even if you take into account the code behind the scenes that is being used to package the commands you're entering, there's still not very much involved. If you are curious about the Visual Basic and Windows API code involved, you can find it in Chapter 16.

There's more that you can do with the MCI overlay driver. You can change the size of the display window:

```
window ovr at 0 0 640 480
```

The window command takes a series of numbers commonly called a rectangle. The first two numbers are the x and y coordinates of the top-left corner, and the next two are the width and height of the rectangle. However, the video is still displaying at default size; to make the video the same size as the window, you need to enter the command:

```
put ovr destinaton at 0 0 640 480
```

You can save this larger, more detailed file with the save command:

```
save ovr test2.tga format tga24
```

You didn't use the freeze command, but that's OK; the save command will freeze the display before it saves. You will need to use the unfreeze command if you want to redisplay live video in the window.

You can also obtain information about the overlay driver from MCI. For example, you can use the where command to find out the size of the destination:

```
where ovr destination
```

MCI responds with 0 0 640 480. If you enter:

```
where ovr video
```

MCI gives the size of the full video buffer: 0 0 720 486.

To end this session, you need to close the overlay device:

```
close ovr
```

There are a number of additional commands supported by the Bravado; the full Bravado command set is shown in Table 13.1.

Table 13.1. MCI Command set for Bravado 16 digital video overlay.

Command	Parameter(s)	Comments
open		Open the bravado mci driver
	alias alias_name	
	parent hwnd	
	style ####	
	style child	
	style overlapped	
	style popup	
	type device_type	
close		Close the bravado mci driver
info		Get information about the bravado mci driver.
	product	truevision bravado mci v1.0
	window text	[video window caption]
	capability	get capabilities of the mci driver.
	device type	Returns: overlay
	windows	Returns: 1

continues

Table 13.1. continued

Command	Parameter(s)	Comments
	can eject	Returns: false
	can play	Returns: false
	can record	Returns: false
	compound device	Returns: false
	uses files	Returns: false
	can freeze	Returns: true
	can stretch	Returns: true
	has audio	Returns: true
	has video	Returns: true
	can save	Returns: true
set (*1)		Control bravado video and
	video	audio functions.
	audio	**on	off**
	source	**all	left	right on	off**
	volume	**1	2	3**
	balance	**#**
	bass	**#**
	treble	**#**
	hue	**#**
	brightness	**#**
	contrast	**#**
	saturation	**#**
	key color	**#### (rgb color format)**
status (*2)		Get current bravado video and
	video	audio settings.
	audio	Returns: true	false (on	off)
	source	Returns: true	false (on	off)
	volume	Returns: 1|2|3
	balance	Returns: #
	bass	Returns: #
	treble	Returns: #
	hue	Returns: #
	brightness	Returns: #
	contrast	Returns: #
	saturation	Returns: #

Command	Parameter(s)	Comments
	key color	Returns: #
	stretch	Returns: ####
	ready	Returns: true | false
	window handle	Returns: true | false
	media present	Returns: [handle of current window]
	mode	Returns: true
		Returns: stopped
freeze		Grab the currently displayed bravado video.
unfreeze		Display live video in the bravado window.
put		Defines the source, destination, and frame (video acquisition) rectangles.
	destination	
	destination at [rectangle]	
	frame	
	frame at [rectangle]	
	source	
	source at [rectangle]	
	video	
	video at [rectangle]	
where		Get the current source, destination, and frame (video acquisition) rectangles.
	destination	
	frame	[rectangle]
	source	[rectangle]
	video	[rectangle]
		[rectangle]

continues

329

Table 13.1. continued

Command	Parameter(s)	Comments
window (*3)	**handle**	Specify the window and/or
	handle default	window state used for video
	state hide	display.
	state iconic	
	state maximized	
	state minimize	
	state minimized	
	state no activate	
	state no action	
	state normal	
	state show	
	text	
	fixed	
	stretch	
	at rectangle	
load (*4)		Load an image into the video
	[filename]	buffer.
	at [rectangle]	
	format tga|mmp	
save (*5)		Save the video buffer.
	[filename]	
	at [rectangle]	
	format tga16|tga24|mmp	

*1 All parameters except VIDEO and AUDIO are Bravado driver extensions to the MCI spec.

*2 All parameters except VIDEO, MEDIA PRESENT, MODE, READY, and WINDOW HANDLE are Bravado driver extensions to the MCI spec.

*3 The AT parameter is a Bravado driver extension to the MCI spec.

*4 The FORMAT parameter is a Bravado driver extension to the MCI spec.

*5 The FORMAT parameter is a Bravado driver extension to the MCI spec.

Table 13.2 shows all of the command strings I entered for the overlay session, and the response generated by MCI. I even included one error to show how that is handled. These commands and responses were collected during a session with the MCI test program, mcitest.exe. You can also use it to test any MCI device or element; it is not limited to use with overlay video.

Table 13.2. A sample session with video overlay commands.

Result	Command	Response from MCI
OK	open overlay style popup alias ovr	1
OK	window ovr state show	\<null\>
OK	freeze ovr	\<null\>
OK	save ovr test.tga format tga24	\<null\>
OK	unfreeze ovr	\<null\>
OK	window ovr at 0 0 640 480	\<null\>
OK	put ovr destination at 0 0 640 480	\<null\>
OK	freeze ovr	\<null\>
OK	save ovr test2.tga format tga24	\<null\>
Error	unfreeze	The specified command requires an alias, file, driver, or device name. Please supply one.
OK	unfreeze ovr	\<null\>
OK	where ovr destination	0 0 640 480
OK	where ovr source	0 0 0 0
OK	where ovr video	0 0 720 486
OK	load ovr test.tga	\<null\>

continues

Table 13.2. continued

Result	Command	Response from MCI
OK	unfreeze ovr	<null>
OK	window ovr at 0 0 320 240	<null>
OK	save ovr test3.tga at 0 0 160 120	<null>
OK	close ovr	<null>

The full set of commands supported by the Bravado 16 MCI overlay driver is shown in Table 13.1. The Bravado MCI driver conforms to the Video Overlay driver specification published by Microsoft. Rectangles are expressed in the form:

```
x y width height
```

with a space between the parameters. Parameters listed as # are in the range 0-255. Parameters listed as ## are in the range 0-65536. Parameters listed as #### are in the range 0-4294967295.

Parameters in brackets are variables that you must specify when you use the command.

Command Messages

Command messages are a more detailed and more powerful way to work with MCI, especially if you are programming in C. Instead of using plain-language commands such as open overlay or close overlay, command messages use Window messages to accomplish their tasks.

The command message interface uses the function mciSendCommand to send messages and receive information from MCI. For example, the following source code for the function get_number_of_devices uses mciSendCommand to query all devices in the system to see if they are open. If it is successful, it returns the value returned by MCI. Otherwise, it returns zero.

```
int PASCAL NEAR get_number_of_devices(void)

{
```

```
MCI_SYSINFO_PARMS sysinfo;
DWORD dwDevices;

/* Set things up so that MCI puts the number of
 *open devices directly
 * into <nDevices>.
 */
sysinfo.lpstrReturn = (LPSTR)(LPDWORD)&dwDevices;
sysinfo.dwRetSize = sizeof(DWORD);

if (mciSendCommand(MCI_ALL_DEVICE_ID, MCI_SYSINFO,
                   MCI_SYSINFO_OPEN ¦
        MCI_SYSINFO_QUANTITY,
            (DWORD)(LPMCI_SYSINFO_PARMS)&sysinfo) != 0)
    return 0;
else
    return (int)dwDevices;
}
```

Look more closely at what is going on in this example. The first thing to notice are the variable declarations at the top of the function:

```
MCI_SYSINFO_PARMS sysinfo;
DWOND dwDovi000;
```

The variable sysinfo uses a data type that is declared as a structure in mmsystem.h:

```
/* parameter block for MCI_SYSINFO command message */
typedef struct tagMCI_SYSINFO_PARMS {
    DWORD    dwCallback;
    LPSTR    lpstrReturn;
    DWORD    dwRetSize;
    DWORD    dwNumber;
    UINT     wDeviceType;
    UINT     wReserved0;
} MCI_SYSINFO_PARMS;
typedef MCI_SYSINFO_PARMS FAR * LPMCI_SYSINFO_PARMS;
```

This structure contains variables that are used to send and receive information. The address of the structure is one of the arguments to mciSendCommand:

```
DWORD WINAPI mciSendCommand (UINT uDeviceID, UINT uMessage,
                             DWORD dwParam1, DWORD dwParam2);
```

The parameters for mciSendCommand are shown in Table 13.3.

Table 13.3. Parameters for mciSendCommand.

Parameter	Description
uDeviceID	This is the device ID of the device that is to receive the command. There are two special cases: use **NULL** when you are opening a device, and use **MCI_ALL_DEVICE_ID** when you want to address all devices.
uMessage	This is the message you are sending. Typical digital video messages include such things as **MCI_OPEN**, **MCI_CLOSE**, and **MCI_FREEZE**.
dwParam1	Specifies flags. Flags are used to signal that certain actions or results are required. For example, you could use the flag **MCI_WAIT** with a **MCI_OPEN** message to specify that you want MCI to complete the open before returning control. The equivalent with a command string would be "open digital video wait."
dwParam2	Specifies a pointer to a parameter block for the command. The parameter block is a structure that contains elements relevant to the message. In the example above, the system information parameter block is used. The block used varies for different messages.

Before calling mciSendCommand in the example, you need to assign some values to particular members of the sysinfo structure:

```
sysinfo.lpstrReturn = (LPSTR)(LPDWORD)&dwDevices;
sysinfo.dwRetSize = sizeof(DWORD);
```

You can now call mciSendCommand. The device ID is set to MCI_ALL_DEVICE_ID, the message is MCI_SYSINFO, the flags are set to MCI_SYSINFO_OPEN | MCI_SYSINFO_QUANTITY (combined, this results in getting the *number* of open devices instead of the *names* of the open devices), and the results will be placed in the sysinfo structure:

```
mciSendCommand(MCI_ALL_DEVICE_ID, MCI_SYSINFO,    MCI_SYSINFO_OPEN |
               MCI_SYSINFO_QUANTITY,    (DWORD)(LPMCI_SYSINFO_PARMS)&sysinfo)
```

This is just a small taste of the command message interface to MCI. Appendix B is a reference to the messages and structures that are needed to use command messages with digital video and overlay devices.

Authoring and Programming Alternatives

You don't use MCI alone, however, to work with multimedia files. MCI is an interface, a method of accessing multimedia functionality. That gives us just two of the three elements of the chain. There is the object of the action—a multimedia device such as digital video—and the opening to get to it, MCI. What is lacking is a tool—a a development environment, a programming language, or an authoring package.

In this section, you'll look at some of the alternatives available. These include visual programming languages, authoring packages, presentation packages, animation software, scripting languages, and programming languages. As you will see, each method has both strengths and weaknesses. Which you use will depend on a variety of factors.

Visual Programming Language: Visual Basic

There are a number of programming languages that use a visual metaphor for programming, but the most used and best known is Visual Basic. It was one of those rare instant success stories—all the more remarkable because it came at a time when it seemed like all of the revolutionary advances in personal computing had already happened.

It's not an exaggeration to say that Visual Basic represented a revolution in programming. Not only did it bring Windows programming to anyone who needed it, it also gives access to the Windows API. Before Visual Basic came along, you needed to program in something like C to get at the power of the Windows API. This was a significant advantage: instead of writing tons of code to handle the Windows interface overhead in order to use a few API functions, a programmer could rely on Visual Basic to handle all of the overhead. Instead of taking days or weeks to write a simple application, a programmer could do it in minutes or hours.

Visual Basic is ideal for many Windows programming tasks. It's strength is in its WYSIWYG (What You See Is What You Get) interface—if you need a check box (individual window elements are called *controls),* you just plop one down on a window. Visual Basic will handle all of the overhead. For digital video programming, Visual Basic is most useful when you just need to access MCI in simple ways:

➤ Playing video files.

➤ Managing overlay display and capture of individual frames.

➤ Simple multimedia utilities—image browsers, file utilities, and so on.

In addition, Visual Basic can be extended by competent C programmers in powerful and interesting ways, including the creation of custom controls.

If you need to add hypertext capabilities, or want sophisticated control over MCI, look elsewhere because Visual Basic does not support hypertext, and it does not allow use of the notify flag (MCI can notify a window when a particular multimedia even, such as completion of playback, occurs).

Be sure to get the Professional Edition of Visual Basic, 2.0 or later, because it contains a large amount of very useful custom controls.

Authoring Packages: Interactive

Interactive, from HSC, is a high-level authoring package that also offers some scripting control for MCI access. Most of your application design is done by placing or rearranging icons in a flow chart. A typical Interactive session is shown in Figure 13.6.

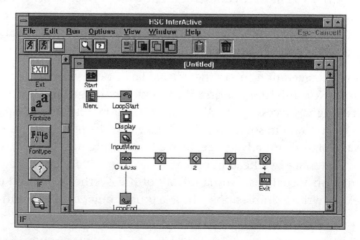

Figure 13.6. Typical Interactive design session.

The important features to note are the vertical row of icons at the left of the window, and the icon-based flow chart. To add icons to the flow chart, you just click and drag them from the row of icons to the desired position in the chart. Some icons, such as the Menu icon, expand into a series of icons. This makes it very easy to structure your programs.

To control what an icon does, double-click it. This opens a content editor specific to that type of icon. This allows you to specify things like filenames for image, position on the screen, special transition effects, and so forth. A typical content editor is shown in Figure 13.7.

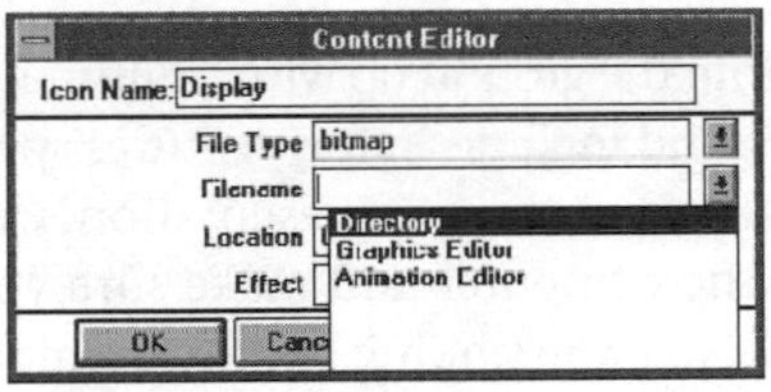

Figure 13.7. Typical Interactive content editor dialog box.

HSC Interactive offers a subset of the tool found in Icon Author, a high end (and much more expensive) authoring system. The strength of both packages lies in the ease with which you can quickly develop interactive multimedia presentations. It's relatively easy to set up icons, all in a row, and then assign bitmaps, colors, AVI files, etc. to them using content editors.

Interactive also has some weaknesses you should know about. It is not very good for putting large amounts of text on the screen—you can only put one line of text to the screen per icon. This is fine for titles and bulleted lists, but does not work for anything more text-intensive than that. Another weakness involves placement of resource files, like bitmaps or animations. HSC puts hard-coded paths into a special file for all resources. If you plan to publish or distribute your application, your users will have to use those same paths. This makes Interactive more suitable for situations where you have complete control, such as sales presentations, board room presentations, kiosks, self-running demos, and similar applications.

Presentation Packages: Compel

Presentation packages have been around for a long time, and many of them have tried to ride the multimedia bandwagon. After all, multimedia has a lot of impact, and the best presentations need to have impact to be—well, compelling.

Existing presentation packages have one problem, however: they were coded before the advent of multimedia. Many of them have done a very good job of integrating multimedia into the package, but a new product has just been introduced that redefines the use of multimedia in presentations. It's called Compel, and it's from the same folks who brought us Multimedia Toolbook: Asymetrix.

Compel was built from the ground up with multimedia in mind, and it shows. The interface is smooth, and includes many features specifically for multimedia. For example, before you try to run your presentation, Compel will scan the multimedia capabilities of the computer and make sure you have all of the media available that you need. No more finding out in the middle of the third slide that you don't have the right sound card in your machine. Compel will also "package" your presentation for transfer to other machines.

Compel is a solid package, and should challenge the current crop of presentation packages strongly. Let's take a look at how easy it is to add a digital video file to a Compel presentation.

Figure 13.8 shows a typical working screen in Compel—there is a toolbar at the top, several palettes are displayed, and the slide itself is in the background. Nothing very different so far. Notice that the button "View Video" at the bottom of the slide is selected (it has sizing handles visible).

The Effects menu has a selection called Media Links that you can use to open a dialog box shown in Figure 13.9.

It contains two lists: triggering events on the left, and actions on the right. We can pick from the list of triggering events (in this case, "When Clicked"), and then pick from the available actions. Naturally, we want Play Digital Video, as shown in Figure 13.10.

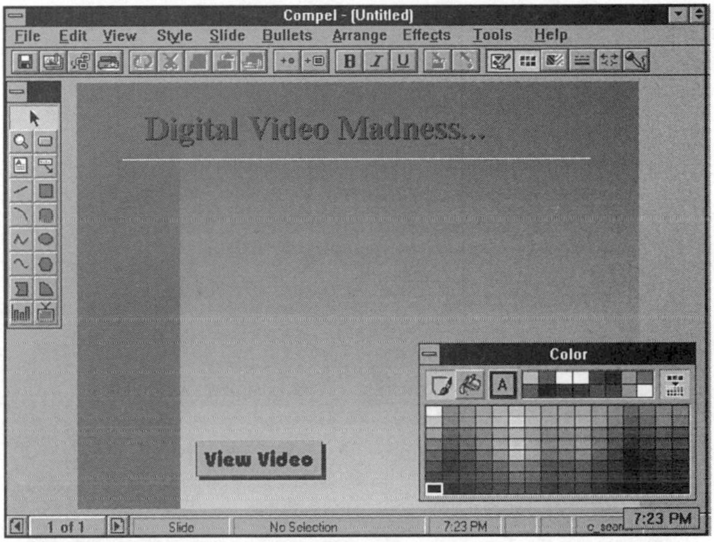

Figure 13.8. A typical Compel window.

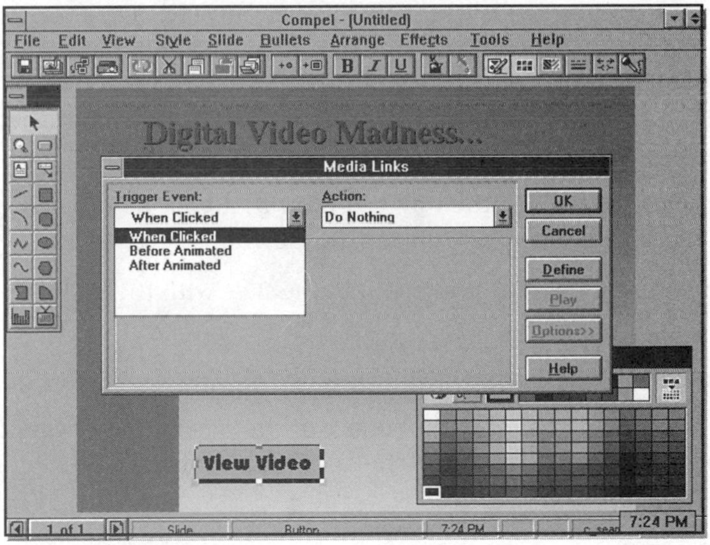

Figure 13.9. Compel Media Links dialog box.

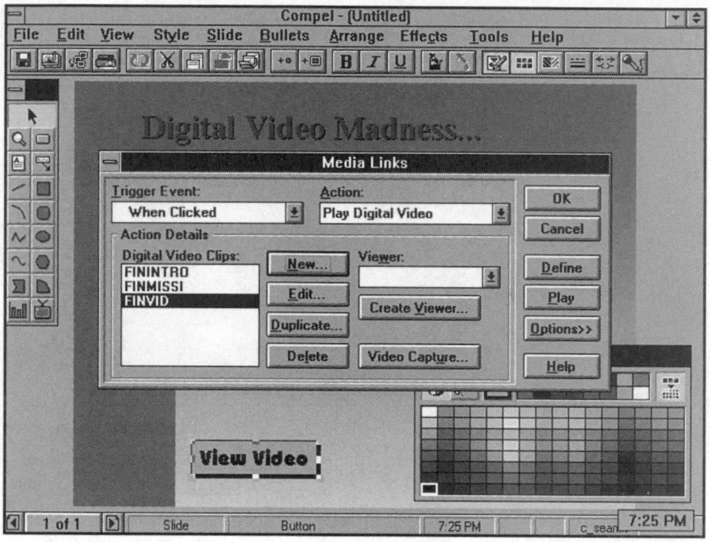

Figure 13.10. Selecting digital video as a Media Link in Compel.

We can establish a fine level of control over the playback of the video file, as shown in Figure 13.11. We can select a start frame, an end frame, create a name for the clip, test the beginning and ending portions of the selection, play the file, and so on. This gives you complete control over the multimedia aspects of your presentation.

Once you have the clip the way you want it, it appears as a generic viewer. You can assign names to viewer objects, as shown in Figure 13.12.

When you play the slide presentation, the slide with the View Video button looks like Figure 13.13.

Clicking the View Video button plays the video, as shown in Figure 13.14.

This example touches only the surface of the capabilities of Compel. If you are looking for an easy yet powerful way to use multimedia in your presentation, check this out!

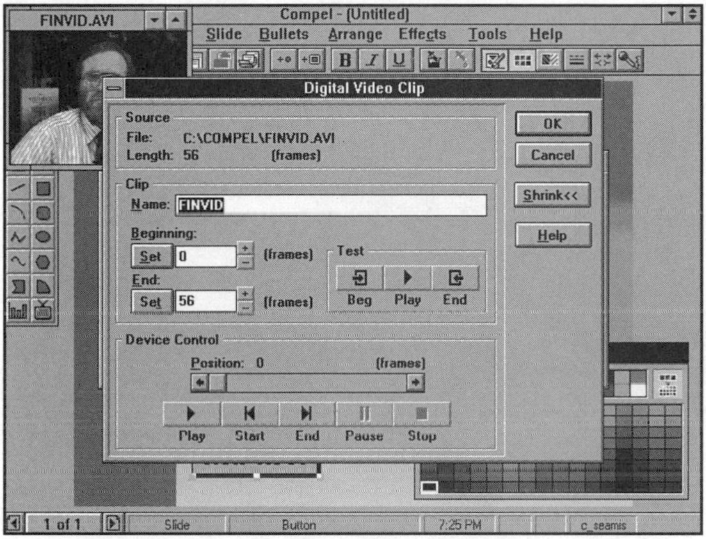

Figure 13.11. Testing and selecting a digital video clip.

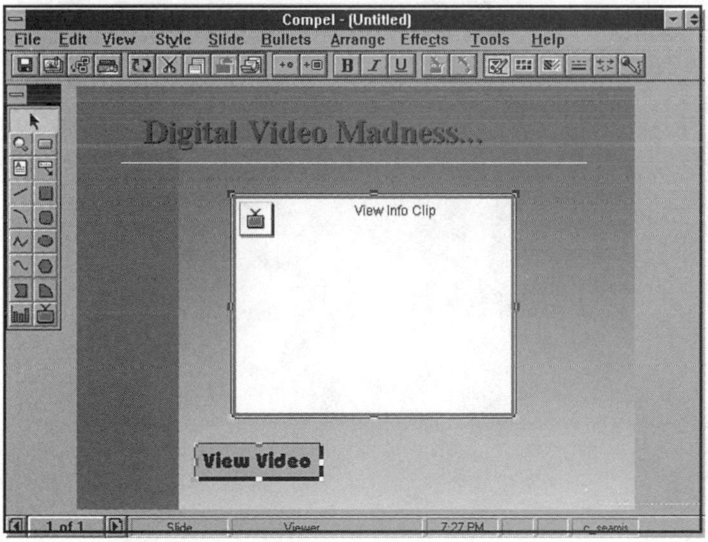

Figure 13.12. A viewer object in Compel.

Figure 13.13. The slide while running the presentation.

Figure 13.14. The slide after clicking the View Video button.

Animation Software: Animation Works Interactive

One of the best animation packages for business-style animation is Animation Works Interactive. It combines a solid set of animation capabilities with a strong business orientation. (See chapter 6 for a closer look at this product.)

Adding video to an animation is straightforward; there are even two ways to do it. You can either create a "Video Event" or you can use MCI command strings.

Figure 13.15 shows a typical Animation Works screen. It shows a presentation which has already had its graphic elements and actors put into position; all we need to add is the video. The Event menu has a selection for Video. Clicking it opens the Video Event dialog box (see Figure 13.16).

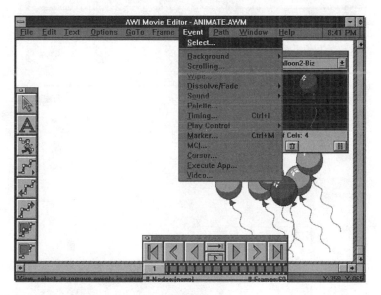

Figure 13.15. Typical Animation Works screen.

The Video Event editor supports both playback and overlay devices. Unlike Compel, it does not support video capture directly, but you could easily run VidCap if necessary; this is, after all, Windows. You can select a file to play, and position the playback rectangle on the screen (see Figure 13.17).

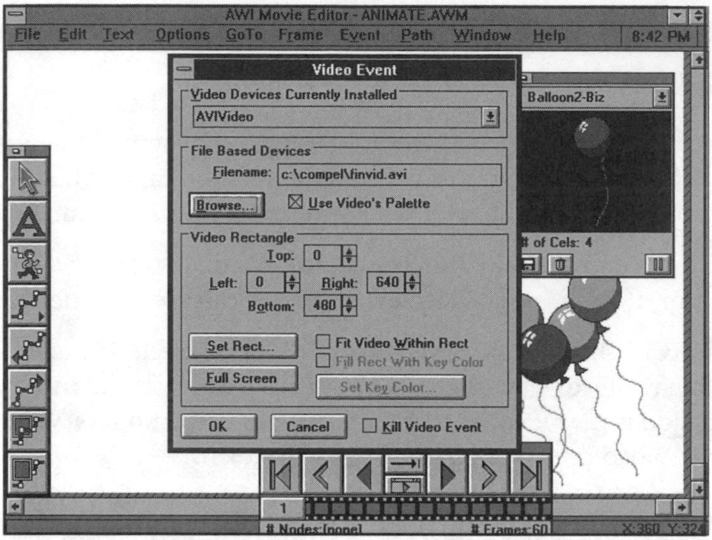

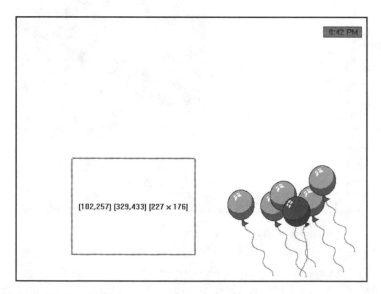

Figure 13.16. Video Event editor.

Figure 13.17. Positioning the video window.

When you play the animation, everything happens at once: the balloons flut-
ter upward along their predefined paths, and the video plays in the background

(see Figure 13.18). I tested this program on a 486/66 DX2, and it played very smoothly.

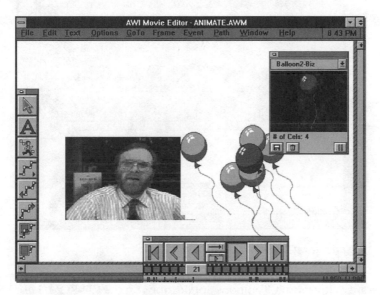

Figure 13.18. Video playback in Animation Works.

You can also use MCI command strings to play video files or control overlay devices. The Event menu has a selection called "MCI" that pops up a window (see Figure 13.19). You can enter one or a series of MCI commands in the window, and you can save to and load from disk.

When the frame containing the MCI commands is reached, the commands are sent to MCI. If you use a "wait" flag, the animation will wait until the command is carried out. Otherwise, the animation continues on while the MCI commands are executed. In that case, synchronization will be somewhat loose between the animation and the video or sound.

Scripting Language: Toolbook

Toolbook is a very powerful package, and it is hard to stuff it into one category or another. You can use it as an authoring package to create simple but impressive presentations, or you can use it like a programming language to create sophisticated custom applications, or you can use a combination of these two methods. Toolbook is a multi-layered product—appropriate for a multimedia authoring/programming tool.

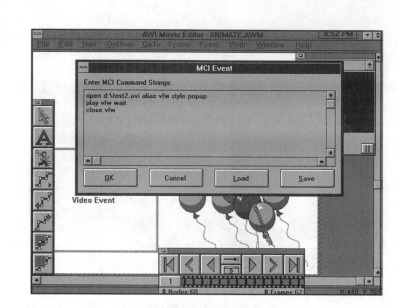

Figure 13.19. Entering MCI commands in Animation Works.

There are many sample Toolbook applications on the CD-ROM. I use Toolbook frequently when I need to create a multimedia presentation or application. I like its power and flexibility, but it takes some time to learn how to use it effectively. Unlike some programs, the time you take to learn Toolbook is time well spent. Because Toolbook is a WYSIWYG development program, the screen looks like whatever you want to to look like; there is no specific design metaphor, such as the icons in Interactive. One of the best-known applications developed with Toolbook is Multimedia Beethoven. A sample screen is shown in Figure 13.20. Note how the screen designer was free to create a unique layout specifically for Multimedia Beethoven.

Let's take a quick look at the multi-layered architecture of Toolbook development. At the highest layer, you can simply put objects where you want them to create a look that suits your application. Objects include such things as text boxes, buttons, bitmaps, and painted objects (circles, lines, and so on). You can then use simple scripts to make the objects do what you need done. Most scripts are called *handlers*. This means that they handle events. For example, you might write a script for a button that handles a button down event. You can even create your own events with the send command, so you are not limited to the obvious Windows-interface events such as key presses and mouse clicks.

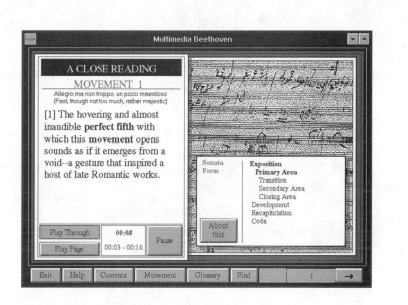

Figure 13.20. Sample screen from the Toolbook-developed Multimedia Beethoven.

Toolbook's strengths include powerful text-handling capabilities (including hypertext linking), full multimedia support including callback, a very powerful and sophisticated scripting language, and excellent technical support. Toolbook does have some weaknesses, too. The manual for the current edition (Version 1.53 as we went to press) is weak, and you will probably need to take advantage of that excellent technical support to learn some of the subtler techniques of scripting. The weak documentation is almost offset by a large and useful set of scripting examples. Most important of these is one called Multimedia Widgets. It includes a wide variety of useful objects—buttons that load bitmaps, buttons to play multimedia files using MCI, and lots of other useful code. Best of all, you can simply copy a widget from the sample to your own application. This provides a medium level of functionality; if you want to use the full multimedia power of Toolbook, you'll need to invest some time to learn the ins and outs of the scripting language.

Programming Language: C/C++

The most flexible and powerful way to program for multimedia is, of course, C/C++. At the same time, the most challenging, frustrating and limiting way to program for multimedia is, of course, C/C++. It all depends on your point of view.

If you want a multimedia program that runs with great speed, C is your answer. If you want to develop a multimedia program quickly, C is *not* your answer. If you want detailed control over playback of video files, or the way that the screen is laid out, C is your answer. If you want to make changes to anything quickly, C is out.

This will change to a degree with the introduction of Visual C from Microsoft. Adding many of the advantages of Visual Basic to C, it will allow you to develop with the best of both worlds: the power and flexibility of C, and the development speed of a WYSIWYG environment.

14

OLE Basics:
Working with
Media Player

In Chapter 2, you saw how easy it is to use Media Player to embed video objects in a document. In this chapter, I'll show you how other programs can be used in place of Media Player to provide different capabilities for the embedded object.

Media Player provides a base level of functionality for video objects: you can link, you can embed, and you can play the file. About the fanciest thing you can do with Media Player is to select only a portion of the video file for embedding. Media Player allows you to select a start point and end point other than the beginning and ending of the file you are embedding.

Working with OLE: Media Blitz

OLE isn't just video files; it will work with all kinds of multimedia files, including images and sounds. If you use OLE, you can avoid programming—OLE allows you to dress up documents and applications quickly and without much fuss.

Media Player is just one example of an application that you can use as a media object editor. Many commercial programs also give you this capability. You may have used Paintbrush (pbrush.exe), for example, as an object editor in Windows.

One product that makes maximum use of OLE is Media Blitz, from Asymetrix. It does some of the same things that Media Player does, but in much more powerful ways. For example, Media Player will allow you to adjust the starting and end points of a media clip. With Media Blitz, you can include a variety of clips in an OLE object. You can easily combine a video clip, a musical score in a MIDI file, and a series of bitmaps into a single, easy-to-play OLE object.

Take a look at how this can be done. Start with an application called ClipMaker. It allows you to assemble a collection of clips, and to set beginning and end points for each clip. Clips can be MIDI, Wave, video, or animation files, or CD audio. Figure 14.1 shows a typical ClipMaker window, with two clips already selected and their beginning and ending points set.

Note that the middle portion of the ClipMaker window is designed to allow you to easily edit the clip. It includes controls for playing just the first few or last few seconds of the clip to check your work, and it allows you to specify the clip beginning and ending points numerically. The bottom portion of the window is used to select the type of clip and to play, rewind, etc., the entire clip. The MIDI clip in Figure 14.1 has been edited to a total of 10 seconds; using ClipMaker, I was able to start and end the clip right on the beat. The video clip is 140 frames at 15 frames per second, or 9.33 seconds long. You'll see why I made them different lengths in a moment.

Figure 14.1. ClipMaker with two clips loaded.

Next you go to the ScoreMaker application (see Figure 14.2). With ScoreMaker, you can combine various clips into a complete multimedia presentation. You can load several clip files, and have multiple scores available at the same time. In Figure 14.2, there are three clips loaded and arranged on the timeline at the bottom of the window:

➤ The MIDI clip that I created in ClipMaker (10 seconds out of 15 total in the file).

➤ The video clip that I created in ClipMaker (9.33 seconds out of 24.2 total in the file).

➤ A bitmap, which will be displayed for a total of 11 seconds.

If you look closely at Figure 14.2, the three bands at the bottom of the window represent, from top to bottom, the MIDI clip, the video clip, and the bitmap.

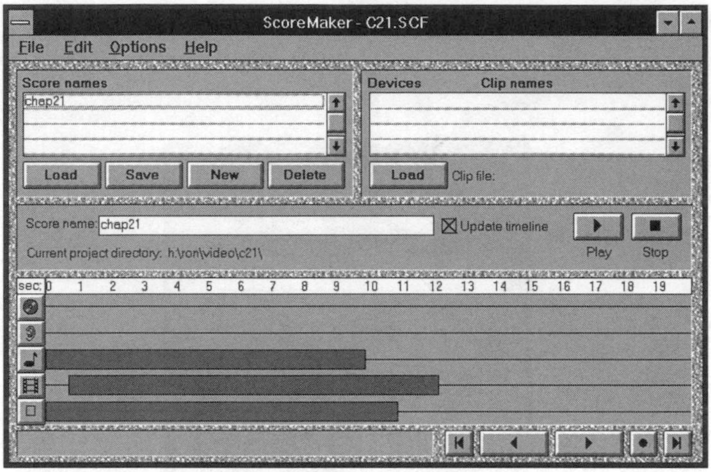

Figure 14.2. ScoreMaker with three clips in the timeline.

The bitmap is new; I did not add the bitmap to ClipMaker. I added it to ScoreMaker after I added the two clips in the ClipMaker file. You can use both complete files and ClipMaker clips in a score. In fact, you can even do most of the things you can do in ClipMaker with ScoreMaker. I find that using ClipMaker first allows me to focus on the job of selecting good clips, which I can use later in ScoreMaker.

You can easily play the score for testing by clicking the Play button in the middle of the ScoreMaker window; playback is shown in Figure 14.3. As you can see, the bitmap serves as a background, while the AVI video file plays in the foreground. As shown in the timeline, the bitmap is displayed at the same time the music starts. After a .7 second delay, the AVI file plays. The AVI file and the music end at the same time, 10 seconds into the score. The bitmap remains displayed for one second after playback ends. This provides an easy transition for the viewer, rather than an abrupt end to both music and visuals.

Once a score is complete, you can easily use OLE to add the score to any application that supports OLE. To incorporate a score this way, open ScorePlayer (see Figure 14.4) and load a score file. Then simply use the Edit/Copy menu selection to put the media object on the clipboard, just as you did with Media Player. Then you can use the Edit/Paste command to paste the media object into your application.

Figure 14.3. A score being played.

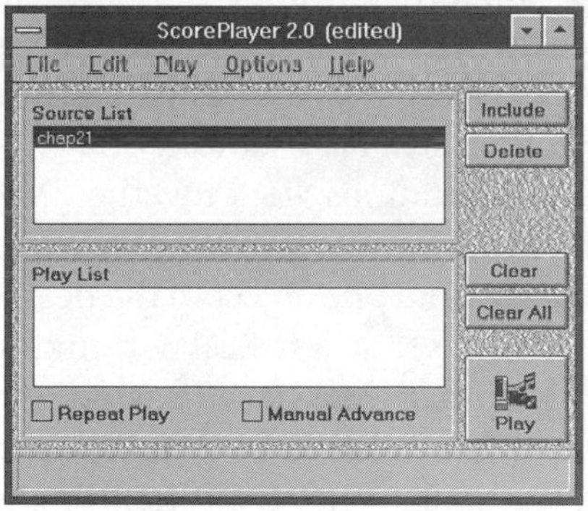

Figure 14.4. ScorePlayer with a score file loaded.

The Future of OLE: Version 2.0

Microsoft has big plans for the future of OLE. Version 2.0 threatens to dramatically change the way we work with computers. It goes much further than the

current implementations of OLE. At a recent conference where the new OLE was discussed, Microsoft made it clear that they would like Version 2.0 to create nothing less than a revolution in computing.

And what might that revolution look like? Today, even working in Windows, most of what you do is based on whatever application you happen to be working in. If you want to write a letter, you use a word processor. If you want to do some calculations, you load up a spreadsheet such as Excel or 1-2-3. If you want to create an illustration, you run CorelDRAW! or Freehand. OLE 2.0 would like to change all that. It would like to make the document the center of your computing. No matter what you are doing, you would do it in a single document. If you want to do a graphic illustration, the document's menu and tool bar changes to graphic-oriented choices. If you need some calculations—presto-chango, your menu is now appropriately configured. As you move through your document, the menu will reflect whatever application you chose for that part of the document. You can edit the various kinds of data—images, text, spreadsheets, and so forth—without leaving your document.

That's because OLE 2.0 will offer you the capability of seamless linking and embedding—once it is supported by application developers. Thus, the *potential* is there to change the way we work with our computers. We have yet to see the results, but Microsoft is making it as easy as possible for developers to add OLE 2.0 support to their applications. For example, one obvious and important issue is how well all of these applications work together. Microsoft has opened a lab where software vendors can work together to make sure that you can, indeed, move seamlessly and easily from one object to the next in your document. Nonetheless, OLE 2.0 is nothing less than a radical re-thinking of how we use our computers, and it seems likely that we'll have to wrestle with the fallout from the changes through a few future versions of OLE. Like most ambitious new metaphors for computing, document-centered computing will have to evolve based on real-world "testing."

15

Basic Programming: MCI in Multimedia Viewer

For several years, the best-kept secret in multimedia programming was a Microsoft program called Viewer. With the release of Version 2.0, now called Multimedia Viewer, Microsoft is moving this once-a-dinosaur into the multimedia mainstream. It is worth a serious look if your authoring or programming tasks meet the right criteria.

To be a good candidate for Viewer, a multimedia project should:

➤ Have large amounts of text.

➤ Need Viewer's text search capabilities.

➤ Be suitable for breaking into small (one or two pages in size) topics.

By large amounts of text, I mean one of two things: either the application simply has a lot of text (ten, a hundred, or even thousands of pages), or that the ratio of text to other media is large. For projects with very small amounts of text, almost any multimedia authoring tool will work. For intermediate amounts of text, and text applications that don't require search capabilities, Toolbook is excellent. When text becomes the predominant medium, however, Viewer becomes the authoring system of choice.

I need to add a note of caution to that last statement. Even though Viewer is well suited to such projects, it has some built-in limitations that may be problematic. You should look at Viewer carefully before you choose it for a project. Although Viewer 2.0 goes far beyond Version 1.0, it still has a way to go before it provides excellent ease of use.

A little history lesson will make this clearer. In Version 1.0, Viewer was basically an unusual programming environment. You used complex and numerous codes to indicate what you wanted to do. That's bad enough, of course; we'd all like WYSIWYG instead of strange codes. But Viewer 1.0 took things a step further into the strange: it required that you use Microsoft Word RTF files as input. This meant that you had to struggle with things like hidden text, footnotes with obscure meanings, and embedded commands right in your document. It worked, but the frustration level was high.

There are many subtle differences and many multimedia improvements in Viewer 2.0 that mask its connections to Viewer 1.0. For example, Viewer 2.0 still uses strange, embedded codes, but now there are tools that allow you to click options in a dialog box and then write the codes for you. This makes Viewer accessible to a much wider audience, even if it's still not a WYSIWYG application.

With all of this in mind, you'll spend the rest of this chapter experimenting with Viewer 2.0. This will give you a good idea of what it is like to work with Viewer and its capabilities.

The new tools actually make Viewer an easy way to create a multimedia application. It is particularly well suited to converting existing documents to multimedia because you can just load the existing document, formatting and all, into Word for Windows. By pressing a hot key combination, you can easily access the Viewer 2.0 Tools.

I surprised myself by liking Viewer; I usually prefer to work with WYSIWYG tools. Viewer adds some key functionality that other multimedia tools simply don't have. Its most important strengths are its capability to organize and search through text, the ease with which you can add hyperlinks, and the ease with which you can add multimedia to a text document.

If you can manage to bend your thinking to Viewer's unique way of working with text and multimedia, you just might find it a useful addition to your multimedia tool kit.

Working with Viewer 2.0

Viewer consists of several parts; the two parts you'll use the most are the Project Editor and the Topic Editor. The Project Editor collects all of the files related to a project—text and multimedia files—and enables you to configure the project. The Topic Editor is accessible via a hot key while you work in Word for Windows; you can use the Topic Editor to integrate Viewer 2.0 features into your text relatively easily.

Viewer Project Editor

Figure 15.1 shows the Project Editor window. It includes a toolbar with the most commonly used functions and a large working area where two kinds of files are listed: text files and baggage files. The text files are all listed as RTF files, a special format used by Viewer and supported by all versions of Microsoft Word. Baggage files are almost any kind of multimedia files. The Project Editor includes a compiler, and the baggage files will be included as resources by the compiler.

Certain kinds of files, such as videos, cannot be loaded as resources—they are so large that it doesn't make sense.

Figure 15.1. Viewer Project Editor.

Figure 15.1 shows one RTF file listed: **c:\ron\video\c25\c25_vwr.rtf**. To create a sample viewer file, I took the source for a portion of a chapter in this book, saved it as an RTF file, and built a Viewer application from that file. For fun, I chose the chapter about Toolbook. You might think that Viewer and Toolbook are competitors, but in reality each is best at different things. They complement one another. If I had a text-intensive application, I would probably prefer to use Viewer for the title. If I had many multimedia files to integrate, I'd use Toolbook because it is stronger at that.

Most of the "action" in Viewer development occurs in your word processor. Technically, you can use any word processor that supports RTF files, but the best one to use is Word for Windows. This takes you as close as possible to WYSIWYG development. Any text formatting you apply, from paragraph spacing to the color of the text, will be carried forward into the RTF file, and, ultimately, to the final application. Figure 15.2 shows the start of a file in Word for Windows. It shows the table of contents for the Viewer application (which is about Toolbook—I couldn't resist).

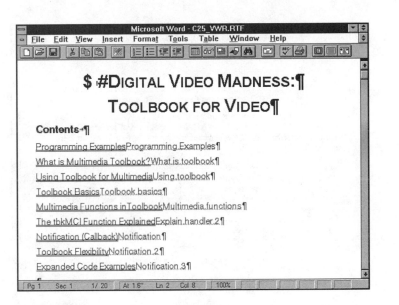

Figure 15.2. Marked text in a text file destined for Viewer.

There are a few things worth noting in this illustration. Look at a close-up of a portion of the window in Figure 15.2, which shows the text at full size. As you can see, there are two kinds of text: text that is double underlined, and text that has a dotted underline. The double underlined text is text that is "hot." That is, the text will trigger a hyperlink when it is clicked. The text with the dotted underline specifies where to jump to. This is called a *context string,* and somewhere in the project each of these context strings must be defined.

The most basic Viewer title consists of topics and context strings. A topic is defined with hard page breaks, as shown by the horizontal lines in Figure 15.3. All of the text in one topic is displayed in a single window. If there is more text than can fit in the window, Viewer will add scroll bars to the window. The topic title is at the top, just under the horizontal bar. See that dollar sign and number sign to the left of the title? Those are Viewer codes. The dollar sign means there is a topic title embedded, and the number sign indicates an embedded context string. At runtime, topic titles are displayed in a special part of the window, and context strings are used as jump destinations.

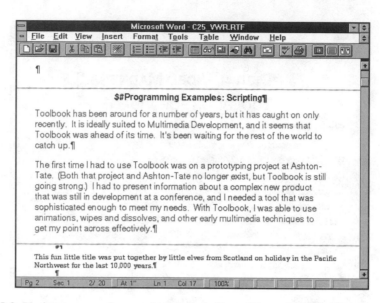

Figure 15.3. Various arcane signs and symbols indicate Viewer features in text.

To add or edit topics and context strings, you can use the Viewer Topic Editor. It is accessed with a hot key from within Word for Windows. To use the Topic Editor, you select the appropriate text and press the hot key (the default combination is Ctrl+Shift+T). The Topic Editor window has two parts—a list of elements that were in the text you selected, and specific information about each element. (See Figure 15.4.)

The way that Viewer stores this information in your text is a bit funky, but it works. Figure 15.5 shows the Word for Windows View menu, which has a selection for displaying footnotes—that's where Viewer keeps the information it needs about Viewer elements. (See Figure 15.6.)

That's the essence of how Viewer works. You operate on the text content of your title in a word processor, and the codes for the various links and jumps are stored in obscure codes. In Viewer 1.0, this was a nightmare of memorization. With Viewer 2.0, you can use the Topic Editor to create Viewer elements—including display of video files.

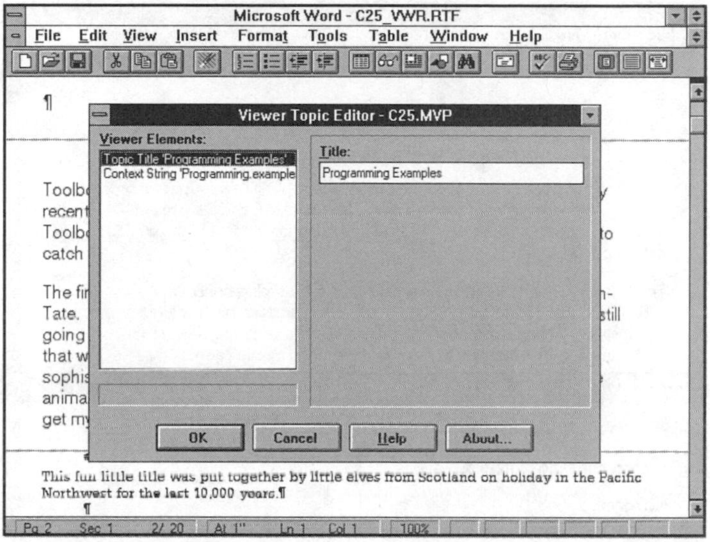

Figure 15.4. The Viewer Topic Editor.

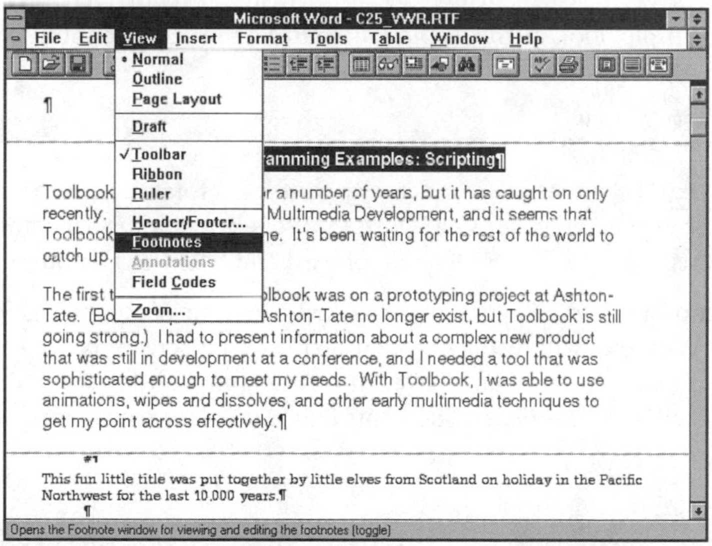

Figure 15.5. Accessing Viewer information with the Footnote pane.

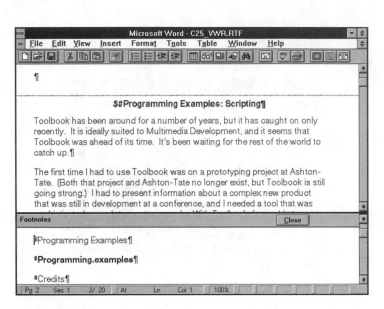

Figure 15.6. Topic titles and context strings in the Footnote pane.

For example, look at the Topic Editor in Figure 15.7. It shows two viewer elements:

```
Hot Spot 'Open a movie!'
Command 'PaneID(qchPath, 'PlayMovie>LowerLft',0)
```

The second element, Command, actually contains a total of three commands, as you can see at the upper-right of Figure 15.7. The two additional commands enable buttons that you can use to step forward and backward through the video.

The commands, like context strings, exist in your document as *hidden text*. Word for Windows will display hidden text on your screen, but it won't print, and it won't show up in your Viewer title after compilation. The hidden text is used to store Viewer elements. The Topic Editor takes care of creating the hidden text.

Note

Although the Topic Editor will do the work for you, there is nothing stopping you from typing in Viewer commands, hot spots, context strings, etc. manually. Unless you're already an experienced user of Viewer 1.0, you will probably want to avoid doing that at all costs.

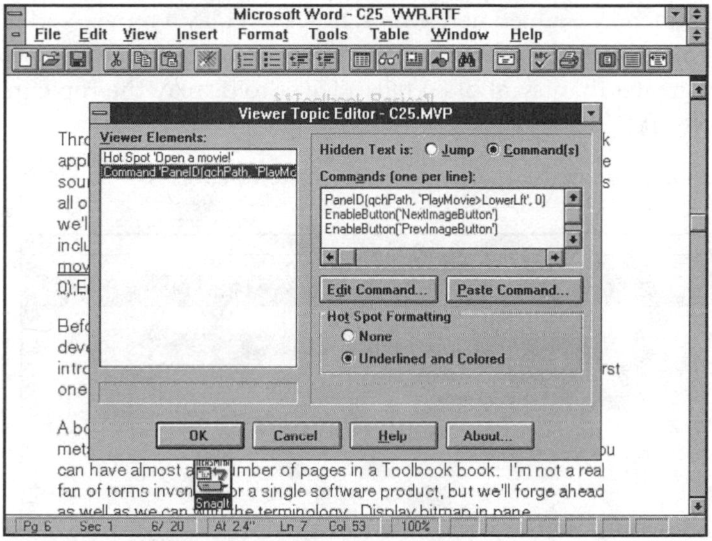

Figure 15.7. Adding a video to Viewer 2.0.

The Topic Editor allows you to edit commands in a convenient way (see Figure 15.8). By clicking the Edit Command button, you display a series of list boxes containing the valid input for each element of a command.

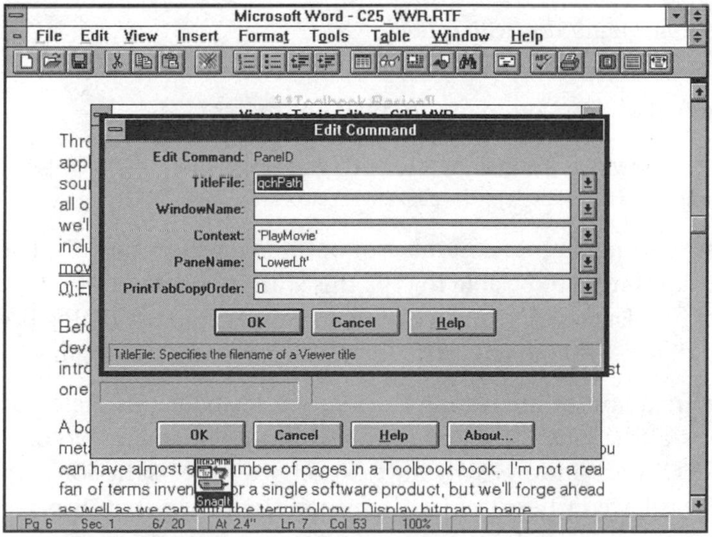

Figure 15.8. Editing a command.

The command we added here won't, however, play a movie—all it will do is underline the text "Play a movie!" at runtime, and jump to the PlayMovie context string. The greater than symbol (>) tells Viewer to display the topic in the pane called "Lowerlft."

The real action occurs at the PlayMovie context, as shown in Figure 15.9.

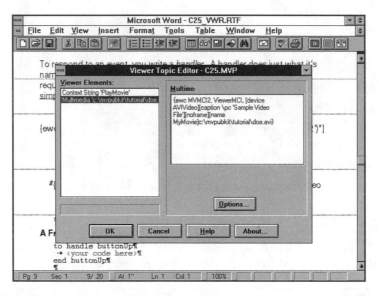

Figure 15.9. Playing a Video, with options.

The actual Viewer command for playing the movie is:

```
{ewc MVMCI2, ViewerMCI, [device AVIVideo][caption \pc 'Sample Video
File'][noframe][name MyMovie]c:\mvpubkit\tutorial\doe.avi}
```

This text string defines a number of options for the video display and playback. You don't need to be able to type this stuff in, however. See that little Options button in Figure 15.9? A click on it reveals a very busy dialog box that you can use to define the characteristics for video playback. (See Figure 15.10.)

There are a host of interesting things to note about this dialog box. For example, look at the tabs at the top of the window—there are two operating systems listed! One is Windows, which we expect; the other is the Sony XA CD-ROM player. If you haven't heard of it, it's a small CD player that displays only text and images. It runs Modular Windows, and you can use Viewer to program titles for it.

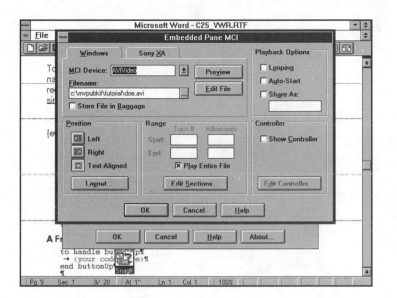

Figure 15.10. Setting options for playing an AVIVideo.

But all we'll need for now is the ability to program for Windows as we know it. This dialog, by the way, applies to a variety of different multimedia data types, not just Video. You can also use it for CD Audio, MM Movies, Sequences, and Wave Audio by selecting the appropriate device in the MCI Device list box. Other important elements of playback that you can control include:

Position—the video can be placed at the left or right margins, or it can be aligned with the text. If you elect to specify Layout options, you can specify the position and content of a caption (see Figure 15.11), define the image size, and put a frame around the image. Captions can be multi-line.

Range—You can select a range to play; this feature isn't particularly useful with video files because it is oriented toward tracks and times, not frames.

Controller—If desired, you can show a controller for controlling playback. If you elect not to show the controller, the user can play the video by simply clicking the image to start and pause playback.

Playback options—This allows you to loop or automatically start playback.

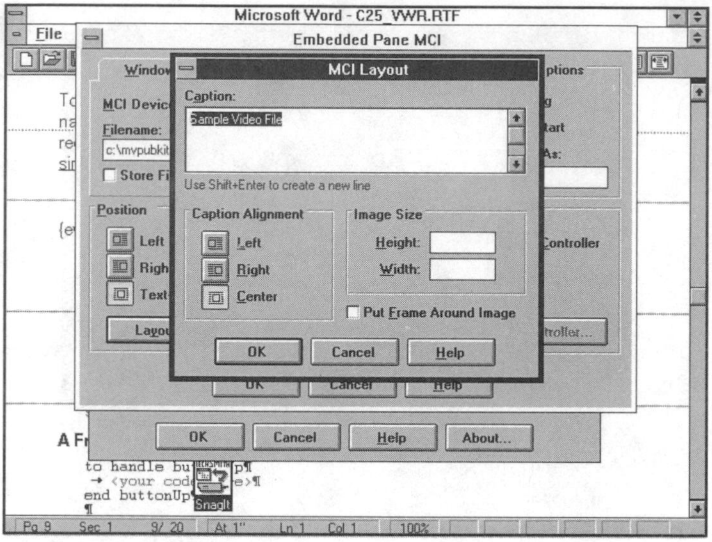

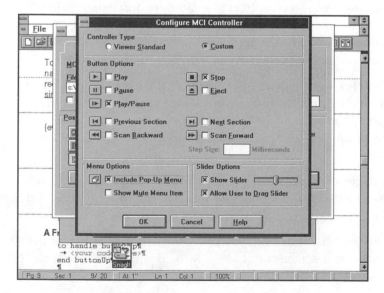

Figure 15.11. MCI Layout dialog.

The controller is highly configurable, as shown in Figure 15.12.

Figure 15.12. Configuring the MCI controller.

You can determine which of nine different button appears on the controller, and you can also add a pop-up menu and a slider showing position in the file.

I found these dialog boxes to be a very convenient way to set the options for video playback in Viewer. The resulting command string is long and complex, but it does the job well.

Once you have set the options, created commands, hot spots, jumps, topic titles, context strings and all of the other Viewer elements you need for your title, you can compile the project in the Project Editor. Errors are automatically logged to a file for review.

Once the title is compiled, you can run it. The first topic in most cases is a table of contents. A table of contents is really nothing more than a series of jumps to the various main topics, as shown in Figure 15.13.

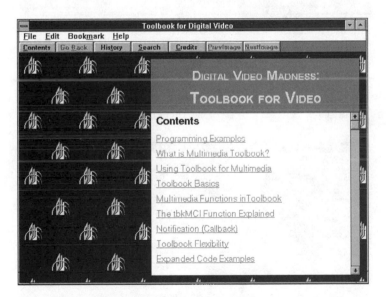

Figure 15.13. A running Viewer application.

You can't see it in black and white, but the underlined text is in green; the combination of underline and color is used to indicate that this is jump text—if you click it, you'll jump to the topic indicated in the hidden text we saw in Figure 15.2.

Clicking jump text takes you right to the topic, as shown in Figure 15.14.

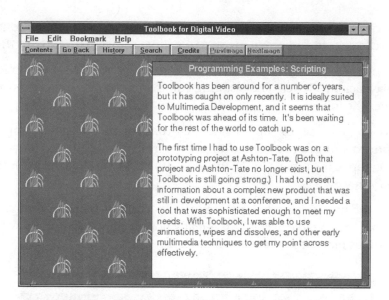

Figure 15.14. A simple topic displayed in Viewer.

If the topic contains more text than can be displayed in the active window, Viewer automatically adds scroll bars, as shown in Figure 15.15.

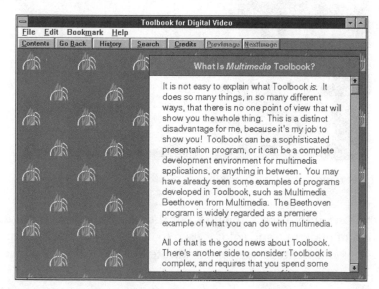

Figure 15.15. Scroll bars are automatically supplied as needed.

You can create hot spots that don't jump to a new topic, but merely display additional information, as shown in Figure 15.16.

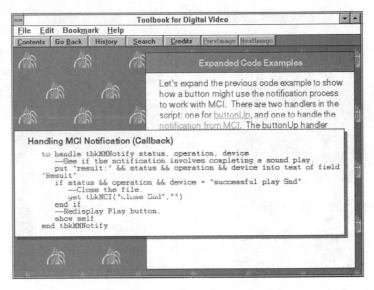

Figure 15.16. Displaying additional text information with a hot spot.

Figure 15.17 shows the text with the hot spot for displaying the video file that we looked at earlier. Note that the text is underlined; this indicates that it is a hot spot.

Clicking the hot text causes the video to be displayed. If you recall, the command for displaying it calls for it to appear in the pane LowerLft, which is a separate pane from the one the text is displayed in. This allows us to have both the text and the video displayed at the same time, as shown in Figure 15.18.

The video can be played by clicking it (without a controller, that's the only way to play it). The video will remain displayed either until we move to another topic, or until we put something else into the LowerLft pane.

Configuring Viewer

Before compiling your title, you can configure a wide range of parameters in Viewer. These parameters are found on the Section menu, as a series of choices.

(See Figure 15.19.) Many of these menu items correspond to special sections in the Viewer title; these are enclosed in square brackets and capitalized.

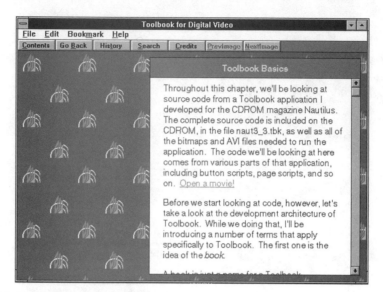

Figure 15.17. The hot spot for playing a video.

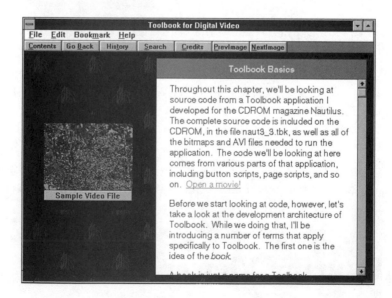

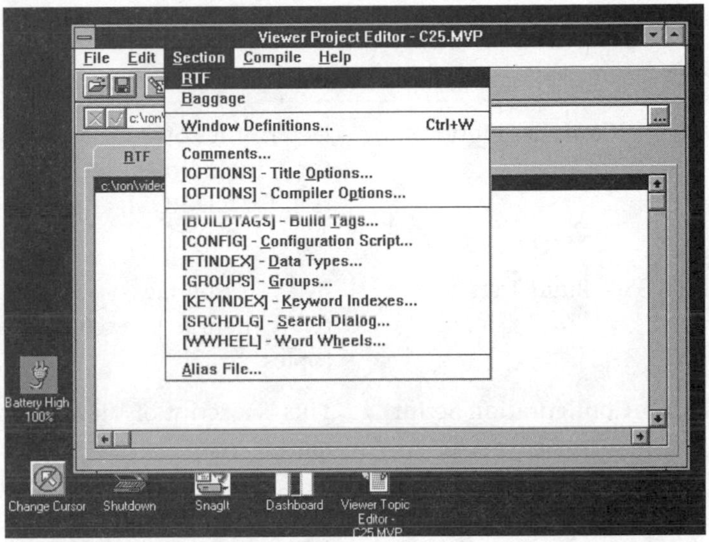

Figure 15.19. Viewer Section menu with selections.

The various entries on the Section menu are listed in Table 15.1.

Table 15.1. The Viewer Section Menu selections.

Menu item	Description
RTF	Displays RTF file list in work area.
Baggage	Displays baggage files in work area.
Window Definitions	Used for defining the number, type, location, and characteristics of master window, subsidiary windows, and panes.
Comments	You can enter comments about the title here.
[OPTIONS] – Title Options	Establishes several options for the title, including copyright notice and icon file.

continues

Table 15.1. continued

Menu item	Description
[OPTIONS] – Compiler Options	Determines options for compile time, including aliases, optimization for CD-ROM, and file compression.
[BUILDTAGS] – Build Tags	By assigning tags, you can selectively include or exclude groups of topics.
[CONFIG] – Configuration Script	This is a script of Viewer commands that is executed at runtime to set up the title. This is where you can, for example, define buttons for your title.
[FTINDEX] – Data Types	Each data type is supported by a DLL; the data type definitions for standard and custom data types are entered here.
[GROUPS] – Groups	Topics can be grouped, and Viewer supports some special operation for groups. You define your groups here, and define whether or not a group is searchable.
[KEYINDEX] – Keyword Indexes	If you need multiple keyword indexes, define them here.
[SRCHDLG] – Search Dialog	You can customize the search process to a limited degree here.
[WWHEEL] – Word Wheels	Word wheels are list boxes with predefined lists of words you can select.

The Title Options dialog box is shown in Figure 15.20. This particular option allows you to determine how material copied from your title will be annotated with copyright information. It also allows you to add a citation that will also be copied automatically to the clipboard, and to determine the icon for your title.

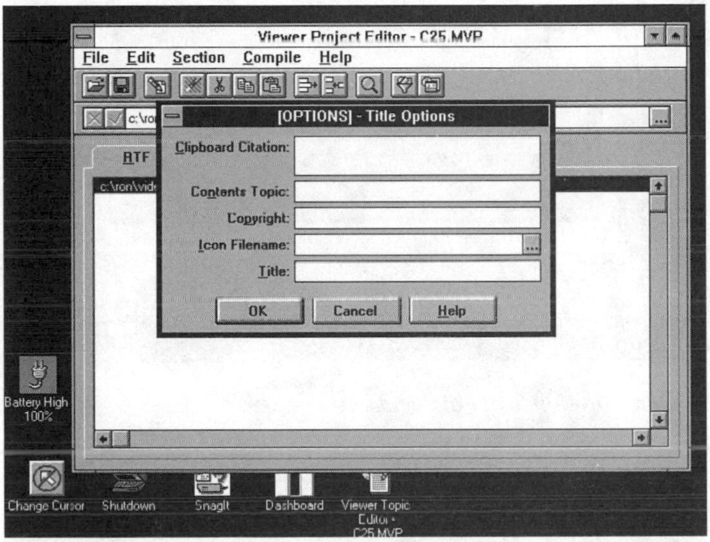

Figure 15.20. Title Options dialog box.

One of the most important selections on the Section menu is [CONFIG]. This opens the configuration script, as shown in Figure 15.21.

Viewer 2.0 is configurable; you can create and add you own DLLs to enhance or expand Viewer's capabilities. If you are a C programmer, or if you have one or more C programmers on your staff, this means that Viewer, despite its occasional clunkiness, offers capabilities that many other multimedia authoring/programming environments don't. If you have a text-intensive title that you want to customize heavily, Viewer becomes a very viable option. One popular title that uses heavy customization on top of the basic Viewer engine is Cinemania, from Microsoft. Figure 15.22 shows a sample Cinemania screen. In this screen, the customization is evident in the nonstandard controls, including the now-famous "remote control" window. Note the extensive range of search capabilities, including genre, MPAA ratings, director, performers, awards, dates, and ratings. In addition to the obvious cosmetic changes, Cinemania also includes extensive internal additions to the Viewer text search engine in DLLs.

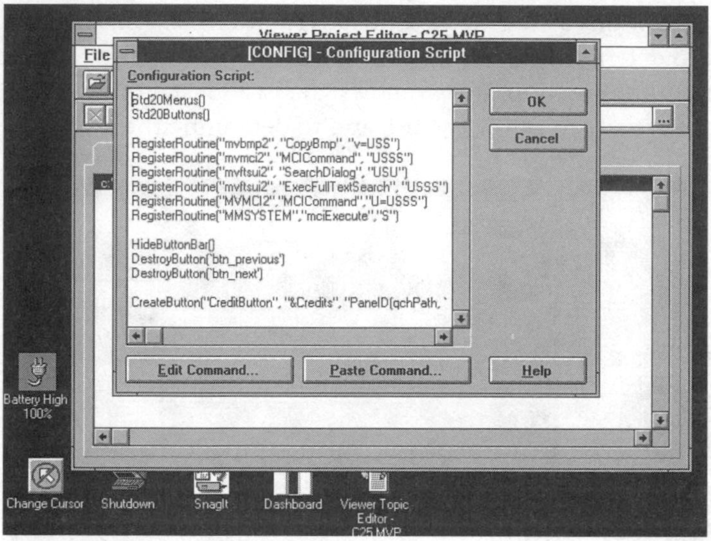

Figure 15.21. Configuration Script dialog box.

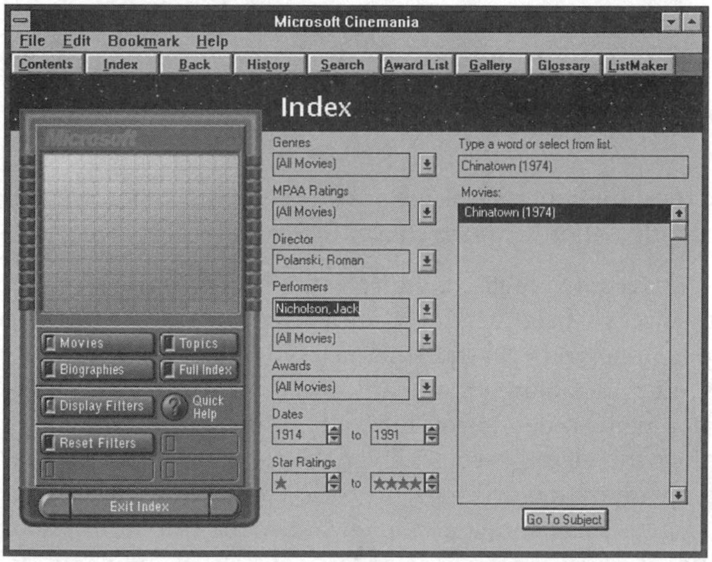

Figure 15.22. Cinemania, a commercial title created with Viewer.

To add a standard or custom DLL to Viewer, you use the `RegisterRoutine` command (see Figure 15.21). Other commands in this configuration script destroy some standard buttons, and create new ones.

Figure 15.23 shows the Cinemania remote control in a different context: displaying a still from the film *Chinatown*. By clicking the speaker icon, you can hear a line from the film. Sadly, Cinemania does not include any video clips in the 1992 version. Microsoft is attempting to negotiate for the rights to some video clips for future versions of the product.

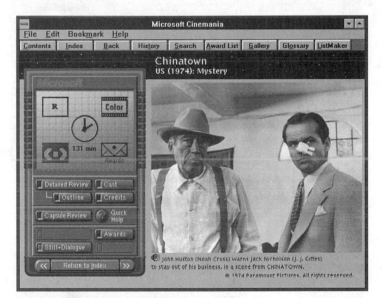

Figure 15.23. Another Cinemania screen.

Even without customization, however, the Viewer interface is highly configurable. Figure 15.24 shows a typical configuration dialog box. This one is for the master window; there are separate configuration dialogs for windows and panes.

The dialog box allows you to set a variety of configuration options, including background color or bitmap, the border, the size, minimum margin requirements and others. You can also define a nonscrolling region and position it in several different ways within the master window. Figure 15.25 shows a layout window, where you can define the size and relationship of the various windows and panes in your applications. To change the size or location of a window or

pane, just click and drag. Figure 15.25 shows two panes at the left of the screen; there is a bitmap for the background, and the master window has a nonscrollable region at the top.

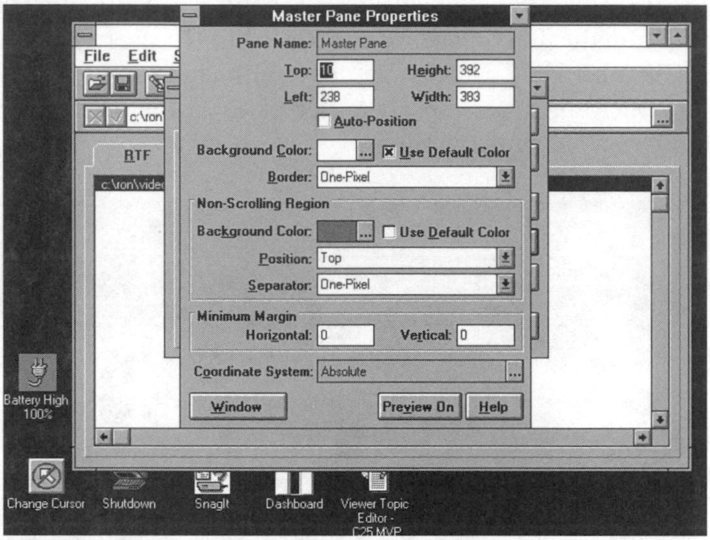

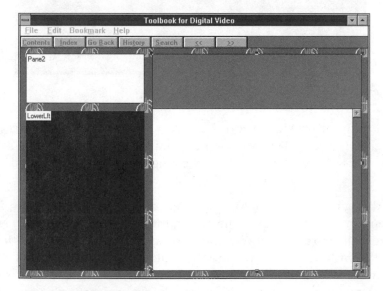

Figure 15.24. Configuring the Viewer master window.

Figure 15.25. Previewing the layout of windows and panes.

The viewer package comes with a variety of sample projects on a CD-ROM, and you can both learn from these projects and re-use the code they contain. For example, one project contains a useful extension to Viewer that allows you to put hot spots in a scrolling list. The scrolling list extension can be used in a variety of ways, and allows the user to select from very large numbers of items in a list. This is similar to the list choices offered in Cinemania.

Summary

Viewer is a complex and powerful tool. It uses a unique interface for development. Don't be put off by the differences; Viewer offers a lot of functionality for anyone developing multimedia titles with a lot of text content. It is extremely easy to use if your requirements are modest—just create topics, context strings, and add the bitmaps, movies, or other multimedia elements you want.

If you want to develop sophisticated titles, Viewer can also be ideal. However, the effort for a complex title is very large. Keeping track of all the topics, contexts, and multimedia files can be an enormous chore. However, the flexibility of Viewer allows you to create true one-of-a-kind titles that can be very impressive, as Cinemania demonstrates.

16

Advanced Programming: MCI in Visual Basic

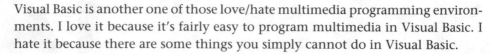
Visual Basic is another one of those love/hate multimedia programming environments. I love it because it's fairly easy to program multimedia in Visual Basic. I hate it because there are some things you simply cannot do in Visual Basic.

Unlike Toolbook, Visual Basic does not yet support multimedia in a tightly integrated fashion. That will probably change over time, of course, but for the time being it's important to know what you can and cannot do with multimedia in Visual Basic.

What you can do with multimedia in Visual Basic:

➤ Use most of the MCI string commands. The bulk of the MCI commands are directly accessible using mciExecute and mciSendString.

➤ Easily and directly call Windows API functions. Visual Basic makes it very easy to declare and call API functions. You can even create user-defined data types that make it ultra-easy to access data structures. Easy access to data structures allows you to read video files directly, and we will use that capability to examine the inner workings of AVI files.

What you cannot do with multimedia in Visual Basic:

➤ Incorporate callbacks (anything having to do with the notify flag). Because Visual Basic doesn't support callbacks at all, this is also a general limitation of the product. As we'll see, this places a few important limitations on what you can do with standard Visual Basic controls in multimedia applications. Visual Basic simply does not provide function addresses, so there is no simple work-around to this problem. There are some third party products, such as Spy-Works VB (Desaware, 408-377-4770), that allow you to incorporate callbacks.

In this chapter you'll look at the code for two multimedia applications built with Visual Basic. The first is a video system tester, and the second enables you to read the contents of AVI files.

Video Tester Application

The Video Tester application that I have included here should be doubly useful to you. It is a good introduction to the use of multimedia objects in Visual Basic, and it is a useful program as well. In this section, you'll learn how to use the Video Tester, and then you'll take a close look at the code behind the program.

Concepts Behind VIDTEST

Visual Basic comes with a multimedia control, mci.vbx, but I have chosen not to use it for a number of reasons. The primary reason involves the limitations of mci.vbx—there are many useful multimedia operations that are not accessible through mci.vbx. I strongly prefer using MCI string commands in almost all situations. Once you know how to declare the basic multimedia functions from the Windows API—`mci Execute`, `mciSendString`, `mciErrorString`—you can do many more things with multimedia.

For detailed information on using these functions, see the section below, "Using Windows API Multimedia Functions." The information in that section is tailored for Visual Basic, but almost all of the information also applies to any application that supports your ability to call Windows API functions.

As I mentioned at the beginning of this chapter, Visual Basic does not support *callbacks*. A callback function is a function that you specify to receive a call at a later time. For example, when you use the `notify` flag with MCI commands, the notification has to go somewhere. That somewhere is a function you specify. Because Visual Basic won't let you specify functions (that is, it does not support function addresses as an argument type), there's no way to specify the callback function.

Here's an example of a situation that really needs a callback capability. While you are playing a video file, it would be nice to update a slider to show the current frame position. With a callback capability, you can do this. Toolbook has tightly integrated callback capabilities that allow you to do all kinds of sophisticated multimedia programming.

Note

Asymetrix, the company that created Toolbook, has provided a book of video widgets that demonstrate how this is done; you'll find it on the CD-ROM in the Toolbook directory. The filename is **vidwidgt.tbk**. With that file are the latest versions of Toolbook's multimedia DLLs, which support some of the nifty callback capabilities in **vidwidgt.tbk**.

Using VIDTEST

The Video Tester application is, for the most part, self-explanatory. The opening screen is shown in Figure 16.1. It contains four menu selections (**F**ile, **V**iew, **Z**oom, **O**ptions), and a single but inactive button. Until you open a video file, most functionality is inactive.

Figure 16.1. The opening window of Video Tester.

Opening a file will display the first frame of the video in a window, and it will also display some information about the video file. The information shown was obtained using simple MCI command strings; no fancy programming was required. The video shown is a sample file from the Video for Windows CD-ROM, **email.avi**.

The Zoom menu is an easy way to scale the video image for different playback sizes, as shown in Figure 16.3. You can zoom by factors of .5x, 1x, 2x, 3x, or 4x. You can also specify a particular zoom factor by clicking the Custom option.

The Test Playback button will play the video file, and then check how many frames were skipped, as shown in Figure 16.4. All of this is accomplished with MCI command strings, as I'll show you later in this chapter.

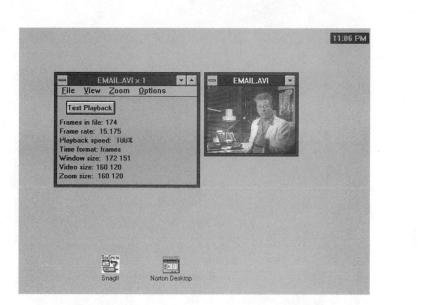

Figure 16.2. Video information displayed in the Video Tester.

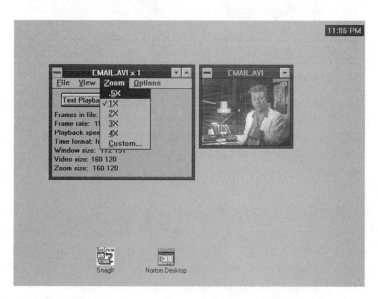

Figure 16.3. Changing the zoom factor.

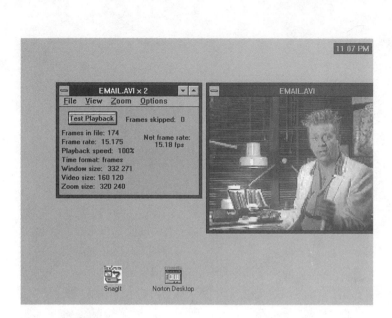

Figure 16.4. Reporting playback statistics.

The View menu offers some interesting possibilities: two forms of a floating controller for video operations. Figure 16.5 shows the controller for seeking directly to a frame by number, and Figure 16.6 shows the controller for scrolling through video frames.

You may sometimes find that these controllers don't work quite the way you would expect them to. This comes from a flaw in the interaction between Visual Basic and MCI, and is unavoidable. For example, moving to the last frame may not take you to the last frame—it may take you to the last key frame instead. Clicking the Last button a second time should get you to the last frame if this happens.

All of the preceding functionality was implemented with standard MCI command strings, using calls to `mciExecute` and `mciSendString`. One additional bit of functionality borrows heavily from the second application in this chapter, RiffWalker. Using functions such as `mmioAscend` and `mmioDescend`, the Video Tester is able to extract a great deal of detailed information about the AVI file and display it in a window, as shown in Figure 16.7. This capability is available by clicking View/File Statistics on the menu.

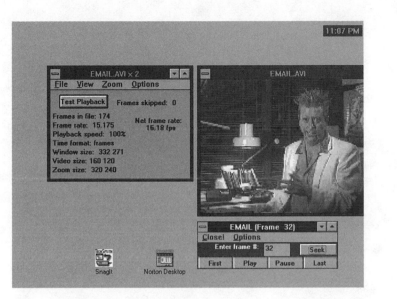

Figure 16.5. Seek-to-frame floating controller.

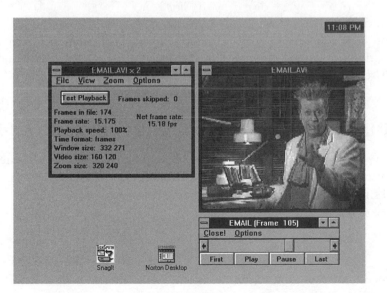

Figure 16.6. Scrolling floating controller.

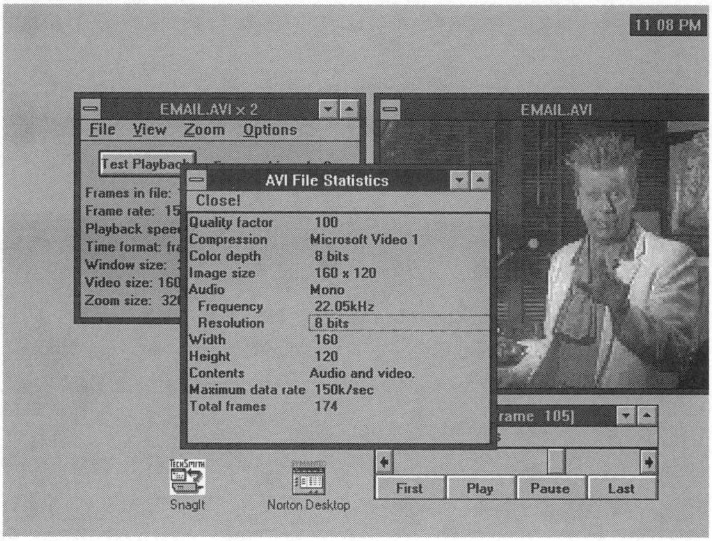

Figure 16.7. Displaying file statistics with Video Tester.

The code used to extract the text string for the compression method may not work on all machines; it depends on exactly how and where the configuration information for various codecs is stored. Check the source code if you have problems. The relevant code is in the module chunk.bas.

Using Windows API Multimedia Functions

There are two Windows API functions that are used throughout the Video Tester application: mciExecute and mciSendString. A third function, mciGetErrorString, is used several times to get a description when an error occurs.

mciExecute

This is the easiest function to use, but it is also somewhat limited. To use it, you only need to constuct the appropriate command string and use it as an argument for mciExecute. Here is a sample call from the Video Tester application:

```
result% = mciExecute("close AVIFile")
```

As you can see, the function returns an integer. If the return value is zero, there was no error; any other number is an error code.

The main limitation of working with `mciExecute` is that you cannot get any return values from MCI. Many MCI command strings return information about MCI or MCI devices that can be very useful. In those cases, you will need to use `mciSendString`.

However, you can do a lot with `mciExecute`. For example, the following sequence will open a file, position the playback window, play the video, and close it when done.

```
result% = mciExecute("open " + AVIFile + " alias aviFile")
result% = mciExecute("put AVIFile window at 100 100 160 120")
result% = mciExecute("put aviFile destination at 0 0 160 120")
result% = mciExecute("realize aviFile normal")
result% = mciExecute("break aviFile on 27")
result% = mciExecute("window aviFile state show")
result% = mciExecute("play AVIFile wait")
```

This sequence opens the file specified by the variable `AVIFile`, and assigns the alias `aviFile` to the device. It then positions the playback window and positions the image within the window. It realizes the palette, sets the Escape key as the break key, and displays the playback window. It then plays the file using the wait keyword, so that nothing else will interfere with playback.

`mciExecute` will display a message box if an error occurs, informing the user of anything that goes wrong. If you don't want the user to see these errors, or if you want to handle them yourself, you'll need to use `mciSendString` instead.

mciSendString

To get the most out of the command string interface, you'll need to use `mciSendString`. It takes more arguments than `mciExecute`, but it packs more power as well. The following bit of code shows a typical way to use `mciSendString`. The example obtains the handle of the window containing the video image.

```
Dim ReturnString As String * 1024

result2& = mciSendString("status aviFile window handle",
➥ ReturnString, 1024, 0)
```

Note that `mciSendString` returns a long integer. Note also that I declared a fixed-length string to receive the returned information from MCI, the variable `ReturnString`. This variable will contain a string with the handle for the window. Some MCI commands take this as an argument, and you can save the value in a

global variable for later use. For example, the window command allows you to specify the window that is to be used for playback:

```
result% = mciExecute("window AVIFile handle "+WindowHandle)
```

You'll need to handle any errors yourself. An error exists when the return value for mciSendString is nonzero. Use mciGetErrorString to get text information about the error.

mciGetErrorString

As with mciSendString, mciGetErrorString uses a fixed-length string to receive the text information. The following bit of code shows mciSendString and mciGetErrorString used together.

```
Dim ErrorString As String * 1024
Dim ReturnString As String * 1024

result2& = mciSendString("status aviFile window handle",
➥ ReturnString, 1024, 0)
WindowHandle$ = ReturnString

If result2& = 0 Then
    ' Switch windows and play video.
    result% = mciExecute("window AVIFile handle " + FormHandle$)
    result% = mciExecute("play AVIFile wait")
Else
    result% = mciGetErrorString(result2&, ErrorString, 1024)
    Label1.Caption = "Error: " + ErrorString$
End If

'...intervening code here...

' Restore old window handle.
result% = mciExecute("window AVIFile handle " + WindowHandle$)
```

In the example above, mciSendString is used to obtain the handle of the current playback window. If there is an error, we report it as the caption of the object Label1. If there is no error, we use a form handle (stored as a string) as the new playback window. Later, after the video has played, we switch back to the old window.

The following code, taken from mmsystem.h, defines the MCI error codes. If you want to handle specific codes, use the approptiate numbers in your Visual Basic code.

```
#define MCIERR_BASE                   256

/* MCI error return values */
#define MCIERR_INVALID_DEVICE_ID        (MCIERR_BASE + 1)
#define MCIERR_UNRECOGNIZED_KEYWORD     (MCIERR_BASE + 3)
#define MCIERR_UNRECOGNIZED_COMMAND     (MCIERR_BASE + 5)
#define MCIERR_HARDWARE                 (MCIERR_BASE + 6)
#define MCIERR_INVALID_DEVICE_NAME      (MCIERR_BASE + 7)
#define MCIERR_OUT_OF_MEMORY            (MCIERR_BASE + 8)
#define MCIERR_DEVICE_OPEN              (MCIERR_BASE + 9)
#define MCIERR_CANNOT_LOAD_DRIVER       (MCIERR_BASE + 10)
#define MCIERR_MISSING_COMMAND_STRING   (MCIERR_BASE + 11)
#define MCIERR_PARAM_OVERFLOW           (MCIERR_BASE + 12)
#define MCIERR_MISSING_STRING_ARGUMENT  (MCIERR_BASE + 13)
#define MCIERR_BAD_INTEGER              (MCIERR_BASE + 14)
#define MCIERR_PARSER_INTERNAL          (MCIERR_BASE + 15)
#define MCIERR_DRIVER_INTERNAL          (MCIERR_BASE + 16)
#define MCIERR_MISSING_PARAMETER        (MCIERR_BASE + 17)
#define MCIERR_UNSUPPORTED_FUNCTION     (MCIERR_BASE + 18)
#define MCIERR_FILE_NOT_FOUND           (MCIERR_BASE + 19)
#define MCIERR_DEVICE_NOT_READY         (MCIERR_BASE + 20)
#define MCIERR_INTERNAL                 (MCIERR_BASE + 21)
#define MCIERR_DRIVER                   (MCIERR_BASE + 22)
#define MCIERR_CANNOT_USE_ALL           (MCIERR_BASE + 23)
#define MCIERR_MULTIPLE                 (MCIERR_BASE + 24)
#define MCIERR_EXTENSION_NOT_FOUND      (MCIERR_BASE + 25)
#define MCIERR_OUTOFRANGE               (MCIERR_BASE + 26)
#define MCIERR_FLAGS_NOT_COMPATIBLE     (MCIERR_BASE + 28)
#define MCIERR_FILE_NOT_SAVED           (MCIERR_BASE + 30)
#define MCIERR_DEVICE_TYPE_REQUIRED     (MCIERR_BASE + 31)
#define MCIERR_DEVICE_LOCKED            (MCIERR_BASE + 32)
#define MCIERR_DUPLICATE_ALIAS          (MCIERR_BASE + 33)
#define MCIERR_BAD_CONSTANT             (MCIERR_BASE + 34)
#define MCIERR_MUST_USE_SHAREABLE       (MCIERR_BASE + 35)
#define MCIERR_MISSING_DEVICE_NAME      (MCIERR_BASE + 36)
#define MCIERR_BAD_TIME_FORMAT          (MCIERR_BASE + 37)
#define MCIERR_NO_CLOSING_QUOTE         (MCIERR_BASE + 38)
#define MCIERR_DUPLICATE_FLAGS          (MCIERR_BASE + 39)
#define MCIERR_INVALID_FILE             (MCIERR_BASE + 40)
#define MCIERR_NULL_PARAMETER_BLOCK     (MCIERR_BASE + 41)
#define MCIERR_UNNAMED_RESOURCE         (MCIERR_BASE + 42)
#define MCIERR_NEW_REQUIRES_ALIAS       (MCIERR_BASE + 43)
#define MCIERR_NOTIFY_ON_AUTO_OPEN      (MCIERR_BASE + 44)
#define MCIERR_NO_ELEMENT_ALLOWED       (MCIERR_BASE + 45)
#define MCIERR_NONAPPLICABLE_FUNCTION   (MCIERR_BASE + 46)
#define MCIERR_ILLEGAL_FOR_AUTO_OPEN    (MCIERR_BASE + 47)
#define MCIERR_FILENAME_REQUIRED        (MCIERR_BASE + 48)
#define MCIERR_EXTRA_CHARACTERS         (MCIERR_BASE + 49)
#define MCIERR_DEVICE_NOT_INSTALLED     (MCIERR_BASE + 50)
#define MCIERR_GET_CD                   (MCIERR_BASE + 51)
#define MCIERR_SET_CD                   (MCIERR_BASE + 52)
```

```
#define MCIERR_SET_DRIVE                 (MCIERR_BASE + 53)
#define MCIERR_DEVICE_LENGTH             (MCIERR_BASE + 54)
#define MCIERR_DEVICE_ORD_LENGTH         (MCIERR_BASE + 55)
#define MCIERR_NO_INTEGER                (MCIERR_BASE + 56)

#define MCIERR_WAVE_OUTPUTSINUSE         (MCIERR_BASE + 64)
#define MCIERR_WAVE_SETOUTPUTINUSE       (MCIERR_BASE + 65)
#define MCIERR_WAVE_INPUTSINUSE          (MCIERR_BASE + 66)
#define MCIERR_WAVE_SETINPUTINUSE        (MCIERR_BASE + 67)
#define MCIERR_WAVE_OUTPUTUNSPECIFIED    (MCIERR_BASE + 68)
#define MCIERR_WAVE_INPUTUNSPECIFIED     (MCIERR_BASE + 69)
#define MCIERR_WAVE_OUTPUTSUNSUITABLE    (MCIERR_BASE + 70)
#define MCIERR_WAVE_SETOUTPUTUNSUITABLE  (MCIERR_BASE + 71)
#define MCIERR_WAVE_INPUTSUNSUITABLE     (MCIERR_BASE + 72)
#define MCIERR_WAVE_SETINPUTUNSUITABLE   (MCIERR_BASE + 73)

#define MCIERR_SEQ_DIV_INCOMPATIBLE      (MCIERR_BASE + 80)
#define MCIERR_SEQ_PORT_INUSE            (MCIERR_BASE + 81)
#define MCIERR_SEQ_PORT_NONEXISTENT      (MCIERR_BASE + 82)
#define MCIERR_SEQ_PORT_MAPNODEVICE      (MCIERR_BASE + 83)
#define MCIERR_SEQ_PORT_MISCERROR        (MCIERR_BASE + 84)
#define MCIERR_SEQ_TIMER                 (MCIERR_BASE + 85)
#define MCIERR_SEQ_PORTUNSPECIFIED       (MCIERR_BASE + 86)
#define MCIERR_SEQ_NOMIDIPRESENT         (MCIERR_BASE + 87)

#define MCIERR_NO_WINDOW                 (MCIERR_BASE + 90)
#define MCIERR_CREATEWINDOW              (MCIERR_BASE + 91)
#define MCIERR_FILE_READ                 (MCIERR_BASE + 92)
#define MCIERR_FILE_WRITE                (MCIERR_BASE + 93)

/* all custom device driver errors must be >= than this value */
#define MCIERR_CUSTOM_DRIVER_BASE        (MCIERR_BASE + 256)
```

Video Tester Source Code Commentary

I have included the complete source code for the Video Tester later in this chapter, in the section "Complete Source Code." The source code is also included on the CD-ROM in the Visual Basic directory.

In this section, I will comment on the Hows and Whys of coding multimedia, especially video, for Visual Basic. This section is arranged according the various forms used in the Video Tester application.

The Main Form

The main form for this application is `vid2test.frm`. This is a revised version of a video test application I uploaded to CompuServe in January, 1993. This version incorporates major revisions to that program.

There are four menu choices and one button on the main form. Most choices are inactive until you open a video file using the File/Open menu selection.

Most of the code for the main form is actually located in the code modules, `module1.bas` and `chunk.bas`. Most of the MCI-related code actually found in the main form is contained in the menu choice, Select Video for Test. There are three things you can do in this menu selection:

➤ Open the video file.

➤ Position the video window for playback.

➤ Obtain information about the video file for display.

Opening and Positioning Video

The complete code for the "Select Video for Test" menu item can be found later in this chapter, under the heading VID2TEST.FRM. If you have Visual Basic 2.0, Professional Edition, you can also view the code on your computer. The code begins with this line:

```
Sub SelectCtl_Click ()
```

We'll look at this particular piece of code very closely because it contains most of the elements of working with multimedia in Visual Basic and serves as a good example.

The subroutine starts with two declarations we've seen already:

```
Dim ReturnString As String * 1024
Dim ErrorString As String * 1024
```

These fixed-length strings are used to hold return values for `mciSendString` and `mciGetErrorMessage`.

We need to check to see if a video file is already open before we try to open another one. One way to do this is to check for an error when we send a command string to the alias we'll be using for the video device. The alias, established in the open command, is `aviFile`.

```
result2& = mciSendString("capability aviFile device type",
➥ ReturnString, 1024, 0)
If result2& <> 0 Then
     ' device not opened.
Else
     result% = mciExecute("close AVIFile")
End If
```

The preceding code will close a previously opened file. We know a file is open when the command `capability aviFile device type` is successful—it won't work unless there is an open file with that alias.

After this little bit of housekeeping, we can use a common dialog to open a file.

```
CMDialog1.Action = 1

AVIFile = CMDialog1.Filename
AVIFileTitle = CMDialog1.Filetitle
If AVIFile = "" Then
     Exit Sub
End If
```

Several things happened in this part of the code. We opened a common dialog for a File Open, and then we saved both the fully qualified path name and the filename in global variables. We'll use the fully qualified path name for opening the file, and we'll use the filename alone as a title for the playback window.

I'll skip ahead in the code, past a section that accesses the video file for various bits of information, to the actual opening of the file for playback:

```
result2& = mciSendString("open " + AVIFile + " alias aviFile",
➥ ReturnString, 1024, 0)
```

This is a simple open; we're not using any special window styles, such as child or popup. We're using the default window style, which is overlapped. Figure 16.2 shows an overlapped window.

A long section of code with numerous calls to `mciSendString` and `mciExecute` follows, but only if the open was successful. We'll examine each call individually. Each call is followed by a description.

```
If result2& = 0 Then
     result% = mciExecute("set AVIFile seek exactly on")
```

If there was no error, we can start to process the MCI commands. The first one sets `seek exactly` to `on`. This will force the video driver to seek to exactly the frame we are seeking. If `seek exactly` is `off`, the video driver will seek to the key frame preceding the frame we want.

```
result2& = mciSendString("status AVIFile length", ReturnString, 1024, 0)
Label4.Caption = " Frames in file: " + ReturnString
TotalFrames = Val(ReturnString)
```

This sequence gets the length of the AVI file, and displays the results on the form in the object Label4. It also stores the value in a global variable, TotalFrames.

```
result2& = mciSendString("status AVIFile nominal frame rate",
➥ ReturnString, 1024, 0)
Label5.Caption = " Frame rate: " + Str$(Val(ReturnString) / 1000)
FrameRate = Val(ReturnString) / 1000
```

Next, we obtain the frame rate. To get a figure in frames per second, we must divide by 1,000. The value is stored in the global variable FrameRate.

```
result2& = mciSendString("status AVIFile speed", ReturnString, 1024, 0)
Label6.Caption = " Playback speed: " + Str$(Val(ReturnString) / 10) + "%"
```

This sequence gets the speed factor for the file. Because we haven't changed the speed setting, it will be 1,000. To represent this as a percentage, we must divide by 10.

```
result2& = mciSendString("status AVIFile time format",
➥ ReturnString, 1024, 0)
Label7.Caption = " Time format: " + ReturnString
```

This gets the default time format from the file, which is usually frames. Time can also be formated in milliseconds.

SetAVIWindow

This is a call to a subroutine that sets up the AVI playback window. It used several MCI calls with mciSendString to determine the current window and image sizes, and stores them in global variables. The complete code for the subroutine follows.

```
Sub SetAVIWindow ()
    Dim ReturnString As String * 1024
    Dim ErrorString As String * 1024

    result2& = mciSendString("where AVIFile window",
➥ ReturnString, 1024, 0)
    WindowWidth = Val(parse(ReturnString, 3))
    WindowHeight = Val(parse(ReturnString, 4))
    Form1.Label8.Caption = " Window size: " + Str$(WindowWidth) +
Str$(WindowHeight)
    result2& = mciSendString("where AVIFile destination",
➥ ReturnString, 1024, 0)
    Form1.Label9.Caption = " Video size: " + Mid$(ReturnString, 5, 8)
    ' Extract window width/height information.
```

```
        ClientWidth = Val(parse(ReturnString, 3))
        ClientHeight = Val(parse(ReturnString, 4))
        MoreWidth = WindowWidth - ClientWidth
        MoreHeight = WindowHeight - ClientHeight
        If ClientHeight > 0 Then
            Form1.Label10.Caption = " Zoom size: " +
➡Str$(ClientWidth * ZoomFactor) + Str$(ClientHeight * ZoomFactor)
        End If
End Sub
```

The first call to mciSendString requests the position and size of the playback window. This information comes as four space-separated numbers in a string. For example, the return string might look like this:

116 132 332 279

This specifies a window located 116 pixels from the left edge of the screen, 132 pixels from the top edge, and that is 332 pixels wide by 279 pixels high. These dimensions include any menu bar, caption, border, and so on that are present in the window.

I wrote a simple function, Parse, that extracts a given item in a space-separated list. This is used to extract the window width and height, and the values are stored in global variables. The values are also displayed on the form.

The next call to mciSendString requests the size and position of the video image using the destination parameter. The result is, once again, four numbers in a space-separated list. This time, the first two numbers refer to the position of the image inside the playback window. The second two numbers specify the size of the image. Given the window numbers in the previous example, likely values for the image might be:

0 0 320 240

Note that the image is positioned at 0,0—the top left corner of the playback window. The size of the image—320x240—is smaller than the values for the window. This is because the window values included things such as borders and captions.

The values for the image size are also stored in global variables, as are the differences between the window size and the image size. Depending on exactly what screen resolution and system font size are involved, the difference between these two sets of numbers can change dramatically, so it is critical to store them if we plan to change the size of the playback window and image. We need to keep track of the size difference so we don't cut off part of the image, or leave blank space around the image.

Finally, if a valid `ClientHeight` was found, the size of the image is displayed on the main form.

That concludes the `SetAVIWindow` subroutine. The following lines of code are executed next in the `SelectCtl_Click` subroutine:

```
result% = mciExecute("put AVIFile window at " + Str$(CInt(WindowLeft)) +
➡ Str$(CInt(WindowTop)) + Str$(CInt(ClientWidth * ZoomFactor +
➡ MoreWidth)) + Str$(CInt(ClientHeight * ZoomFactor + MoreHeight)))
```

This places the window at the same location it was at, but it does add the zoom factor. If you want to establish a different initial position for the playback window, this is the place to do it.

```
result% = mciExecute("put aviFile destination at 0 0 " +
➡ Str$(CInt(ClientWidth * ZoomFactor)) +
➡ Str$(CInt(ClientHeight * ZoomFactor)))
```

This call to `mciExecute` establishes the initial position of the image in the playback window. We're really doing no more than putting it where it already is, but you could easily modify the initial position to suit your own needs here.

```
result% = mciExecute("realize aviFile normal")
```

This establishes the palette of the video file. This gives you the best color rendition, but it may cause palette flash if you are working in 8-bit color. You can avoid palette flash (which occurs whenever you change palettes) by using `"realize aviFile background"` instead. However, this may cause undesirable color problems if there is much of a difference between the current palette and the video's palette. Realizing a palette as background is best done when you know what the preceding palette was, and you also know that the current palette is compatible with it.

```
result% = mciExecute("break aviFile on 27")
```

It's nice to be able to stop a video once it starts to play. We'll be playing the video with the wait parameter, and if we don't establish a break method, the user will be unable to stop playback. The values for keys and mouse clicks are located in windows.h, and are summarized in table 16.1.

```
result% = mciExecute("window aviFile state show")
```

This command causes the playback window to appear on-screen. You can also show it minimized as an icon. To do so, use the command string `"window aviFile state show minimized"`.

If there is an error, the error message is displayed on the main form:

```
result% = mciGetErrorString(result2&, ErrorString, 1024)
Label2.Caption = "Error: " + ErrorString$
```

Table 16.1. Values for break keys.

Key	Value (Hex)	Value (decimal)
LBUTTON	0x01	1
RBUTTON	0x02	2
CANCEL	0x03	3
MBUTTON	0x04	4
BACK	0x08	8
TAB	0x09	9
CLEAR	0x0C	12
RETURN	0x0D	13
SHIFT	0x10	16
CONTROL	0x11	17
MENU	0x12	18
PAUSE	0x13	19
CAPITAL	0x14	20
ESCAPE	0x1B	27
SPACE	0x20	32
PRIOR	0x21	33
NEXT	0x22	34
END	0x23	35
HOME	0x24	36
LEFT	0x25	37
UP	0x26	38
RIGHT	0x27	39

Key	Value (Hex)	Value (decimal)
DOWN	0x28	40
SELECT	0x29	41
PRINT	0x2A	42
EXECUTE	0x2B	43
SNAPSHOT	0x2C	44
INSERT	0x2D	45
DELETE	0x2E	46
HELP	0x2F	47
NUMPAD0	0x60	96
NUMPAD1	0x61	97
NUMPAD2	0x62	97
NUMPAD3	0x63	99
NUMPAD4	0x64	100
NUMPAD5	0x65	101
NUMPAD6	0x66	102
NUMPAD7	0x67	103
NUMPAD8	0x68	104
NUMPAD9	0x69	105
MULTIPLY	0x6A	106
ADD	0x6B	107
SEPARATOR	0x6C	108
SUBTRACT	0x6D	109
DECIMAL	0x6E	110
DIVIDE	0x6F	111
F1	0x70	112
F2	0x71	113

continues

Table 16.1. continued

Key	Value (Hex)	Value (decimal)
F3	0x72	114
F4	0x73	115
F5	0x74	116
F6	0x75	117
F7	0x76	118
F8	0x77	119
F9	0x78	120
F10	0x79	121
F11	0x7A	122
F12	0x7B	123
F13	0x7C	124
F14	0x7D	125
F15	0x7E	126
F16	0x7F	127
F17	0x80	128
F18	0x81	129
F19	0x82	130
F20	0x83	131
F21	0x84	132
F22	0x85	133
F23	0x86	134
F24	0x87	135
NUMLOCK	0x90	144
SCROLL	0x91	145

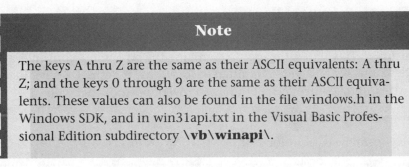

Note

The keys A thru Z are the same as their ASCII equivalents: A thru Z; and the keys 0 through 9 are the same as their ASCII equivalents. These values can also be found in the file windows.h in the Windows SDK, and in win31api.txt in the Visual Basic Professional Edition subdirectory **\vb\winapi**.

Accessing Video Information

There's a short bit of code in the SelectCtl_Click subroutine that we passed over in the above discussion. It's just four lines of code:

```
mmHandle = mmioOpen(AVIFile, 0&, 2&)
SetupGrid Form4
WalkFile Form4
result% = mmioClose(mmHandle, 0)
```

The first function call, to mmioOpen, opens the AVI file for input/output. This is a very different way to open an AVI file, and I explain it in much greater detail later in this chapter, in the section on the RiffWalker application. The mmioOpen function opens the file for reading and writing, not for playing.

While the file is open, there is a call to SetupGrid and to WalkFile. The SetupGrid subroutine merely puts some text labels into a grid on Form4.frm. The WalkFile subroutine does some very interesting things with the mmioAscend and mmioDescend multimedia API functions. Basically, they allow us to move through the AVI file, reading the right-sized chunks of data. The WalkFile subroutine looks at each chunk of data, and if it is the right kind of chunk, it extracts meaningful data and puts it into that grid on form4.frm. The details on these functions can be found in the Riffwalk section.

There is a lot of information in the AVI file that can only be reached in this manner. I won't say that using the mmio functions is trivial, because it's not, but if you are careful, and take some time to understand the structure of the AVI file, you can move around within the file successfully. The RiffWalk application allows you to experiment in a non-lethal situation with any AVI file.

The Floating Controller

A frequently requested feature in applications that work with video files is a float-ing controller. This allows the user to configure the screen in a convenient way, with the controller and video in different locations, if desired. I have incorpo-rated two kinds of controllers. Both have a row of buttons that will:

➤ Move to the first frame.

➤ Play from the current location.

➤ Pause playback.

➤ Move to the last frame.

One controller also adds the ability to move to frames by number, and the other uses a scroll bar for moving through the video file.

Seek to Frame

Seeking to a specific frame is easy to do. A single call to an MCI command will do it:

```
result% = mciExecute("seek aviFile to " + SeekFrame$)
```

All that you need to specify is the frame number to seek to.

Additional code for this version of the floating controller can be found in the section below for form3.frm.

Scroll Bar Seeking

Seeking with the scroll bar adds a little bit of complexity, but not a lot. The first thing to do is to set the scroll maximum value to the total number of frames.

```
HScroll1.Max = TotalFrames
```

Next, we must determine the current file position, and make that the start-ing value for the scroll bar.

```
result2& = mciSendString("status aviFile position",
➥ ReturnString, 1024, 0)
HScroll1.Value = Val(ReturnString)
```

For good measure, I also put the filename and current position as the cap-tion for the playback window:

```
NewName$ = Left$(AVIFiletitle, Len(AVIFiletitle) - 4)
Form3.Caption = NewName$ + " (Frame " + ReturnString + ")"
```

If the value of the scroll bar changes, we need to seek to the new frame number:

```
result% = mciExecute("seek aviFile to " + Str$(HScroll1.Value))
```

Module1.bas Code

The module `module1.bas` has a number of useful subroutines in it. These include the functions listed in Table 16.2.

Table 16.2. Subroutines in module1.bas.

Subroutine	Description
AdjustWindow	This subroutine gets the current size and position of the window and video image, updates global variables with the values, and then calls ResetAVIWindow.
Parse	This function extracts a given item from a list of space-separated items.
ResetAVIWindow	This function updates some global variables and updates window size information on the main form.
PlayTestFile	This subroutine plays an open AVI file from the current frame number.
SendMCI	This function handles the calculation of the net frame rate using MCI commands.
SetAVIWindow	This is a variation on the ResetAVIWindow subroutine that is needed by certain routines.

In addition to the functions and subroutines, `module1.bas` also contains a number of API function declarations and global variable declarations. The API functions declared are listed in Table 16.3.

Table 16.3. Ron's Standard Set of Multimedia API Functions.

Function	Description
sndPlaySound	This function, although not used in this application, is a very handy one to have around. It allows you to play Wave files quickly and easily.
mciSendString	Used whenever there is either text being returned from MCI, or a need to check for an error condition.
mciGetErrorString	Used to get text descriptions of errors.
mciExecute	Simple calls to MCI use this function.
GetActiveWindow	This is handy for obtaining window handles. You never know when you'll run into an API function that can't live without a window handle!

These functions constitute my standard set of most-used functions. I automatically include them because I almost always use all of them.

This is a good opportunity to look at the arguments you'll need to supply for these functions.

sndPlaySound

```
Declare Function sndPlaySound Lib "mmsystem" (ByVal SoundName As String,
➥ ByVal Flags As Integer) As Integer
```

This function takes two arguments:

Argument	Data type	Description
SoundName	String	The name of the sound file, or a variable containing the sound data (flag SND_MEMORY).
Flags	Integer	The flags specify how MCI treats the sound information. The valid flags are shown in Table 16.4.

Table 16.4. Flags for SndPlaySound.

Flag	Value	Description
SND_SYNC	0x00	Play the sound synchronously (default)
SND_ASYNC	0x01	Play the sound asynchronously
SND_NODEFAULT	0x02	Don't use the default sound if the requested sound file is not found.
SND_MEMORY	0x04	The sound is loaded into memory, and the contents of the string variable contain the sound data. You can load the sound data into a variable by simply opening the file, reading the data into a variable, and closing the file.
SND_LOOP	0x08	Loop the sound continuously until the next call to SndPlaySound.
SND_NOSTOP	0x10	Don't stop playing any currently playing sound.

mciSendString

```
Declare Function mciSendString Lib "mmsystem" (ByVal MCI_Command As String,
➥ ByVal ReturnString As String, ByVal ReturnLength As Integer,
➥ ByVal Handle As Integer) As Long
```

This function takes four arguments:

Argument	Data type	Description
MCI_Command	String	This can be any valid MCI command string.
ReturnString	Fixed-length string	This is a container for the return value, if any, from MCI.
ReturnLength	Integer	You must specify the length of the return container so that memory is not overwritten!

Argument	Data type	Description
Handle	Integer	Normally, you'll use zero for this argument. It is the handle to a callback function, something you can't use in Visual Basic.

mciGetErrorString

```
Declare Function mciGetErrorString Lib "mmsystem" (ByVal MCI_Error
➥ As Long, ByVal ErrorString As String, ByVal ReturnLength As Integer)
➥ As Integer
```

This function takes three arguments:

Argument	Data type	Description
MCI_Error	Long	The error number returned by mciSendString.
ErrorString	Fixed-length string	This is a container for the return value, if any, from MCI.
ReturnLength	Integer	You must specify the length of the return container so that memory is not overwritten!

mciExecute

```
Declare Function mciExecute Lib "mmsystem" (ByVal MCI_Command As String)
➥ As Integer
```

This function takes one argument:

Argument	Data type	Description
MCI_Command	String	This can be any valid MCI command string.

GetActiveWindow

```
Declare Function GetActiveWindow Lib "User" () As Integer
```

This function takes no arguments.

Chunk.bas Code

Most of the code in this module was transplanted from the RiffWalker application, so I won't cover a lot of detail here—especially the low-level details of the mmio functions, which are explained later, in the RiffWalker section. There are, however, some higher-level things going on in this module that are worth a brief look.

One subroutine that I referred to earlier, WalkFile, is contained in the chunk.bas module. The source code, other than the part that sets up the width of a grid, is very obscure:

```
Sub WalkFile (GridForm As Form)
    GridForm.Grid1.ColWidth(1) = GridForm.Grid1.Width * .6
    GridForm.Grid1.ColWidth(0) = GridForm.Grid1.Width * .4

    DescendChunk
    DescendChunk
    DescendChunk

    AscendChunk
    DescendChunk
    DescendChunk

    AscendChunk
    DescendChunk

    AscendChunk
    DescendChunk
    DescendChunk

    AscendChunk
    DescendChunk
End Sub
```

However, this series of function calls is anything but arbitrary. The sequence of calls was determined by the structure of the AVI file. In the section on the RiffWalker application, we'll explore what happens when you execute this exact sequence of ascend and descend calls. As you will see, the result is that we arrive at just those header chunks that tell us important facts about the AVI file.

There is also an API function declaration that is worth commenting on. I use the function GetPrivateProfileString to get some information from the control.ini and system.ini files. The declaration is more than a little bit daunting:

```
' Declare function for getting info from control.ini and system.ini
Declare Function GetPrivateProfileString Lib "Kernel"
➥ (ByVal lpApplicationName As String, ByVal lpKeyName As String,
➥ ByVal lpDefault As String, ByVal lpReturnedString As String,
➥ ByVal nSize As Integer, ByVal lpFileName As String) As Integer
```

This function takes six arguments:

Argument	Data type	Description
lpApplicationName	String	This is the application name to search for in the .INI file. These are the names that are within square brackets in .INI files, such as [drivers].
lpKeyName	String	This is the key name you want to search for in the section relating to the application name.
lpDefault	String	This is the default value to be used if the application name or key name is not found.
lpReturnedString	String	This is a container for the returned profile string.
nSize	Integer	You must specify the length of the return container so that memory is not overwritten!
lpFileName	String	This is the .INI file that you want to get the profile string from.

Summary

The Video Tester shows you how to integrate video into Visual Basic applications. There are some limitations on what you can do, most notably the inability to work with callback functions. However, within these limits, Visual Basic offers easy access to Windows API functions as a means of controlling digital video.

Complete Source Code: Video Tester

This section includes the *complete* source code for the Video Tester applications. The code is divided by forms, and the code for each form is listed as a continuous stream of code. As you know, this is not how the code is accessed in Visual Basic. The handlers for various objects can be identified by the opening line of each section of code.

For example, the code for the Test Playback button is from vid2test.frm, and begins with

```
Sub Command1_Click ()
```

This identifies the code as that which will be executed when the Command1 button is clicked. This allows you to find the code for appropriate portions of each form.

If you wish to look at or modify the code, you will need Version 2.0 of Visual Basic, Professional Edition. The application incorporates two .VBX files:

```
cmdialog.vbx
grid.vbx
```

These files must be installed into your Windows system directory, usually **c:\windows\system**.

VID2TEST.FRM

```
Sub AboutCtl_Click ()
    AboutForm.Show 1
End Sub

Sub AnyFrameCtl_Click ()
    Dim ReturnString As String * 1024
    Dim ErrorString As String * 1024

    Form3.Text1.Visible = True
    Form3.Command1.Visible = True
    Form3.Label2.Visible = True
    Form3.HScroll1.Visible = False
    Form3.Label2.Caption = "Enter frame #:"

    Form3.Show 0

End Sub

Sub Command1_Click ()
    Label1.Visible = False
    Label2.Visible = False
    result% = mciExecute("seek aviFile to 0")
    PlayTestFile True
    SendMCI "status AVIFile frames skipped"
```

```
        result% = mciExecute("seek aviFile to 0")
        Label1.Visible = True
        Label2.Visible = True
    End Sub

    Sub CustomCtl_Click ()
        Form2.Show 1
        If ClientHeight > 0 Then
         Label10.Caption = " Zoom size: " + Str$(CInt(ClientWidth *
    ➥ ZoomFactor)) + Str$(CInt(ClientHeight * ZoomFactor))
        End If
        ZoomPoint5.Checked = False
        Zoom1.Checked = False
        Zoom2.Checked = False
        Zoom3.Checked = False
        Zoom4.Checked = False
        CustomCtl.Checked = True
    End Sub

    Sub FirstFrameCtl_Click ()
        Dim ReturnString As String * 1024
        Dim ErrorString As String * 1024

        result% = mciExecute("seek AVIFile to 0")
    End Sub

    Sub Form_Load ()
        Dim pth As String
        ZoomFactor = 1#
        PlayWinCtl.Checked = True
        PlayScreenCtl.Checked = False
        Zoom1.Checked = True
    End Sub

    Sub FrameStepCtl_Click ()
        Dim ReturnString As String * 1024
        Dim ErrorString As String * 1024

        Form3.HScroll1.Visible = True
        Form3.Text1.Visible = False
        Form3.Command1.Visible = False
        Form3.Show 0
    End Sub

    Sub PlayScreenCtl_Click ()
        PlayMethod = " fullscreen"
        PlayWinCtl.Checked = False
        PlayScreenCtl.Checked = True
        Form3.PlayWinCtl.Checked = False
        Form3.PlayScreenCtl.Checked = True
    End Sub
```

```vb
Sub PlayWinCtl_Click ()
    PlayMethod = " window"
    PlayWinCtl.Checked = True
    PlayScreenCtl.Checked = False
    Form3.PlayWinCtl.Checked = True
    Form3.PlayScreenCtl.Checked = False
End Sub

Sub QuitCode_Click ()
    Dim ReturnString As String * 1024
    Dim ErrorString As String * 1024

    result2& = mciSendString("capability aviFile device type",
➥ ReturnString, 1024, 0)
    If result2& <> 0 Then
          ' device not opened.
    Else
          result% = mciExecute("close AVIFile")
    End If
End Sub

Sub SelectCtl_Click ()
    Dim ReturnString As String * 1024
    Dim ErrorString As String * 1024

    result2& = mciSendString("capability aviFile device type",
➥ ReturnString, 1024, 0)
    If result2& <> 0 Then
     ' device not opened.
    Else
     result% = mciExecute("close AVIFile")
    End If

    CMDialog1.Action = 1

    AVIFile = CMDialog1.Filename
    AVIFileTitle = CMDialog1.Filetitle
    If AVIFile = "" Then
     Exit Sub
    End If

    Label2.Caption = ""
    Label1.Caption = ""

    mmHandle = mmioOpen(AVIFile, 0&, 2&)
    SetupGrid Form4
    WalkFile Form4
    result% = mmioClose(mmHandle, 0)

    result2& = mciSendString("open " + AVIFile + " alias aviFile",
➥ ReturnString, 1024, 0)
```

```
    If result2& = 0 Then
      result% = mciExecute("set AVIFile seek exactly on")

      Command1.Enabled = True
      ViewMenu.Enabled = True
      Form1.Caption = CMDialog1.Filetitle + " x" + Str$(ZoomFactor)
      ' File exists.  OK to get info about it.
      result2& = mciSendString("status AVIFile length",
➡ ReturnString, 1024, 0)
      Label4.Caption = " Frames in file: " + ReturnString
      TotalFrames = Val(ReturnString)
      result2& = mciSendString("status AVIFile nominal frame rate",
➡ ReturnString, 1024, 0)
      Label5.Caption = " Frame rate: " + Str$(Val(ReturnString) / 1000)
      FrameRate = Val(ReturnString) / 1000
      result2& = mciSendString("status AVIFile speed",
➡ ReturnString, 1024, 0)
      Label6.Caption = " Playback speed: " + Str$(Val(ReturnString)
➡ / 10) + "%"
      result2& = mciSendString("status AVIFile time format",
➡ ReturnString, 1024, 0)
      Label7.Caption = " Time format: " + ReturnString
      SetAVIWindow
      result% = mciExecute("put AVIFile window at " +
➡ Str$(CInt(WindowLeft)) + Str$(CInt(WindowTop)) +
➡ Str$(CInt(ClientWidth * ZoomFactor + MoreWidth)) +
➡ Str$(CInt(ClientHeight * ZoomFactor + MoreHeight)))
      result% = mciExecute("put aviFile destination at 0 0 " +
➡ Str$(CInt(ClientWidth * ZoomFactor)) + Str$(CInt(ClientHeight *
➡ ZoomFactor)))
      result% = mciExecute("realize aviFile normal")
      result% = mciExecute("break aviFile on 27")
      result% = mciExecute("window aviFile state show")
      result% = mciExecute("seek AVIFile to 0")
      AnyFrameCtl.Enabled = True
      FirstFrameCtl.Enabled = True
      FrameStepCtl.Enabled = True
      ShowStatCtl.Enabled = True

    Else
      ' Report error.
      result% = mciGetErrorString(result2&, ErrorString, 1024)
      Label2.Caption = "Error: " + ErrorString$
      Command1.Enabled = False
      ViewMenu.Enabled = False
      Label4.Caption = ""
      Label5.Caption = ""
      Label6.Caption = ""
      Label7.Caption = ""
      Label8.Caption = ""
      Label9.Caption = ""
```

```
        End If
End Sub

Sub ShowStatCtl_Click ()
    Form4.Show 1
End Sub

Sub Zoom1_Click ()
    ZoomFactor = 1#
    Form1.Caption = Form1.CMDialog1.Filetitle + " x" + Str$(ZoomFactor)
    If ClientHeight > 0 Then
     Label10.Caption = " Zoom size: " + Str$(ClientWidth * ZoomFactor) +
➥ Str$(ClientHeight * ZoomFactor)
    End If
    AdjustWindow
    ZoomPoint5.Checked = False
    Zoom1.Checked = True
    Zoom2.Checked = False
    Zoom3.Checked = False
    Zoom4.Checked = False
    CustomCtl.Checked = False
End Sub

Sub Zoom2_Click ()
    ZoomFactor = 2#
    Form1.Caption = Form1.CMDialog1.Filetitle + " x" + Str$(ZoomFactor)
    If ClientHeight > 0 Then
     Label10.Caption = " Zoom size: " + Str$(ClientWidth * ZoomFactor) +
➥ Str$(ClientHeight * ZoomFactor)
    End If
    AdjustWindow
    ZoomPoint5.Checked = False
    Zoom1.Checked = False
    Zoom2.Checked = True
    Zoom3.Checked = False
    Zoom4.Checked = False
    CustomCtl.Checked = False
End Sub

Sub Zoom3_Click ()
    ZoomFactor = 3#
    Form1.Caption = Form1.CMDialog1.Filetitle + " x" + Str$(ZoomFactor)
    If ClientHeight > 0 Then
     Label10.Caption = " Zoom size: " + Str$(ClientWidth * ZoomFactor) +
➥ Str$(ClientHeight * ZoomFactor)
    End If
    AdjustWindow
    ZoomPoint5.Checked = False
    Zoom1.Checked = False
    Zoom2.Checked = False
    Zoom3.Checked = True
```

```
        Zoom4.Checked = False
        CustomCtl.Checked = False
    End Sub

    Sub Zoom4_Click ()
        ZoomFactor = 4#
        Form1.Caption = Form1.CMDialog1.Filetitle + " x" + Str$(ZoomFactor)
        If ClientHeight > 0 Then
         Label10.Caption = " Zoom size: " + Str$(ClientWidth * ZoomFactor) +
➥ Str$(ClientHeight * ZoomFactor)
        End If
        AdjustWindow
        ZoomPoint5.Checked = False
        Zoom1.Checked = False
        Zoom2.Checked = False
        Zoom3.Checked = False
        Zoom4.Checked = True
        CustomCtl.Checked = False
    End Sub

    Sub ZoomPoint5_Click ()
        ZoomFactor = .5
        Form1.Caption = Form1.CMDialog1.Filetitle + " x" + Str$(ZoomFactor)
        If ClientHeight > 0 Then
         Label10.Caption = " Zoom size: " + Str$(CInt(ClientWidth *
➥ ZoomFactor)) + Str$(CInt(ClientHeight * ZoomFactor))
        End If
        AdjustWindow
        ZoomPoint5.Checked = True
        Zoom1.Checked = False
        Zoom2.Checked = False
        Zoom3.Checked = False
        Zoom4.Checked = False
        CustomCtl.Checked = False
    End Sub
```

FORM2.FRM

```
Sub DoneCtl_Click ()
    Unload Form2
End Sub

Sub Form_Load ()
    OldZoom% = ZoomFactor * 10
    HScroll1.Value = OldZoom%
    Form2.Label1.Caption = Str$(ZoomFactor)
End Sub

Sub Form_Unload (Cancel As Integer)
    Dim ReturnString As String * 1024
    Dim ErrorString As String * 1024
```

```
    ZoomFactor = Val(Label1.Caption)
    Form1.Caption = Form1.CMDialog1.Filetitle + " x" + Label1.Caption

    If ZoomFactor = 0 Then
        ZoomFactor = 1
    End If
    AdjustWindow
End Sub


Sub HScroll1_Change ()
    If SettingUpForm Then
        Exit Sub
    End If

    Label1.Caption = HScroll1.Value / 10
End Sub
```

FORM3.FRM

```
Sub Command1_Click ()
    Dim ReturnString As String * 1024
    Dim ErrorString As String * 1024

    SeekFrame$ = Text1.Text
    If Val(SeekFrame$) > TotalFrames Then
        SeekFrame$ - Str$(TotalFrames)
        Text1.Text = Str$(TotalFrames)
    End If

    result% = mciExecute("seek aviFile to " + SeekFrame$)
    result2& = mciSendString("status aviFile position",
➥ ReturnString, 1024, 0)
    NewName$ = Left$(Form1.CMDialog1.Filetitle,
➥ Len(Form1.CMDialog1.Filetitle) - 4)
    Form3.Caption = NewName$ + " (Frame " + Str$(Val(ReturnString)) + ")"
End Sub

Sub Command2_Click ()
    Dim ReturnString As String * 1024
    Dim ErrorString As String * 1024

    result% = mciExecute("seek AVIFile to start")
    UpdateScroll
End Sub

Sub Command3_Click ()
    PlayVideoFromHere
End Sub
```

```
Sub Command4_Click ()
    Dim ReturnString As String * 1024
    Dim ErrorString As String * 1024

    result% = mciExecute("seek AVIFile to " + Str$(TotalFrames))
    UpdateScroll
End Sub

Sub Command5_Click ()
    Dim ReturnString As String * 1024
    Dim ErrorString As String * 1024

    result% = mciExecute("pause AVIFile")
    UpdateScroll
    Form3.HScroll1.Value = CurrentFrame
End Sub

Sub ExitCtl_Click ()
    Unload Form3
End Sub

Sub Form_Activate ()
    Dim ReturnString As String * 1024
    Dim ErrorString As String * 1024

    result2& = mciSendString("status aviFile position",
 ➥ ReturnString, 1024, 0)
    NewName$ = Left$(AVIFiletitle, Len(AVIFiletitle) - 4)
    Form3.Caption = NewName$ + " (Frame " + ReturnString + ")"

    HScroll1.Max = TotalFrames
    Form3.Command1.Enabled = True
    If Form3.HScroll1.Visible Then
        Form3.HScroll1.Enabled = True
    End If
End Sub

Sub Form_Resize ()
    ResetAVIWindow
End Sub

Sub HScroll1_Change ()
    Dim ReturnString As String * 1024
    Dim ErrorString As String * 1024

    result% = mciExecute("seek aviFile to " + Str$(HScroll1.Value))
    UpdateScroll
End Sub

Sub PlayScreenCtl_Click ()
    PlayMethod = " fullscreen"
```

```
    Form1.PlayWinCtl.Checked = False
    Form1.PlayScreenCtl.Checked = True
    PlayWinCtl.Checked = False
    PlayScreenCtl.Checked = True
End Sub

Sub PlayVideoFromHere ()
    If HScroll1.Visible = True Then
        HideScroll = True
        HScroll1.Visible = False
    End If
    If Command1.Visible = True Then
        HideButton = True
        Label2.Visible = False
        Text1.Visible = False
        Command1.Visible = False
    End If
    PlayTestFile False
    If HideScroll Then
        HScroll1.Visible = True
        HideScroll = False
    End If
    If HideButton Then
        Label2.Visible = True
        Text1.Visible = True
        Command1.Visible = True
        HideButton = False
    End If
End Sub

Sub PlayWinCtl_Click ()
    PlayMethod = " window"
    Form1.PlayWinCtl.Checked = True
    Form1.PlayScreenCtl.Checked = False
    PlayWinCtl.Checked = True
    PlayScreenCtl.Checked = False
End Sub

Sub UpdateScroll ()
    Dim ReturnString As String * 1024
    Dim ErrorString As String * 1024

    result2& = mciSendString("status aviFile position",
➥ ReturnString, 1024, 0)
    CurrentFrame = Val(ReturnString)
    NewName$ = Left$(AVIFiletitle, Len(AVIFiletitle) - 4)
    Form3.Caption = NewName$ + " (Frame " + Str$(CurrentFrame) + ")"
End Sub
```

FORM4.FRM

```
Sub CloseFormCtl_Click ()
    form4.Hide
End Sub
```

ABOUT.FRM

```
Sub Command1_Click ()
    Unload AboutForm
End Sub
```

MODULE1.BAS

```
' Declare the various functions we can use for mci stuff.
' Playing sounds.
Declare Function sndPlaySound Lib "mmsystem" (ByVal SoundName
➥ As String, ByVal Flags As Integer) As Integer
' Sending strings to mci.
Declare Function mciSendString Lib "mmsystem" (ByVal MCI_Command
➥ As String, ByVal ReturnString As String, ByVal ReturnLength
➥ As Integer, ByVal Handle As Integer) As Long
' Getting error messages.
Declare Function mciGetErrorString Lib "mmsystem" (ByVal MCI_Error
➥ As Long, ByVal ErrorString As String, ByVal ReturnLength
➥ As Integer) As Integer
' Sending strings to mci, no return messages.
Declare Function mciExecute Lib "mmsystem" (ByVal MCI_Command As String)
➥ As Integer
' Get handle of current window.
Declare Function GetActiveWindow Lib "User" () As Integer

Global ZoomFactor As Double
Global aviFile As String
Global aviFileTitle As String
Global TotalFrames As Integer
Global FrameRate As Double
Global NetFrameRate As Double
Global ClientHeight As Integer
Global ClientWidth As Integer
Global WindowHeight As Integer
Global WindowWidth As Integer
Global MoreHeight As Integer
Global MoreWidth As Integer
Global PlayMethod As String
Global WindowTop As Integer
Global WindowLeft As Integer
Global CurrentFrame As Integer
```

```
Global Wnd As Integer
Global SettingUpForm As Integer

Sub AdjustWindow ()
    Dim ReturnString As String * 1024
    Dim ErrorString As String * 1024

    ' Get current coordinates of window.
    result2& = mciSendString("where AVIFile window",
➥ ReturnString, 1024, 0)
    WindowLeft = Val(parse(ReturnString, 1))
    WindowTop = Val(parse(ReturnString, 2))
    ' Adjust playback window for new zoom size.
    result% = mciExecute("put AVIFile window at " +
➥ Str$(CInt(WindowLeft)) + Str$(CInt(WindowTop)) +
➥ Str$(CInt(ClientWidth * ZoomFactor + MoreWidth)) +
➥ Str$(CInt(ClientHeight * ZoomFactor + MoreHeight)))
    result% = mciExecute("put aviFile destination at 0 0 " +
➥ Str$(CInt(ClientWidth * ZoomFactor)) +
➥ Str$(CInt(ClientHeight * ZoomFactor)))
    ResetAVIWindow
End Sub

Function parse (Argument As String, Position As Integer)
    Dim FromPos As Integer
    FromPos = 1
    For i% = 1 To Position - 1
        NextArg = InStr(FromPos, Argument, " ")
        FromPos = NextArg + 1
    Next i%
    NextArg = InStr(FromPos, Argument, " ")
    If NextArg <> 0 Then
        parse = Mid$(Argument, FromPos, NextArg - FromPos)
    Else
        parse = Mid$(Argument, FromPos, 10)
    End If
End Function

Sub PlayTestFile (Wait As Integer)
    Dim ReturnString As String * 1024
    Dim ErrorString As String * 1024

    ' Get current coordinates of window.
    result2& = mciSendString("where AVIFile window",
➥ ReturnString, 1024, 0)
    WindowLeft = Val(parse(ReturnString, 1))
    WindowTop = Val(parse(ReturnString, 2))
    result% = mciExecute("put AVIFile window at " +
➥ Str$(CInt(WindowLeft)) + Str$(CInt(WindowTop)) +
➥ Str$(CInt(ClientWidth * ZoomFactor + MoreWidth)) +
➥ Str$(CInt(ClientHeight * ZoomFactor + MoreHeight)))
```

```
        result% = mciExecute("put aviFile destination at 0 0 " +
➥ Str$(CInt(ClientWidth * ZoomFactor)) +
➥ Str$(CInt(ClientHeight * ZoomFactor)))
        result% = mciExecute("realize aviFile normal")
        result% = mciExecute("break aviFile on 27")
        result% = mciExecute("window aviFile state show")
        If Wait Then
            result% = mciExecute("play AVIFile wait" + PlayMethod)
        Else
            result% = mciExecute("play AVIFile" + PlayMethod)
        End If
End Sub

Sub ResetAVIWindow ()
    Dim ReturnString As String * 1024
    Dim ErrorString As String * 1024

    result2& = mciSendString("where AVIFile window",
➥ ReturnString, 1024, 0)
    WindowWidth = Val(parse(ReturnString, 3))
    WindowHeight = Val(parse(ReturnString, 4))
    Form1.Label8.Caption = " Window size: " + Str$(WindowWidth) +
➥ Str$(WindowHeight)
    ' Extract window width/height information.
    If ClientHeight > 0 Then
        Form1.Label10.Caption = " Zoom size: " +
➥ Str$(ClientWidth * ZoomFactor) + Str$(ClientHeight * ZoomFactor)
    End If
End Sub

Sub SendMCI (MCI_String As String)
    Dim ReturnString As String * 1024
    Dim ErrorString As String * 1024

    result2& = mciSendString(MCI_String, ReturnString, 1024, 0)
    If result2& = 0 Then
        ' Convert return string to a number.
        FramesSkipped& = Val(ReturnString)
        ' Calculate Actual Frame rate.
        NetFrameRate = ((TotalFrames - FramesSkipped&) / TotalFrames) *
➥ FrameRate
        Form1.Label1.Caption = "Frames skipped: " + Str$(FramesSkipped&)
        NetFrameRate = CInt(NetFrameRate * 100) / 100
        Form1.Label2.Caption = "Net frame rate: " +
➥ Left$(Str$(NetFrameRate), 6) + " fps"
    Else
        result% = mciGetErrorString(result2&, ErrorString, 1024)
        Form1.Label2.Caption = "Error: " + ErrorString$
    End If
End Sub
```

```
Sub SetAVIWindow ()
    Dim ReturnString As String * 1024
    Dim ErrorString As String * 1024

    result2& = mciSendString("where AVIFile window",
➥ ReturnString, 1024, 0)
    WindowWidth = Val(parse(ReturnString, 3))
    WindowHeight = Val(parse(ReturnString, 4))
    Form1.Label8.Caption = " Window size: " + Str$(WindowWidth) +
➥ Str$(WindowHeight)
    result2& = mciSendString("where AVIFile destination",
➥ ReturnString, 1024, 0)
    Form1.Label9.Caption = " Video size: " + Mid$(ReturnString, 5, 8)
    ' Extract window width/height information.
    ClientWidth = Val(parse(ReturnString, 3))
    ClientHeight = Val(parse(ReturnString, 4))
    MoreWidth = WindowWidth - ClientWidth
    MoreHeight = WindowHeight - ClientHeight
    If ClientHeight > 0 Then
        Form1.Label10.Caption = " Zoom size: " + Str$(ClientWidth *
➥ ZoomFactor) + Str$(ClientHeight * ZoomFactor)
    End If
End Sub
```

CHUNK.BAS

```
Type ChunkInfo
    ChunkID As String * 4
    ChunkSize As Long
    FormType As String * 4
    ChunkDataOffset As Long
    ChunkFlags As Long
End Type

Type DisplayInfo
    DType As Long
    TextDesc As String * 2048
End Type

Type ISBJData
    TextDesc As String * 2048
End Type

Type WaveFormat
    FormatType As Integer
    Channels As Integer
    Sample As Long
    Bytes As Long
    Block As Integer
    Bits As Integer
End Type
```

☐419

```
Type AviHeader
    MicroSecPerFrame As Long
    MaxBytesPerSec As Long
    Reserved1 As Long
    Flags As Long
    TotalFrames As Long
    InitialFrames As Long
    Streams As Long
    SuggestedBufferSize As Long
    AWidth As Long
    AHeight As Long
    AScale As Long
    ARate As Long
    AStart As Long
    ALength As Long
End Type

Type GeneralInfo
    Flags As Long
    IOProc As String * 4
    IOProcAddress As Long
    ErrorCode As Integer
    IOLocal As Integer
    BufferSize As Long
    Buffer As String
    BNext As String
    EndRead As String
    EndWrite As String
    BufferOffset As Long
    DiskOffset As Long
    GenInfo(4) As Long
    Reserved1 As Long
    Reserved2 As Long
    mmHandle As Integer
End Type

Type BitMapHeader
    bsize As Long
    BWidth As Long
    BHeight As Long
    Planes As Integer
    BitCount As Integer
    Compression As Long
    SizeImage As Long
    XPelsPerMeter As Long
    YPelsPerMeter As Long
    ClrUsed As Long
    ClrImportant As Long
End Type
```

```
Type StreamHeader
    Type As String * 4
    Handler As String * 4
    Flags As Long
    Reserved1 As Long
    InitialFrames As Long
    SScale As Long
    Rate As Long
    Start As Long
    Length As Long
    SuggestedBufferSize As Long
    Quality As Long
    SampleSize As Long
End Type

Global mmHandle As Integer
Global ErrorInfo As GeneralInfo
Global FileInfo As ChunkInfo
Global WaveData As WaveFormat
Global Streaminfo As StreamHeader
Global VideoInfo As BitMapHeader
Global CRLF As String
Global AVIInfo As AviHeader
Global DisplayEncounter As Integer
Global DISPInfo As DisplayInfo
Global ISBJInfo As ISBJData
Global sresult As String

' Declare the various functions we can use for mci stuff.
' Function for opening a RIFF file.
Declare Function mmioOpen Lib "mmsystem" (ByVal Filename As String,
➥ ByVal Junk As Long, ByVal Flags As Long) As Integer
Declare Function mmioDescend Lib "mmsystem" (ByVal Handle As Integer,
➥ mmInfo As ChunkInfo, ParentInfo As Long, ByVal Flags As Integer)
➥ As Integer
Declare Function mmioAscend Lib "mmsystem" (ByVal Handle As Integer,
➥ mmInfo As ChunkInfo, ByVal Flags As Integer) As Integer
Declare Function mmioRead Lib "mmsystem" (ByVal Handle As Integer,
➥ mmInfo As Any, ByVal BytesToRead As Long) As Long
Declare Function mmioSeek Lib "mmsystem" (ByVal Handle As Integer,
➥ ByVal Offset As Long, ByVal Origin As Integer) As Long
Declare Function mmioClose Lib "mmsystem" (ByVal Handle As Integer,
➥ ByVal Flags As Integer) As Integer

' Declare function for getting info from control.ini and system.ini
Declare Function GetPrivateProfileString Lib "Kernel" (ByVal
➥ lpApplicationName As String, ByVal lpKeyName As String,
➥ ByVal lpDefault As String, ByVal lpReturnedString As String,
➥ ByVal nSize As Integer, ByVal lpFileName As String) As Integer
```

```
Sub AscendChunk ()
    If mmHandle <> 0 Then
     result% = mmioAscend(mmHandle, FileInfo, 0)
     If result% = 0 Then
     Else
         ' Error.
         If result% = 265 Then
          'End of file.  No more chunks!"
         Else
          'Unknown error.  Watch out!"
         End If
     End If
    Else
     'No file is open."
    End If
End Sub

Sub CheckData (GridForm As Form)
    Dim bsize As Long
    Dim temp As String * 1024
    Dim temp2 As String

    GridForm.Grid1.Col = 1
    If FileInfo.ChunkID = "strh" Then
     ChunkType = "AVIHeader"
      ' Get stream header data.
     result# = mmioRead(mmHandle, Streaminfo, FileInfo.ChunkSize)
     If result# <> FileInfo.ChunkSize Then
         'Failed to read AVI stream header.
     Else
         If Asc(Streaminfo.Handler) > 0 Then
          ' Get description of codec from control.ini, if available.
          res% = GetPrivateProfileString("drivers", "VIDC." +
➥Streaminfo.Handler, Streaminfo.Handler, temp, 1024, "system.ini")
          temp2 = parse(temp, 1)
          res% = GetPrivateProfileString("drivers.desc", temp2,
➥Streaminfo.Handler, temp, 1024, "Control.ini")

          ' Display results.
          GridForm.Grid1.Row = 0
          GridForm.Grid1.Text = Str$(Streaminfo.Quality / 100)

          GridForm.Grid1.Row = 1
          GridForm.Grid1.Text = temp

         End If
     End If
    End If

    If FileInfo.ChunkID = "strf" Then
     ChunkType = "AVIFormat"
```

```
       ' Get stream format data.
       ' Determine if audio or video format.
       If Streaminfo.Type = "auds" Then
           IsWaveFile = True
       Else
           '"vids" chunk.
           IsWaveFile = False
           ' Display video information.
           result# = mmioRead(mmHandle, VideoInfo, 40)
           If result# <> 40 Then
            'Failed to read AVI stream format (type:
➥ " + StreamInfo.Type + ")."
          Else
            ' Display results.
            GridForm.Grid1.Row = 2
            GridForm.Grid1.Text = Str$(VideoInfo.BitCount) + " bits"

            GridForm.Grid1.Row = 3
            GridForm.Grid1.Text = Str$(VideoInfo.BWidth) + " x" +
➥ Str$(VideoInfo.BHeight)
          End If
       End If
     End If

     If IsWaveFile Then
      ' Get format chunk?
      If FileInfo.ChunkID = "fmt " Or FileInfo.ChunkID = "strf" Then
          ' Get data about this file.
          result# = mmioRead(mmHandle, WaveData, FileInfo.ChunkSize)
          If result# <> FileInfo.ChunkSize Then
            'Failed to read Wave file format."
          Else
            ' Display results.
            If WaveData.Channels = 1 Then
                sresult = "Mono"
            Else
                sresult = "Stereo,"
            End If
            GridForm.Grid1.Row = 4
            GridForm.Grid1.Text = sresult

            GridForm.Grid1.Row = 5
            GridForm.Grid1.Text = Str$(WaveData.Sample / 1000) + "kHz"

            GridForm.Grid1.Row = 6
            GridForm.Grid1.Text = Str$(WaveData.Bits) + " bits"
          End If
      End If
     End If
```

```
        If FileInfo.ChunkID = "avih" Then
          ' Display file information.
          result# = mmioRead(mmHandle, AVIInfo, FileInfo.ChunkSize)
          If result# <> FileInfo.ChunkSize Then
              'Failed to read main AVI header."
          Else
              ' Display results.
              If AVIInfo.Streams = 1 Then
               sresult = "Video; no audio."
              Else
               sresult = "Audio and video."
              End If
               GridForm.Grid1.Row = 7
               GridForm.Grid1.Text = Str$(AVIInfo.AWidth)

               GridForm.Grid1.Row = 8
               GridForm.Grid1.Text = Str$(AVIInfo.AHeight)

               GridForm.Grid1.Row = 9
               GridForm.Grid1.Text = sresult

               GridForm.Grid1.Row = 10
               GridForm.Grid1.Text =
➥ Str$(CInt(AVIInfo.MaxBytesPerSec / 1024)) + "k/sec"

               GridForm.Grid1.Row = 11
               GridForm.Grid1.Text = Str$(AVIInfo.TotalFrames)
          End If
        End If
End Sub

Sub DescendChunk ()
    If mmHandle <> 0 Then
     result% = mmioDescend(mmHandle, FileInfo, 0, 0)
     If result% = 0 Then
         CheckData Form4
     Else
         ' Error.
         If result% = 265 Then
          'End of file.  No more chunks!"
         Else
          'Unknown error.  Watch out!"
         End If
     End If
    Else
     'No file is open."
    End If
End Sub
```

```
Sub SetupGrid (GridForm As Form)
    GridForm.Grid1.Col = 0

    GridForm.Grid1.Row = 0
    GridForm.Grid1.Text = "Quality factor"

    GridForm.Grid1.Row = 1
    GridForm.Grid1.Text = "Compression method"

    GridForm.Grid1.Row = 2
    GridForm.Grid1.Text = "Color depth"

    GridForm.Grid1.Row = 3
    GridForm.Grid1.Text = "Image size"

    GridForm.Grid1.Row = 4
    GridForm.Grid1.Text = "Audio"

    GridForm.Grid1.Row = 5
    GridForm.Grid1.Text = "  Frequency"

    GridForm.Grid1.Row = 6
    GridForm.Grid1.Text = "  Resolution"

    GridForm.Grid1.Row = 7
    GridForm.Grid1.Text = "Width"

    GridForm.Grid1.Row = 8
    GridForm.Grid1.Text = "Height"

    GridForm.Grid1.Row = 9
    GridForm.Grid1.Text = "Contents"

    GridForm.Grid1.Row = 10
    GridForm.Grid1.Text = "Maximum data rate"

    GridForm.Grid1.Row = 11
    GridForm.Grid1.Text = "Total frames"
End Sub

Sub WalkFile (GridForm As Form)
    GridForm.Grid1.ColWidth(1) = GridForm.Grid1.Width * .6
    GridForm.Grid1.ColWidth(0) = GridForm.Grid1.Width * .4

    DescendChunk
    DescendChunk
    DescendChunk

    AscendChunk
    DescendChunk
    DescendChunk
```

```
        AscendChunk
        DescendChunk

        AscendChunk
        DescendChunk
        DescendChunk

        AscendChunk
        DescendChunk
End  Sub
```

RIFFWalker Application

And now, as the Monty Python crew used to say, for something entirely different. In the preceding sections of this chapter, I stressed the relative ease with which you could access MCI commands and video functionality. In this section, we'll work at a lower level, with the resulting increase in the degree of difficulty.

The RiffWalker application does just what its name suggests: it walks through the data in an AVI file. An AVI file is actually a RIFF file, you see, and we'll need to use standard RIFFing techniques to find our way. Along the way, you'll learn a lot about the internal structure of RIFF files, and about AVI files in particular. I can't cover everything you'll need to know here, however, so I suggest you turn to the Microsoft Video for Windows Development Kit, available directly from Microsoft, for more information.

Concepts Behind RiffWalk

The RiffWalker application uses the mmio functions to open, read, navigate, and then close an AVI file. This is a completely different way of accessing an AVI file than MCI command strings.

Unlike many kinds of files, you must have a fairly intimate knowledge of an AVI file's structure before you can get any information out of it. The file is separated into chunks, and each chunk has a specific structure that you must know if you are to read the chunk.

The chunks are nested in a hierarchy, which complicates things a bit. Instead of reading chunks serially—chunk one, chunk two, and so on—you have to navigate much more carefully through the file. The basic structure of a RIFF file, and the details of AVI files, is complex. To make sense out of the Using RiffWalk section, however, a basic understanding of RIFF files, and how AVI data is stored in the RIFF file, is needed.

The following diagram shows the basic nested, hierarchical structure of a RIFF file with AVI data in it. The highest level is the RIFF chunk—the whole file is one RIFF chunk. The next level consists of three chunks: two LIST chunks, and an idx1 (index) chunk.

The first list chunk contains the avih (AVI header) chunk, which in turn contains a LIST chunk with the stream header chunks. There will be one such LIST chunk for the video stream, and another for the audio stream. There will be additional LIST chunks for any additional streams.

Following all of the header chunks, we find the second LIST chunk, which contains the actual video and audio data in a moviE chunk. This contains further subchunks containing data; at the lowest level is single frame data.

Finally, the file may or may not contain an optional index chunk. The index chunk, if present, allows for much faster access to specific frames because it provides an index to the location of the chunks for individual frames.

A general outline of the RIFF chunks in an AVI File follows. The four-letter names in uppercase are *Chunk IDs,* and the lowercase ones are called *Form Types.* If a chunk has a form type, you can count on there being some sub-chunks at the next lower level in the hierarchy.

```
RIFF ('AVI '
    LIST ('hdrl'
          'avih'(<Main AVI Header>)
          LIST ('strl'
                'strh'(<Stream header>)
                'strf'(<Stream format>)
                'strd'(additional stream header data)
                . (additional streams, if any)
                .
                .
                )
          .
          .
          .
          )
    LIST ('movi'
          {SubChunk ¦ LIST('rec '
                SubChunk1
                SubChunk2
```

```
                    .
                    .
                    .
                 )
            .
            .
            .
           }
            .
            .
            .
             )
       ['idx1'<AVIIndex>]
        )
```

I'll provide more detail about the content of chunks, particularly the header chunks, in the later sections of this chapter. You'll also see some structure as a result of the following tutorial on using RiffWalker. Finally, the best way to get a good grasp on AVI file structure is to spend some time using RiffWalker on your own, ascending and descending until the overall structure starts to make some sense.

You may want to refer back to this illustration of the structure of a RIFF file as you read the following section.

Using RiffWalk

The RiffWalker screen is shown in Figure 16.8. It contains a large area at the top for messages and information, and a number of text boxes that will tell us things we want to know about the AVI file. There are also three buttons: Go Top, Descend, and Ascend.

To open an AVI file, click on the File/Open menu selection and choose a file using the common dialog that is presented to you. When the file is opened successfully, you'll see a message specifying the file name, and the handle that was returned for the file. The handle is also placed in the text box labelled "Result code." Each call to an mmio function returns a result code, and it is displayed in this same box. (See Figure 16.9.)

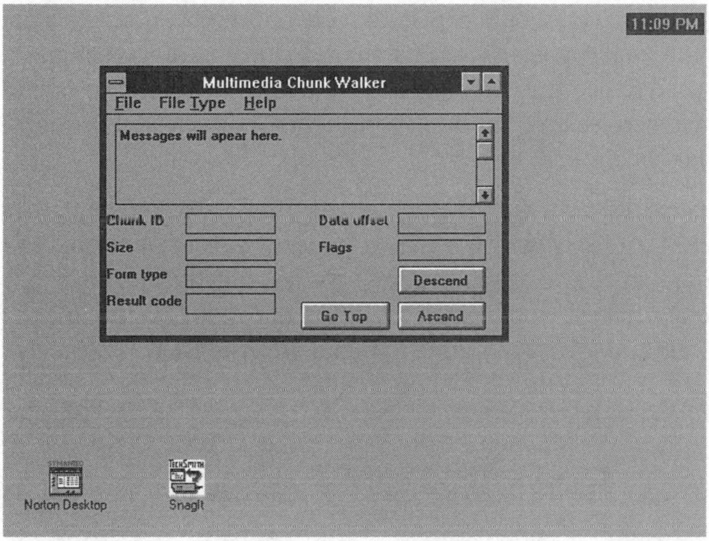

Figure 16.8. The opening window of RiffWalker.

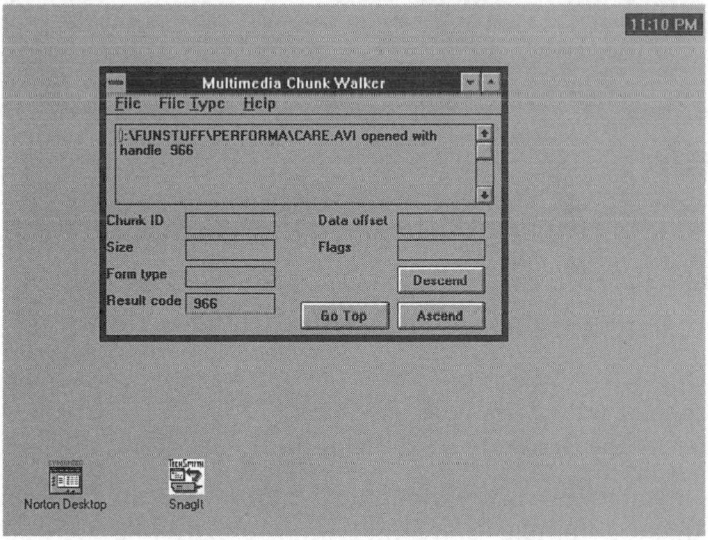

Figure 16.9. RiffWalk after a file has been opened.

Once the file is open, the next order of business is to descend to the next level of the hierarchy. If you refer back to the structure of the RIFF file in the

preceding section, you would expect to see a Chunk ID of "RIFF" and a form type of "AVI ". Note that there are four characters in both chunk types and form types. A space is used to pad the "AVI " form type. The "AVI " form type is also an exception to the lowercase used for other form types. Technically, the entire AVI data set is one large chunk.

Figure 16.10 shows the RiffWalk screen after a single click on the Descend button. What we see is exactly what we expected to see: A chunk ID of "RIFF", a form type of "AVI ", and a result code of zero meaning: no error. The size of the chunk also is what we would expect: it's the complete file size, minus 8 bytes for the Chunk ID and form type (note the data offset of 8).

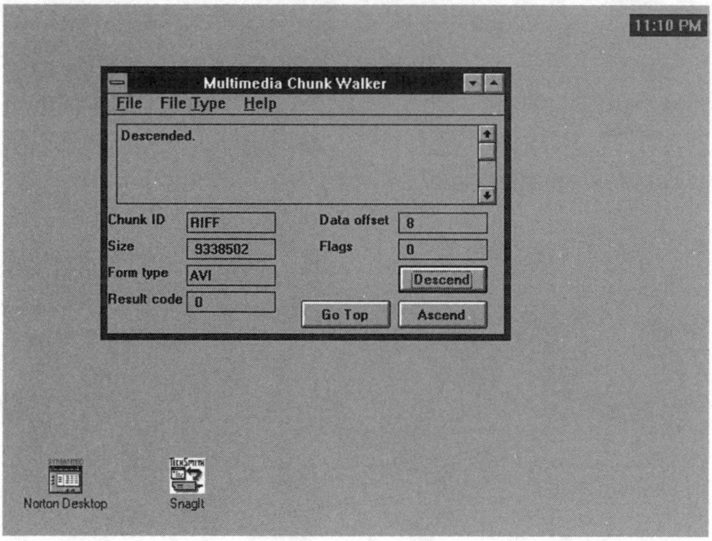

Figure 16.10. RiffWalk after a single click of the Descend button.

Because there was a form type, we expect to find a sub-chunk if we descend again. A click of the Descend button yields the results shown in Figure 16.11.

Again, if you refer back to the outline of a RIFF file in the preceding section, you'll see that the chunk ID and form type are exactly what we would expect. We are now 20 bytes into the file (there were some bytes used to store the size of the chunks). The chunk ID is "LIST", and the form type is "hdrl". So far, no surprises.

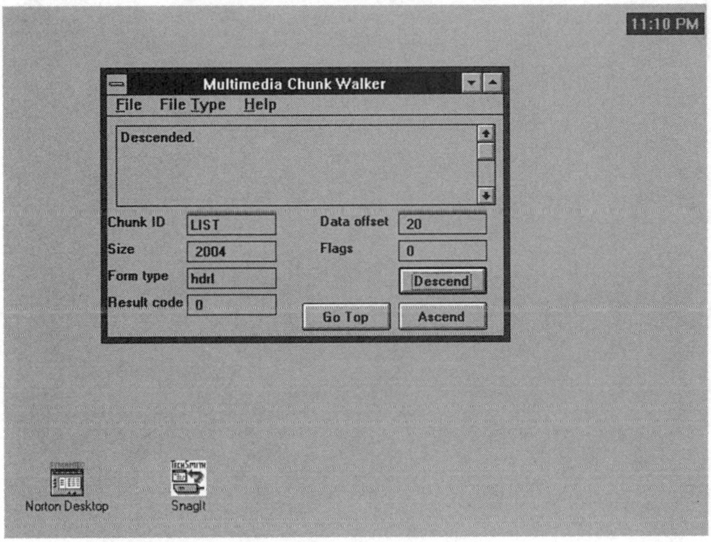

Figure 16.11. A second click of the Descend button.

We'll click Descend again because there was a form type and that tells us to expect another sub-chunk. You don't want to try to descend when there isn't another sub-chunk; that will get things totally out of alignment, and you can no longer reliably ascend and descend on chunk boundaries. The result of the descent is shown in Figure 16.12.

This time, we see something a little different. The chunk ID is now lower-case, and there is no form type. Note also that there is lots of information displayed in the message area at the top of the window. We can see that the maximum data rate for this file is 154K/second, and that there are 961 frames in the file. This and the remaining information was obtained from the "avih" chunk. As we'll see in the section "RIFF Structures," the structure of this chunk is easily accessible in Visual Basic. We use a user-defined data type to define the contents of the structure, which makes it easy to decode the contents.

There is no form type here, so it is time to click the Ascend button, with the results shown in Figure 16.13. Actually, there are no results, as no data is read. All we get is a result code, zero, telling us that we ascended successfully. To get anywhere, we'll now need to click the Descend button again. The result is shown in Figure 16.14.

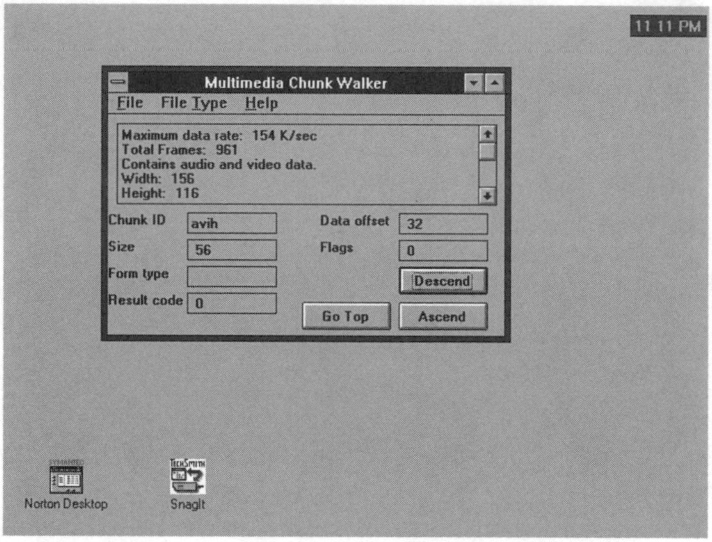

Figure 16.12. RiffWalk after a third click of the Descend button.

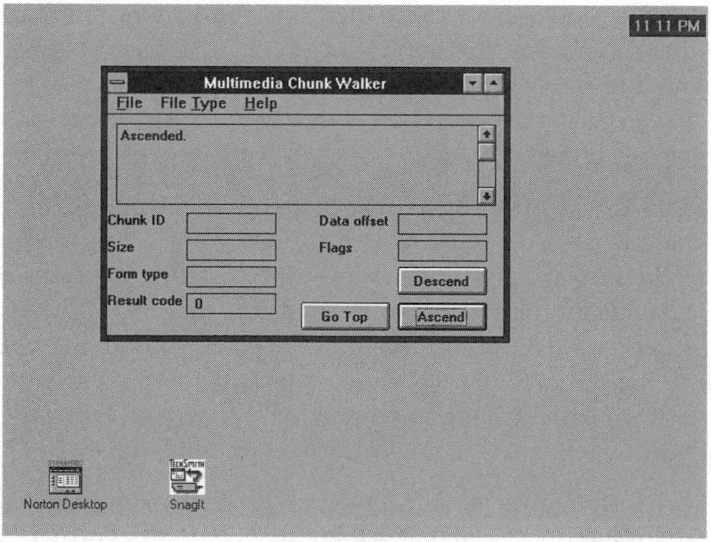

Figure 16.13. RiffWalk after clicking the Ascend button.

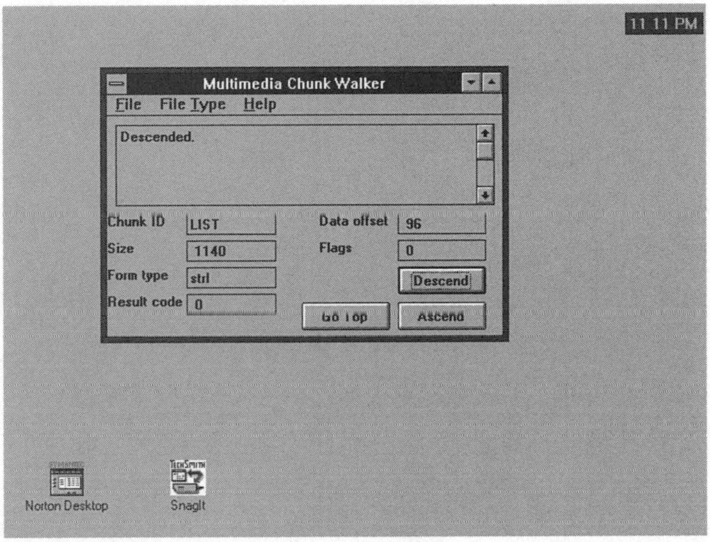

Figure 16.14. RiffWalk after beginning the second descent.

The contents of Figure 16.14 are just what we would expect to see: a chunk ID of "LIST" and a form type of "strl". The entire chunk is 1,140 bytes long. We expect to see two video header chunks, and two audio header chunks within this LIST chunk. So far, we are a mere 96 bytes into the AVI file, as shown in the Data offset box. Because there is a form type, we will click the Descend button again. The result is shown in Figure 16.15, where we find the "strh" header as expected. This chunk has no form type, and thus no sub-chunks, so we see a second chunk of information about the AVI file. We learn such things as the quality factor (100) and the compression method (MSVC). The compression method can be specified more exactly by using the function GetPrivateProfileString to access the driver name associated with MSVC in system.ini (in the section [drivers]), and then using the driver name to get the driver description from control.ini (in the section [drivers.desc]). The code for accomplishing this can be found in the Video Tester application earlier in this chapter, in the code for chunk.bas.

We can continue to navigate through the AVI file in this same manner, Ascending when there is no form type, and descending when there is. You can, of course, ascend before descending completely, and you will then descend at the higher level that leaves you at. You can also ascend several levels and then descend. Doing so, naturally, requires that you know where you are as you do so. If you go completely wrong, and get lost, or find yourself getting to chunk after chunk of similar video or audio data, click the Go Top button and start over.

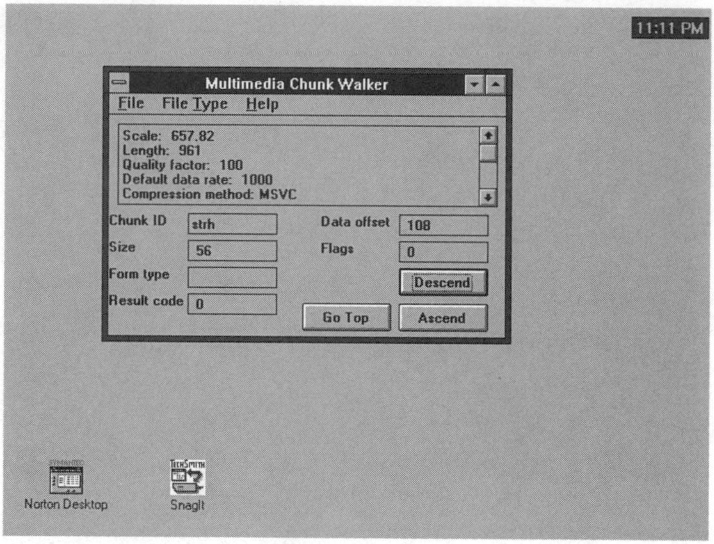

Figure 16.15. Descending into a data chunk.

When you get past all of the header information, you'll see another LIST chunk, as shown in Figure 16.16.

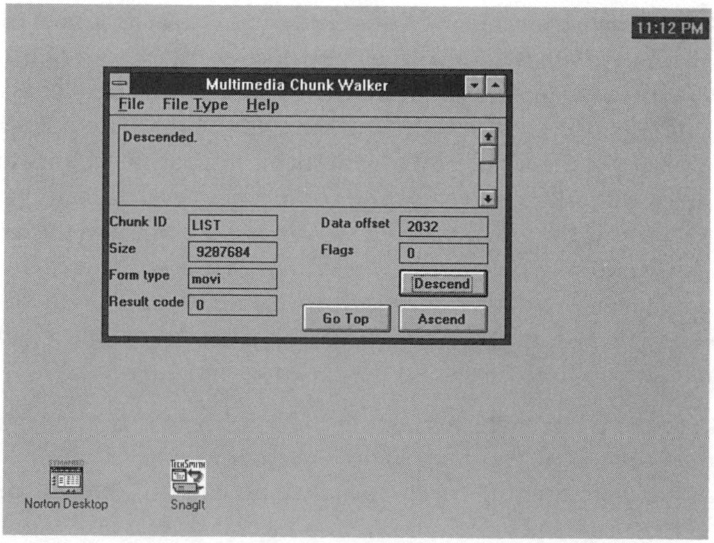

Figure 16.16. The LIST chunk containing the video and audio data.

At this point, the Data offset is 2032; we're just 2K bytes into the file (2032 plus eight bytes for the two four-character codes and eight more for the size, a long integer). The form type of this chunk is `"movi"` which tells us we have found the video/audio data. Clicking the Descend button again takes us to a subchunk with a form type of `"rec "`. This is a single record, as shown in Figure 16.17.

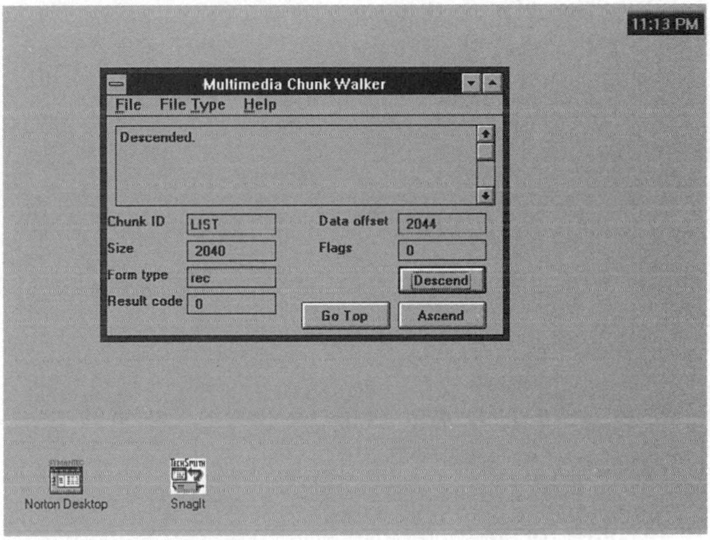

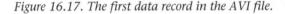

Figure 16.17. The first data record in the AVI file.

Note that the chunk size is 2040; minus the eight bytes for the two four-character codes, that makes 2K. That tells us that the file was probably saved with Padding for CD-ROM turned on, so we can expect to see some padding chunks. The Chunk ID for these pads is `"JUNK"`.

Figure 16.18 shows a data chunk, with a chunk ID of `"01wb"`.

The following summary shows a LIST chunk, form type rec, that contains three sub-chunks—video data, audio data, and a JUNK chunk:

```
Chunk ID: LIST
Chunk Size: 14328
Form Type: rec

     Chunk ID: 00AM
     Chunk Size: 12712

     Chunk ID: 01wb
     Chunk Size: 1195
```

```
Chunk ID: JUNK
Chunk Size: 392
```

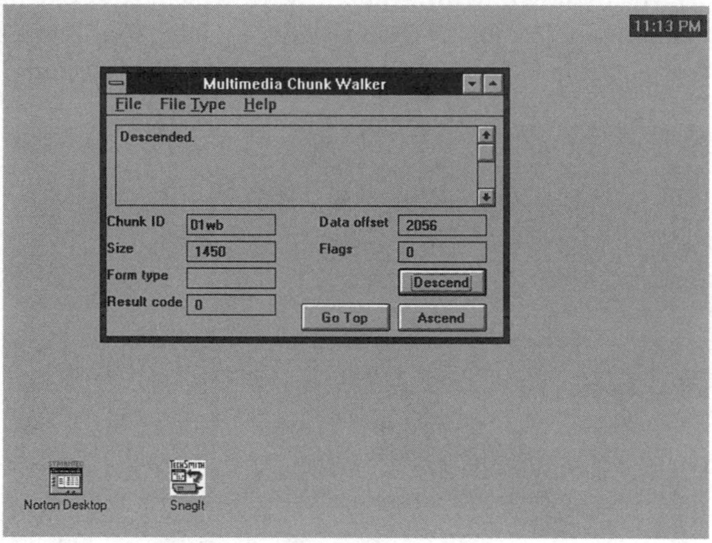

Figure 16.18. A data chunk in the AVI file.

You may see chunks of only audio data before you see chunks with both audio and video data. There is so much more video data than audio data that the audio usually needs a "running start" to avoid breakup of the audio while video data is being read. This audio offset is one of the many things defined in the header section, so that playback code knows how to synchronize the two data streams. The audio-only chunks will be much smaller than the chunk illustrated above, often a mere 2K bytes, as in Figure 16.18.

Programming with the mmio Functions

Now that we have seen how RiffWalk works, it's time to see why it works the way it does. There are three steps involved in explaining RiffWalk:

➤ Using the mmio functions.

➤ Contents of the RIFF structures for an AVI file.

➤ Accessing the RIFF structures with Visual Basic code.

The Visual Basic declarations for the `mmio` functions are included in the code for chunk.bas:

```
Declare Function mmioOpen Lib "mmsystem" (ByVal Filename As String,
➥ ByVal Junk As Long, ByVal Flags As Long) As Integer

Declare Function mmioDescend Lib "mmsystem" (ByVal Handle As Integer,
➥ mmInfo As ChunkInfo, ParentInfo As Long, ByVal Flags As Integer)
➥ As Integer

Declare Function mmioAscend Lib "mmsystem" (ByVal Handle As Integer,
➥ mmInfo As ChunkInfo, ByVal Flags As Integer) As Integer

Declare Function mmioRead Lib "mmsystem" (ByVal Handle As Integer,
➥ mmInfo As Any, ByVal BytesToRead As Long) As Long

Declare Function mmioSeek Lib "mmsystem" (ByVal Handle As Integer,
➥ ByVal Offset As Long, ByVal Origin As Integer) As Long

Declare Function mmioClose Lib "mmsystem" (ByVal Handle As Integer,
➥ ByVal Flags As Integer) As Integer
```

The arguments for these functions are critical to correct usage.

```
Declare Function mmioOpen Lib "mmsystem" (ByVal Filename As String,
➥ ByVal Junk As Long, ByVal Flags As Long) As Integer
```

The return value is a handle that must be used in all subsequent references to the open file. This function takes three arguments:

Argument	Data type	Description
Filename	String	The name of the file to open.
Junk	Long	This parameter only applies to memory files and other special uses of mmioOpen. Use NULL as a value in all cases for Visual Basic use.
Flags	Long	These flags specify the options for the open operations. The flags are listed in Table 16.5.

Table 16.5. Flags for mmioOpen function.

Flag	Value	Description
MMIO_READ	0x00000000	open file for reading only
MMIO_WRITE	0x00000001	open file for writing only
MMIO_READWRITE	0x00000002	open file for reading and writing
MMIO_COMPAT	0x00000000	compatibility mode
MMIO_EXCLUSIVE	0x00000010	exclusive-access mode
MMIO_DENYWRITE	0x00000020	deny writing to other processes
MMIO_DENYREAD	0x00000030	deny reading to other processes
MMIO_DENYNONE	0x00000040	deny nothing to other processes

```
Declare Function mmioDescend Lib "mmsystem" (ByVal Handle As Integer,
➥ mmInfo As ChunkInfo, ParentInfo As Long, ByVal Flags As Integer)
➥ As Integer
```

The return value is an integer that will be zero if no error occurs. This function takes four arguments:

Argument	Data type	Description
Handle	Integer	The handle returned by the mmioOpen function.
mmInfo	ChunkInfo	The data structure that will contain the results of the descent.
ParentInfo	Long	The data structure of the parent chunk. Optional; in most cases, use NULL.
Flags	Integer	These flags specify the options for the descend operation. The flags are listed in table 16.6.

Table 16.6. Flags for mmioDescend function.

Flag	Value	Description
MMIO_FINDCHUNK	0x0010	Find a chunk by ID
MMIO_FINDRIFF	0x0020	Find a RIFF chunk
MMIO_FINDLIST	0x0040	Find a LIST chunk

```
Declare Function mmioAscend Lib "mmsystem" (ByVal Handle As Integer,
➥ mmInfo As ChunkInfo, ByVal Flags As Integer) As Integer
```

The return value is an integer that will be zero if no error occurs. This function takes three arguments:

Argument	Data type	Description
Handle	Integer	The handle returned by the mmioOpen function.
mmInfo	ChunkInfo	The data structure previously filled by mmioDescend.
Flags	Integer	Note used; set to zero.

```
Declare Function mmioRead Lib "mmsystem" (ByVal Handle As Integer,
➥ mmInfo As Any, ByVal BytesToRead As Long) As Long
```

The return value is an integer that will be zero if no error occurs. This function takes three arguments:

Argument	Data type	Description
Handle	Integer	The handle returned by the mmioOpen function.
mmInfo	User Type	Buffer to hold data read from the file. Will be a user-defined type appropriate to the type of chunk being read.
BytesToRead	Long	The chunk size.

```
Declare Function mmioSeek Lib "mmsystem" (ByVal Handle As Integer,
➥ ByVal Offset As Long, ByVal Origin As Integer) As Long
```

The return value is a long that specified the new position in the file, or -1 if an error occurs. This function takes three arguments:

Argument	Data type	Description
Handle	Integer	The handle returned by the mmioOpen function.
Offset	Long	Number of bytes to move from origin.
Origin	Integer	Three possible values: SEEK_SET (0; beginning of file), SEEK_CUR (1; current position), and SEEK_END (2; end of file).

```
Declare Function mmioClose Lib "mmsystem" (ByVal Handle As Integer,
➥ ByVal Flags As Integer) As Integer
```

The return value is an integer that will be zero if no error occurs. This function takes two arguments:

Argument	Data type	Description
Handle	Integer	The handle returned by the mmioOpen function.
Flags	Integer	Options for close operation; see Table 16.7.

Table 16.7. Flags for mmioClose function.

Flag	Value	Description
MMIO_FHOPEN	0x0010	Close MMIO file handle, but not DOS file handle

For examples of the use of the mmio functions, see the code for Video Tester, module chunk.bas, and RiffWalk, module chunk.bas.

RIFF Structures

The key to accessing the data in the AVI file is knowledge of the C structures that are used to store the data. In this section, I've included both the C declarations for the various structures, and a sample Visual Basic user-defined type to access it.

The Main AVI Header LIST

The file begins with the main header. In the AVI file, this header is identified with "avih" four-character code. In the section on using RiffWalker, this is the chunk we reached with three clicks of the Descend button. The C structure for this chunk looks like this:

```
typedef struct {
    DWORD   dwMicroSecPerFrame;
    DWORD   dwMaxBytesPerSec;
    DWORD   dwReserved1;
    DWORD   dwFlags;
    DWORD   dwTotalFrames;
    DWORD   dwInitialFrames;
    DWORD   dwStreams;
    DWORD   dwSuggestedBufferSize;
    DWORD   dwWidth;
    DWORD   dwHeight;
    DWORD   dwScale;
    DWORD   dwRate;
    DWORD   dwStart;
    DWORD   dwLength;
} MainAVIHeader;
```

A Visual Basic user-defined data type for accessing this structure would look something like this:

```
Type AviHeader
    MicroSecPerFrame As Long
    MaxBytesPerSec As Long
    Reserved1 As Long
    Flags As Long
    TotalFrames As Long
    InitialFrames As Long
    Streams As Long
    SuggestedBufferSize As Long
    AWidth As Long
    AHeight As Long
    AScale As Long
    ARate As Long
```

```
      AStart As Long
      ALength As Long
End Type
```

Note that the Visual Basic structure substitutes Visual Basic data types, such as Long, for the C data types. The meaning of the various terms used in the structure is explained in Table 16.8.

Table 16.8. Elements of main AVI header structure 'avih'.

Element	Description
dwMicroSecPerFrame	Specifies the period between video frames. This value indicates the overall timing for the file.
dwMaxBytesPerSec	Specifies the approximate maximum data rate of the file. This value indicates the number of bytes per second the system must handle to present an AVI sequence as specified by the other parameters contained in the main header and stream header chunks.
dwFlags	Contains any flags for the file. The following flags are defined: AVIF_HASINDEX Indicates the AVI file has an "idx1" chunk. AVIF_MUSTUSEINDEX Indicates the index should be used to determine the order of presentation of the data. AVIF_ISINTERLEAVED Indicates the AVI file is interleaved. AVIF_WASCAPTUREFILE Indicates the AVI file is a specially allocated file used for capturing real-time video. AVIF_COPYRIGHTED Indicates the AVI file contains copyrighted data.
dwTotalFrames	Specifies the total number of frames of data in file.

Element	Description
dwInitialFrames	Used for interleaved files. If you are creating interleaved files, specify the number of frames in the file prior to the initial frame of the AVI sequence in this field.
dwStreams	Specifies the number of streams in the file. For example, a file with audio and video has two streams.
dwSuggestedBufferSize	Specifies the suggested buffer size for reading the file. Generally, this size should be large enough to contain the largest chunk in the file. If set to zero, or if it is too small, the playback software will have to reallocate memory during playback which will reduce performance. For an interleaved file, the buffer size should be large enough to read an entire record and not just a chunk.
dwWidth	Width of the AVI file in pixels.
dwHeight	Height of the AVI file in pixels.
dwScale	Specifies the general time scale that the file will use. In addition to this time scale, each stream can have its own time scale.
dwRate	The time scale in samples per second is determined by dividing dwRate by dwScale.
dwStart	Starting time of the AVI file. The dwStart field is usually set to zero. The units are defined by dwRate and dwScale.
dwLength	Length of the file. The units are defined by dwRate and dwScale.

The Stream Header ("strl") Chunks

The main header is followed by one or more "strl" chunks; a "strl" chunk is required for each data stream. Each "strl" chunk must contain a stream header and stream format chunk. Stream header chunks are identified by the four-character code "strh" and stream format chunks are identified with the four-character code "strf". In addition to the stream header and stream format chunks, the "strl" chunk might also contain a stream data chunk. Stream data chunks are identified with the four-character code "strd".

The C structure for a strl chunk looks like this:

```
typedef struct {
    FOURCC  fccType;
    FOURCC  fccHandler;
    DWORD   dwFlags;
    DWORD   dwReserved1;
    DWORD   dwInitialFrames;
    DWORD   dwScale;
    DWORD   dwRate;
    DWORD   dwStart;
    DWORD   dwLength;
    DWORD   dwSuggestedBufferSize;
    DWORD   dwQuality;
    DWORD   dwSampleSize;
} AVIStreamHeader;
```

A Visual Basic user-defined data type for accessing this structure would look something like this:

```
Type StreamHeader
    Type As String * 4
    Handler As String * 4
    Flags As Long
    Reserved1 As Long
    InitialFrames As Long
    SScale As Long
    Rate As Long
    Start As Long
    Length As Long
    SuggestedBufferSize As Long
    Quality As Long
    SampleSize As Long
End Type
```

Note that the string elements of the Visual Basic structure are fixed-length strings.

The stream header specifies the type of data the stream contains, such as audio or video, by means of a four-character code.

Table 16.9. Elements of stream header structure 'strl'.

Element	Description
fccType	Set to "vids" if the stream it specifies contains video data. It is set to "auds" if it contains audio data.
fccHandler	Contains a four-character code describing the installable compressor or decompressor used with the data.
dwFlags	Contains any flags for the data stream. The AVISF_DISABLED flag indicates that the stream data should be rendered only when explicitly enabled by the user. The AVISF_VIDEO_PALCHANGES flag indicates palette changes are embedded in the file.
dwInitialFrames	Used for interleaved files. If you are creating interleaved files, specify the number of frames in the file prior to the initial frame of the AVI sequence in this field.

The remaining fields describe the playback characteristics of the stream. These factors include the playback rate (dwScale and dwRate), the starting time of the sequence (dwStart), the length of the sequence (dwLength), the size of the playback buffer (dwSuggestedBuffer), an indicator of the data quality (dwQuality), and sample size (dwSampleSize).

Some of the fields in the stream header structure are also present in the main header structure. The data in the main header structure applies to the whole file while the data in the stream header structure applies only to a stream.

A stream format ("strf") chunk must follow a stream header ("strh") chunk. The stream format chunk describes the format of the data in the stream. For video streams, the information in this chunk is a BITMAPINFO structure (including palette information if appropriate). For audio streams, the information in this chunk is a WAVEFORMATEX or PCMWAVEFORMAT structure.

You can use the following Visual Basic structure for the audio stream format chunk (WAVEFORMAT) of most AVI files:

```
Type WaveFormat
    FormatType As Integer
    Channels As Integer
    Sample As Long
    Bytes As Long
    Block As Integer
    Bits As Integer
End Type
```

You can use the following Visual Basic structure for the video stream format chunk (BITMAPINFO) of most AVI files:

```
Type BitMapHeader
    BSize As Long
    BWidth As Long
    BHeight As Long
    Planes As Integer
    BitCount As Integer
    Compression As Long
    SizeImage As Long
    XPelsPerMeter As Long
    YPelsPerMeter As Long
    ClrUsed As Long
    ClrImportant As Long
End Type
```

The "strl" chunk might also contain a stream data ("strd") chunk. If used, this chunk follows the stream format chunk. The format and content of this chunk is defined by installable compression or decompression drivers. Typically, drivers use this information for configuration. Applications that read and write RIFF files do not need to decode this information. They transfer this data to and from a driver as a memory block.

An AVI player associates the stream headers in the LIST "hdrl" chunk with the stream data in the LIST "movi" chunk by using the order of the "strl" chunks. The first "strl" chunk applies to stream 0, the second applies to stream 1, and so forth. For example, if the first "strl" chunk describes the wave audio data, the wave audio data is contained in stream 0. Similarly, if the second "strl" chunk describes video data, the video data is contained in stream 1.

The LIST "movi" Chunk

The RiffWalker applications don't access any of the data chunks in the "movi" chunk, but I'll provide an overview of how the information is stored so you'll be able to make some sense out of what you find in the AVI files. This information borrows almost directly from the technical information released by Microsoft for AVI file formats. This information changes as new technologies become available. The best place to find the latest information is on CompuServe, in the WINEXT (Windows Extensions) forum. Section 2 is reserved for development issues related to Video for Windows. End-user questions are not appropriate in this forum.

Following the header information is a LIST "movi" chunk that contains chunks of the actual data in the streams—the pictures and sounds. The data chunks can reside directly in the LIST "movi" chunk or they might be grouped into "rec " chunks. The "rec " grouping implies that the grouped chunks should be read from disk all at once. This is used only for files specifically interleaved to play from CD-ROM.

Like any RIFF chunk, the data chunks contain a four-character code to identify the chunk type. The four-character code for each chunk consists of the stream number and a two-character code that defines the type of information encapsulated in the chunk.

An audio data chunk has the following format (the ## in the format represents the stream number):

```
WAVE  Bytes    '##wb'
      BYTE     abBytes[];
```

Video data can be compressed or uncompressed DIBs. An uncompressed DIB has BI_RGB (the C macro is: #define BI_RGB 0L) specified for the biCompression field in its associated BITMAPINFO structure. A compressed DIB has a value other than BI_RGB specified in the biCompression field.

A data chunk for an uncompressed DIB contains RGB video data. These chunks are identified with a two-character code of "db" (db is an abbreviation for DIB bits). Data chunks for a compressed DIB are identified with a two-character code of "dc" (dc is an abbreviation for DIB compressed). Neither data chunk will contain any header information about the DIBs. The data chunk for an uncompressed DIB has the following form:

```
DIB  Bits    '##db'
     BYTE    abBits[];
```

The data chunk for a compressed DIB has the following form:

```
Compressed DIB    '##dc'
     BYTE            abBits[];
```

Video data chunks can also define new palette entries used to update the palette during an AVI sequence. These chunks are identified with a two-character code of "pc" (pc is an abbreviation for palette change). The following data structure is defined palette information:

```
typedef struct {
    BYTE            bFirstEntry;
    BYTE            bNumEntries;
    WORD            wFlags;
    PALETTEENTRY    peNew;
} AVIPALCHANGE;
```

The bFirstEntry field defines the first entry to change and the bNumEntries field specifies the number of entries to change. The peNew field contains the new color entries.

A video stream with palette changes must have the AVITF_VIDEO_PALCHANGES flag set in the dwFlags field of the stream header. This flag indicates that this video stream contains palette changes and warns the playback software that it will need to animate the palette.

For examples of the use of the various structures, and some additional data structures that are useful for reading AVI files, see the code for Video Tester, module chunk.bas, and RiffWalker, module chunk.bas.

Summary

I've covered a lot of territory in this section, but in reality I have only touched on the most basic issues involved with the guts of an AVI file. For example, I have not even touched on the subject of writing AVI files. There's good reason for that: it is not an activity for mere mortals. It's a complex area, and requires a substantial amount of information to do correctly. Microsoft has provided numerous code examples in the Microsoft Video for Windows Development Kit, which is supplied in electronic form on the CD-ROM. You'll find it ready to be installed in the directory VFW-DK.

The Development Kit contains a wealth of useful information, and is being made available to you in this way at no charge by Microsoft. It includes complete documentation in electronic form.

Complete Source Code

This section includes the *complete* source code for the RiffWalker application. The code is divided by forms, and the code for each form is listed as a continuous stream of code. As you know, this is not how the code is accessed in Visual Basic. The handlers for various objects can be identified by the opening line of each section of code.

For example, the code for the Descend button is from chunk.frm, and begins with

```
Sub Command1_Click ()
```

This identifies the code as that which will be executed when the Command1 button is clicked. This allows you to find the code for appropriate portions of each form.

If you wish to look at or modify the code, you will need Version 2.0 of Visual Basic, Professional Edition. The application incorporates one .VBX file:

```
cmdialog.vbx
```

This file must be installed into your Windows system directory, usually **c:\windows\system**.

CHUNK.FRM

```
Sub AboutCtl_Click ()
    Form3.Show 1
End Sub

Sub AudioCtl_Click ()
    CMDialog1.FilterIndex = 2
    CMDialog1.Filename = "*.wav"
    VideoCtl.Checked = False
    AudioCtl.Checked = True
End Sub

Sub CheckData ()
    Dim bsize As Long

    If FileInfo.FormType = "WAVE" Then
        IsWaveFile = True
    End If

    If FileInfo.ChunkID = "strh" Then
        ChunkType = "AVIHeader"
```

```
                ' Get stream header data.
            result# = mmioRead(mmHandle, StreamInfo, FileInfo.ChunkSize)
            If result# <> FileInfo.ChunkSize Then
                Text1.Text = "Failed to read AVI stream header."
                Text7.Text = Str$(result#)
            Else
                ' Display results.
                sresult$ = "Scale: " + Str$(StreamInfo.SScale / 100) + CRLF
                sresult$ = sresult$ + "Length: " + Str$(StreamInfo.Length) +
➥ CRLF + "Quality factor: " + Str$(StreamInfo.Quality / 100) + CRLF +
➥ "Default data rate: " + Str$(StreamInfo.Rate / 1000) + CRLF
                sresult$ = sresult$ + "Compression method: " +
➥ StreamInfo.Handler + CRLF
                Text1.Text = sresult$
            End If
            ' Determine if audio or video format.
            If StreamInfo.Type = "auds" Then
                IsWaveFile = True
            Else
                '"vids" chunk.
                IsWaveFile = False
                ' Display video information.
            End If
        End If
        If FileInfo.ChunkID = "strf" Then
            ChunkType = "AVIFormat"
            ' Get stream format data.
            ' Determine if audio or video format.
            If StreamInfo.Type = "auds" Then
                IsWaveFile = True
            Else
                '"vids" chunk.
                IsWaveFile = False
                ' Display video information.
                result# = mmioRead(mmHandle, VideoInfo, 40)
                If result# <> 40 Then
                    Text1.Text = "Failed to read AVI stream format (type: " +
➥ StreamInfo.Type + ")."
                    Text7.Text = Str$(result#)
                Else
                    ' Display results.
                    sresult$ = "Header size: " + Str$(VideoInfo.bsize) + CRLF
                    sresult$ = sresult$ + "Color depth: " +
➥ Str$(VideoInfo.BitCount) + " bits. " + CRLF
                    sresult$ = sresult$ + "Image size: " +
➥ Str$(VideoInfo.BWidth) + " x" + Str$(VideoInfo.BHeight) + CRLF +
➥ "Compression method: " + Str$(VideoInfo.Compression)
                    Text1.Text = sresult$
                End If
            End If
        End If
    End If
```

```
    If IsWaveFile Then
        ' Get format chunk?
        If FileInfo.ChunkID = "fmt " Or FileInfo.ChunkID = "strf" Then
            ' Get data about this file.
            result# = mmioRead(mmHandle, WaveData, FileInfo.ChunkSize)
            If result# <> FileInfo.ChunkSize Then
                Text1.Text = "Failed to read Wave file format."
                Text7.Text = Str$(result#)
            Else
                ' Display results.
                sresult$ = "Audio data is "
                If WaveData.Channels = 1 Then
                    sresult$ = sresult$ + "mono,"
                Else
                    sresult$ = sresult$ + "stereo,"
                End If
                sresult$ = sresult$ + " at " +
➥ Str$(WaveData.Sample / 1000) + "kHz," + CRLF +
➥ "with a sample resolution of " + Str$(WaveData.Bits) + " bits."
                Text1.Text = sresult$
            End If
        End If
    End If
    If FileInfo.ChunkID = "avih" Then
            ' Display file information.
            result# = mmioRead(mmHandle, AVIInfo, FileInfo.ChunkSize)
            If result# <> FileInfo.ChunkSize Then
                Text1.Text = "Failed to read main AVI header."
                Text7.Text = Str$(result#)
            Else
                ' Display results.
                sresult$ = "Maximum data rate: " +
➥ Str$(CInt(AVIInfo.MaxBytesPerSec / 1024)) + " K/sec" + CRLF
                sresult$ = sresult$ + "Total Frames: " +
➥ Str$(AVIInfo.TotalFrames) + CRLF
                If AVIInfo.Streams = 1 Then
                    sresult$ = sresult$ +
➥ "Video data only; no audio track."
                Else
                    sresult$ = sresult$ + "Contains audio and video data."
                End If
                sresult$ = sresult$ + CRLF + "Width: " +
➥ Str$(AVIInfo.AWidth) + CRLF
                sresult$ = sresult$ + "Height: " +
➥ Str$(AVIInfo.AHeight) + CRLF
                Text1.Text = sresult$
            End If
    End If
    If FileInfo.ChunkID = "DISP" Or FileInfo.ChunkID = "ISBJ" Then
        sresult$ = ""
        If FileInfo.ChunkSize > 2048 Then
```

```
                  sresult$ = sresult$ + "Display chunk type: " +
➡ Str$(DISPInfo.DType) + CRLF
                  sresult$ = "Chunk data is too large to read.
➡ May not be text!" + CRLF + CRLF
          Else
              ' Display text.
              If FileInfo.ChunkID = "ISBJ" Then
                  ' Use a different structure.
                  result# = mmioRead(mmHandle, ISBJInfo, FileInfo.ChunkSize)
                  If result# <> FileInfo.ChunkSize Then
                      Text1.Text = "Failed to read ISBJ chunk correctly."
                      Text7.Text = Str$(result#)
                  Else
                      sresult$ = sresult$ + "Chunk contents: " +
➡ ISBJInfo.TextDesc
                  End If
              Else
                  result# = mmioRead(mmHandle, DISPInfo, FileInfo.ChunkSize)
                  If result# <> FileInfo.ChunkSize Then
                      Text1.Text = "Failed to read DISP chunk correctly."
                      Text7.Text = Str$(result#)
                  Else
                      sresult$ = sresult$ + "DISP chunk type: " +
➡ Str$(DISPInfo.DType) + CRLF
                      If DISPInfo.DType = 1 Then
                          sresult$ = sresult$ + "Chunk contents: " +
➡ DISPInfo.TextDesc
                      End If
                  End If
              End If
          End If
          ' Display results.
          Text1.Text = sresult$
      End If
End Sub

Sub ClearText ()
    ' Clear text boxes.
    Text2.Text = ""
    Text3.Text = ""
    Text4.Text = ""
    Text5.Text = ""
    Text6.Text = ""
End Sub

Sub CloseCtl_Click ()
    If mmHandle > 0 Then
        result% = mmioClose(mmHandle, 0)
        Text7.Text = Str$(result%)
        If result% = 0 Then
            Text1.Text = "File closed successfully."
```

```
        Else
            Text1.Text = "*** Danger!*** Error closing file!"
        End If
        mmHandle = 0
        OpenCtl.Enabled = True
        CloseCtl.Enabled = False
        IsWaveFile = False
    End If
    ' Clear text boxes.
    Text2.Text = ""
    Text3.Text = ""
    Text4.Text = ""
    Text5.Text = ""
    Text6.Text = ""
End Sub

Sub Command1_Click ()
    If mmHandle <> 0 Then
        result% = mmioDescend(mmHandle, FileInfo, 0, 0)
        Text7.Text = Str$(result%)
        If result% = 0 Then
            Text2.Text = FileInfo.ChunkID
            Text3.Text = Str$(FileInfo.ChunkSize)
            Text4.Text = FileInfo.FormType
            Text5.Text = Str$(FileInfo.ChunkDataOffset)
            Text6.Text = Str$(FileInfo.ChunkFlags)
            Text1.Text = "Descended."
            CheckData

        Else
            ' Error.
            If result% = 265 Then
                Text1.Text = "End of file.  No more chunks!"
            Else
                Text1.Text = "Unknown error.  Watch out!"
            End If
        End If
    Else
        Text1.Text = "No file is open."
    End If
End Sub

Sub Command2_Click ()
    If mmHandle <> 0 Then
        result% = mmioAscend(mmHandle, FileInfo, 0)
        Text7.Text = Str$(result%)
        If result% = 0 Then
            Text1.Text = "Ascended."
        Else
            ' Error.
            If result% = 265 Then
```

```
                        Text1.Text = "End of file.  No more chunks!"
                Else
                        Text1.Text = "Unknown error.  Watch out!"
                End If
            End If
        Else
            Text1.Text = "No file is open."
        End If
        ClearText
End Sub

Sub Command3_Click ()
    If mmHandle > 0 Then
        result& = mmioSeek(mmHandle, 0, 0)
        If result& = -1 Then
            Text1.Text = "Could not seek to beginning of file."
        Else
            Text1.Text = "Positioned at top of file."
            Text7.Text = Str$(result&)
        End If
    End If
    ClearText
    DisplayEncounter = 0
End Sub

Sub ExitCtl_Click ()
    If mmHandle > 0 Then
        result% = mmioClose(mmHandle, 0)
    End If
    End
End Sub

Sub Form_Load ()
    Form1.Top = 0
    Form1.Left = 0
    CMDialog1.Filter = "Video (*.avi)¦*.AVI¦Audio (*.wav)¦*.WAV"
    CMDialog1.FilterIndex = 1
    CMDialog1.Filename = "*.avi"
    VideoCtl.Checked = True
    AudioCtl.Checked = False
    CRLF = Chr(13) + Chr(10)
End Sub

Sub Form_Unload (Cancel As Integer)
    If mmHandle > 0 Then
        result% = mmioClose(mmHandle, 0)
    End If
End Sub

Sub HelpCtl_Click ()
    Form2.Show
```

```
End Sub

Sub OpenCtl_Click ()
    If mmHandle <> 0 Then
        Text1.Text = "File already open.  Close it first."
        Exit Sub
    End If

    CMDialog1.Action = 1
    AVIFile = CMDialog1.Filename
    'AVIFile = "c:\ron\video\anger.avi"

    If Len(AVIFile) > 0 Then
        mmHandle = mmioOpen(AVIFile, 0&, 2&)
        Text7.Text = Str$(mmHandle)
        If mmHandle = 0 Then
            Text1.Text = "Unable to open " + AVIFile
        Else
            Text1.Text = AVIFile + " opened with handle " + Str$(mmHandle)
        End If
        CloseCtl.Enabled = True
        OpenCtl.Enabled = False
    End If
End Sub

Sub VideoCtl_Click ()
    CMDialog1.FilterIndex = 1
    CMDialog1.Filename = "*.avi"
    VideoCtl.Checked = True
    AudioCtl.Checked = False
End Sub
```

CHUNK2.FRM

```
Sub Form_Load ()
    Form2.Top = 0
    Form2.Left = (640 * 15) - Form2.Width

DS = "Introduction" + Chr(13) + Chr(10)
DS = DS + "--------------------" + Chr(13) + Chr(10)
DS = DS + "The key to understanding RIFF files is two-fold:
➥ knowing how the file is put "
DS = DS + "together, and knowing
➥ the C structures that are used to organize the data stored "
DS = DS + "in the file.  An overview of the layout of a RIFF file
➥ is included below." + Chr(13) + Chr(10) + Chr(13) + Chr(10)

DS = DS + "Instructions" + Chr(13) + Chr(10) + Chr(13) + Chr(10)
DS = DS + "--------------------" + Chr(13) + Chr(10)
DS = DS + "To get started, you can try the following sequence;
```

```
➥ it hits the high points." + Chr(13) + Chr(10) + Chr(13) + Chr(10)
DS = DS + "* Descend three times, to move through the 'RIFF', 'LIST',
➥ and 'avih' chunks.  This will display the AVI header info.
➥  Among other things, note if the file has both video and audio
➥ streams, or just video." + Chr(13) + Chr(10) + Chr(13) + Chr(10)
DS = DS + "* Ascend once, to move to the end of the first LIST chunk,
➥ then descend twice (second LIST chunk, then to 'strh' chunk—"
DS = DS + "that's the video stream header chunk.  You'll see info about
➥ the video stream.  " + Chr(13) + Chr(10) + Chr(13) + Chr(10) +
➥ "* Then ascend/descend to get to the video "
DS = DS + "format chunk.  You'll see video format information displayed."
➥ + Chr(13) + Chr(10) + Chr(13) + Chr(10)
DS = DS + "* If there is an audio stream,  you can ascend/descend "
DS = DS + "to the 'LIST' chunk for the stream, then descend to the audio
➥ stream header info ('strh' Chunk ID).  " + Chr(13) + Chr(10) +
➥ Chr(13) + Chr(10) + "* Then ascend/descend "
DS = DS + "to the audio format chunk, where you will see info about the
➥ audio stream, such as sample frequency." + Chr(13) + Chr(10) +
➥ Chr(13) + Chr(10)
DS = DS + "You're on your own from there; I haven't worked out additional
➥ stuff yet, but feel free to experiment.
➥  The file is only open for reading "
DS = DS + "the entire time.  Oh yeah -- the mmio functions don't
➥ automatically close a file, so I've tried to put a mmioClose call
➥ anywhere you might try to leave the program, but it won't hurt to
➥ Close on your way out! " + Chr(13) + Chr(10) + Chr(13) + Chr(10)

DS = DS + "Tech info" + Chr(13) + Chr(10)
DS = DS + "--------------------" + Chr(13) + Chr(10)
DS = DS + "(The following technical information is from Microsoft:)"
➥ + Chr(13) + Chr(10) + Chr(13) + Chr(10)
DS = DS + "AVI files use the AVI RIFF form. The AVI RIFF form is
➥ identified by the four-character "
DS = DS + "code 'AVI '. All AVI files include two mandatory LIST chunks.
➥ These chunks define "
DS = DS + "the format of the streams and stream data. AVI files
➥ might also include an index "
DS = DS + "chunk. This optional chunk specifies the location of
➥ data chunks within the file. An "
DS = DS + "AVI file with these components has the following form:"
➥ + Chr(13) + Chr(10) + Chr(13) + Chr(10)
DS = DS + "RIFF ('AVI ' " + Chr(13) + Chr(10)
DS = DS + "      LIST ('hdrl'" + Chr(13) + Chr(10)
DS = DS + "              ." + Chr(13) + Chr(10)
DS = DS + "              ." + Chr(13) + Chr(10)
DS = DS + "              ." + Chr(13) + Chr(10)
DS = DS + "              )" + Chr(13) + Chr(10)
DS = DS + "      LIST ('movi' " + Chr(13) + Chr(10)
DS = DS + "              ." + Chr(13) + Chr(10)
DS = DS + "              ." + Chr(13) + Chr(10)
DS = DS + "              ." + Chr(13) + Chr(10)
```

```
DS = DS + "              )" + Chr(13) + Chr(10)
DS = DS + "      ['idx1'<AVI Index>]" + Chr(13) + Chr(10)
DS = DS + "      )" + Chr(13) + Chr(10)
DS = DS + "" + Chr(13) + Chr(10)
DS = DS + "The LIST chunks and the index chunk are subchunks of the
➥ RIFF 'AVI ' chunk. The "
DS = DS + "'AVI ' chunk identifies the file as an AVI RIFF file.
➥ The LIST 'hdrl' chunk defines the "
DS = DS + "format of the data and is the first required list chunk.
➥ The LIST 'movi' chunk "
DS = DS + "contains the data for the AVI sequence and is the second
➥ required list chunk. The "
DS = DS + "'idx1' chunk is the optional index chunk. AVI files must
➥ keep these three "
DS = DS + "components in the proper sequence. " + Chr(13) + Chr(10)
➥ + Chr(13) + Chr(10)
DS = DS + "The LIST 'hdrl' and LIST 'movi' chunks use subchunks
➥ for their data. The"
DS = DS + " following example shows the AVI RIFF form expanded with the
➥ chunks needed to "
DS = DS + "complete the LIST 'hdrl' and LIST 'movi' chunks:" + Chr(13)
➥ + Chr(10) + Chr(13) + Chr(10)
DS = DS + "RIFF ('AVI '" + Chr(13) + Chr(10)
DS = DS + "        LIST ('hdrl'" + Chr(13) + Chr(10)
DS = DS + "              'avih'(<Main AVI Header>)" + Chr(13) + Chr(10)
DS = DS + "              LIST ('strl'" + Chr(13) + Chr(10)
DS = DS + "                    'strh'(<Stream header>)" + Chr(13) + Chr(10)
DS = DS + "                    'strf'(<Stream format>)" + Chr(13) + Chr(10)
DS = DS + "                    'strd'(additional header data)"
➥ + Chr(13) + Chr(10)
DS = DS + "                    ." + Chr(13) + Chr(10)
DS = DS + "                    ." + Chr(13) + Chr(10)
DS = DS + "                    ." + Chr(13) + Chr(10)
DS = DS + "              )" + Chr(13) + Chr(10)
DS = DS + "              ." + Chr(13) + Chr(10)
DS = DS + "              ." + Chr(13) + Chr(10)
DS = DS + "              ." + Chr(13) + Chr(10)
DS = DS + "        )" + Chr(13) + Chr(10)
DS = DS + "LIST ('movi'" + Chr(13) + Chr(10)
DS = DS + "        {SubChunk | LIST('rec '" + Chr(13) + Chr(10)
DS = DS + "                     SubChunk1" + Chr(13) + Chr(10)
DS = DS + "                     SubChunk2" + Chr(13) + Chr(10)
DS = DS + "                     ." + Chr(13) + Chr(10)
DS = DS + "                     ." + Chr(13) + Chr(10)
DS = DS + "                     ." + Chr(13) + Chr(10)
DS = DS + "                )" + Chr(13) + Chr(10)
DS = DS + "           ." + Chr(13) + Chr(10)
DS = DS + "           ." + Chr(13) + Chr(10)
DS = DS + "           ." + Chr(13) + Chr(10)
DS = DS + "        }" + Chr(13) + Chr(10)
DS = DS + "     ." + Chr(13) + Chr(10)
```

```
DS = DS + "          ." + Chr(13) + Chr(10)
DS = DS + "              ." + Chr(13) + Chr(10)
DS = DS + "    )" + Chr(13) + Chr(10)
DS = DS + "    ['idx1'<AVIIndex>]" + Chr(13) + Chr(10)
DS = DS + ")" + Chr(13) + Chr(10) + Chr(13) + Chr(10)
DS = DS + "To obtain more technical information about AVI RIFF files,
➥ download the file "
DS = DS + "VFW.ZIP from the Compuserve forum WINEXT, in library 2.
➥  There is also a file "
DS = DS + "of samples in another ZIP file, VFWX.ZIP.
➥  These samples are for C, but they contain "
DS = DS + "lots of useful information about the structures inside the
➥ RIFF file." + Chr(13) + Chr(10) + Chr(13) + Chr(10)
DS = DS + "The source code showing how I used VB user-defined types
➥ to access the "
DS = DS + "various C structures are declared in chunk.bas, along with
➥ the various multimedia "
DS = DS + "DLL function declrations.  The logic for determining what
➥ chunk is what is in the procedure 'CheckData' on the form Chunk1."
➥ + Chr(13) + Chr(10) + Chr(13) + Chr(10)
DS = DS + "This is just a first draft, so don't take the actual code too
➥ seriously. <grin>  I don't code that much in "
DS = DS + "Visual Basic, and I'm a little rusty." + Chr(13) + Chr(10)
➥ + Chr(13) + Chr(10)

DS = DS + "Advertising" + Chr(13) + Chr(10)
DS = DS + "--------------------" + Chr(13) + Chr(10)
DS = DS + "If you would like more information along the same lines,
➥ I'd like to recommend some books "
DS = DS + "I have written on this and related topics.  The first is
➥ 'Multimedia Madness,' from Sams "
DS = DS + "Publishing.  It covers just about every hardware and
➥ software aspect of multimedia, including things like "
DS = DS + "animation, video capture, high-res video, CD-ROM disks,
➥ image creation and editing, file types, digital sound, "
DS = DS + "MIDI hardware and software, sequencers -- etc., etc., etc."
➥ + Chr(13) + Chr(10) + Chr(13) + Chr(10)
DS = DS + "The second is one I am still writing, and the title is still
➥ not decided.  Titles under discussion include 'Video Visions' and
➥ 'Video Madness.'  The book will cover a range of "
DS = DS + "topics centered around digital video -- evaluations of capture
➥ boards, inside info on compression, "
DS = DS + "programming tips (including Toolbook, Visual Basic, and
➥ multimedia authoring), desktop production, "
DS = DS + "high-end video post-production techniques, and integrating
➥ digital video in existing applications." + Chr(13) + Chr(10)
DS = DS + ""

Text1.Text = DS

End Sub
```

```
Sub Form_Resize ()
    Text1.Height = Form2.ScaleHeight
    Text1.Width = Form2.ScaleWidth
End Sub

Sub ReturnCtl_Click ()
    Unload Form2
End Sub
```

CHUNK3.FRM

```
Sub Command1_Click ()
    Unload Form3
End Sub
```

CHUNK.BAS

```
Type ChunkInfo
    ChunkID As String * 4
    ChunkSize As Long
    FormType As String * 4
    ChunkDataOffset As Long
    ChunkFlags As Long
End Type

Type DisplayInfo
    DType As Long
    TextDesc As String * 2048
End Type

Type ISBJData
    TextDesc As String * 2048
End Type

Type WaveFormat
    FormatType As Integer
    Channels As Integer
    Sample As Long
    Bytes As Long
    Block As Integer
    Bits As Integer
End Type

Type AviHeader
    MicroSecPerFrame As Long
    MaxBytesPerSec As Long
    Reserved1 As Long
    Flags As Long
    TotalFrames As Long
    InitialFrames As Long
```

```
        Streams As Long
        SuggestedBufferSize As Long
        AWidth As Long
        AHeight As Long
        AScale As Long
        ARate As Long
        AStart As Long
        ALength As Long
End Type

Type GeneralInfo
        Flags As Long
        IOProc As String * 4
        IOProcAddress As Long
        ErrorCode As Integer
        IOLocal As Integer
        BufferSize As Long
        Buffer As String
        BNext As String
        EndRead As String
        EndWrite As String
        BufferOffset As Long
        DiskOffset As Long
        GenInfo(4) As Long
        Reserved1 As Long
        Reserved2 As Long
        mmHandle As Integer
End Type

Type BitMapHeader
        BSize As Long
        BWidth As Long
        BHeight As Long
        Planes As Integer
        BitCount As Integer
        Compression As Long
        SizeImage As Long
        XPelsPerMeter As Long
        YPelsPerMeter As Long
        ClrUsed As Long
        ClrImportant As Long
End Type

Type StreamHeader
        Type As String * 4
        Handler As String * 4
        Flags As Long
        Reserved1 As Long
        InitialFrames As Long
        SScale As Long
        Rate As Long
```

```
        Start As Long
        Length As Long
        SuggestedBufferSize As Long
        Quality As Long
        SampleSize As Long
End Type


Global mmHandle As Integer
Global ErrorInfo As GeneralInfo
Global FileInfo As ChunkInfo
Global WaveData As WaveFormat
Global IsWaveFile As Integer
Global StreamInfo As StreamHeader
Global VideoInfo As BitMapHeader
Global CRLF As String
Global AviInfo As AviHeader
Global DisplayEncounter As Integer
Global DISPInfo As DisplayInfo
Global ISBJInfo As ISBJData


' Declare the various functions we can use for mci stuff.
' Playing sounds.
Declare Function sndPlaySound Lib "mmsystem" (ByVal SoundName As String,
➥ ByVal Flags As Integer) As Integer
' Sending strings to mci.
Declare Function mciSendString Lib "mmsystem" (ByVal MCI_Command
➥ As String, ByVal ReturnString As String, ByVal ReturnLength
➥ As Integer, ByVal Handle As Integer) As Long
' Getting error messages.
Declare Function mciGetErrorString Lib "mmsystem" (ByVal MCI_Error
➥ As Long, ByVal ErrorString As String, ByVal ReturnLength
➥ As Integer) As Integer
' Sending strings to mci, no return messages.
Declare Function mciExecute Lib "mmsystem" (ByVal MCI_Command As String)
➥ As Integer
' Get handle of current window.
Declare Function GetActiveWindow Lib "User" () As Integer
' Function for opening a RIFF file.
Declare Function mmioOpen Lib "mmsystem" (ByVal Filename As String,
➥ ByVal Junk As Long, ByVal Flags As Long) As Integer
Declare Function mmioDescend Lib "mmsystem" (ByVal Handle As Integer,
➥ mmInfo As ChunkInfo, ParentInfo As Long, ByVal Flags As Integer)
➥ As Integer
Declare Function mmioAscend Lib "mmsystem" (ByVal Handle As Integer,
➥ mmInfo As ChunkInfo, ByVal Flags As Integer) As Integer
Declare Function mmioRead Lib "mmsystem" (ByVal Handle As Integer,
➥ mmInfo As Any, ByVal BytesToRead As Long) As Long
Declare Function mmioSeek Lib "mmsystem" (ByVal Handle As Integer,
➥ ByVal Offset As Long, ByVal Origin As Integer) As Long
Declare Function mmioClose Lib "mmsystem" (ByVal Handle As Integer,
➥ ByVal Flags As Integer) As Integer
```

17

Multimedia Authoring: Interactive

HSC Interactive can be either easy or frustrating to use. If you use it for the kinds of things it does well, it's easy to use. If you try to go too far, however, you'll run into a brick wall. Thus, the key to using Interactive is to know what it's best at and avoid the rest.

The examples in this chapter will show you how Interactive works and what it is good at. Figure 17.1 shows the basic Interactive screen, with a list of icons on the left and a toolbar at the top. The work area is the large open area.

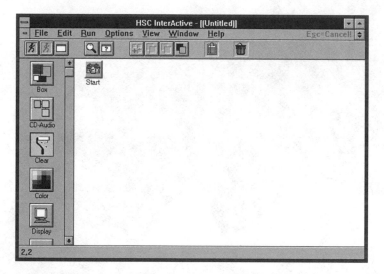

Figure 17.1. HSC Interactive screen.

Notice that the work area contains a single icon. Simply stated, to create an Interactive application, you drag various kinds of icons from the list on the left into the work area, and arrange them like a flow chart. When the application runs, the program will follow the flow chart, executing various actions that are defined for each icon.

Table 17.1 lists the basic icons that are used in Interactive.

Table 17.1. Interactive Icons.

Icon type	Description
Box	Draws a filled or outlined box. If you use the Color icon to specify a fill color of TRANSPARENT, the underlying screen display will show through the interior of the box.
CD-Audio	The CD-Audio and other multimedia icons are made up of multiple MCI icons. (In Interactive, this is called a composite icon.) Each individual MCI icon executes an MCI command and gets a return code (if any) as well as an error code and matching error message. You can use MCI icons to support multimedia data types not formally supported in Interactive.
Clear	The Clear icon clears the screen to a specified color.
Color	The Color icon sets the outline and fill color for graphics and text displays. You can create text with a transparent fill color so that the text appears to lie directly on top of the current display.
Display	Each Display icon you use can display a bitmap, vector graphic, or an animation routine.
Exit	An Exit icon causes an exit from a loop, a composite icon, or the program.
Fontsize	The Font Size icon sets the height, width, and boldness of the characters generated by the Write icon. If you do not use a Font Size icon or a Font Type icon, the smallest available size of the System type font is in effect for text displays. If you use a Font Type icon to change the font, and do not use a Font Size icon, the smallest available size of the selected font is in effect.
Fonttype	The Font Type icon sets the font and other attributes of characters when the Write icon displays text. See Font Size icon for more information.

continues

465

Table 17.1. continued

Icon type	Description
IF	The IF icon controls the execution flow of an application. Because the IF icon forms a branch in the structure, you can build or paste an icon to the right of the IF icon.
InputMenu	The Input Menu icon is used to get input from the user. Specifically, it lets the user choose from one of two or more options on the screen. These options are usually menu choices or multiple choice answers to a question.
Menu	The Menu icon is a composite icon; it includes other icons. A menu provides choices of several activities or options. See Figure 17.7 for an example of a menu icon, and see table 17.2 for descriptions of the icons in the menu composite.
	The Menu composite is only a framework. You must add other icons to the structure to tailor it to your needs. For example, by default there are four branches; you can cut or paste to change the number of branches.
MIDI	A composite of MCI icons. See CD-Audio icon.
Pause	The Pause icon causes execution to pause for a specified period of time. Acceptable values are real numbers greater than 0, such as 3 or .5.
WaveAudio	A composite of MCI icons. See CD-Audio icon.
Write	The Write icon displays text or the value stored in a system variable on the screen. Only one line of characters can be displayed by each Write icon. This is a significant limitation, and needs to be addressed in future versions of the program. To set the font type, font size, and/or color that are used to generate the characters on the screen, precede the Write icon with a Font Type icon, a Font Size icon, and/or a Color icon. If you do not use these icons, the system default font, size, and color are in effect.

In the Menu composite, a Display icon typically precedes an Input Menu icon. (For an example, look ahead to Figure 17.7.) The Display icon displays the menu (a graphic file) on the screen. You then use the InputMenu icon's Content Editor to define hot spots. Each hot spot has an ID number that is used to determine which branch to take. The hot spot ID number is stored in a system variable, @_SELECTION.

The Input Menu icon is usually followed by a Choices composite. The Choices composite contains several IF icons, each of which compares the value in @_SELECTION to a number such as 1, 2, 3, and so forth. If @_SELECTION - 1, the first IF icon tests true and the branch below is executed. If @_SELECTION = 2, the second IF icon tests true and the branch below is executed, and so on.

The icons that make up a Menu composite are listed in Table 17.2.

Table 17.2. Menu composite icons.

Menu Icon	Description
Menu Icon	Marks the beginning of the Menu composite. The Content Editor contains only a Composite Name text box to let you customize the name of the composite.
LoopStart Icon	Marks the beginning of the loop within the Menu composite. Does not have a Content Editor.
Display Icon	Displays a graphic file that is the menu screen.
Input Menu Icon	Defines areas of the screen that are selectable. Each selection area has a unique ID number that is placed in the system variable @_SELECTION when it is clicked.
Choices Icon	Marks the beginning of the Choices composite within the Menu composite.
1,2,3, and 4 Icons	These are the four IF icons built into the Menu composite. Each of these icons marks the beginning of a different branch. If the 1 icon, 2 icon, or 3 icon test true, the corresponding branch is executed. After a non-exit branch completes, the loop begins again and the menu is redisplayed.

continues

Table 17.2. continued

Menu Icon	Description
Exit Icon	Allows the user to exit from the menu composite. Execution flows out of the loop to the icon below the lead icon in the Menu composite.
LoopEnd Icon	Marks the end of the loop within the Menu composite. This icon is executed if one of the first three branches (icon 1, icon 2, or icon 3) is executed. After the Loop End icon, execution returns to the beginning of the loop within the Menu composite.

Using Digital Video with Interactive

The icon-based nature of Interactive makes it relatively simple to add digital video to your applications. In this section, we'll build a simple interactive video player. It will allow you to play, pause, or stop video playback of an AVI file. In addition, we'll add some controls to go to the first or last frame of the video.

If you are more interested in overlay video, you could use this example as a template for controlling overlay video easily. To make the change, simply use overlay string commands instead of digital video commands.

Creating the Application

The first step in creating this application is to design a menu screen. Interactive allows you to define hot spots on an underlying graphic image. We'll need a backdrop for the video display and control buttons. A simple background graphic is shown in Figure 17.2.

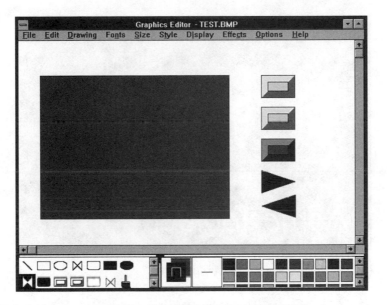

Figure 17.2. A simple menu graphic for Interactive.

This background graphic was created using the graphic editor supplied with Interactive. You could use any kind of suitable graphic image as a background for your menu, including scanned images, 3-D images, and so on. This enables you to control the degree of sophistication for your application; you are not limited by Interactive's built-in capabilities. For example, we could also use the image in Figure 17.3 as a background. This shows a wood background, with pictures of routers as icons for clicking. It would be suitable for displaying videos that show various features of routers in a sales demonstration.

To add the image background, you click the Display icon in the icon list at the left of the Interactive window, and drag it to the Start icon (see Figure 17.1). You then double-click the Display icon to open its Content Editor, as shown in Figure 17.4. You will define the hot spots when you insert the InputMenu icon, later in the flow chart.

Now that we have a background, we can add the MCI icons needed to display a movie in a specific location. I use the icons shown in Figure 17.5.

Each icon's content editor contains a single MCI string command needed to set up the display of the video images. Figure 17.6 shows the Content Editor for the first MCI icon, a Query icon.

Cutting
Edging
Finishing
Acme Tools

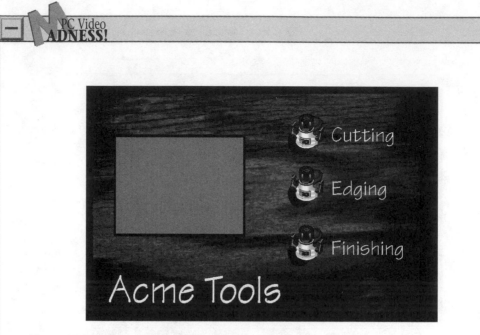

Figure 17.3. An alternate menu graphic for Interactive.

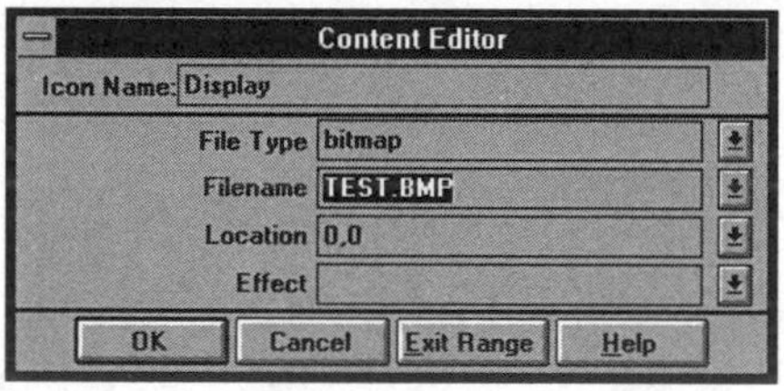

Content Editor
Icon Name: Display
File Type bitmap
Filename TEST.BMP
Location 0,0
Effect
OK
Cancel
Exit Range
Help

Figure 17.4. The Content Editor dialog for a Display icon.

The effect of this icon is to send the command `query iconauthor window` and to place the handle for the current window in the variable `@win`. This variable is used later when you open the file, to denote the parent window of the playback window.

Note that the icon name, Query, is an editable property of the icon. This allows you to create your own icons. The other fields in the Content Editor are described in Table 17.3.

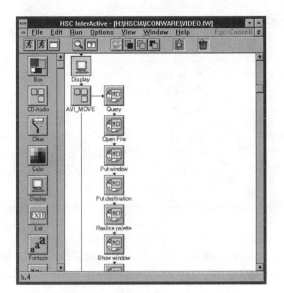

Figure 17.5. MCI icons for displaying a digital video file.

Figure 17.6. Content Editor for the Query MCI icon.

Table 17.3. MCI Icon Content Editor fields.

Field	Description
MCI Command	You can enter any single MCI command here. Any command that you could use with mciSendString is suitable.
MCI Result	If the MCI command returns a result message, you can specify a variable to hold it. The default value is no variable name.

continues

Table 17.3. continued

Field	Description
MCI Error Number	This is the variable that will be used to store any error number that is returned. The default value is `@error_number`.
MCI Error Message	This is the variable that will be used to store any error message that is associated with the returned error number. The default value is `@error_message`.

There are a total of six MCI icons that I used to set up the video for playback. The remaining five do not use the MCI Result field. The MCI command strings for all six icons are shown in Table 17.4.

Table 17.4. MCI Icons for displaying video in Interactive

Icon #	MCI string command
1	query iconauthor window
2	open i:\mania\monmulcd.avi type avivideo style child parent @win alias avi
3	put avi window at 51 71 320 240
4	put avi destination at 0 0 320 240
5	realize avi normal
6	window avi state show

These six commands result in the display of the first frame of the video sequence at the size and position we require. A brief description of the purpose and actions of each icon is included in Table 17.5.

Table 17.5. Purpose of MCI Icons for video display.

Icon #	Description
1	Obtains handle for the current window. This is not a standard MCI command, but is support added by Interactive.
2	Opens the specified video file as a child of the Interactive window and assigns the alias "avi."
3	Places the window at the coordinates 51,71 in the parent window and sizes the window at 320 by 240 pixels.
4	Places the playback image at the upper left of the playback window (0,0) and sizes the image at 320 by 240 pixels.
5	Realizes the palette for the movie.
6	Displays the playback window; the result on the screen is the first frame of the video sequence in a borderless window, displayed on top of the graphic background.

Menu Control

Thus far, we have opened the video file and displayed the first frame. Now we can add some VCR-style control to the program using hot spots. The first step is to click on the Menu icon in the icon list to the left of the Interactive window, and drag it to the last icon in the flow chart. This adds a whole series of icons because the Menu icon is actually a composite icon consisting of a number of individual icons. To make the menu do what we want it to do, we use the Content Editor for each icon to edit its contents. The result is shown in Figure 17.7.

Note that the flow through the menu icon group begins with a Loop Start icon, and ends with a Loop End icon. This means that the menu will loop endlessly unless you provide some kind of exit.

The first icon in the menu group is in InputMenu icon. The content editor for this icon allows us to specify hot spots on the screen. Each hot spot will have an ID number than can be used to branch within the menu. Each icon with a question mark on it represents one ID number for a hot spot. In this example, there are five possible choices:

Resume—starts playback.

Pause—pauses playback.

Close file—closes the file, and then flows to an Exit icon.

Go first—moves to the first frame in the video and displays it.

Go last—moves to the last frame in the video and displays it.

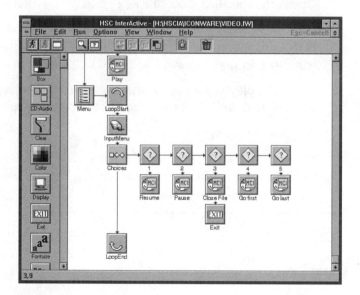

Figure 17.7. Menu structure.

If control flows to the Exit icon, the loop will be exited, and that ends the program as well because there are no more icons to flow to.

The Content Editor for the InputMenu icon is shown in Figure 17.8. Note that the selection areas are defined by rectangular coordinates. That is, there are four numbers, two specifying the upper-left corner of the hot spot, and two specifying width and height. It would be tedious to determine and enter the numbers, of course, so Interactive provides an Input Template Editor to place the hot spots above the underlying image (see Figure 17.9).

Each branch of the menu causes one MCI command to be executed; the commands are listed in Table 17.6.

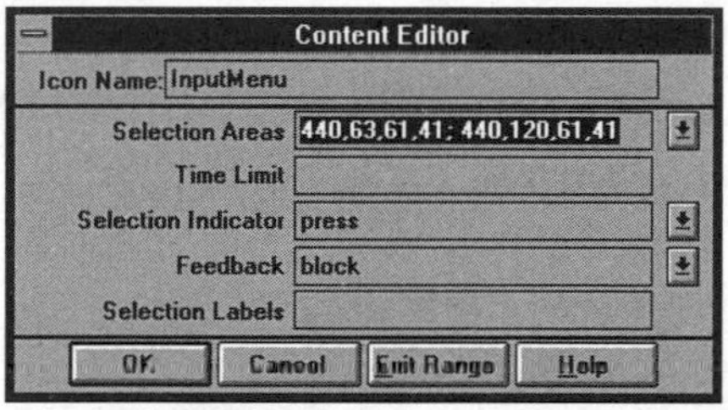

Figure 17.8. Content Editor for InputMenu icon.

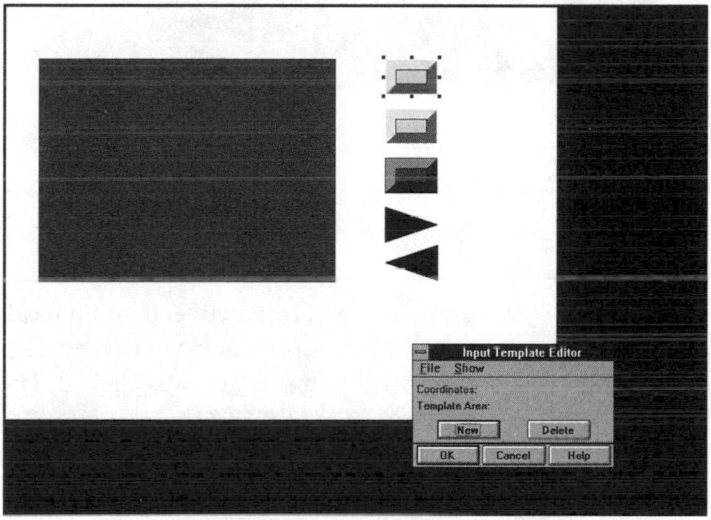

Figure 17.9. Interactive Input Template Editor.

Table 17.6. MCI commands for Interactive example.

Menu Branch	MCI Command
1	Play AVI
2	Pause AVI
3	Close AVI
4	Seek AVI to 0
5	Seek AVI to end

475

When the application is running, the screen includes the background bitmap and the video image, as shown in Figure 17.10.

Figure 17.10. Interactive application using a video sequence.

There are other ways to handle video in Interactive. If you'll recall the Acme Tools example, we did not need to control playback; we needed to play one of three video sequences, depending on which hot spot was clicked. The icon flow diagram for such a situation is shown in Figure 17.11.

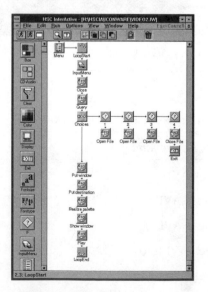

Figure 17.11. Interactive application with different menu structure.

In this example, there is a single list of MCI icons that handles opening the file, positioning the window, and so on. This list of icons is contained within the menu structure. The InputMenu icon feeds into four possible branches. Three branches contain an MCI icon with an Open command; each branch opens a different file. After the file is opened, flow returns to the list of MCI icons, which position the window and play the file. Note that I have added an icon that closes any open AVI file inside the loop. This allows you to interrupt playback of one file to begin playback of another file. All icons share the same alias, "avi."

During playback, the video image is scaled and placed in the gray rectangle, as shown in Figure 17.12.

Figure 17.12. Sample application screen.

Summary

If you are looking for a simple and easy way to integrate video into multimedia applications, Interactive is a good choice. It does have some limitations, however, and you should evaluate it carefully to make sure it will meet your needs.

For example, if you plan to distribute your application widely, the runtime module isn't as convenient to use as it should be. For example, you have to put full pathnames into your application. This means that you can't install an Interactive program onto a different hard drive letter than the one you created it on—

the drive letter is part of the application. I have spoken with the technical people at HSC about this, and there is some hope that the next version will deal with these kinds of limitations.

The ideal project for Interactive will be run on a limited number of PCs, will not need to display much text, and needs to get written right away. If your project fits this profile, Interactive may be an excellent solution.

Interactive inherits many of its features (and some of its limitations) from IconAuthor, a high-end multimedia authoring system. If you have a very sophisticated application, and need fancy data-handling and storage, IconAuthor might meet your needs if Interactive can't.

Multimedia Scripting: Toolbook

Toolbook has been around for a number of years, but it has caught on only recently. It is ideally suited to multimedia development, and it seems that Toolbook was ahead of its time. It's been waiting for the rest of the world to catch up.

The first time I had to use Toolbook was on a prototyping project at Ashton-Tate. (Both that project and Ashton-Tate no longer exist, but Toolbook is still going strong.) I had to present information about a complex new product that was still in development at a conference, and I needed a tool that was sophisticated enough to meet my needs. With Toolbook, I was able to use animations, wipes and dissolves, and other early multimedia techniques to get my point across effectively.

What Is Multimedia Toolbook?

It is not easy to explain what Toolbook *is*. It does so many things, in so many different ways, that there is no one point of view that will show you the whole thing. This is a distinct disadvantage for me, because it's my job to show you! Toolbook can be a sophisticated presentation program, or it can be a complete development environment for multimedia applications, or anything in between. You may have already seen some examples of programs developed in Toolbook, such as Multimedia Beethoven from Multimedia. The Beethoven program is widely regarded as a premiere example of what you can do with multimedia.

All of that is the good news about Toolbook. There's another side to consider: Toolbook is complex, and requires that you spend some time learning the ins and outs of its programming concepts. It takes a while to become proficient, but I have felt that the time is well spent.

Using Toolbook for Multimedia

If you have any facility with programming, you might want to make Toolbook your first choice on most multimedia projects. While it is a little more complex than a typical authoring package, once you learn how to work with it you may find that you prefer it even for applications that do not, strictly speaking, require its full features set. There's a very simple reason for this: Toolbook integrates multimedia better than almost any other multimedia tool; often, this integration shows up in subtle ways. For example, one of the most powerful capabilities of the MCI interface is the ability to receive messages from multimedia processes when they are complete. Toolbook has built-in sophisticated support for this capability; an example of its use is included in the code samples in this chapter, in the section *The Toolbook Project: Video Capture Cards.*

Thus, even though Toolbook might take a little longer to learn, and even if you have to write more code than you would with an authoring package, the combination of a tight integration with MCI and the flexibility of its scripting language can still make it the development tool of choice.

Toolbook Basics

Throughout this chapter, we'll be looking at source code from a Toolbook application I developed for the CD-ROM magazine Nautilus. The complete source code is included on the CD-ROM, in the file naut3_3.tbk, as well as all of the bitmaps and AVI files needed to run the application. The code we'll be looking at here comes from various parts of that application, including button scripts, page scripts, and so on.

Before we start looking at code, however, let's take a look at the development architecture of Toolbook. While we're doing that, I'll be introducing a number of terms that apply specifically to Toolbook. The first one is the idea of the *book.*

A *book* is just a name for a Toolbook application. Toolbook uses a page metaphor—you can have almost any number of pages in a book, and you can have almost any number of pages in a Toolbook book. I'm not a real fan of terms invented for a single software product, but we'll forge ahead as well as we can with the terminology.

The second thing to keep in mind about Toolbook is that it operates with *events.* An event is, as you might suggest, anything that happens—mouse clicks, mouse movements, key presses. For example, if you click on a button, that's an event. Well, actually, it's two events—a buttonDown event, and a buttonUp event. If you need to you can distinguish between these two events, but most of the time you can just stick with one or the other. For years I wrote code that looked for the buttonDown event, until I encountered a situation (in naut3_3.tbk, of all places) that made it clear that buttonUp is a better general choice. The reasons are too technical to go into here; you'll have to take my word for it.

So we have a few facts about Toolbook at hand now: it is based on pages, and it responds to events. Let's look at how Toolbook responds to a typical event.

To respond to an event, you write a *handler*. A handler does just what its name suggests: it handles an event. The code for a handler has two required parts: a beginning and an end:

```
to handle buttonUp

end buttonUp
```

The first line of this code is the beginning of a handler; note the English-like syntax, including the preposition *to*. This is typical of Toolbook code, as you will see as we move toward more complex statements. Note also that we specify the event we want to handle: buttonUp. The second line of code is the end of the handler, of course. Whatever you want your handler to do goes between these two statements.

> ### Note
>
> Handlers are placed in the *script* of an object. Any object can have a script. A script is nothing more than a place to put the code associated with an object.

You might want your handler to play a sound file. Toolbook has a series of multimedia functions and commands that you can use; the easiest method for most situations is to use the command string interface. The Toolbook function tbkMCI allows you to pass command strings directly to MCI, as shown in the following handler that plays a wave file when a button is clicked:

```
to handle buttonUp
    get tbkMCI("play c:\windows\chime.wav",self)
end buttonUp
```

Let's take a moment to look at this function; it could well be the one you'll use most with Toolbook (or its cousin, tbkMCIchk, which we'll look at in a moment). The formal declaration for tbkMCI looks like this:

```
tbkMCI("<MCI command & parameters> [wait]",<Object ID>)
```

There are three parts to this function. The first is the MCI command and its parameters; see the chapter on MCI for details about constructing valid MCI command strings. The second part is the optional wait flag. MCI uses a wait flag, but this is different. With Toolbook, you can use a wait flag with *any* MCI command. When you use it, Toolbook will wait for the MCI command to complete before executing the next line of Toolbook code.

> **Note**
>
> This is an example of the tight integration of Toolbook and MCI. Although it will often be perfectly safe to use a wait flag with most other products that support MCI command strings, it's nice to know that Toolbook itself is waiting to get the notification as well.

Speaking of notification, that's what the third part of the function is for. You can specify an object that is to be notified when the MCI process completes. This notification will occur whether or not you use the wait flag, but it makes more sense to use it when you don't use the wait flag. That way, your application can continue while the MCI process executes. For example, if a very long sound file is playing, you might want to have a button that stops playback. It wouldn't make much sense to have that button active when no sound is playing; you could route the notification that the sound has completed to that button and have it hide itself.

Let's pause the discussion for a moment while I point out something about Toolbook. The process I just described, with its notifications and hiding of oneself, are typical of the flexibility built into Toolbook. This means that there is almost always more than one way to accomplish a given task. The novice can get confused by this; the experienced Toolbook programmer learns the ins and outs and can make the best use out of the resources at hand. What seems like a handicap for the new user is raw power for the experienced programmer. If you decide to learn Toolbook, keep these facts in mind!

Let's expand the previous code example to show how a button might use the notification process to work with MCI. There are two handlers in the script: one for buttonUp, and one to handle the notification from MCI. The buttonUp handler does three things: it opens the file, it plays the file, and it hides itself. Why hide the button? It probably says something like "Play," and there's nothing more to do while we're playing. The notification handler does two things: if the notification was, indeed, for playing a sound, it closes the sound file. Then it shows the button again, ready to play the sound once more. The code for this application can be found on the CD-ROM in the directory **\tb\code1**.

```
to handle buttonUp
      -- Clear result field.
      put "" into text of field "Result"
      --Set file name in a variable.
      put "c:\windows\chime.wav" into SndFile
      --Open the sound file; don't want to be notified.
      get tbkMCIchk("open"&&SndFile&&"alias Snd","")
      --See if the file was opened.
      if It <> ""
            --Play the sound file, and notify me when done.
            get tbkMCI("play Snd",self)
            --Hide the Play button.
            hide self
      else
            --Could not open file.
            put "Result: Could not open file." into text of field "Result"
      end if
end buttonUp

to handle tbkMMNotify status, operation, device
      --See if the notification involves completing a sound play.
      put "result:" && status && operation && device into text of field "Result"
      if status && operation && device = "successful play Snd"
            --Close the file.
            get tbkMCI("close Snd","")
      end if
      --Redisplay Play button.
      show self
end tbkMMNotify
```

Let's look at each line of these scripts to see what's going on, the buttonUp handler first. The first line of code is:

```
put "" into text of field "Result"
```

I created a field where we will store the result of our MCI process. This simply blanks the text field, clearing whatever might have been there before. Just basic "good housekeeping." The next line of code stores the name of the file we want to play in a variable SndFile:

```
put "c:\windows\chime.wav" into SndFile
```

If the filename had been typed into a text field by the user, we could just as easily get the filename from the field:

```
-- Alternate code example:
put text of field FileField into SndFile
```

Once again, this demonstrates the English-like syntax of Toolbook script commands. Now we can open the file:

```
get tbkMCI("open" && SndFile && "alias Snd","")
```

The MCI command string will open the indicated file, and give it the device alias Snd. There is no request for notification. Note that we say `get tbkMCI()`. `tbkMCI` is a function, and that means it returns a result. If you think it's strange that we aren't storing the result in a variable, I'll explain. In a language such as C or Visual Basic, you can put the return value of a function into a variable using the equal sign as an assignment operator: `result = GetData()`. In Toolbook, if you do not specify a variable, the value is placed in a default variable called `It`. The very next line of code checks the value of `It`:

```
if It <> ""
```

If `It` is not null (that is, empty), the file was opened, and we can play it. The value returned by `tbkMCI` on an open command is a device number. Device numbers typically start at 1 for the first device, 2 for second, and so on. To play the file after it is successfully opened, we again use `tbkMCI`:

```
get tbkMCI("play Snd",self)
```

This will play the sound, using the alias we established. In addition, we have requested that this button be notified when the sound has completed playing. Next, the `buttonUp` handler hides the button:

```
hide self
```

If the file could not be opened, we put an error message into the text field "Result":

```
put "Result: Could not open file." into text of field "Result"
```

That completes the `buttonUp` handler.

Now we turn our attention to the handler for notification. Notice that there's more here than for the `buttonUp` handler. There are some parameters that are passed to the handler:

```
to handle tbkMMNotify status, operation, device
```

The event name is `tbkMMNotify`, and this is the standard name for the notification event. The handler expects three parameters:

status   This conveys the result of the MCI process. We're looking for successful.

operation   This describes what was done. We sent a play command, so we expect to see play.

device   This is the device that just completed the action. We are only interested in the waveaudio device.

Before we do anything with these values, we will display them in a text field:

```
put "result:" && status && operation && device into text of field "Result"
```

Figure 18.1 shows what the sample application looks like when it plays a file successfully.

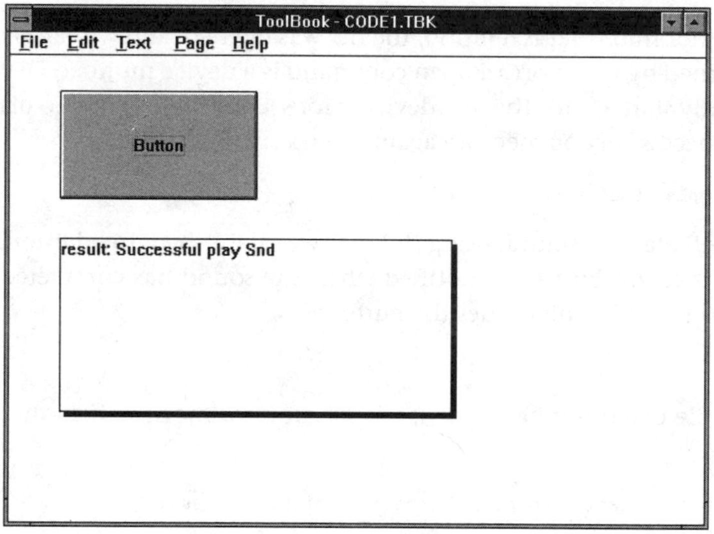

Figure 18.1. Successful playing of a multimedia file.

To determine that what we want is what has in fact happened, we compare the parameters to what we expect:

```
if status && operation && device = "successful play Snd"
```

Note that we used the alias that we assigned earlier to refer to the device. If the result is "successful play Snd", we close the file, without a request for notification:

```
get tbkMCI("close Snd","")
```

Finally, in case the user wants to play the sound again, we show the button:

```
show self
```

That's all there is to it!

If we wanted to modify this file to play a digital video AVI file, all we have to do is change the filename. The alias `"Snd"` won't make sense, of course, but the script will play the AVI file; try it and see. In fact, it will play almost any multimedia file, because the MCI commands we used—open, play, and close—are supported by nearly every MCI device. One device that does not support the play command is overlay video, by the way.

Toolbook Event Handling

One of the most important things to know about Toolbook is this: events move in a predictable way through the various objects in Toolbook.

An event first goes to the object immediately involved—like a button click going to a button first. If that object handles the event, that's all there is to it; an event, once handled, is over. If that first object does not handle the event, it is passed up to the next higher object. There are some simple rules for determining what that next higher object is. We'll use a `buttonUp` event and trace it through the object hierarchy.

The lowest possible objects are the ones that you place on a Toolbook window—buttons, text fields, bitmaps, etc. If you put a handler for `buttonUp` in one of these objects, the event gets handled there. There is one exception: if you want to pass the event up the chain, you can use the forward command:

```
to handle buttonUp
    put "Buttons up!" into text of field MyField
    forward
end buttonUp
```

After putting the text in the field, this handler will pass the `buttonUp` event to the next level.

There are two possibilities for the next level: `page` and `group`. A `page` is just that: one of the pages in the Toolbook application. A `group` is any group of objects, and a `group` can contain different kinds of objects. For example, a `group` can contain a button and a text field. For example, you might want to group three radio buttons into a group to make it easier to manage them. Toolbook does not

automatically turn radio buttons on and off (by Windows convention, only one radio button in a group is on at one time). For example, suppose we had three radio buttons in a group (see Table 18.1).

Table 18.1. Sample radio buttons.

Button #	Button name	Button text
1	PlaySound	Play Sound
2	PlayMovie	Play Movie
3	PlayVideo	Play Video

We don't need to put any code in the button scripts, but we do need to write some code in the script for the group, since the group will be receiving the buttonUp message:

```
-- Code for a group of radio buttons

to handle buttonUp
    if target is button "PlaySound"
        set checked of button PlayMovie to False
        set checked of button PlayVideo to False
        set checked of button PlaySound to True
        put "sound1.wav" into text of field "FileName"
    end if

    if target is button "PlayMovie"
        set checked of button PlayMovie to True
        set checked of button PlayVideo to False
        set checked of button PlaySound to False
        put "movie1.mmm" into text of field "FileName"
    end if

    if target is button "PlayVideo"
        set checked of button PlayMovie to False
        set checked of button PlayVideo to True
        set checked of button PlaySound to False
        put "video1.avi" into text of field "FileName"
    end if
    send buttonUp to "OpenButton"
end buttonUp
```

There are several points of interest in this script. First of all, note how we distinguish which button in the group was clicked—we refer to it by name:

```
if target is button "PlayVideo"
```

Note also that target refers to the object that initially received the click. This is what makes it possible to use the buttonUp event effectively at higher levels of the hierarchy: Information is preserved. There are just two kinds of statements used in this handler. We are either setting the "checked" properties of the buttons, or putting a filename into a text field.

And then there is that one strange line of code right at the end of the handler:

```
send buttonUp to "OpenButton"
```

Yes, you can send events to objects. The button "OpenButton" might contain some code to open the file:

```
to handle buttonUp
    -- Declare system (global) variable
    system DeviceID
    -- Open file.
    put tbkMCI("open"&&text of field "FileName"&& alias mciFile","")
➥ into DeviceID
end buttonUp
```

This handler first declares a system variable, DeviceID. We then put the results of the open attempt into DeviceID. Other handlers and scripts can access DeviceID to determine if there is indeed an open file to work with.

We might also have a handler at the page level. If we wanted this handler to get the buttonUp event, we would need to add a "forward" command to the buttonUp handler in the group. The page script might look something like this:

```
to handle buttonUp
    -- Declare system (global) variable
    system FileOpen

    if target is group "PlayFile"
        if DeviceID <> ""
            get tbkMCI("play mciFile","")
        end if
    end if

    if target is group "CloseFile"
        if DeviceID <> ""
            get tbkMCI("close mciFile","")
            put "" into DeviceID
```

```
        end if
    end if
end buttonUp
```

This script determines which group the `buttonUp` event came from, and takes an appropriate action.

Toolbook now adds a twist to the process, and we must digress for a moment. You can have one or more backgrounds in a Toolbook application. A background is a lot like a page—you can put objects on it, you can write handlers for it and put them in the background's script. The background, however, can be the background for multiple pages. In other words, if you put objects on the background, they will appear on all pages associated with that background. You can have more than one background. For example, you might want to use one background for the first 10 pages, and a different background for the next 8 pages, and yet another background for just the last page.

If an event does not get handled at the page level, or if it is not handled by an object placed directly on the background, Toolbook will look for a handler in the background's script. If the background doesn't handle the event, Toolbook looks in the script for the entire book. (The book script is a good place for events like `"enterBook"` and `"leaveBook"`.)

And if the event still doesn't get handled, Toolbook goes to the top of the hierarchy: the Toolbook system book. If the event has no handler there, you'll get an error telling you there is no handler for an event.

Toolbook Programming: OpenScript

We have looked at the architecture of Toolbook, and we have seen some examples of code, but it's worth a moment to look at the syntax of `OpenScript`, the official name for Toolbook's language.

The basic elements of `OpenScript` are summarized in Table 18.2.

Table 18.2. Toolbook OpenScript elements.

Elements	Description
Variable	Toolbook variables are almost, but not quite, like variables in other languages. The important difference is that Toolbook doesn't distinguish variable types. A variable can contain a number, a string, a date, etc. You don't have to worry about what type the data is; you can just store it in the variable. Instead of the equal sign, Toolbook uses the "put" command. For example, "put 27 into MyVariable."
Expression	An expression in Toolbook is similar to expressions in other languages. Some of the expression operators are different. For example, "&" concatenates, and "&&" concatenates by putting a space in the middle.
Function	Toolbook functions, like functions in other languages, return a value. The return value, like variables, is not typed.
Statement	Any single line of code.
Command	Any line of code besides a "to handle" or "end" statement. Typical commands are "put," "hide," and "get."
Control structure	Toolbook has more control structures than most languages. This has to do with the event-based nature of Toolbook. The best-known structure is, of course, if/then/else. A complete list of Toolbook control structures is in Table 18.3.
Object	Objects are the "things" you can put on a Toolbook page, as well as pages, books, and backgrounds. The valid objects are listed in Table 18.4.

continues

Table 18.2. continued

Elements	Description
Property	Any attribute of an object. Properties can be modified or checked, and are the basis of much of OpenScript programming. For example, a button can have a "checked" property which you can set to True or False. A button could also have a caption property that determines what caption appears on the button.
Event	Loosely speaking, an event is anything that happens. There are two kinds of events: built-in Windows system events, such as mouse clicks, and user-generated events that you create with the "send" command.
Handler	A series of commands that determines how Toolbook handles events. Handlers go in scripts, and just about any object can have a script.
Script	A place where handlers reside. To access an object's script, either click on the Script button in the object properties dialog (F6), or Control-Double-Click the object.

Table 18.3. Toolbook control structures.

Structure	Description
if/then/else	This is the standard workhorse of the computer world. The if statement evaluates an expression and executes the appropriate branch of code.
step/by	Full syntax is step <variable> from <start> to <finish> [by <steps>]. Basically the same as a for/next loop in BASIC.

Structure	Description
while	Loops as long as an expression evaluates to True.
do/until	Executes a series of statements until an expression evaluates to True. Opposite of "while."
conditions/when/else	Similar to a CASE or switch statement. Selects one of several branches based on evaluation of an expression.
start spooler	Contains print-related statements. You can print all, some (continuous or discontinuous), or one page(s).
linkDLL	Allows you to access almost any Windows DLL file.
translateWindowMessage	Allows you to process messages for a given window. Within the control structure, you can generate Toolbook events for processing either before or after the intercepted message. This allows you to get down to the system level with Toolbook.

Table 18.4. Toolbook objects.

Object	Description
Button	Can be any of the standard Windows button types, including, for example, push buttons, check boxes, and radio buttons.
Field	A text field. Can be single or multi-line, with or without scroll bars, etc.
Record Field	A special type of field used to implement database functionality.

continues

Table 18.4. continued

Object	Description
Hotword	One or more words linked to form an object. Usually, you create hotwords to establish hypertext links.
Graphic	There are two kinds of graphics—ones that you draw using Toolbook's painting tools, and ones that you import, such as bitmaps.
Group	Two or more objects can be joined to form a group. An object in a group retains its identity, and its scripts will still execute. The group acts like any other object: it can have a script to handle events.
Page	A Toolbook program can have one or more pages. The commas go to page n, go to previous page, go to next page, and go to page <name> can be used to navigate pages.
Background	A Toolbook program can have one or more backgrounds. A background persists from page to page unless you create a new background.
Book	The entire Toolbook program is called a book. Like pages and backgrounds, the book itself can have a script and handle events.

The Toolbook Project: Video Capture Cards

As far as digital video is concerned, the most important and useful feature in Toolbook is notification. Because Toolbook can communicate in both directions with MCI, we can establish detailed control over video in a Toolbook application.

In this section, we will look at a major portion of the code for a complete Toolbook application. The application is a "column" I "wrote" for the CD-ROM magazine *Nautilus*, for their March 1993 edition. The application illustrates the results of a comparison between several video capture cards, so it is useful on several different levels. It is a good example of how to incorporate video into a Toolbook application, and it is also full of useful information about digital video.

We'll limit our examination to the code related to digital video and MCI, although I'll include enough Toolbook sample code to give you a good idea of what is involved in creating a video application with Toolbook from scratch.

Project Code

I wrote a lot of code to implement this application. This is typical of a Toolbook application in which you want to have a relatively tight degree of control over multimedia files or objects. The plus side is that you can design the application to look and operate exactly the way you want it to. The minus side is that you have to write the code to do that. Fortunately, once written, the code can be re-used effectively for future projects.

Book Script

The highest level of the Toolbook object hierarchy is the book. Thus, I chose to put all handlers that might be called anywhere in the book at the book level. There are quite a few handlers in the book script, as shown in Table 18.5.

Table 18.5. EnterBook script handlers.

Handler	Description
enterBook	Handles setting up all kinds of things we'll need later in the book. It also takes care of arranging the initial appearance of the book.
to get pathName	A user-created function that is used to get the pathname of the current working directory. This is useful when looking for files.
PlayWave	Opens and plays a .WAV file.

continues

Table 18.5. continued

Handler	Description
OpenAVI	Opens an .AVI file. It is a lot more complex than PlayWave.
PlayAVI	Plays an already-open .AVI file.
AdjustMagnification	Changes the playback size of the .AVI file.
RedisplayAVI	Redraws the .AVI playback window to make sure that the image displays correctly. Without it, palette changes and screen redraws could really mess up the .AVI window.
PauseAVI	Pauses playing of an .AVI file.
ResumeAVI	Resumes playing of a paused .AVI file.
CloseWave	Closes an open .WAV file.
CloseAVI	Closes an open .AVI file.
nextPage	Moves to the next page.
prevPage	Moves to the previous page.
GoTop	Moves to the first page.

Let's look at the code for each handler in detail.

EnterBook Handler

The enterBook script is executed only once, at the time we start up the Toolbook application. It is normally used to initialize system variables, arrange the page display, and for any other one-time setup actions. The full text of the enterBook handler is listed in code Listing 18.1.

Listing 18.1. enterBook handler.

```
to handle enterBook
    — Declare system variables.
    system PlayingWave
    system PlayingAVI
```

```
        system MuteAVIAudio
        system AVIMagnification
        system KeepAVISize
        system fPath
        system DisplayButtons
        system AVIWindowType
        system AVICenter
        system MainBounds
        system AVIIdle

        — Link in function from tbkwin.dll.
        linkDLL "tbkwin.dll"
            STRING pageFromClient(STRING, INT, STRING)
        end

        — Initialize system variables.
        set AVICenter to False
        set AVIMagnification to 1
        set PlayingWave to False
        set PlayingAVI to False
        set RetainImage to False
        set MuteAVIAudio to False
        set KeepAVISize to False
        set DisplayButtons to False
        set AVIWindowType to "overlapped"
        set fPath to pathName(name of this book)
        set sysBooks to (fPath & "tbkmm.sbk")
        set sysChangesDb to false
        set AVIIdle to false

        — Hide some stuff we don't want to show at startup.
        set syslockscreen to True
        hide button "OpenButton" of this background
        hide button "ResultButton" of this background
        hide group "ButtonGroup" of this background
        hide group "BoxGroup" of this background
        hide menubar

        — Set size of page for current screen resolution.
        send sizetopage
        — Initialize one more system variable.
        put bounds of mainWindow into MainBounds
        set syslockscreen to False
end
```

This script has five distinct sections (see Table 18.6):

Table 18.6. EnterBook handler sections.

Section	Description
Declare system variables	If you plan to use a variable in more than one handler, you need to declare it as a system variable. You must declare it as a system variable in every handler where it is used. Otherwise, it is treated as a local variable.
Link DLL	You can use functions from almost any valid Windows DLL file in Toolbook. In this case, we will later need to use the pageFromClient function from the DLL file tbkwin.dll. You must declare each function from each DLL that you plan to use.
Initialize system variables	Many of the system variables are Boolean—that is, they are either True or False. These must have an initial value.
Hide stuff	The opening screen doesn't require a number of buttons and object groups that are normally visible on the background, so we hide them. We set the system variable syslockscreen to True to temporarily disable screen updates. When we are done hiding, we set it to False to re-enable screen updates. This is a very useful trick when you are hiding/showing/moving a number of objects.
Set page size	The actual page size can vary with changes in font size and screen resolution. This command places the Toolbook window at the center of the screen and insures that the Window size matches the page size.

OpenAVI Handler

Now we come to the first handler that works with MCI. It's a long one, and it shows how to work closely with window sizes in both Toolbook and MCI. The complete script is shown in code Listing 18.2.

Listing 18.2. OpenAVI handler.

```
to handle OpenAVI fName
    -- Declare system variables.
    system PlayingAVI
    system PlayX
    system PlayY
    system PlayWidth
    system PlayHeight
    system MuteAVIAudio
    system RectAVI
    system RectWindowAVI
    system AVIMagnification
    system TotalFrames
    system FrameRate
    system PlayingTime
    system BaseX
    system BaseY
    system BaseWidth
    system BaseHeight
    system WindowX
    system WindowY
    system WindowWidth
    system WindowHeight
    system MainOffset
    system BaseXOffset
    system BaseYOffset
    system MainBounds
    system KeepAVISize
    system DisplayButtons
    system AVIWindowType
    system MainX
    system MainY
    system MainWidth
    system MainHeight
    system AVICenter

    -- Close any open AVI file with same alias.
    if PlayingAVI
        get tbkMCIchk("close vfwFile","",1)
        set PlayingAVI to false
    end
```

continues

Listing 18.2. continued

```
-- Open the AVI file.
get tbkMCIchk("open"&& fName && "alias vfwFile style" \
    && AVIWindowType && "parent" && sysWindowHandle,"",1,1)

-- If unable to open, break out of handler.
if It = ""
    break OpenAVI
end

— Establish defaults.
get tbkMCIchk("set vfwFile time format frames","",1)
get tbkMCIchk("set vfwFile seek exactly on","",1)
set PlayingAVI to true
put position of mainWindow into MainOffset
put bounds of mainWindow into MainBounds
get tbkMCIchk("where vfwFile window","",1)
put it into RectWindowAVI
get tbkMCIchk("where vfwFile destination","",1)
put it into RectAVI

— Extract width and height information from RectAVI
set BaseX to word 1 of RectAVI
set BaseY to word 2 of RectAVI
set BaseWidth to word 3 of RectAVI
set BaseHeight to word 4 of RectAVI
set WindowWidth to word 3 of RectWindowAVI
set WindowHeight to word 4 of RectWindowAVI

set BaseXOffset to item 1 of MainOffset
set BaseYOffset to item 2 of MainOffset

set MainX to item 1 of MainBounds
set MainY to item 2 of MainBounds
set MainWidth to item 3 of MainBounds
set MainHeight to item 4 of MainBounds
set MainWidth to MainWidth-MainX
set MainHeight to MainHeight-MainY

-- Establish adjustment for variations from screen I designed on.
set AdjXFactor to (MainWidth)/584
set AdjYFactor to (MainHeight)/411

-- Get infc from file.
put tbkMCIchk("status vfwFile length","",1) into TotalFrames

put tbkMCIchk("status vfwFile nominal frame rate","",1)/1000 into FrameRate
set PlayingTime to TotalFrames/FrameRate
```

```
        -- Are we keeping current size, or changing it?
    if not KeepAVISize
        set PlayX to floor((320*AdjXFactor-BaseWidth)/2) + floor((BaseXOffset+5))
        set PlayY to floor((240*AdjYFactor-BaseHeight)/2) + floor((BaseYOffset+22))
        set PlayWidth to BaseWidth
        set PlayHeight to BaseHeight
    else
        set PlayX to PlayX + floor((BaseXOffset+5)*AdjXFactor)
        set PlayY to PlayY + floor((BaseYOffset+22)*AdjYFactor)
    end if

        -- Are we centering for playback?
    if AVICenter
        -- Set file to play centered in current window.
        if AVIWindowType = "child"
            set PlayX to floor((MainWidth-BaseWidth)/2)
            set PlayY to floor((MainHeight-BaseHeight)/2)
        else
            set PlayX to floor((MainWidth-BaseWidth)/2) + floor((BaseXOffset+5))
            set PlayY to floor((MainHeight-BaseHeight)/2) + floor((BaseYOffset+22))
        end if
        set PlayWidth to BaseWidth
        set PlayHeight to BaseHeight
    end if

        -- Make sure we are withing allowable sizes.
    if PlayWidth > 320
        set PlayWidth to 320
    end
    if PlayHeight > 240
        set PlayHeight to 240
    end

        -- Position the AVI file for playback and display first frame.
    set WindowX to WindowWidth-PlayWidth
    set WindowY to WindowHeight-PlayHeight
    get tbkMCIchk("put vfwFile window at" && PlayX && PlayY && PlayWidth+WindowX &&
PlayHeight+WindowY,"",1)
    get tbkMCIchk("put vfwFile destination at 0 0" && PlayWidth && PlayHeight,"",1)
    get tbkMCIchk("realize vfwFile normal","",1)
    get tbkMCIchk("seek vfwFile to 0","",1)
    get tbkMCIchk("window vfwFile state show","",1)

        -- Do we need to display control buttons?
    if DisplayButtons
        — Show buttons for controlling playback.
        show button "PauseVideo" of this background
```

continues

501

Listing 18.2. continued

```
        show button "ResumeVideo" of this background
        show button "CloseVideo" of this background
    end if

    -- Check to see if audio should be played.
    if MuteAVIAudio
        get tbkMCIchk("setaudio vfwFile off","",1)
    else
        get tbkMCIchk("setaudio vfwFile on","",1)
    end if

end
```

There is a lot going on in this handler, and some of it isn't very pretty. We'll look at each section of code closely to find out what's going on.

First, however, we need to establish how this handler gets called. A handler like enterBook gets called when we enter a book. A handler like buttonUp gets called when a mouse button goes up. OpenAVI is a custom handler, and it has a custom event. To call this handler, we simple put the statement

```
send PlayAVI
```

to create a PlayAVI event. The event will bubble up through the object hierarchy until it hits the PlayAVI handler in the book script.

The handler starts with the usual system variable declarations. There is a very large number of global variables. Toolbook does not have structures (like C) or user-defined types (like Visual Basic), so we simply wind up with a large number of globals. There are two major groups of globals: toggles that we already saw in the enterBook script, and containers for measurements. We need to keep track of the window size (main window, playback window), the location of the playback window (default location, new location), how playback will be handled (AVICenter, DisplayButtons), and many other measurements.

Following the variable declarations, we check to see if there is already an open AVI file:

```
if PlayingAVI
    get tbkMCIchk("close vfwFile","",1)
    set PlayingAVI to false
end
```

Notice that I used the Toolbook function `tbkMCIchk` instead of `tbkMCI`. `tbkMCIchk` adds options for error checking, but is otherwise identical to `tbkMCI`. Note that there is a third parameter, the number one, in the call to `tbkMCIchk`. This insures that if an error occurs, MCI will display an error message explaining the problem. If we did not want error messages displayed, we would use zero instead of one.

The variable `PlayingAVI` is used to determine if an AVI file is already open.

We can now open the AVI file with another call to `tbkMCIchk`. The syntax of the call is:

```
get tbkMCIchk("open"&& fName && "alias vfwFile style" \
    && AVIWindowType && "parent" && sysWindowHandle,"",1,1)
```

Note the use of the line continuation character, `"\"`. For a typical call, the MCI command string looks something like this:

```
open c:\windows\scr_sav.avi alias vfwFile style overlapped parent 23
```

The default window type, overlapped, was set in the `enterBook` script.

If we are unable to open the file, the rest of the script makes no sense, so we check to make sure that a valid device ID was returned. If not, we break out of the handler.

Once the file is open, we need to get information about the file and stuff it into variables. We also need to establish some defaults. The following two MCI commands set the desired time format and seek method:

```
get tbkMCIchk("set vfwFile time format frames","",1)
get tbkMCIchk("set vfwFile seek exactly on","",1)
```

The frame time format insures that we'll receive length data in terms of frames. By setting "seek exactly" on, we will be able to seek to the exact frame number, rather than to key frames.

We also store information about both the Toolbook application's main window and the video default window in variables. Both Toolbook and MCI use rectangles to store this information. A rectangle consists of four numbers, separated by spaces: top coordinate, left coordinate, width, and height. For example, the string `"0 0 160 120"` describes a rectangle whose top left corner is at the coordinate 0,0, and which is 160 pixels wide and 120 pixels high. The statement:

```
put bounds of mainWindow into MainBounds
```

stores rectangle information for the main window in the variable MainBounds, and the statements:

```
get tbkMCIchk("where vfwFile window","",1)
put it into RectWindowAVI
get tbkMCIchk("where vfwFile destination","",1)
put it into RectAVI
```

store information about the AVI file window and destination in the variables RectWindowAVI and RectAVI.

It is important to be aware of the difference between "where vfwFile window" and "where vfwFile destination". We are requesting this data right after opening the file, so both commands will return default values. The *window* rectangle describes the window that will be used for playback. A window rectangle includes space for such things as the window caption and borders. The *destination* rectangle is the portion of the window that will be used for the image. This does not include caption or borders. In fact, when we set the destination rectangle, it can be very small, so that the images play back at a size smaller than the containing window. It can also be large, so that playback is larger than the containing window. In the former case, the window background will surround the images. In the latter case, only a portion of the image will show in the window. This will become clearer when we set the window and destination for playback.

The next section of code illustrates how easy it is to work with strings in Toolbook. Each rectangle consists of four numbers, separated by spaces. If we wanted to extract the numbers in C or BASIC, we would need to use functions like strtok() or Left$(). In Toolbook, it's as easy as saying:

```
set BaseX to word 1 of RectAVI
set BaseY to word 2 of RectAVI
```

Once we have all of the global variables stuffed with the appropriate numbers for the AVI file, we can get additional information about the file with MCI commands. The following statements get the file length (in frames) and frame rate, and calculate the total playing time:

```
put tbkMCIchk("status vfwFile length","",1) into TotalFrames
put tbkMCIchk("status vfwFile nominal frame rate","",1)/1000 into FrameRate
set PlayingTime to TotalFrames/FrameRate
```

The following section of code looks obscure, and that's because I decided to add some things that were just not easy to do. I wanted to be able to play back the AVI file in a number of ways—without changing the default sizes, centered in the Toolbook window (no matter where it might have been moved on the screen), with a new size, and so on. Taking all of the relevant factors into consideration produces some not very readable code, unfortunately. This capability should really be hidden as a user-defined function.

Just before we position the AVI file, we check to make sure that the window size is within allowable limits. I chose to not allow the playback window to be larger than 320 by 240 pixels; if you have a very fast machine, you might want to try a larger size.

Now we can position the file for initial playback:

```
get tbkMCIchk("put vfwFile window at" && PlayX && PlayY \
    && PlayWidth+WindowX && PlayHeight+WindowY,"",1)
get tbkMCIchk("put vfwFile destination at 0 0" && PlayWidth \
    && PlayHeight,"",1)
get tbkMCIchk("realize vfwFile normal","",1)
get tbkMCIchk("seek vfwFile to 0","",1)
get tbkMCIchk("window vfwFile state show","",1)
```

These statements are the core of the OpenAVI handler. Other than the `"open"` command, these are the only other essential MCI commands used in this handler. Together with the open command, they represent the minimum set of commands for controlling playback method and position. Let's look at each in turn.

```
get tbkMCIchk("put vfwFile window at" && PlayX && PlayY \
    && PlayWidth+WindowX && PlayHeight+WindowY,"",1)
```

This command concerns itself with the AVI playback *window*. This is the containing window, and it can be larger or smaller than the playback *images*. When the variables are translated into strings, the command looks something like this:

```
put vfwFile window at 60 75 160 120
```

Once we have positioned the playback window, we can position the image space within that window using *destination:*

```
get tbkMCIchk("put vfwFile destination at 0 0" && PlayWidth \
    && PlayHeight,"",1)
```

Note that I have made the origin of the destination 0,0 as a default. This insures that the images will always start at the top left corner of the playback window. The `PlayWidth` and `PlayHeight` have been set to match the containing window, so the images will fit snugly in the playback window.

If you are using AVI files that were recorded with 8-bits of color depth (that is, 256-color files), you must realize the palette of the file. Most of the time, you will realize the palette normally:

```
get tbkMCIchk("realize vfwFile normal","",1)
```

You could also `"realize vfwFile background"`, but the results are not predictable unless you created a custom palette with the expectation of realizing it as a background palette.

> **Note**
>
> You shouldn't actually use 256-color palettes. When you set the palette in VidCap, use no more than 236 colors. Windows reserves 20 colors for its own use.

I like to display the first frame of the video in the window. The command

```
get tbkMCIchk("seek vfwFile to 0","",1)
```

takes care of this automatically. We are now ready to display the window:

```
get tbkMCIchk("window vfwFile state show","",1)
```

You can also use the `"window"` command to minimize or maximize the playback window.

The remainder of the handler takes care of displaying control buttons (Pause, Play, Close) which control AVI playback. The code for these buttons simply generates events—`PauseAVI`, `PlayAVI`, and `CloseAVI`—located in the book script. The last statements in the handler determine if the audio portion of the file will be heard. They use the `"setaudio"` MCI command:

```
if MuteAVIAudio
    get tbkMCIchk("setaudio vfwFile off","",1)
else
    get tbkMCIchk("setaudio vfwFile on","",1)
end if
```

Now everything is ready for playback!

PlayAVI Handler

The `OpenAVI` handler is the most complex of the AVI-related handlers in the book script. That's because it does a lot besides just opening the file. It has to read data from the file, perform calculations, and so on. Once this is all done, however, the rest of the handlers are comparatively short and to the point.

The PlayAVI handler is a good case in point (see code Listing 18.3). The OpenAVI handler accesses global variables; PlayAVI only two. It also demonstrates a safety net used in all of the MCI-related handlers: if the file is not open, don't try to do anything—break out of the script.

Listing 18.3. PlayAVI handler.

```
to handle PlayAVI WaitAVI
    system MuteAVIAudio
    system PlayingAVI
    local CurrentFrame

    if not PlayingAVI
        break PlayAVI
    end if

    — Check to see if audio should be played.
    if MuteAVIAudio
        get tbkMCIchk("setaudio vfwFile off","",1)
    else
        get tbkMCIchk("setaudio vfwFile on","",1)
    end if

    if WaitAVI
        — End playback with a mouse click.
        get tbkMCIchk("break vfwFile on 1","",1)
        get tbkMCIchk("play vfwFile wait","",1)
    else
        get tbkMCIchk("play vfwFile",uniquename of this background,1)
    end if
end
```

PlayAVI does do one thing that OpenAVI does: it takes care of turning Audio on and off. By monitoring the value of MuteAVIAudio in all appropriate handlers, we can make sure that we will catch any changes in the value of this variable. The variable itself is set in a checkbox.

Note that the PlayAVI handler takes a parameter, WaitAVI. If this is set to True, two things change. One, the file will be played with the wait flag, and two, we add the statement before actually playing the file. The MCI command "break" allows us to specify keys or mouse clicks that will halt playback. The value of one means that a click of the left mouse button will stop playback.

If `WaitAVI` is false, we play the file with the statement:

```
get tbkMCIchk("play vfwFile",uniquename of this background,1)
```

The MCI portion is trivial: `"play vfwFile"`. We have asked for notification to be sent to the background with the phrase `"uniquename of this background"`. See the Background Scripts section later to see how to handle notification of playback.

PauseAVI Handler

Listing 18.4. PauseAVI handler.

```
to handle PauseAVI
    system PlayingAVI

    if not PlayingAVI
        break PauseAVI
    end if

    get tbkMCIchk("pause vfwFile","",1)
    send RedisplayAVI
end
```

The handler for pausing is one of the simplest in this group. Other than making sure that there is, indeed, a file open, we make a single MCI call:

```
get tbkMCIchk("pause vfwFile","",1)
```

We also generate an event with `"send RedisplayAVI"`. It is not at all obvious why we should have to send a redisplay event, however. You would probably expect to be able to simply pause the file, and resume playback at some point. However, palette adjustments can make a mess of things. The reasons for sending `RedisplayAVI` will be clearer when we look at the code for handling the event.

ResumeAVI Handler

Listing 18.5. ResumeAVI handler.

```
to handle ResumeAVI
    system PlayingAVI
    system MuteAVIAudio
```

```
        if not PlayingAVI
            break ResumeAVI
        end if

        send redisplayAVI
        get tbkMCIchk("play vfwFile",uniquename of this background,1)
end
```

Resuming is as easy as pausing; there is a single MCI command:

```
get tbkMCIchk("play vfwFile",uniquename of this background,1)
```

This repeats the PlayAVI command, but ResumeAVI is simpler than PlayAVI, and does less error checking. In other words, it's faster, but should only be used where the error checking is not required.

RedisplayAVI Handler

Listing 18.6. RedisplayAVI handler.

```
to handle RedisplayAVI
    system PlayingAVI
    system PlayX
    system PlayY
    system PlayWidth
    system PlayHeight
    system PlayingAVI
    system WindowX
    system WindowY
    system WindowWidth
    system WindowHeight
    system MuteAVIAudio

    if not PlayingAVI
        break RedisplayAVI
    end if

    — Check to see if audio should be played.
    if MuteAVIAudio
        get tbkMCIchk("setaudio vfwFile off","",1)
    else
        get tbkMCIchk("setaudio vfwFile on","",1)
    end if
```

continues

Listing 18.6. continued

```
    get tbkMCIchk("pause vfwFile","",1)
    put tbkMCIchk("status vfwFile position","",1) into CurrentFrame
    set CurrentFrame to CurrentFrame - 1
    get tbkMCIchk("seek vfwFile to "&CurrentFrame,"",1)
    get tbkMCIchk("put vfwFile window at" && PlayX && PlayY && PlayWidth+WindowX
&& PlayHeight+WindowY,"",1)
    get tbkMCIchk("put vfwFile destination at 0 0" && PlayWidth &&
PlayHeight,"",1)
    get tbkMCIchk("window vfwFile state show","",1)
    get tbkMCIchk("realize vfwFile normal","",1)
end
```

RedisplayAVI is a handler that shouldn't have to exist, but it is essential none-theless. It is needed whenever we are dealing with 8-bit color and the nasty palette changes that go with it.

If you are not familiar with how 8-bit color works, here's a brief description. Using 8 bits, we can come up with 256 different combinations, ranging from 0000-0000 to 1111-1111. This gives us 256 colors. However, just any 256 colors is very limiting. What if we had an image that was all subtle shades of blue, for example, and we only had a handful of blue colors out of the 256? To give better color fidelity, Windows allows us to pick those 256 colors from a much larger pool of colors.

Colors are defined as RGB (Red, Green, Blue) values. There are 256 possible values for each of the red, green, and blue components. Pure red would be represented by (255, 0, 0). A value of zero means none, and a value of 255 means full intensity of that color. Using this system, we can have more than 16 million different colors. We create a palette of 256 of them, and refer to each palette entry by number. To change to a new palette, we just put new color values in the palette. For example, to create a palette for an image consisting of subtle shades of blue, we might load the palette with a large number of blue colors, with a few left over for the colors on the desktop—menus, window captions, borders, and so on.

Here's where the "palette problem" comes in. If we already have an image on the screen that uses Palette A, and then switch to Palette B, the first image may wind up looking like garbage with the new palette. We can't have one palette for part of the screen, and another palette for a different part of the screen.

When we open and display an AVI file, if you recall, we must realize its palette with the "realize vfwFile normal" command. This makes the palette of the AVI file the current palette. If you have another AVI file open and visible, its colors will change. If you have an image file open in a paint program, its color will change. After the AVI file plays, and the focus goes to some other object or window, the palette switches back. This can make a mess of the AVI file window. In certain situations, especially those involving AVI files with palette changes or combinations of video and animation, failure to account for this can render playback useless. Hence, the need for RedisplayAVI.

The actual code for the RedisplayAVI handler evolved over time. The original code was much simpler, but as I created more complex AVI files, I found the need to try more and more tricks to get it to play correctly. For that reason, I can't explain the need for every line of code in there; some of the lines were added in a desperate attempt to get a file to play. When something worked, I left it in—the process was as simple and inelegant as that. Because I was using the initial retail release of Video for Windows, I suspect that there were some unanticipated interactions between Windows, Toolbook, and Video for Windows. (As an aside, I'll mention an experience I had recently while coding for MCI in C. A section of code that worked fine on a 486/35 DX machine failed utterly on a 486/66 DX2 machine—messages were being processed more quickly on the faster machine, effectively changing the order in which messages were received by both Windows and MCI.)

In other words, the code is a "work-around," a bit of weird-looking but effective code that does what's needed. If you try this with a different authoring package, you will probably find that you'll need to make slight adjustments to balance the display of your AVI file.

AdjustMagnification Handler

Listing 18.7. AdjustMagnification handler.

```
to handle AdjustMagnification Amount
    system PlayingAVI
    system PlayX
    system PlayY
    system PlayWidth
    system PlayHeight
    system BaseX
    system BaseY
    system BaseWidth
    system BaseHeight
    system AVIMagnification
```

continues

Listing 18.7. continued

```
    set AVIMagnification to Amount

    set PlayX to PlayX+floor((PlayWidth-floor(BaseWidth*AVIMagnification))/2)
    set PlayY to PlayY+floor((PlayHeight-floor(BaseHeight*AVIMagnification))/2)
    set PlayWidth to floor(BaseWidth*AVIMagnification)
    set PlayHeight to floor(BaseHeight*AVIMagnification)

    if not PlayingAVI
        break AdjustMagnification
    end if

    get tbkMCIchk("status vfwFile mode","",1)
    if It = "playing"
        send RedisplayAVI
        send ResumeAVI
    else
        send RedisplayAVI
    end if
end
```

Wouldn't it be nice to be able to change the size of the AVI playback window, even while a file is playing? I thought so too, and thus the handler called AdjustAVIMagnification. It puts the new image on the screen centered at the same place the original image was centered. If you want to use this handler in your own code, you could easily adjust the code to use coordinates you specify. After adjusting the coordinates, it generates a RedisplayAVI event. If the file is already playing, it also generates a ResumeAVI event.

CloseAVI Handler

Listing 18.8. CloseAVI handler.

```
to handle CloseAVI
    system PlayingAVI

    if not PlayingAVI
        break CloseAVI
    end if
```

```
        get tbkMCIchk("close vfwFile","",1)
        set PlayingAVI to false
        hide button "PauseVideo" of this background
        hide button "ResumeVideo" of this background
        hide button "CloseVideo" of this background
end
```

The PlayAVI and ResumeAVI handlers set up playback so that the background
will receive the notification event when playback is complete. As we'll see in the
background script, the notification handler generates a CloseAVI event which is
processed by the CloseAVI handler. It does three things:

➤ Uses MCI to close the AVI file

➤ Sets the global variable PlayingAVI to False

➤ Hides the buttons used to control the AVI file (Pause, Play, Close)

Wave Handlers

There are several multimedia-related handlers in the book script that don't have
anything to do with video, but they are definitely worth a look. Video playback
has many, many more options than audio playback. Compare the relative simplicity of the PlayWave and CloseWave handlers to their video equivalents.

Listing 18.9. PlayWave handler.

```
to handle PlayWave fName
    system PlayingWave
    if PlayingWave
        get tbkMCIchk("close wave","",1)
        set PlayingWave to false
    end if
    set PlayingWave to true
    get tbkMCIchk("open"&& fName && "alias wave","",1)
    get tbkMCIchk("break wave on 27","",1)
    — Set up notify so file will be closed when done playing.
    get tbkMCIchk("play wave",uniquename of this background,1)
end
```

Listing 18.10. CloseWave handler.

```
to handle CloseWave
    system PlayingWave

    if not PlayingWave
        break CloseWave
    end if

    system PlayingWave
    get tbkMCIchk("close wave","",1)
    set PlayingWave to false
end
```

Miscellaneous Handlers in Book Script

There are several other handlers in the book script. There are two for handling
page changes, which use sysLockScreen to control updating of the screen. With the
screen locked, page changes are much faster—most page changes involve all kinds
of object hiding, showing, and moving. There is also a simple handler for getting
the pathname of the directory where the application resides.

Listing 18.11. Miscellaneous handlers in book script.

```
to handle nextPage
    set syslockscreen to true
    go to next page
    set syslockscreen to false
end

to handle prevPage
    set syslockscreen to true
    go to previous page
    set syslockscreen to false
end

to handle GoTop
    set syslockscreen to True
    go to page 1
    set syslockscreen to false
end
```

```
to get pathName fileSpec
    step i from charCount(fileSpec) to 1 by -1
        if (char i of fileSpec = "\");break step;end
        clear char i of fileSpec
    end step
    return (fileSpec)
end pathName
```

Background Scripts

One of my favorite handlers is in the background script. It handles the tbkMMNotify event—the notification from MCI that something has happened. It takes three parameters, listed in Table 18.7.

Table 18.7. tbkMMNotify parameters.

Parameter	Description
status	Contains information about the result of the MCI process. We're looking for the word "successful" in this example, but you could also check for other conditions if you wanted to handle errors on your own.
operation	The process that completed varies; we are interested in completion of playing.
device	We want to make sure that we only handle events related to devices we are interested in.

Using these three parameters, we can determine exactly what is going on within MCI, and take appropriate action. In the handler for tbkMMNotify, we are interested in just two specific situations. We want to know if a wave file has completed playing, and we want to know if an AVI file has completed playing. The full handler is shown in code Listing 18.12.

Listing 18.12. Handler for tbkMMNotify.

```
to handle tbkMMNotify status, operation, device
    system TotalFrames
    local FramesSkipped
    system PlayingTime

    --
    if status && operation && device = "successful play wave"
        send CloseWave
    end if

    if status && operation && device = "successful play vfwFile"
        put tbkMCIchk("status vfwFile frames skipped","",1) \
            into FramesSkipped
        put ceiling(((TotalFrames-FramesSkipped)/PlayingTime) \
            * 1000)/1000&&"fps ("&FramesSkipped&&"skipped)" \
            into text of field "ResultBox" of this background
        get tbkMCIchk("seek vfwFile to 0","",1)
        put tbkMCIchk("status vfwFile position","",1) \
            into text of field "CurrentFrame" of this background
    end if
end
```

If we are notified that a Wave file has completed playing, we just close the file. Handling an AVI file is more complex; no surprise there. Let's look at the statements in the handler relating to AVI files one line at a time.

The first line checks to see how many frames were skipped during playback:

```
put tbkMCIchk("status vfwFile frames skipped","",1) \
    into FramesSkipped
```

During playback, if the defaults are set appropriately for Media Player, MCI will skip video frames if it gets behind. The command `"status vfwFile frames skipped"` returns the number of frames skipped. This command was not included in the documentation for Video for Windows Version 1.0, by the way, but it is very useful when you are trying to determine how well suited your hardware is for video playback.

The next statement performs a calculation to determine the net playback rate, based on the total number of frames, the number of frames skipped, and the total playing time of the file:

```
put ceiling(((TotalFrames-FramesSkipped)/PlayingTime) \
    * 1000)/1000&&"fps ("&FramesSkipped&&"skipped)" \
    into text of field "ResultBox" of this background
```

We will not close the AVI file after playing it; we will, however, "rewind" it to the first frame:

```
get tbkMCIchk("seek vfwFile to 0","",1)
```

Finally, we put the current frame number into a text field reserved for that information:

```
put tbkMCIchk("status vfwFile position","",1) \
    into text of field "CurrentFrame" of this background
```

If you want to update the current frame indicator during playback, you can write an *idle handler*. The idle handler is called whenever the system is idle. This can be quite often, so you don't want to put any heavy-duty or time-consuming code in an idle handler—it would slow the system down. (You could also use a timer to do this, because a timer would be called less often than an idle handler and would put less overhead on the system.)

I used a global variable, AVIIdle, as a toggle to turn this feature on and off. That way, if a user's machine is so slow that reporting the current position causes frames to be skipped, the feature can be turned off. The idle handler code is shown in code Listing 18.13.

Listing 18.13. An idle handler.

```
to handle idle
    system PlayingAVI
    system AVIIdle

    if not AVIIdle
        break idle
    end if

    if PlayingAVI
        put tbkMCIchk("status vfwFile position","",1) \
            into text of field "CurrentFrame" of this background
    end if

end
```

Page Scripts

You can also put a script into each page. The two most common events that have handlers in page scripts are enterPage and leavePage. The scripts for the five pages in the sample application are explained below.

Page 1

The script for the first page is shown in code Listing 18.14. It repeats a lot of what we have seen already: declaring variables, hiding and showing objects, and setting values for variables. In addition, it generates some events that will be handled in the book script, marked in bold text in the following statements:

```
set AVICenter to True
send OpenAVI "pony2.avi"
send PlayAVI True
set AVICenter to False
send CloseAVI
```

Note that the AVI file will play centered in the Toolbook window because we set the global variable AVICenter to True.

In addition, this handler sets some defaults for the rest of the book:

```
set KeepAVISize to False
set DisplayButtons to True
set AVIWindowType to "overlapped"
```

Any page could set different values for itself. However, these values are used throughout the book. If we did change the values, it would be wise to create a handler for a "ResetAVIDefaults" event:

```
to handle ResetAVIDefaults
    set KeepAVISize to False
    set DisplayButtons to True
    set AVIWindowType to "overlapped"
    set MuteAVIAudio to False
end
```

The enterPage handler ends with a command to move to the next page:

```
go to next page
```

gives the user no choice: after completing page 1 business, Toolbook will advance automatically to the second page.

Listing 18.14. Page 1 handlers.

```
to handle enterPage
      system PlayX
      system PlayY
      system PlayWidth
      system PlayHeight
      system KeepAVISize
      system DisplayButtons
      system PlayingTime
      set DisplayButtons to False
      system AVIWindowType
      system AVICenter

      set syslockscreen to True
      show field "BlueField"
      hide button "TopButton" of this background
      hide button "PrevButton" of this background
      hide button "EndButton" of this background
      hide button "ExitButton" of this background
      hide button "Nextbutton" of this background
      hide button "PauseVideo" of this background
      hide button "ResumeVideo" of this background
      hide button "CloseVideo" of this background
      hide rectangle "BackRect" of this background

      set KeepAVISize to True
      set PlayX to 190
      set PlayY to 130
      set PlayWidth to 200
      set PlayHeight to 120
      hide field "BlueField"
      show field "ClickField"
      set syslockscreen to false

      set AVIWindowType to "child"

      set AVICenter to True
      send OpenAVI "pony2.avi"
      send PlayAVI True
      set AVICenter to False

      set syslockscreen to True
      hide field "ClickField"
      show button "TopButton" of this background
      show button "PrevButton" of this background
      show button "EndButton" of this background
      show button "ExitButton" of this background
      show button "Nextbutton" of this background
      set syslockscreen to False
```

continues

Listing 18.14. continued

```
        send CloseAVI
        set KeepAVISize to False
        set DisplayButtons to True
        set AVIWindowType to "overlapped"

        go to next page
end
```

Page 2

Most of the code for enterPage and leavePage handlers on page 2 is concerned with housekeeping tasks—hiding and showing the correct objects. There are also a few statements that set the correct default values for some objects, including the radio buttons "checked" property and the default text in a text field. Note that the leavePage handler resets MuteAVIAudio to False, and sets the "checked" property to False as well.

Listing 18.15. Page 2 handlers.

```
to handle enterPage
     system waveFile
     system PageInstructions
     system MainBounds

     show rectangle "BackRect" of this background
     show group "IntroText"
     show field "ResultBox" of this background
     show button "ResultButton" of this background
     show group "ButtonGroup" of this background
     show group "BoxGroup" of this background
     show button "OpenButton" of this background
     set checked of button Spigot to True
     set checked of button Promotion to False
     set checked of button Bravado to False
     put "" into text of field "ResultBox" of this background
     put "spigot.avi" into text of field "AVIFileName" of this background
end

To handle leavePage
     system MuteAVIAudio
```

```
      send CloseAVI
      set syslockscreen to True
      hide field "ResultBox" of this background
      hide button "ResultButton" of this background
      hide rectangle "BackRect" of this background
      hide group "IntroText"
      hide group "ButtonGroup" of this background
      hide group "BoxGroup" of this background
      set checked of button "muteaudio" of this background to false
      set MuteAVIAudio to False
      put "" into text of field "ResultBox" of this background
      set syslockscreen to False
end
```

Page 3

Page 3 is a different kind of page. There are no digital video files; just some bitmaps to deal with. However, the code used here is instructive. Asymetrix uses the kinds of commands to open, display, and close bitmaps that MCI used. This makes it easy to work with bitmaps alongside more obvious multimedia file types like video and sound. This script only includes the command to close the bitmap:

```
get tbkBitmap("close bmp")
```

Refer to the Object Scripts section below (Page 3, View Bitmap Button, code Listing 18.16), for details of opening and displaying bitmaps with Toolbook. The script also includes an example of the powerful translateWindowsMessage capability.

Listing 18.16. Page 3 handlers.

```
to handle enterPage
      system ShowingSpigot
      set ShowingSpigot to True
      hide rectangle "BackRect" of this background
end

to handle leavePage
      send CloseBitmapWindow
end

to handle CloseBitmapWindow hwnd, wmsg, sparam, lplo, lphi
      get tbkBitmap("close bmp")
end
```

Page 4

The script for page 4 is similar to the script for page 2. There is an additional button for displaying an AVI file; otherwise, it's just a matter of hiding and showing the right objects, and putting the right values in variables and text fields. The `leavePage` script closes any AVI that we may have left open.

Listing 18.17. Page 4 handlers.

```
to handle enterPage
    set syslockscreen to True
    show group "IntroText"
    show group "ButtonGroup" of this background
    show group "BoxGroup" of this background
    put "jbird.avi" into text of field "AVIFileName" of this background
    set checked of button ProMotion to True
    set checked of button Spigot to False
    set checked of button Bravado to False
    set checked of button Blow to False
    hide field "Madness"
    hide field "Chicken"
    show field "JBird2"
    show button "OpenButton" of this background
    set syslockscreen to false
end

to handle leavePage
    set syslockscreen to true
    hide group "BoxGroup" of this background
    hide group "ButtonGroup" of this background
    hide button "OpenButton" of this background
    send CloseAVI
    set syslockscreen to false
end
```

Page 5

Page 5 is also a little different, but not much. The big news here is that we use the `enterPage` handler to open a specific AVI file. We also enforce audio on:

```
set MuteAVIAudio to False
```

Unlike other pages, page 5 hides the "Pause" and "Close" buttons, and does not display any information about the video file—this page uses the AVI file the way you might in an interactive training package—the video is there to be seen and heard, but there is no need to tell the user about the file, or to give him the ability to manipulate it. It's there for the information only. Of course, if you play the AVI file, you'll quickly realize it's really there for fun. (I have no intention of going into the used-car-salesman business.)

Page 5 also happens to be the last page in the book; the ontorPago script hides some buttons that don't make sense on the last page, such as the one for moving to the next page.

Listing 18.18. Page 5 handlers.

```
to handle enterPage
    system MuteAVIAudio

    set syslockscreen to true
    hide button "NextButton" of this background
    hide button "EndButton" of this background
    hide rectangle "BackRect" of this background
    set syslockscreen to false
    set MuteAVIAudio to False
    send OpenAVI "trust2.avi"
    hide button "PauseVideo" of this background
    hide button "CloseVideo" of this background
end

to handle leavePage
    set syslockscreen to true
    show button "NextButton" of this background
    show button "EndButton" of this background
    set syslockscreen to false
    send CloseAVI
end
```

Object Scripts

A number of the individual objects on various pages have scripts that are instructive to look at. I'll only include the most important and useful ones here. If you have Toolbook, I have included the complete source code with the application.

Page 3, View Bitmap Button

This script displays a bitmap file, and then translates Windows messages to find out when you are ready to close the bitmap file. The first order of business is to open the bitmap file with a call to a special Toolbook function, `tbkBitmap`:

```
get tbkBitmap("open v_rac8c.bmp alias bmp style popup parent" \
    && sysClientHandle)
```

Note that the command string is just like the kind you use with MCI. However, MCI isn't involved: this is just how Toolbook implemented support for bitmap files. The parallels to MCI command strings make it easy to use. In this case, we are displaying the bitmap in a window that is a popup, and a child of the main application window. To display the open bitmap, use the `"window"` command:

```
get tbkBitmap("window bmp state show")
```

If desired, you could use this command to maximize or minimize the bitmap window. We also need the handle for the popup window that contains the bitmap:

```
set Bitwindow to tbkBitmap("status bmp window")
```

This puts the handle in the variable `Bitwindow`. We need the window handle to use `TranslateWindowMessage`. The numbers in the handler refer to specific Windows messages (see Table 18.8).

Table 18.8. Translating windows messages.

Number	Message	Description
257	WM_KEYUP	Any "typewriter" keypress.
261	WM_SYSKEYUP	Any system keypress, such as Control, Alt, etc.
514	WM_LBUTTONUP	Left mouse button up.
517	WM_RBUTTONUP	Right mouse button up.

If any of these messages occur, we will generate the event `CloseBitmapWindow`. The handler is located in the script for page 3 (see code listing 18.19), and, as its name implies, it closes the bitmap file. Note that only mouse clicks that are actually in the window will be intercepted and translated; we need a `"send CloseBitmapWindow"` statement in the `leavePage` handler for page 3 to make sure the bitmap is closed.

Listing 18.19. Displaying bitmaps from files.

```
to handle buttonUp
    set ShowingSpigot to True
    hide group "BravadoText"
    show group "SpigotText"
    get tbkBitmap("open v_rac8c.bmp alias bmp style popup
parent"&&sysClientHandle)
    get tbkBitmap("window bmp state show")
    set Bitwindow to tbkBitmap("status bmp window")
    TranslateWindowMessage for BitWindow
        after 257 send CloseBitmapWindow
        after 261 send CloseBitmapWindow
        after 514 send CloseBitmapWindow
        after 517 send CloseBitmapWindow
    end
end
```

Toolbook Multimedia Support

If you haven't already gotten the idea that Toolbook's support for multimedia is both complete and well-designed, I'm providing a summary of the multimedia functionality you can find in Toolbook. Table 18.9 provides a list of the most useful functions used with Multimedia in Toolbook. Table 18.10 lists the functions that were recently added to enable better handling of video files, as well as other new functions for general multimedia tasks. These functions greatly reduce the amount of code you'll need to write for setting the size and position of video display windows. If you have very specific requirements, you still have the option of sizing and positioning video windows yourself.

If you do not already have the new version of the Toolbook Multimedia DLL (tbkmm.dll), you can download it from the Asymetrix BBS. Check your Toolbook manual for the phone number. It comes with a sample application that shows clearly how to use the new functions. If you own Multimedia Toolbook, I have included the source code for an application on the CD-ROM that uses several of the new functions (master.tbk).

Table 18.9. Toolbook multimedia functions.

Function	Description
HMSfromMillisec	Converts a value in milliseconds into a time string of the format *hh:mm:ss* (hours, minutes, seconds or HMS).
millisecFromHMS	Converts a time string in the format *hh:mm:ss* to milliseconds.
millisecFromMSF	Used with CD audio (Red Book audio). Converts a time string in the format *hh:mm:ss:ff* (hours, minutes, seconds, Red Book frames) to milliseconds.
millisecFromSMPTE	Converts milliseconds into a time string of the format *hh:mm:ss:ff* (hours, minutes, seconds, SMPTE frames).
MSFfromMillisec	Converts milliseconds into a time string of the format *hh:mm:ss:ff* (hours, minutes, seconds, Red Book frames).
SMPTEfromMillisec	Converts milliseconds into a time string of the format *hh:mm:ss:ff* (hours, minutes, seconds, SMPTE frames).
tbkBitmap	Controls display of bitmap files in child, popup, or overlapped windows. Use is similar to tbkMCI. Supports the following MCI-like commands: capability, close, info, open, play, status, and window. There are numerous sub-commands and parameters as well.
tbkBitmapChk	Similar to tbkBitmap, but supports optional error messages.
tbkBmpErrorString	Returns a string for a given error message number.
tbkMCI	Gives complete access to all installed MCI device drivers using the command string interface. See numerous examples throughout this chapter.

Function	Description
tbkMCIchk	Similar to tbkMCI, but supports optional error messages. Numerous examples throughout this chapter.
tbkMMDevices	Specifies which devices were successfully loaded from the [devices] section of tbkmm.ini.
tbkMMErrorString	Returns error message associated with a multimedia error number. Toolbook stores error numbers in the system variable sysErrorNumber automatically.
tbkMMNotify	Not a function, but a message sent to handlers you can specify in calls to tbkMCI and tbkMCIchk. Sent when an MCI process completes.
tbkMMTimer	Not a function, but a message sent to handlers specified in calls to tbkTimerStart function.
tbkMMVersion	Returns version information for tbkmm.dll.
tbkTimerCapability	For requesting information about the capabilities of the installed timer device.
tbkTimerStart	Starts a timer.
tbkTimerStop	Stops a timer.

Table 18.10. New Toolbook multimedia functions.

Function	Description
tbkBitmapCenterWindow	Centers a bitmap relative to a point, a rectangle, or another window.
tbkBitmapGetWindowRect	Gets the bounds of the window for a bitmap in either ToolBook coordinates or pixels.

continues

Table 18.10. continued

Function	Description
tbkBitmapPositionWindow	Sets the position or bounds of the window for a bitmap.
tbkCenterWindow	Centers a window, such as the stage window for a digital video, video overlay, or animation device, relative to a point, a rectangle, or another window.
tbkGetWindowRect	Gets the bounding rectangle of any window in either ToolBook coordinates or pixels.
tbkPositionWindow	Sets the position or bounds of a window, such as the stage window for a digital video, video overlay, or animation device.
tbkMCICenterWindow	Centers a window, such as the stage window for a digital video, video overlay, or animation device, relative to a point, a rectangle, or another window.
tbkMCIGetWindowRect	Gets the bounding rectangle of the window for any MCI device that uses a window in either ToolBook coordinates or pixels.
tbkMCIPositionWindow	Sets the position or bounds of a window, such as the stage window for a digital video, video overlay, or animation device.

Afterthoughts

I hope that I have been able to convey the true power and flexibility that Multimedia Toolbook offers. Multimedia functionality is well integrated into the product, and if you can imagine a task you can probably find a way to do it with

Toolbook. I feel obliged to warn you that it can take some effort to become proficient with Toolbook, but I have always found that the time spent learning about Toolbook was amply rewarded with useful skills and clever multimedia tricks. If you want the best balance between power and ease of use, Toolbook is worth a very close examination.

19

Programming Examples: C/C++

I got my start in programming with lowly BASIC, and moved from there to languages such as dBASE. This was in the early '80s, when being able to program at all was considered a really great accomplishment. But that faded pretty quickly, and it wasn't long before the folks who could program in C let us know that they were the *real* programmers; the rest of us were just fooling around.

To see just how impressive a knowledge of C programming really was, I decided to try it for myself. I will grant that it's not as easy to learn as, say, dBASE, but it's not all that hard, either; it just takes some time to learn the ins and outs. As with any language, there will always be a stellar few who know every nuance, and C does have more nuances than the average language, but it's a very approachable subject for anyone with any kind of prior programming experience.

Once I had learned my way around in C, I ran into the next set of *real* programmers: Windows programmers. Maybe I ought to say GUI (Graphical User Interface) programmers because the Mac programmers I knew were pretty aloof and crusty, too. They just used their lofty position to do more fun things. Well, the years have caught up with these folks—now that you can run down to your local bookstore and buy a book explaining how to program for Windows, you realize that even this is within the skill range of mere mortals.

I have to admit that I'd never actually managed to sit down and write a Windows application in C, because about the time I decided it would be a really great accomplishment, Visual Basic came out. I like to accomplish things as much as the next person, but let's face it: if I could do it in Visual Basic, I was not going to do it in C.

But there are some things that really, really, require C to work. One of those things (at least so far) is a screen saver. You can't write screen savers in just any old language. You need a *real* language, and that's C.

When I thought about what kind of a digital video program I might write in C, a screen saver seemed far and away the most needed. Even after finishing it, I still haven't seen another one. I can't figure out why there aren't a bunch of them out there on the market because, well, wait until you see how much fun it is. If you don't feel up to the C programming part, you can just run the screen saver and have fun with it—it's on the CD-ROM. My favorite way to run the screen saver is without blanking the screen; it creates interesting designs on your desktop, as shown in Figure 19.1.

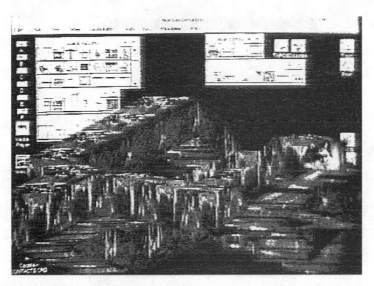

Figure 19.1. The video screen saver in action.

Using Video Screen Saver

The video screen saver is on both the floppy disk and the CD-ROM. It's in a ZIP file, vidsaver.exe, in the directory **<CD drive>:\vidsaver**. To use it, you'll need to:

1. Make the Windows 3.1 installation directory your current directory (usually **c:\windows**).

2. vidsaver.exe is a self-extracting archive file. If you run it from the floppy drive **A:**, type in **a:\vidsaver\vidsaver** and press the enter key. If you run it from the CD-ROM, and assuming your CD-ROM is drive **D:**, type in **d:\vidsaver\vidsaver** and press Enter.

3. This will put a copy of the screen saver file into your Windows directory. If you want to install the vidsaver source and make file, follow the instructions in the section, "The Screen Saver Code."

The screen saver is easy to use; it will now automatically appear in the list of screen savers when you run the Desktop applet in Control Panel. See Figure 19.2, which shows a typical Control Panel with a Desktop icon.

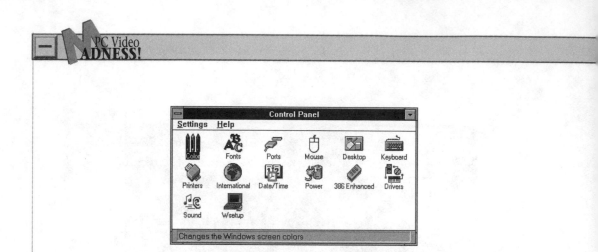

Figure 19.2. Windows Control Panel with Desktop applet icon.

Double-click the Desktop icon, which brings up the Desktop dialog box, as shown in Figure 19.3.

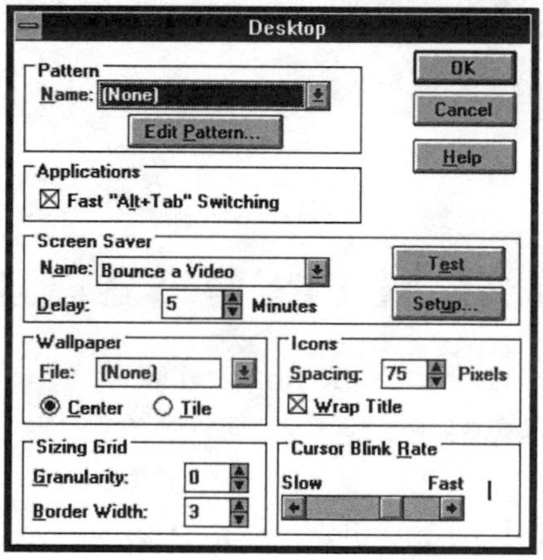

Figure 19.3. Desktop dialog box.

The screen saver information is located at the middle of the dialog box. Click the pulldown arrow to see a list of available screen savers (see Figure 19.3) and click "Bounce a Video." That's the video screen saver. For information on configuring the Video Saver, see the section "Setup Dialog Explained" later in this chapter.

> ## Note
>
> Video Saver requires that you have the runtime version of Video for Windows installed. If you do not, see Appendix A.

What Does Video Saver Do?

Video Saver creates a window and plays the video file you specify in that window. During playback, Video Saver moves the window randomly around the screen. If you tell Video Saver to blank the screen, it will make the entire screen black and then move the playback window randomly. If you tell it not to blank the screen, it will play the video on top of the existing screen image, but without erasing images as it moves randomly. Most videos wind up creating rather interesting patterns with this technique.

Setup Dialog Explained

The configuration dialog box for Video Saver is shown in Figure 19.4. It contains a number of parameters that can be used in two ways: to tailor Video Saver to your system's capabilities, or to achieve interesting and unusual visual effects. Some of these settings control capabilities that are not obvious, but have dramatic effects.

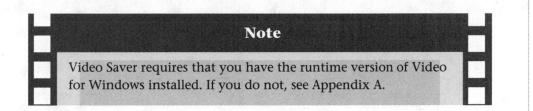

Figure 19.4. Video Saver configuration dialog box.

The complete list of configurable options for Video Saver are shown in Table 19.1.

Table 19.1. Configuring Video Saver

Dialog item	Description
Max pixels/move	Vidsaver moves the video playback window by shifting its position by a variable number of pixels. The number you enter here is the maximum number of pixels the playback window can move at one time. For smaller displays (like 640x480) or less powerful computers, smaller numbers like 3-5 work best. On a 486/66, numbers up to 25 are interesting, although anything over 12 or so makes the movement jumpy. Larger numbers are amusing but not very easy on the eyes. <grin> If you enter an invalid value a default value will be saved to the configuration file (control.ini is used).
Between delay	Use this to specify a delay between replays of the video. For small values, there will be a short delay before the next playback. For larger values, the delay increases. The delay is approximately in tens of milliseconds, so for a 1 second delay you would enter 100. This method of playback sets a time equal to the length of the file playback plus the time you specify. There is always some small slice of time required to read the file from disk before it actually starts to play, so you can never get a truly seamless, continuous loop this way. If you want the tightest possible loop, check the "Continuous repeat" box.
Move delay	This specifies how long to delay before moving the playback window to its next position. Small values mean that the playback window moves slowly around the screen. Large values mean that

Dialog item	Description
	the window moves quickly. Values are approximately in milliseconds (the value is used to set a timer). The number of pixels per move has some effect on speed as well. The best value for your computer depends on a variety of factors. If you are under powered, larger numbers (up to about 500) will be better; it takes CPU time to move the playback window around, and on a slow machine that CPU time is needed for playing the AVI file. If you have a fast machine, you can make this number as small as you can live with—if the playback window moves too fast, it can make playback choppy, or it can be hard to view the video as it sweeps wildly across the screen.
Magnification %	The magnification factor you use depends on computer speed, screen size, and personal taste. If you have a very fast 486, you can probably use 200% or even 300% safely. For slower hardware, 100% or even 50% may be needed. It also depends on the file—you won't want to magnify a file that is 320x240, for example, unless you've got a Pentium under the hood.
Random rate	This number controls how often the playback window changes direction. The lower the number, the more often direction changes. This setting is purely a matter of personal taste. Very small numbers create a bouncing image that is amusing but hard to watch. Numbers around 35 give a random effect but enough continuity to make the video watchable. Numbers over 100 allow the video to move in straight lines for extended periods. With screen blanking turned off, this often results in attractive patterns on the screen.
Filename	You can specify any valid AVI file here. By default, Vidsaver uses c:\windows\scr_sav.avi.

continues

537

Table 19.1. continued

Dialog item	Description
Blank screen	(Check box) There are two basic modes for Vidsaver. If you check this box, the screen will go black when the screen saver starts, and the playback window will move around randomly according to the parameters you have set. If you leave this box unchecked, the screen will not be blanked, and the behavior of the screen saver is different. Instead of simply moving the window against the background, previous images of the window are retained, sort of like leaving a trail of used windows behind. This often creates some very interesting patterns over time.
Mute audio	(Check box) If you are playing an AVI file that has an audio track, and you don't want to hear it over and over, check this box. The video portion will still play, of course.
Continuous repeat	If you simply want the video to play over and over with a minimum delay between each playback, check this box.
Password options	This works just like it would for any other screen saver. Use it if you want to require a password for clearing the screen saver.

Windows Screen Savers

There are two kinds of screen savers. The latest version of Windows, 3.1, incorporates one kind of screen saver easily. Support for these screen savers is built right into Windows itself. Some of the most challenging aspects of screen saver programming are built right into Windows itself, making our job easier. Naturally, this is the kind of screen saver we'll write.

The other kind of screen saver is a roll-your-own, where you are responsible for everything that happens. This is not the kind of screen saver we'll write. I believe strongly in the Lazy Programmer theory.

According to this theory, a person becomes a programmer because he or she is fundamentally a lazy person. You might object to this idea if you have ever seen a programmer working long hours to get a program to run. You would be missing a very important point about programmers if you did. The idea behind programming is that, once written, it runs with almost no effort (on the programmer's part, that is; armies of data entry operators are not the programmer's concern). Thus, even if it takes a lot of effort to get the program to run, there is a big payoff at the end. Thus, programmers program because that allows them to do things once, and then let a machine handle it forever after.

Now, there are a couple of things wrong with these assumptions, but human nature being what it is, most of us programmers go ahead and program anyway.

Still, allowing for reality, my approach to this screen saver project is pretty straightforward: I don't write code I don't have to, I use whatever tools will simplify the job, and I build my own tools whenever necessary, which is most of the time. Some of the other projects in the book, such as the MCI Command Processor, were built as tools to support the Screen Saver project. You see, a programmer is only as good as his tools, and a good programmer can always build his own tools.

The Parts of a Screen Saver

The typical screen saver has five basic sections. Each section has a different character, and a different job to do. First we'll look at the specifics of building a screen saver, and then see how to fit digital video into a screen saver. The full code for the screen saver can be found on the CD-ROM, and is printed in full in the Screen Saver Code section, later in this chapter.

Globals

It takes a ton of global variables to make a screen saver work, and there doesn't seem to be much you can do about that. It's partly the price of being in Windows, and it's partly to keep track of everything going on. You'll need some standard globals for communications with Windows, and some to maintain your own internal information.

ScreenSaverProc()

This is the main procedure for processing messages that get sent to the screen saver. It's here that you create the playback window, initialize for playback, handle timer messages, and so on.

ScreenSaverConfigureDialog()

This is a procedure that handles all messages associated with the configuration dialog box.

Miscellaneous Housekeeping

We'll need some miscellaneous functions to handle various tasks related to the screen saver. For example, we'll need to read configuration information from control.ini, where it's stored.

Screen Saver Stuff

Last, and far from least, we'll need the actual code that does the screen saver stuff. That's where most of the code goes that deals with digital video.

Video Screen Savers

A video screen saver, or for that matter almost any multimedia screen saver, pushes the limits of what a screen saver can handle. In some ways, it's a miracle that it works at all. When I didn't see any video screen savers anywhere, I thought that maybe it wasn't possible, or that it wasn't stable enough or reliable enough. As it turns out, the way that screen savers are implemented in Windows 3.1 works really well with almost all kinds of multimedia. However, you have to take a few precautions, especially with a video screen saver.

The reason is simple: multimedia, and video in particular, can place heavy demands on your PC. If the demands are too high, it can be difficult to cancel the screen saver with mouse movements, mouse clicks, or keystrokes—the CPU will be so busy, it will miss them entirely. Of course, eventually the screen saver will be interrupted, but it's important to think about the demands we're putting on the system, and provide at least a way for the user to modify playback so the screen saver doesn't take too much processing time.

There are several ways to limit overuse of resources:

➤ Minimize overhead.

➤ Reduce data rates.

➤ Avoid "multi" in the media.

➤ Optimize, optimize, optimize.

Let's look a little more closely at each technique.

Minimize overhead—Because the video is placing so much demand on system resources, we need to avoid adding too much additional demand. For example, the video screen saver moves a window around on the screen. If we move the window frequently, that puts more load on the system. If we move it less frequently, we reduce the load. Of course, there's a price to pay: if we go too far, the sense of continuous motion gets lost. The best choice is to include variable settings in the configuration dialog box to allow the user to tune the screen saver for his or her machine's capabilities.

Reduce data rates—There's not much you can do about the CPU power required to handle such things as decompression, but you do have some control over data rates. Playing a video at a smaller size cuts the amount of data dramatically, for example. You can also use lower frame rates to achieve the same result.

Avoid "multi" in the media—If one data-hungry medium is taxing, two or more media are even more difficult. Muting audio, for example, eliminates a significant chunk of data movement and processing. Admittedly, limiting one's choice of media isn't very exciting. It's a sad fact that multimedia, especially if it involves video, requires a lot of horsepower to manage.

Optimize, optimize, optimize—As with any programming task, and especially in C, taking the time to optimize performance is important. If there is a simple way to do something, use it. If there's a faster but less elegant way to make something happen, use it. Video itself eats up so much processing time that you, as the programmer, need to look for ways to speed things up. You can only go so far, of course, but the best place to look for opportunities for optimization are in the parts of the program that get called most often. With video, that's the playback loop. In the Video screen saver, there are two distinct types of playback. In one, playback is handled within the screen saver itself. In the other, we use a repeat capability built into MCI to handle playback—reducing overhead.

So writing a video screen saver isn't a walk in the park, but if you give the user the ability to tune playback, and are reasonably careful about your code, you won't have any trouble.

There is one other aspect to watch out for, however. Video for Windows is a new technology, and there are sometimes unusual interactions with other new and interesting technologies. Keep an eye out for trouble!

The Screen Saver Code

In this section, we'll take a detailed look at the screen saver code. We'll examine the multimedia portions most closely, but we will also look at the code involved in the screen saver itself.

Listing 19.1 shows the code for the main module in the program, vidsaver.c. This is the only C source module. The other files with source code are:

```
vidsaver.h      Listing 5
vidsaver.dlg    Listing 3
scrnsave.dlg    Listing 4
makefile        Listing 2
```

We'll start by looking at the code in vidsaver.c.

Listing 19.1. VIDSAVER.C.

```
/*  VIDSAVER.C
 *
 *  VIDSAVER is a sample screen saver application. It moves a
 *  playing .AVI file around the screen.  It provides a variety of
 *  options for controlling movement and sound.
 *
 *  (C) Copyright Ron Wodaski 1992-1993.  All rights reserved.
 *
 *  This application was written and compiled using Microsoft C/C++
 *  version 7.0.
 *
 *  You have a royalty-free right to use, modify, reproduce and
 *  distribute the sample files (and/or any modified version) in
 *  any way you find useful, provided that you agree that
 *  the author, Ron Wodaski has no warranty obligations or liability
 *  for any sample application files which are modified.
 */
```

```c
#include <windows.h>
#include <mmsystem.h>
#include "vidsaver.h"
#include <string.h>
#include <stdlib.h>
#include <stdio.h>
#include <time.h>

/* Global used by SCRNSAVE.LIB. Required for all screen savers.
 */
char szAppName[40];


/* Globals specific to VIDSAVER.
 */
char szSpeedName[] = "Speed";
char szDelayName[] = "Delay between file play";
char szSDelayName[] = "Delay between moves";
char szMagnifyName[] = "Magnification";
char szChangeName[] = "Change frequency";
char szBlankitName[] = "Blank Screen";
char szMuteName[]= "Mute Audio";
char szRepeatName[]= "Repeat Play";
char szPlayFileName[]= "Filename to Play";
char szName[]="Bounce a Video";

/* Externals defined in SCRNSAVE.LIB. Required for all screen savers.
 */
HINSTANCE _cdecl hMainInstance;
HWND _cdecl hMainWindow;
char _cdecl szName[TITLEBARNAMELEN];
char _cdecl szIsPassword[22];
char _cdecl szIniFile[MAXFILELEN];
char _cdecl szScreenSaver[22];
char _cdecl szPassword[16];
char _cdecl szDifferentPW[BUFFLEN];
char _cdecl szChangePW[30];
char _cdecl szBadOldPW[BUFFLEN];
char _cdecl szHelpFile[MAXFILELEN];
char _cdecl szNoHelpMemory[BUFFLEN];
UINT _cdecl MyHelpMessage;
HOOKPROC _cdecl fpMessageFilter;

WORD wElapse;           // speed parameter
WORD wTimer;            // timer id
BOOL bBottom;           // TRUE if frog at bottom of screen
int xPos;               // current x position
int yPos;               // current y position
int xPosInit;           // initial x position
```

continues

Listing 19.1. continued

```
int yPosInit;          // initial y position
int xVelocInit;        // x initial velocity
int nGravity;          // acceleration factor
BOOL bSound;           // sound on/off flag
BOOL bPause;           // stick at bottom of screen?
BOOL bPassword;        // password protected?

WORD wMaxSpeed=25;                        // Maximum # pixels per window move
int ChangeFreq=100;                   // Determines how often change num pixels
char szReturnString[STRLEN];          // buffer for messages from mciSendString
char szWindowHandle[16];              // buffer for string of window handle
char szCommandString[STRLEN];         // buffer for MCI command strings
char szProgName[]="VideoSaver";   // Program name

char szFileToPlay[STRLEN];                // Buffer for name of file to play.
char szWinTitle[STRLEN];                  // Buffer for playback window caption
char szPlayWidth[8];                      // Buffer for playback window width
char szPlayHeight[8];                     // Buffer for playback window height
long  wPlayWidth;                         // Playback window width
long  wPlayHeight;                        // Playback window height
WORD wMagnification=200;                  // Magnification factor
BOOL bMuteAudio=0;                        // Toggle for muting audio
BOOL bRepeatPlay=0;                       // Toggle for Continuous repeat
BOOL bBlankScreen=1;                      // Toggle for blanking screen
int wAdjWidth, wAdjHeight;                // Difference between window/client
                                          // area sizes
int wTop=0, wLeft=0;                      // X,Y coordinates for playback window
                                          // create

HWND hScrWnd;                 // Handle for playback window
WNDCLASS wcScrApp;            // Class for playback window
FILE *FileOpen;               // File open pointer for fopen call
RECT lpScreen;                // For screen rectangle
RECT lpWindowSize;            // For playback window rectangle
RECT lpClientSize;            // For playback window client area rectangle
long wWidth, wHeight;         // Initial size of playback window

WORD wTimerShort;       // timer id for interval on window move
int ShortTime=100;               // default length of timer
WORD wTimerLong;        // timer id for interval on file play
int DelayTime=250;               // default length of timer
UINT PlayingTime;                // Length of AVI file in ms

/* Toggle for repainting during calls to MoveWindow() */
static BOOL RepaintToggle=FALSE;


/* ScreenSaverProc - Main entry point for screen saver messages.
 * This function is required for all screen savers.
```

```
 *
 * Params:  Standard window message handler parameters.
 *
 * Return:  The return value depends on the message.
 *
 *  Note that all messages go to the DefScreenSaverProc(), except
 *  for ones we process.
 */
LONG FAR PASCAL ScreenSaverProc(HWND hWnd, UINT msg, WPARAM wParam, LPARAM lParam)
{
    RECT rc;                          // Rectangle for erasing background

    switch (msg)
    {
        case WM_CREATE:
        {
            /* Load the strings from the STRINGTABLE */
            GetIniEntries();

            /* Load the initial bounce settings. */
            GetIniSettings();

                srand((unsigned)time(NULL));   // Seed random # generation.

                /* Make default window size one-fourth screen size.  */
                GetWindowRect(GetDesktopWindow(),&lpScreen);
                wWidth  = (long)(lpScreen.right-lpScreen.left)/4;
                wHeight = (long)(lpScreen.bottom-lpScreen.top)/4;

                /* Create window class for playback. */
                wcScrApp.lpszClassName=szProgName;
                wcScrApp.hInstance    =hMainInstance;
                wcScrApp.lpfnWndProc  =WndProc;
                wcScrApp.hCursor      =LoadCursor(NULL,IDC_ARROW);
                wcScrApp.hIcon        =NULL;
                wcScrApp.lpszMenuName =NULL;
                wcScrApp.hbrBackground=CreateSolidBrush(RGB(0,255,255));
                wcScrApp.style        =CS_HREDRAW¦CS_VREDRAW;
                wcScrApp.cbClsExtra   =0;
                wcScrApp.cbWndExtra   =0;
                if (!RegisterClass (&wcScrApp))
                return FALSE;

                /* Create playback window. */
                hScrWnd=CreateWindow(szProgName,"VidSaver 0.1c",
                    (WS_POPUP), wLeft, wTop,
                    (int)wWidth,(int)wHeight, hWnd,(HMENU)NULL,
                    (HANDLE)hMainInstance,(LPSTR)NULL);
```

continues

545

Listing 19.1. continued

```
                /* Get sizes of Window & Client area for later calculations. */
                GetWindowRect(hScrWnd,&lpWindowSize);
                GetClientRect(hScrWnd,&lpClientSize);

                /* Setup for playback. */
                PlayingTime = SetupPlayback(szFileToPlay);
        MovePlayerRandom(hScrWnd);
                ShowWindow(hScrWnd,SW_SHOWNORMAL);

                /* Create timers.  Note that each time belongs to a different
                    window.  The playback timer belongs to the playback
                    window,
                    and the move timer belongs to the ScreenSaver default
                    window.
                 */
                /* Set a timer for the length of the file plus delay time * 10.
*/
        wTimerLong=SetTimer(hScrWnd,ID_TIMER,PlayingTime+DelayTime*10, NULL);
                /* Set a timer for interval between playback window move. */
        wTimerShort=SetTimer(hWnd, ID_TIMER, ShortTime, NULL);

                /* Play the AVI file! */
        PlayFile(hScrWnd);
            return 0L;
        }

    case WM_TIMER:

                /* Short timer went off; move window to new location. */
            MovePlayer(hScrWnd);
            return 0L;

    case WM_DESTROY:

                /* Clean up; we're out of here. */
                if (FileOpen)
                    mciExecute("close AVIFile");
                /* Kill timers. */
            if(wTimerShort) KillTimer(hWnd,ID_TIMER);
            if(wTimerLong)  KillTimer(hScrWnd,ID_TIMER);
        break;

    case WM_ERASEBKGND:
                if (bBlankScreen)
                    {
            GetClientRect(hWnd,&rc);
            FillRect((HDC)wParam,&rc,(HBRUSH)GetStockObject(BLACK_BRUSH));
                    }
        return 0L;
```

```
            default:
                break;
        }
    /* If we don't handle message, pass it to default procedure. */
    return DefScreenSaverProc(hWnd, msg, wParam, lParam);
}


/* RegisterDialogClasses -- Entry point for registering window
 * classes required by configuration dialog box.
 *
 * Params:  hWnd -- Handle to window
 *
 * Return:  None
 */
BOOL RegisterDialogClasses(HINSTANCE hInst)
{
    return TRUE;
}



/* ScreenSaverConfigureDialog -- Dialog box function for configuration
 * dialog.
 *
 * Params:  hWnd -- Handle to window
 *
 * Return:  None
 */
BOOL FAR PASCAL ScreenSaverConfigureDialog(HWND hDlg,UINT msg,WPARAM wParam,LPARAM
lParam)
{
  static HWND hIDOK;
  static HWND hSetPassword;

    switch (msg)
    {
        case WM_INITDIALOG:
            GetIniEntries();        // Load strings from table.
            GetIniSettings();       // Read from CONTROL.INI

                    /* Set values in dialog box. */
            SetDlgItemInt(hDlg, ID_SPEED,   wMaxSpeed,      FALSE);
            SetDlgItemInt(hDlg, ID_BDELAY,  DelayTime,      TRUE );
            SetDlgItemInt(hDlg, ID_MDELAY,  ShortTime,      TRUE );
            SetDlgItemInt(hDlg, ID_MAGNIFY, wMagnification, TRUE );
            SetDlgItemInt(hDlg, ID_CLEVEL,  ChangeFreq,     TRUE );
                SetDlgItemText(hDlg,ID_FNAME,   szFileToPlay);
            SendDlgItemMessage(hDlg, ID_BLANKIT, BM_SETCHECK, bBlankScreen, NULL);
            SendDlgItemMessage(hDlg, ID_MUTE,    BM_SETCHECK, bMuteAudio,   NULL);
            SendDlgItemMessage(hDlg, ID_CONT,    BM_SETCHECK, bRepeatPlay,  NULL);
```

continues

Listing 19.1. continued

```
            SendDlgItemMessage(hDlg, ID_PASSWORDPROTECTED, BM_SETCHECK,
                bPassword, NULL);
            hSetPassword=GetDlgItem(hDlg, ID_SETPASSWORD);
            EnableWindow(hSetPassword, bPassword);
            hIDOK=GetDlgItem(hDlg, IDOK);
            return TRUE;

    case WM_COMMAND:
        switch (wParam)
        {
            case IDOK:
                            /* User clicked OK button; put values into vari-
ables. */
                    wMaxSpeed       = GetDlgItemInt(hDlg, ID_SPEED,   NULL, FALSE );
                    DelayTime       = GetDlgItemInt(hDlg, ID_BDELAY,  NULL, TRUE );
                    ShortTime       = GetDlgItemInt(hDlg, ID_MDELAY,  NULL, TRUE );
                    wMagnification  = GetDlgItemInt(hDlg, ID_MAGNIFY, NULL, TRUE );
                    ChangeFreq      = GetDlgItemInt(hDlg, ID_CLEVEL,  NULL, TRUE );
                    GetDlgItemText(hDlg,ID_FNAME,   szFileToPlay,   STRLEN);
                    bBlankScreen    = IsDlgButtonChecked(hDlg, ID_BLANKIT        );
                    bRepeatPlay     = IsDlgButtonChecked(hDlg, ID_CONT           );
                    bMuteAudio      = IsDlgButtonChecked(hDlg, ID_MUTE           );
                    bPassword       = IsDlgButtonChecked(hDlg,
ID_PASSWORDPROTECTED);

                            /* Check the values we just loaded! */
                            VerifyIniSettings();

                            /* Put values into CONTROL.INI. */
                    WriteProfileInt(szAppName, szSpeedName,   wMaxSpeed      );
                    WriteProfileInt(szAppName, szDelayName,   DelayTime      );
                    WriteProfileInt(szAppName, szSDelayName,  ShortTime      );
                    WriteProfileInt(szAppName, szMagnifyName, wMagnification );
                    WriteProfileInt(szAppName, szChangeName,  ChangeFreq     );

                    WritePrivateProfileString(szAppName, szPlayFileName,
                     szFileToPlay, szIniFile);

                    WriteProfileInt(szAppName, szBlankitName, bBlankScreen   );
                    WriteProfileInt(szAppName, szMuteName,    bMuteAudio     );
                    WriteProfileInt(szAppName, szRepeatName,  bRepeatPlay     );
                    WriteProfileInt(szAppName, szIsPassword,  bPassword      );

                            /* Close dialog box. */
                    EndDialog(hDlg, TRUE);
                    return TRUE;
```

```
                case IDCANCEL:
                            /* Cancelling dialog box.  Save nothing and close. */
                    EndDialog(hDlg, FALSE);
                    return TRUE;

                case ID_SETPASSWORD:
                {
                    FARPROC fpDialog;
                            /* Get and set password. */
                        if((fpDialog = MakeProcInstance(DlgChangePassword,
                            hMainInstance)) == NULL)
                        return FALSE;
                    DialogBox(hMainInstance, MAKEINTRESOURCE(DLG_CHANGEPASSWORD),
                            hDlg, fpDialog);
                    FreeProcInstance(fpDialog);
                    SendMessage(hDlg, WM_NEXTDLGCTL, hIDOK, 1l);
                    break;
                }

                case ID_PASSWORDPROTECTED:

                            /* Password protection enabled. */
                    bPassword ^= 1;
                    CheckDlgButton(hDlg, wParam, bPassword);
                    EnableWindow(hSetPassword, bPassword);
                    break;

                case ID_HELP:
DoHelp:
#if 0
                    bHelpActive=WinHelp(hDlg, szHelpFile, HELP_CONTEXT,
                                        IDH_DLG_BOUNCER);
                    if (!bHelpActive)
                        MessageBox(hDlg, szNoHelpMemory, szName, MB_OK);
#else
                    MessageBox(hDlg, "Insert your call to WinHelp() here.",
                        szName, MB_OK);
#endif
                    break;
            }
            break;
        default:
            if (msg==MyHelpMessage)        // Context sensitive help msg.
                goto DoHelp;
    }
    return FALSE;
}
```

continues

Listing 19.1. continued

```c
/* GetIniSettings -- Get initial bounce settings from WIN.INI
 *
 * Params:   hWnd -- Handle to window
 *
 * Return:   None
 */
static void GetIniSettings()
{
      /* Load initialization settings from CONTROL.INI. */
    wMaxSpeed = GetPrivateProfileInt(szAppName,szSpeedName,DEF_SPEED,szIniFile);
    DelayTime =
GetPrivateProfileInt(szAppName,szDelayName,DEF_INIT_BDELAY,szIniFile);
    ShortTime =
GetPrivateProfileInt(szAppName,szSDelayName,DEF_INIT_MDELAY,szIniFile);
    wMagnification = GetPrivateProfileInt(szAppName,szMagnifyName,DEF_INIT_MAGNIFY,
                                          szIniFile);
    ChangeFreq =
GetPrivateProfileInt(szAppName,szChangeName,DEF_INIT_CLEVEL,szIniFile);
    GetPrivateProfileString(szAppName, szPlayFileName, DEF_FNAME,szFileToPlay,
                                          STRLEN, szIniFile);
    bBlankScreen = GetPrivateProfileInt(szAppName, szBlankitName,
                                     DEF_BLANKIT,szIniFile);
    bMuteAudio = GetPrivateProfileInt(szAppName, szMuteName,
                                     DEF_MUTE,szIniFile);
    bRepeatPlay = GetPrivateProfileInt(szAppName, szRepeatName,
                                     DEF_CONT,szIniFile);
    bPassword = GetPrivateProfileInt(szAppName, szIsPassword,   FALSE, szIniFile);

     /* Check the values we just loaded! */
     VerifyIniSettings();
}

/* WriteProfileInt - Write an unsigned integer value to CONTROL.INI.
 *
 * Params:   name - szSection - [section] name in .INI file
 *                  szKey      - key= in .INI file
 *                  i          - value for key above
 *
 * Return:   None
 */
static void WriteProfileInt(LPSTR szSection, LPSTR szKey, int i)
{
    char achBuf[40];

    /* write out as unsigned because GetPrivateProfileInt() can't
     * cope with signed values!
     */
    wsprintf(achBuf, "%u", i);
```

```
        WritePrivateProfileString(szSection, szKey, achBuf, szIniFile);
}

void GetIniEntries(void)
{
   //Load Common Strings from stringtable...
   LoadString(hMainInstance, idsIsPassword,   szIsPassword,   22          );
   LoadString(hMainInstance, idsIniFile,      szIniFile,      MAXFILELEN);
   LoadString(hMainInstance, idsScreenSaver,  szScreenSaver,  22          );
   LoadString(hMainInstance, idsPassword,     szPassword,     16          );
   LoadString(hMainInstance, idsDifferentPW,  szDifferentPW,  BUFFLEN   );
   LoadString(hMainInstance, idsChangePW,     szChangePW,     30          );
   LoadString(hMainInstance, idsBadOldPW,     szBadOldPW,     255         );
   LoadString(hMainInstance, idsHelpFile,     szHelpFile,     MAXFILELEN);
   LoadString(hMainInstance, idsNoHelpMemory, szNoHelpMemory, BUFFLEN   );
}

/* PlayFile - Play the AVI file.
 *
 * Params:   hWnd - Window used for playback.
 *
 * Return:   None
 */
static void PlayFile(HWND hWnd)
{
     /* See if the file is open for playing. */
     if (FileOpen){
         /* Go to first frame in file.
         mciExecute("seek AVIFile to 0");

         /* Construct a "put" command string for window and execute it. */
         strcpy(szReturnString,"put AVIFIle window at 0 0 ");
         strcat(szReturnString,szPlayWidth);
         strcat(szReturnString," ");
         strcat(szReturnString,szPlayHeight);
         mciExecute(szReturnString);

         /* Construct a "put" command string for destination and execute it. */
         strcpy(szReturnString,"put AVIFIle destination at 0 0 ");
         strcat(szReturnString,szPlayWidth);
         strcat(szReturnString," ");
         strcat(szReturnString,szPlayHeight);
         mciExecute(szReturnString);

         /* Play the file, either continuously or one time. */
         if (bRepeatPlay)
             mciExecute("play AVIFile window repeat");
         else
             mciExecute("play AVIFile window");
         }

}
```

continues

Listing 19.1. continued

```
/* MovePlayer - Move player (called when short timer goes off).
 *
 * Params:  hWnd - Window used for playback.
 *
 * Return:  None
 */

/* Default values for horizontal and vertical increments for moves. */
static UINT Vinc=1;
static UINT Hinc=1;

static void MovePlayer(HWND hWnd)
{
    int Temp;                // Holder for temporary values.

    /* Toggles for defining current direction. */
    static BOOL Horizontal=TRUE, Vertical=TRUE;

    /* Get a random number. */
    Temp = rand();
    /* If mod zero, time to change direction. */
    if (Temp % ChangeFreq == 0)
        {
        /* Change vectors. */
        Horizontal = !Horizontal;
        Temp = rand();
        Hinc = (Temp % wMaxSpeed)+1;
        }
    /* Get a random number. */
    Temp = rand();
    /* If mod zero, time to change direction. */
    if (Temp % ChangeFreq == 0)
        {
        /* Change vectors. */
        Vertical = !Vertical;
        Temp = rand();
        Vinc = (Temp % wMaxSpeed)+1;
        }

    /* Now that we have established direction and amount, apply them! */
    if (Vertical)
        wTop += Vinc;
    else
        wTop -= Vinc;
    if (Horizontal)
        wLeft += Hinc;
    else
        wLeft -= Hinc;
```

```
        /* Make sure we haven't wandered off of the screen. */
        if (wLeft <= 0)
            {
            wLeft = 1;
            Horizontal = !Horizontal;
            }
        if (wTop <= 0)
            {
            wTop = 1;
            Vertical = !Vertical;
            }

        if (wTop  > (lpScreen.bottom-(int)wPlayHeight))
            {
            wTop = lpScreen.bottom-(int)wPlayHeight;
            Vertical = !Vertical;
            }
        if (wLeft > (lpScreen.right-(int)wPlayWidth))
            {
            Horizontal = !Horizontal;
            wLeft = (lpScreen.right-(int)wPlayWidth);
            }

    /* Are we working with a blank screen or not? */
    if (bBlankScreen)
      SetWindowPos(hScrWnd,HWND_TOP,wLeft,wTop,(int)wPlayWidth+wAdjWidth,(int)wPlayHeight+
                                wAdjHeight,SWP_NOSIZE|SWP_NOZORDER);
    else
      MoveWindow(hScrWnd,wLeft,wTop,(int)wPlayWidth+wAdjWidth,(int)wPlayHeight+wAdjHeight,
                                RepaintToggle);
}

/* MovePlayerRandom - Move player to a random screen location.
 *
 * Params:  hWnd - Window used for playback.
 *
 * Return:  None
 */
static void MovePlayerRandom(HWND hWnd)
{
    /* Get new coordinates. */
    wTop = rand();
    wLeft = rand();

    /* Check to see if new coordinates are within screen; do again if not. */
    while (wTop  > (lpScreen.bottom-(int)wPlayHeight-45))
        wTop = rand();
    while (wLeft > (lpScreen.right-(int)wPlayWidth-25))
        wLeft = rand();
```

continues

Listing 19.1. continued

```
      /* Move Window; method depends on whether we are blanking screen. */
      if (bBlankScreen)
        SetWindowPos(hScrWnd,HWND_TOP,wLeft,wTop,(int)wPlayWidth+wAdjWidth,(int)wPlayHeight+
                    wAdjHeight,SWP_NOZORDER);
      else
        MoveWindow(hScrWnd,wLeft,wTop,(int)wPlayWidth+wAdjWidth,(int)wPlayHeight+wAdjHeight,
                    RepaintToggle);

}

/* WndProc - Default procedure for playback window.
 *
 */
LONG FAR PASCAL WndProc(HWND hWindow,UINT messg,
                        WPARAM wParam,LPARAM lParam)

{

    PAINTSTRUCT ps;

    HDC hDC;                               // Handle to our window DC
    HDC hMemDC;                            // Handle to a memory DC
    BITMAP bm;                             // Bitmap info
    HBITMAP hbmOld;

    switch (messg)
    {
        case WM_PAINT:
            hdc=BeginPaint(hWindow,&ps);

            // Put anything you want to display here.

            if (!FileOpen)
                {
                hbmImage = LoadBitmap(hMainInstance, szDIBName);

                /* Get bitmap size
                 */
                GetObject(hbmImage, sizeof(bm), (LPSTR)&bm);

                hDC = GetDC(hScrWnd);
                hMemDC = CreateCompatibleDC(hDC);
                hbmOld = SelectObject(hMemDC, hbmImage);

                if(hbmOld)
                    {
                    /* Blit the image in the new position
                     */
                    BitBlt(hDC,                             // dest DC
                        0,0,                                // dest origin
```

```
                              bm.bmWidth,bm.bmHeight,    // dest extents
                              hMemDC,                    // src DC
                              0,0,                       // src origin
                              SRCCOPY );                 // ROP code

                    SelectObject(hMemDC, hbmOld);
                DeleteDC(hMemDC);
                ReleaseDC(hScrWnd, hDC);
                    }

            }

        ValidateRect(hWindow,NULL);
        EndPaint(hWindow,&ps);
        break;

    case WM_TIMER:
        /* Timer went off; play AVI file again if we are not auto repeating. */
        if (!bRepeatPlay && FileOpen)
            PlayFile(hScrWnd);
     return 0L;
        break;

    case WM_DESTROY:
        PostQuitMessage(0);
        break;
    default:
        return(DefWindowProc(hWindow,messg,wParam,lParam));
  }
  return(0L);
}

/* SetupPlayback - Set up the Playback window and perform file housekeeping.
 *
 * Params:  AVIFile - name of AVI file to open and set up.
 *
 * Return:  Unsigned integer - Playing time in milliseconds.
 */
UINT SetupPlayback(char * AVIFile)
{
    DWORD Result;
    UINT FrameRate, FrameTotal;
    char *tempchar;
    char szMessage[]="  AVI playback file not found:  ";

    /* Verify that file exists. */
    FileOpen = fopen(AVIFile, "r");

    if (FileOpen)
        {
```

continues

Listing 19.1. continued

```
                fclose(FileOpen);

                /* Get string copy of window handle. */
                _itoa(hScrWnd, szWindowHandle, 10);

                /* Get file info. */
                strcpy(szCommandString,"open ");
                strcat(szCommandString,AVIFile);
                strcat(szCommandString," style child parent ");
                strcat(szCommandString,szWindowHandle);
                strcat(szCommandString," alias AVIFile");
                mciExecute(szCommandString);
                mciExecute("set AVIFile time format frames");
                if (bMuteAudio)
                    mciExecute("setaudio AVIFile off");

                /* Get size of frame. */
                Result = mciSendString("where AVIFile window",szReturnString,1024,0);
                tempchar = strtok(szReturnString," ");
                tempchar = strtok(NULL," ");
                tempchar = strtok(NULL," ");
                strcpy(szPlayWidth,tempchar);
                tempchar = strtok(NULL," ");
                strcpy(szPlayHeight,tempchar);

                /* Put width and height into integers. */
                wPlayWidth  = atol(szPlayWidth);
                wPlayHeight = atol(szPlayHeight);

                /* Apply magnification factor. */
                wPlayWidth  = (wPlayWidth  * wMagnification)/100;
                wPlayHeight = (wPlayHeight * wMagnification)/100;

                /* Check to make sure image isn't too big for screen! */
                if (wPlayWidth > (wWidth * 3))
                    wPlayWidth = wWidth * 3;
                if (wPlayHeight > wHeight * 3)
                    wPlayHeight = wHeight * 3;

                /* Put width and hieght back into strings. */
                _ltoa(wPlayWidth,  szPlayWidth, 10);
                _ltoa(wPlayHeight, szPlayHeight, 10);

                /* Resize window to fit frame size. */
                wAdjWidth = (lpWindowSize.right-lpWindowSize.left) - (lpClientSize.right-
                        lpClientSize.left);
                wAdjHeight = (lpWindowSize.bottom-lpWindowSize.top) -
                            (lpClientSize.bottom-
                        lpClientSize.top);
```

```
        mciSendString("status AVIFile length",szReturnString,1024,0);
        FrameTotal = (UINT)atoi(szReturnString);
        strcpy(szWinTitle,szReturnString);

        mciSendString("status AVIFile nominal frame rate",szReturnString,1024,0);
        FrameRate = (UINT)(atoi(szReturnString))/1000;
        _itoa(FrameRate,szReturnString,10);
        strcat(szWinTitle," frames/");
        strcat(szWinTitle,szReturnString);

        _itoa((UINT)(FrameTotal/FrameRate)*1000,szReturnString,10);
        strcat(szWinTitle,"=");
        strcat(szWinTitle,szReturnString);
        return (UINT)(FrameTotal/FrameRate)*1000;

        }
    else
        {
        wPlayWidth  = 240L;
        wPlayHeight = 180L;
        RepaintToggle = TRUE;

    if(wTimerLong)
            DestroyWindow(hScrWnd);
        /* Create new playback window as overlapped. */
        hScrWnd=CreateWindow(szProgName,"Video Saver 1.0",
                    (WS_OVERLAPPED), wLeft, wTop,
                    (int)wPlayWidth, (int)wPlayHeight, hWnd, (HMENU)NULL,
                    (HANDLE)hMainInstance, (LPSTR)NULL);

        /* Get sizes of Window & Client area for later calculations. */
        GetWindowRect(hScrWnd,&lpWindowSize);
        GetClientRect(hScrWnd,&lpClientSize);
        wAdjWidth = (lpWindowSize.right-lpWindowSize.left) - (lpClientSize.right-
                lpClientSize.left);
        wAdjHeight = (lpWindowSize.bottom-lpWindowSize.top) -
                    (lpClientSize.bottom-lpClientSize.top);

        /* Setup for playback. */
        MovePlayerRandom(hScrWnd);

        ShowWindow(hScrWnd,SW_SHOWNORMAL);
    if(wTimerLong)
            KillTimer(hScrWnd,ID_TIMER);

        return 0;
    }
```

continues

Listing 19.1. continued

```
void VerifyIniSettings(void)
{
    /* Make sure that all settings have valid values. */
    if (wMagnification < 10)
        wMagnification = 100;
    if (wMaxSpeed < 1 || wMaxSpeed > 25)
        wMaxSpeed = 5;
    if (ShortTime < 10)
        ShortTime = 10;
    if (DelayTime < 5)
        DelayTime = 5;
    if (ChangeFreq < 25)
        ChangeFreq = 25;

}
```

Listing 19.2. MAKEFILE

```
NAME = vidsaver
SRCS = $(NAME).c
OBJS =

##### C7 Macro #####
C7   = 1

##### Library Macros #####
LIBS = libw slibcew mmsystem scrnsave
MOD  = -AS

##### Include Macro #####
INCLS    = $(NAME).h

##### Resource Macro #####
RCFILES = $(NAME).rc $(NAME).ico $(NAME).dlg scrnsave.dlg

##### DEBUG Macro Defined #####
DEBUG    = 0

##### Build Option Macros #####
!if $(DEBUG)
DDEF = -DDEBUG
CLOPT    = -Zid -Od
MOPT = -Zi
LOPT = /CO /LI /MAP
!else
```

```
DDEF =
CLOPT      = -Os
LOPT =
!endif


##### General Macros #####
DEF  =

##### Tool Macros #####
ASM  = masm -Mx $(MOPT) $(DDEF) $(DEF)
CC   = cl -nologo -c -G2sw -Zp -W3 $(MOD) $(CLOPT) $(DDEF) $(DEF)
LINK = link /NOD /NOE $(LOPT)
RC   = rc $(DDEF) $(DEF)
HC   = hc

##### Inference Rules #####
.c.obj:
    $(CC) $*.c

.asm.obj:
    $(ASM) $*.asm;

.rc.res:
    $(RC) -r $*.rc

##### Main (default) Target #####
goal: $(NAME).exe $(NAME).scr

##### Dependents For Goal and Command Line #####
$(NAME).scr: $(NAME).exe
    copy $(NAME).exe $(NAME).scr
    copy $(NAME).exe c:\windows\$(NAME).scr

$(NAME).exe: $(SRCS:.c=.obj) $(NAME).def $(NAME).res
    $(LINK) @<<
    $(SRCS:.c=.obj) $(OBJS),
    $(NAME).exe,
    $(NAME).map,
    $(LIBS),
    $(NAME).def
<<
    $(RC) -T $(NAME).res
!if $(DEBUG)
!if  !$(C7)
    cvpack -p $(NAME).exe
!endif
    mapsym $(NAME).map
!endif
```

continues

Listing 19.2. continued

```
##### Dependents #####
$(SRCS:.c=.obj):  $(INCLS)
$(NAME).res: $(RCFILES)

##### Clean Directory #####
clean:
    -del *.obj
    -del *.res
    -del *.exe
    -del *.map
    -del *.sym
```

Listing 19.3. VIDSAVER.DLG

```
DLGINCLUDE RCDATA DISCARDABLE
BEGIN
    "VIDSAVER.H\0"
END

DLG_SCRNSAVECONFIGURE DIALOG 44, 49, 189, 142
STYLE DS_MODALFRAME | WS_POPUP | WS_VISIBLE | WS_CAPTION | WS_SYSMENU
CAPTION "VidSaver"
FONT 8, "Helv"
BEGIN
    LTEXT          "Max &pixels/move:", DEF_INIT_MDELAY, 5, 6, 58, 12, NOT WS_GROUP
    EDITTEXT       ID_SPEED, 64, 4, 17, 12
    LTEXT          "&Between delay:", DEF_INIT_MDELAY, 5, 20, 58, 10, NOT
                   WS_GROUP
    EDITTEXT       ID_BDELAY, 64, 19, 17, 12
    LTEXT          "Move &delay:", DEF_INIT_MDELAY, 5, 35, 57, 11, NOT
                   WS_GROUP
    EDITTEXT       ID_MDELAY, 64, 34, 17, 12
    LTEXT          "&Magnification %:", DEF_INIT_MDELAY, 5, 49, 58, 12, NOT
                   WS_GROUP
    EDITTEXT       ID_MAGNIFY, 64, 49, 17, 12
    LTEXT          "&Random Rate:", DEF_INIT_MDELAY, 4, 64, 51, 10, NOT
                   WS_GROUP
    EDITTEXT       ID_CLEVEL, 64, 64, 17, 12
    CONTROL        "&Blank screen", ID_BLANKIT, "Button", BS_AUTOCHECKBOX |
                   WS_GROUP | WS_TABSTOP, 117, 45, 67, 13
    CONTROL        "Mute &audio", ID_MUTE, "Button", BS_AUTOCHECKBOX |
                   WS_TABSTOP, 117, 57, 67, 13
    DEFPUSHBUTTON  "OK", IDOK, 116, 6, 67, 16, WS_GROUP
    PUSHBUTTON     "Cancel", IDCANCEL, 116, 25, 67, 16
```

```
    GROUPBOX        "Password Options", -1, 5, 107, 179, 30
    PUSHBUTTON      "&Set Password...", ID_SETPASSWORD, 115, 116, 66, 16
    CONTROL         "&Password Protected", ID_PASSWORDPROTECTED, "Button",
                    BS_AUTOCHECKBOX | WS_TABSTOP, 9, 120, 78, 10
    LTEXT           "&Filename:", 2004, 4, 90, 46, 8
    EDITTEXT        ID_FNAME, 46, 87, 138, 12, ES_AUTOHSCROLL
    CONTROL         "Continuous &repeat", ID_CONT, "Button", BS_AUTOCHECKBOX |
                    WS_TABSTOP, 117, 71, 72, 10
END
```

Listing 19.4. SCRNSAVE.DLG

```
//#defines...

#define        ID_OLDTEXT        100
#define        ID_NEWTEXT        101
#define        ID_AGAIN          102
#define        ID_PASSWORD       103
#define        ID_ETOLD          104
#define        ID_ETNEW          105
#define        ID_ETAGAIN        106
#define        ID_ETPASSWORD     107
#define        ID_ICON           108
#define        ID_PASSWORDHELP   109


#ifdef RC_INVOKED

DLG_CHANGEPASSWORD    DIALOG      8,16,174,79
FONT 8, "MS Sans Serif"
STYLE WS_POPUP | DS_MODALFRAME | WS_CAPTION | WS_SYSMENU
CAPTION "Change Password"
BEGIN
    LTEXT "&Old Password:", ID_OLDTEXT,       4, 3,80,14
    EDITTEXT  ID_ETOLD,                       84, 3,80,14, ES_PASSWORD
    LTEXT "&New Password:", ID_NEWTEXT,        4,21,80,14
    EDITTEXT  ID_ETNEW,                       84,21,80,14, ES_PASSWORD
    LTEXT "&Retype New Password:", ID_AGAIN,   4,39,80,14
    EDITTEXT  ID_ETAGAIN,                     84,39,80,14, ES_PASSWORD
    DEFPUSHBUTTON "OK", IDOK,                   4,59,40,14
    PUSHBUTTON "&Help", ID_PASSWORDHELP,       64,59,40,14
    PUSHBUTTON "Cancel", IDCANCEL,            124,59,40,14
END


DLG_ENTERPASSWORD     DIALOG      250,175,170,96
FONT 8, "MS Sans Serif"
```

continues

Listing 19.4. continued

```
STYLE WS_POPUP | DS_MODALFRAME | WS_CAPTION | WS_SYSMENU
CAPTION "<name of screensaver>"
BEGIN
    LTEXT "This screen saver is password protected!  You must type in the secret
screen saver password to turn off the screen saver.", -1, 31,3,140,40
    LTEXT "Password:", ID_PASSWORD,              31,45,40,14
    EDITTEXT ID_ETPASSWORD,                       71,45,80,14, ES_PASSWORD
    DEFPUSHBUTTON "OK", IDOK,                      31,66,40,14
    PUSHBUTTON "Cancel", IDCANCEL,                111,66,40,14
    ICON "", ID_ICON,                             3, 3,32,32
END

DLG_INVALIDPASSWORD DIALOG  8,16,174, 79
FONT 8, "MS Sans Serif"
STYLE WS_POPUP | DS_MODALFRAME | WS_CAPTION | WS_SYSMENU
CAPTION "<name of screen saver>"
BEGIN
    ICON "", ID_ICON,                             3, 3, 0, 0
    LTEXT "Incorrect password!\n\nTry again, but I'm beginning to wonder.........",
-1, 40,3,130,40
    DEFPUSHBUTTON "OK!OK!", IDOK,                  70,50,40,14
END
#endif
```

Listing 19.5. VIDSAVER.H

```
/* VIDSAVER.H - Header file for VIDSAVER video screen saver.
 */

/* Include scrnsaver stuff. */
#include <scrnsave.h>

/* IDs for configuration dialog box. */
#define ID_SPEED    101       // Speed of movement (# pixels/move)
#define ID_BDELAY   102       // Delay between playbacks
#define ID_MDELAY   103       // Delay between moves of playback window
#define ID_MAGNIFY  104       // Magnification factor
#define ID_CLEVEL   105       // Frequency of random changes
#define ID_BLANKIT  106       // Screen blanking toggle
#define ID_MUTE     107       // Mute Audio toggle

#define ID_PASSWORDPROTECTED 108  // Password protection toggle
#define ID_SETPASSWORD       109  // Set password
#define ID_HELP              110  // Help
```

```
#define ID_FNAME              111  // Filename for dialog
#define ID_CONT               112  // Continuous replay toggle

#define ID_TIMER 200               // Timer ID
#define STRLEN   256               // Maximum length of certain buffers.

/* Default values for new INI data. */
#define DEF_SPEED         5        // Starting maximum pixels per move
#define DEF_INIT_BDELAY   60       // Starting Between delay
#define DEF_INIT_MDELAY   120      // Starting Move delay
#define DEF_INIT_MAGNIFY  100      // Starting Magnification
#define DEF_INIT_CLEVEL   30       // Starting change level
#define DEF_BLANKIT       TRUE     // Starting Blank Screen state
#define DEF_MUTE          FALSE    // Starting Mute audio state
#define DEF_FNAME         "c:\\windows\\scr_sav.avi"  // Default filename
#define DEF_CONT          FALSE    // Default for continuous repeat

/* Function prototypes
 */
// This is a function from the MM API.
BOOL WINAPI mciExecute (LPCSTR lpstrCommand);

// Window procedure for the playback window.
LONG FAR PASCAL WndProc(HWND,UINT,WPARAM,LPARAM);

// Dialog procedure for configuration dialog.
extern BOOL FAR PASCAL ScreenSaverConfigureDialog(HWND hDlg, UINT msg, WPARAM
wParam, LPARAM lParam);

// A function to open the AVI file and get information about the
//   file.  It uses a number of global variables and structures.
UINT SetupPlayback(char * AVIFile);

// This function loads settings from a string table.
void GetIniEntries(void);

// This function is used to read values from CONTROL.INI.
void GetIniSettings(void);

void MoveImage(HWND hWnd);

// This function is a wrapper for WritePrivateProfileString.
void WriteProfileInt(LPSTR key, LPSTR tag, int i);

// This function is used to play the AVI file from beginning to end.
//    It assumes that the file is already opened and set up with
//    SetupPlayback().
void PlayFile(HWND hWnd);
```

continues

Listing 19.5. continued

```
// This function moves the playback window incrementally while the
//   AVI file is playing.
void MovePlayer(HWND hWnd);

// This function moves the playback window to a random position on
//   the screen.
void MovePlayerRandom(HWND hWnd);

// This function checks to make sure that the initialization settings
//   are OK.
void VerifyIniSettings(void);
```

VIDSAVER.C

The code for this module was written for Microsoft C/C++ Version 7.0. Please note that you have a right to use or re-use the code included here. Such use is given automatically when you purchase the book.

Let's look at the code piece by piece.

Include Files

The first segment of code lists include files that are needed to compile the screen saver. There are four kinds of include files involved: (1) Windows include file, windows.h; (2) multimedia include file, mmsystem.h; (3) local include file, vidsaver.h; (4) standard C include files, string.h, stdlib.h, stdio.h, and time.h.

Global Variables

The include files are followed by a rather long list of global variables. If you haven't coded in C for Windows before, this may be a surprise. However, it's not unusual for a Windows application, and has to do with the way that Windows applications are constructed. A Windows applications sends and received messages, and takes action based on the messages it receives. This is very different from the standard C application, which relies mostly on function calls.

There are two ways to work with such a large number of global values. They can be used as either individual globals, as in this case, or they can be combined into structures. Each approach has value. When all of the globals are individual variables, they are easier to work with. If there are too many, however, you can easily lose track of them. When globals are combined into structures, you have fewer objects to keep track of since you can refer to a group of variables as one object. This is especially important when the number of variables is very large.

There are two kinds of globals used in vidsaver.c. Some globals are required in a screen saver, and some are for use only in the vidsaver module. The following globals are required for any screen saver:

```
/* Externals defined in SCRNSAVE.LIB. Required for all screen savers.
 */
HINSTANCE _cdecl hMainInstance;
HWND _cdecl hMainWindow;
char _cdecl szName[TITLEBARNAMELEN];
char _cdecl szIsPassword[22];
char _cdecl szIniFile[MAXFILELEN];
char _cdecl szScreenSaver[22];
char _cdecl szPassword[16];
char _cdecl szDifferentPW[BUFFLEN];
char _cdecl szChangePW[30];
char _cdecl szBadOldPW[BUFFLEN];
char _cdecl szHelpFile[MAXFILELEN];
char _cdecl szNoHelpMemory[BUFFLEN];
UINT _cdecl MyHelpMessage;
HOOKPROC _cdecl fpMessageFilter;
```

All of these are used within Windows itself to communicate with the screen saver program.

There's no need to discuss all of the globals used in vidsaver.c individually. We'll cover many of them as we look at the various functions in the module. Table 19.2 explains the most important globals.

Table 19.2. Important global variables used in vidsaver.c.

Variable(s)	Description
wMaxSpeed, etc.	These variables are used to control the behavior of the screen saver. Many of these variables are stored in configuration file (control.ini).
hScrWnd	This is a handle for the window used for playback of the video file.

continues

Table 19.2. continued

Variable(s)	Description
RECT variables	These include lpScreen, lpWindowSize, and lpClientSize. They are used to store the rectangle coordinates of various objects. This is a structure with four elements (in two pairs) in it: the x,y coordinates of the object's top left corner, and the x,y coordinates of the bottom right corner.
wTimerShort	This is one of the two time ID variables. It is used to refer to a timer in functions that work with timers.
PlayingTime	This variable holds the duration, in milliseconds, of the video file. This is one of several variables that holds data that is read from the video file after it is opened.

ScreenSaverProc

Following the global variables, we find our first function, ScreenSaverProc. If you are already familiar with Windows programming, you will recognize this function for what it is: a typical Window procedure. The keys are the arguments to the function:

```
ScreenSaverProc(HWND hWnd, UINT msg, WPARAM wParam, LPARAM lParam)
```

These four arguments are always found in window procedures (often referred to as a "window proc"). ScreenSaverProc can be thought of as an extension to the window procedure for the screen saver. Within Windows itself, there is a default procedure that controls the screen saver. Before processing any messages it receives, the default procedure first calls ScreenSaverProc to give it first crack at the messages. If we do not process a message, it goes to DefScreenSaverProc(), the default screen saver procedure. It is mandatory to pass unhandled messages to DefScreenSaverProc.

Table 19.3 describes the purpose of each argument.

Table 19.3. Arguments for ScreenSaverProc

Argument	Purpose
hWnd	This is a window handle. In the case of a screen saver, it is a handle to the main window for the screen saver.
msg	A message code. There are many, many different kinds of messages in Windows. Some common ones include WM_CREATE, WM_PAINT, and WM_DESTROY.
wParam	This is one of two message parameters. Its meaning depends on the message it accompanies.
lParam	This is one of two message parameters. Its meaning depends on the message it accompanies.

The entire contents of the ScreenSaverProc consist of a switch statement. Again, if you are familiar with Windows programming, this is expected. The switch uses the msg parameter to determine which section of code to execute. There are four messages that are handled by ScreenSaverProc:

Message	Description
WM_CREATE	This message is sent when it's time to initialize the screen saver. Windows watches the time since the last activity, and sends this message to ScreenSaverProc.
WM_TIMER	One of the things we do when we initialize is to create a timer associated with the Screen Saver main window. When the timer "goes off," this message is sent to ScreenSaverProc.
WM_DESTROY	When keyboard or mouse activity occurs, this message is sent to ScreenSaverProc, telling it to self-destruct. It's up to us to make sure we do this properly.
WM_ERASEBKGND	This message is sent when it's time to erase the background. That way, if we want to leave the screen intact while our screen saver operates, we can do so.

Now let's take a closer look at what is happening when each of these messages is sent to ScreenSaverProc.

Window Create Message

The code for initialization is by far the longest section of code in ScreenSaverProc. If we consider the code hidden in the functions that are called for the WM_CREATE message, this is even more true.

The first job is to get setup information, including loading some strings (the names of the INI file settings) from a string table and getting configuration settings from control.ini. The two functions that do this are GetIniEntries and GetIniSettings. These are followed by a call to srand to seed the random number generator, and a call to GetWindowRect to get the size of the screen. The default window size, used only for reporting errors, is one-quarter of the screen size.

Next, we handle some Windows overhead—creating a window class for the playback window:

```
/* Create window class for playback. */
wcScrApp.lpszClassName=szProgName;
wcScrApp.hInstance     =hMainInstance;
wcScrApp.lpfnWndProc   =WndProc;
wcScrApp.hCursor       =LoadCursor(NULL,IDC_ARROW);
wcScrApp.hIcon         =NULL;
wcScrApp.lpszMenuName =NULL;
wcScrApp.hbrBackground=CreateSolidBrush(RGB(0,255,255));
wcScrApp.style         =CS_HREDRAW¦CS_VREDRAW¦CS_BYTEALIGNWINDOW;
wcScrApp.cbClsExtra    =0;
wcScrApp.cbWndExtra    =0;
if (!RegisterClass (&wcScrApp))
    return FALSE;
```

There are a couple of things to note. The default window procedure for the window we will create is WndProc. We'll get to this procedure in a bit. For now, it is important to be aware that there are going to be two windows involved, and each window will have a different procedure. The main window for the screen saver is created for us by Windows; that's a service it provides for screen savers. The handle to that window is the handle that was passed to ScreenSaverProc. We are establishing a class for a new window, one that we are going to create ourselves. This created window will be the one where the video file is played. Its handle is stored in the variable hScrWnd, and we create the window with a call to the CreateWindow function:

```
/* Create playback window. */
hScrWnd=CreateWindow(
    szProgName,     // Window class
    "VidSaver 1.0",    // Window caption
    (WS_POPUP),     // Window style
    wLeft,    // Left coordinate
    wTop,      // Top coordinate
    (int)wWidth,    // Width of window
    (int)wHeight,  // Height of window
    hWnd,      // Parent window handle
    (HMENU)NULL,    // Window menu handle (there is none)
    (HANDLE)hMainInstance,    // Program instance handle
    (LPSTR)NULL); // Creation parameters
```

Note that the parent window handle is the screen saver main window, and that we are using the popup style to create the window. We could also make this a child window or an overlapped window by using WS_CHILD or WS_OVERLAPPED. There are no menus.

There are two sizes for a window—one for the overall window, and one for the interior of the window, known as the client window. The overall window size includes the caption bar, any menu that might be present, and the border width. The client area is the inside portion of the window only, excluding these items. We call GetWindowRect and GetClientRect to get the dimensions of the window and the client area. What we are actually interested in is the difference beween these two. We'll use it later.

That completes the Windows housekeeping overhead; now we can handle our own overhead. We call the function SetupPlayback, passing it the Screen Saver window handle and the name of the file to be played. It returns the playing time of the file, which we store in the variable PlayingTime.

```
PlayingTime = SetupPlayback(hWnd, szFileToPlay);
```

There's a lot that happens in this function, so we'll take a moment to look at what it does, and then return to our discussion of ScreenSaverProc.

Setting Up for Playback

The first business for setup is to find out if the specified file exists. If it does, we can go ahead with the (somewhat extensive) setup operation. If it doesn't, we'll write an error message to the playback window. We check for the file with a simple call to fopen. If we open it successfully, we close it and proceed.

There are two ways to work with video files using MCI (the Media Control Interface): command strings, and command messages. Command messages operate at a lower level, while command strings are easier to follow. I chose to use the command string interface because it's easy to work with. There is one complication: we'll have to turn all numbers we use into strings. The first number we need to convert to a string is the handle of the playback window, which we store in the string variable szWindowHandle. We'll integrate this variable into a longer string when we open the file for playback. We need to open the file before we can do anything else with it, such as get information about the file or play it. We use strcpy and strcat to build the complete command from the various pieces available. The code looks like this:

```
/* Get file info. */
strcpy(szCommandString,"open ");
strcat(szCommandString,AVIFile);
strcat(szCommandString," style child parent ");
strcat(szCommandString,szWindowHandle);
strcat(szCommandString," alias AVIFile");
```

Fully assembled, such a string might look like this:

```
open c:\window\scr_sav.avi style child parent 2123 alias AVIFile
```

Let's take a moment to analyze what this string is doing for us. It consists of a command, "open" a device name "c:\windows\scr_sav.avi" and a list of options. There are quite a few options for the open command, and they are explained in detail in Chapter 21. In this case, we are opening the file in a child window. The parent is the window we created just above. So there are actually three windows involved now: the screen saver main window, the popup window we just created, and a child of the popup, where the file will actually play.

Note also that we specified an alias: AVIFile. From now on, we'll need to use this alias to refer to the AVI file, instead of the full pathname.

Once we have the string assembled, there are two methods we can use to pass it to MCI. These involve the functions mciExecute and mciSendString. If we need information back from MCI, we use mciSendString. If we just want MCI to do something, we use mciExecute. In this case, we don't need any information back; we just need the file open, so we'll use mciExecute, passing it the string we assembled:

```
mciExecute(szCommandString);
```

It's that easy to use the command string interface.

Most of the time, AVI files are stored using a time format of frames, but we need to make sure. We can use the command string `"set AVIFile time format frames by using it with mciExecute:"`

```
mciExecute("set AVIFile time format frames");
```

When we loaded the default settings from the configuration file (control.ini), one of the settings was for audio playback. The user can select to mute the audio portion of the file during playback. We check the value of this global variable, and if audio is to be turned off, we use the command `"setaudio"` to switch it off:

```
if (bMuteAudio)
    mciExecute("setaudio AVIFile off");
```

See how easy this is?

Now we need to go poking around in the file to get some information we'll need for playback. Because we need information back, we use mciSendString. The first thing we'll need is informaton about the size of the window for playback:

```
Result = mciSendString("where AVIFile window",szReturnString,STRLEN,0);
```

The return information is placed into the string variable szReturnString. It consists of four numbers separated by spaces. A typical return string might look like `"0 0 160 120"`.

We'll need to get the numbers out of the string and into a series of numeric variables. I used the function strtok, which extracts tokens from strings. The second parameter in the call to strtok tells it what character to use to separate the tokens; in this case, it's a space. Subsequent calls to strtok extract the next token. We are not interested in the first two, just the last two which are the default width and height of the file. The code to accomplish all of this looks like this:

```
tempchar = strtok(szReturnString," ");
tempchar = strtok(NULL," ");
tempchar = strtok(NULL," ");
strcpy(szPlayWidth,tempchar);
tempchar = strtok(NULL," ");
strcpy(szPlayHeight,tempchar);
```

This code puts the third token into the string szPlayWidth, and the fourth token into the string szPlayHeight.

I chose to allow the user to set the magnification factor for playback, so we need to translate these strings into actual numbers. That's accomplished with calls to the atol function which converts strings to longs. The results are stored in the variables wPlayWidth and wPlayHeight.

Now that we have numbers, we can apply the magnification factor.

```
wPlayWidth  = (wPlayWidth  * wMagnification)/100;
wPlayHeight = (wPlayHeight * wMagnification)/100;
```

It is rare to see a playback size of 640 by 480, let alone even larger than that. That may not always be the case once we apply a magnification factor, so I added some code to verify that the image is not too large for the screen. I arbitrarily decided, in fact, that if we are going to bounce the image around on the screen, it shouldn't be any larger than 75% of the screen width and height. If it is, I reduce it to that size.

Once we have the correct starting size, we can put it back into strings with calls to _ltoa, which converts strings to longs. We put the new values back where we got them, in szPlayWidth and szPlayHeight. Later on, we'll constuct a command string to set the playback size to this size.

If you'll recall, earlier we saved the size of the playback window and it's client area. Because we are using a popup window, there is no difference between these two. However, you might want to add the ability to play the video file in an overlapped window and display a caption. To show the AVI file at its correct size, we'll need to know the difference between the window area and the client area. One way to do that is to simply subtract the client coordinates from the window coordinates:

```
wAdjWidth = (lpWindowSize.right-lpWindowSize.left) - (lpClientSize.right-
        lpClientSize.left);
wAdjHeight = (lpWindowSize.bottom-lpWindowSize.top) - (lpClientSize.bottom-
        lpClientSize.top);
```

We could also get the same information using command strings and calls to mciSendString: "where AVIFile window" and "where AVIFile destination." The first command string would tell us the window coordinates, and the second one would tell us the image coordinates. If we were not working in C, this second technique would be useful to know.

There is additional information about the file that we'll need to know. For example, to calculate the playing time, we'll need to know the number of frames in the video. Remember, earlier we set the time format to frames. We can call mciSendString with the command string "status AVIFile length" to get the length in frames. We convert the result to a number and store it in the variable FrameTotal.

Next, we get the frame rate (we want it in frames per second) with the command string "status AVIFile nominal frame rate." To get the playing time, we divide the total number of frames by the frame rate.

That concludes setup. We haven't played the file yet, but we know enough now to do that.

ScreenSaverProc, Part 2

When we return from setup, there are two possibilities: there is an AVI file to play, or we need to display the error message. In either case, we'll still need a timer to tell us when to move the window around the screen, so we use the SetTimer function to create this timer. wTimerShort serves as a handle to the time.

```
wTimerShort=SetTimer(hWnd, ID_TIMER, ShortTime, NULL);
```

Now we can check to see if there is an AVI file to play by checking the variable FileOpen:

```
if (FileOpen)
```

If the file was opened, we'll place the playback window on the screen. Because we'll be moving it around, I chose to place it at a random location. The work is done in the function MovePlayerRandom. We can then use ShowWindow to display the window on the screen.

```
MovePlayerRandom(hScrWnd);
ShowWindow(hScrWnd,SW_SHOWNORMAL);
```

There is a configuration setting for continuous repeat play. If it is checked, then the variable bRepeatPlay will be set to TRUE, and we won't need to set a timer to alert us of the time for each playback. If we do need to start a timer, we do it with a call to the SetTimer function, just as we did for the short timer. However, this time we associate the timer with the playback window, not the screen saver main window. This means that timer messages for file playing will go to the window procedure for the playback window, while timer messages alerting us to move the playback window will go to the screen saver main window.

Now that everything is ready, it's finally time to play the file with a call to a function written for just that purpose:

```
PlayFile();
```

Let's look at this function a little more closely.

Playing the AVI File

The function for playing AVI files, PlayFile, takes no arguments. It assumes that the playback window created when the AVI file was opened is the one we want

to play it in. For safety's sake, PlayFile first checks to make sure there is a file open. If it is, PlayFile constructs a series of MCI command strings and then calls mciExecute. The first command is a "put window" command, to place the playback window where we want it. The second command is a "put destination" command to place the image in the playback window. Strictly speaking, we only need to execute these commands once, but putting them here allows us to stretch and change the playback window to make the screen saver more interesting. I leave that exercise to the reader. Keep in mind that the more overhead you add, the faster your hardware must be to get all the work done and still play the video file without slowing it down too much.

Hint

Look at the code in MovePlayer for calculating the next position of the playback window. How could you modify that code to provide new size coordinates as well?

Here is the code for the first "put" command:

```
strcpy(szReturnString,"put AVIFile window at 0 0 ");
strcat(szReturnString,szPlayWidth);
strcat(szReturnString," ");
strcat(szReturnString,szPlayHeight);
mciExecute(szReturnString);
```

For a typical playback window, the put command might look like this when it is passed to mciExecute:

```
put AVIFile window at 0 0 240 180
```

The put command for the destination is very similar:

```
strcpy(szReturnString,"put AVIFile destination at 0 0 ");
strcat(szReturnString,szPlayWidth);
strcat(szReturnString," ");
strcat(szReturnString,szPlayHeight);
mciExecute(szReturnString);
```

If you did not plan to change the size of the playback window or the image, you could move the preceding code to the setup section of the file. Once these details have been attended to, we can play the file. There are two play modes: regular, and continous repeat. The global variable bRepeatPlay is used in an if statement to determine which method to use. The command string `"play AVIFile window repeat"` causes the file to play repeatedly with no further intervention on our part; the command string `"play AVIFile from 0"` plays the file from the beginning each time the `PlayFile` function is called.

```
/* Play the file, either continuously or one time. */
if (bRepeatPlay)
    mciExecute("play AVIFile window repeat");
else
    mciExecute("play AVIFile from 0");
```

Now we have accomplished two things: we have set up for operations, and we have started playback. If we elected to use continuous repeat, nothing else needs to happen until it's time to quit. We'll get a call from Windows when the mouse or the keyboard is used; see the section, "Window Destroy Message," for a description of what happens when Windows tells us to quit.

If There Is No AVI File

It's possible, of course, that the specified AVI file doesn't exist. We'll need to do something when that happens. Because this is a screen saver, we can have a little fun with displaying the error message.

The first task is to set a default size for the error window:

```
wPlayWidth  = 320L;
wPlayHeight = 240L;
```

When we moved the window while the AVI file was playing, we didn't need to repaint the window because the MCI driver took care of displaying each frame of the video. Because we couldn't find the AVI file, we'll have to make sure that the window gets repainted properly as it is moved. I have reserved a global variable for just that purpose, and we need to set it to TRUE:

```
RepaintToggle = TRUE;
```

I thought it would be nice to create a different kind of window for error conditions. We can create a new window with an overlapped style using the `CreateWindow` function. The original playback window had a popup style, and a popup window has no caption bar. I wanted to have a caption bar for the error window to make it look different from the playback window. If you like the overlapped style for playback, by the way, you can easily change the code and recompile. Note the difference in the following call to `CreateWindow` and the original call:

```
hErrWnd=CreateWindow(szProgName,"Video Saver 1.0",
                        (WS_OVERLAPPED), wLeft, wTop,
                        (int)wPlayWidth, (int)wPlayHeight, hWnd, (HMENU)NULL,
                        (HANDLE)hMainInstance, (LPSTR)NULL);
```

We'll need to get the window and client area sizes for this new window, just as we did for the original window. We also need to recalculate the adjustments for width and height, taking into account the difference in size between the two rectangles.

```
GetWindowRect(hErrWnd,&lpWindowSize);
GetClientRect(hErrWnd,&lpClientSize);
wAdjWidth = (lpWindowSize.right-lpWindowSize.left) - (lpClientSize.right-
            lpClientSize.left);
wAdjHeight = (lpWindowSize.bottom-lpWindowSize.top) - (lpClientSize.bottom-
            lpClientSize.top);
```

Once we have reset the global variables for positioning, we can call `MovePlayerRandom` to place the new window at a random location on the screen, show the window with `ShowWindow`. Then we can return to `ScreenSaverProc`.

If you are wondering where the error message part is, we'll get to that later. I've put the code for displaying the error message in the `WM_PAINT` message handler of `WinProc`, the default procedure for the error window.

Timer Message

There are two timers, one for the screen saver window and one for the playback or error window. The shorter duration timer tells us when to move the playback or error window; the longer duration timer (which is only created if there is a file to play) tells us when to play the file again. This timer message is in the proc for the screen saver main window, `ScreenSaverProc`. All we need to do is to move the playback window to the next location:

```
MovePlayer(hScrWnd);
```

Window Destroy Message

When Windows detects a mouse movement or a keypress, it sends `ScreenSaverProc` a message tellling it to destroy itself. We need to use this opportunity to clean things up. We'll need to free any memory we've used before concluding. Any other windows we created—the playback window and/or the error window—will need to receive their own destroy messages.

There is a fair amount of cleanup to do, too. If we managed to open the AVI file, we'll need to close it with a call to `mciExecute`:

```
if (FileOpen)
    mciExecute("close AVIFile");
```

We'll also need to kill off the short-duration timer, if it exists:

```
if(wTimerShort) KillTimer(hWnd,ID_TIMER);
```

We created at least one and as many as two windows; we'll need to polish them off as well:

```
if (hScrWnd) DestroyWindow(hScrWnd);
if (temp) DestroyWindow(temp);
```

There are three objects that we need to take care of as well, associated with the bitmap and sound resources used in the screen saver. They are only used when there is an error.

```
if( hbmImage ) DeleteObject(hbmImage);
if( lpWave )   UnlockResource(hresWave);
if( hresWave ) FreeResource(hresWave);
```

Finally, just in case we are quitting while the error sound is still playing, we turn off the current sound with a call to sndPlaySound:

```
sndPlaySound(NULL, 0);
```

Erase Background Message

There's one more piece of business handled by ScreenSaverProc: erasing the background. The background is only erased if the global variable bBlankScreen is set to TRUE:

```
if (bBlankScreen)
    {
    GetClientRect(hWnd,&rc);
    FillRect((HDC)wParam,&rc,(HBRUSH)GetStockObject(BLACK_BRUSH));
    }
```

Default Processing of Messages

The messages I've covered here are the only ones that are handled by ScreenSaverProc. However, there may be other messages sent to the main screen saver window. It is critical that these messages get handled! To make sure they are, we need to pass any message we don't process to the default screen saver procedure:

```
return DefScreenSaverProc(hWnd, msg, wParam, lParam);
```

Miscellaneous Screen Saver Functions

There are a few other housekeeping functions in the source for the video screen saver; I'll just mention them briefly here. The code they contain is straightforward, and would be similar for just about any screen saver. See Table 19.4 for information about these functions, and consult the code listings for details about these functions.

Table 19.4. Miscellaneous functions in vidsaver.c.

Function	Description
RegisterDialogClasses	Entry point for registering window classes required by configuration dialog box.
ScreenSaverConfigureDialog	The dialog box procedure for the configuration dialog box. It is responsible for initiallizing the dialog box, which includes putting values in the various text boxes. It also handles setting of passwords, and stores all values in control.ini when you click the OK button.
GetIniSettings	Loads values from control.ini and puts them in global variables.
VerifyIniSettings	Checks to make sure that the default values are within acceptable ranges.
WriteProfileInt	This is actually just a *wrapper function* for the function WritePrivateProfileString. A wrapper function is used to simplify calling of the function it wraps; it also may perform a translation—in this case, from integers to strings.
GetIniEntries	This function simply loads strings from a string table in the resource file.

Function	Description
MovePlayer	This is the function that moves the playback and error windows around the screen. It does a lot of juggling with random numbers to come up with new coordinates for the top left corner of the window. It includes quite a bit of error checking to make sure the window doesn't leave the confines of the screen.
MovePlayerRandom	This function is used to initially place the playback and error windows on the screen. It generates a set of coordinates using random number generation.
PlaceBitmap	This function puts a bitmap into a window at 0,0. Not just any bitmap, however; it uses a bitmap we put into the resource file. The bitmap is defined in vidsaver.rc.
PlaySoundResource	This function plays a sound that we've put into the resource file. Like the bitmap, the sound is defined in vidsaver.rc.

Playback Window Procedure

The window procedure for the playback window, WndProc, looks a lot like ScreenSaverProc. That's because both of them are window procedures. Note that the procedure for the playback window uses the same kind of arguments as ScreenSaverProc:

```
1WndProc(HWND hWnd, UINT messg, WPARAM wParam, LPARAM lParam)
```

Like ScreenSaverProc, WndProc uses a switch statement to determine how to handle the various messages it receives. Unlike ScreenSaverProc, WndProc handles a WM_PAINT message. It receives this message whenever the window rectangle has been

invalidated. Moving and sizing are two typical operations that invalidate a window's rectangle.

There are a few things we need to do to handle a WM_PAINT message:

```
hdc=BeginPaint(hWindow,&ps);

/*   Put your code for painting here. */

ValidateRect(hWindow,NULL);
EndPaint(hWindow,&ps);
```

We only need to handle painting if there is no AVI file playing, so we check to see if the file was opened first. If it was not, and FileOpen is FALSE, we can put the bitmap in the window and play the sound:

```
if (!FileOpen)
    {
    PlaceBitmap(hWindow);
    PlaySoundResource();
    }
```

We created a timer that sends messages to WndProc, so we'll need to handle those messages here. The timer is the long-duration timer; when we get a message, it means that it is time to play the AVI file again. If the repeat capability is set on, we don't need to do anything:

```
if (!bRepeatPlay)
    /* Timer went off; play AVI file again. */
    PlayFile(hScrWnd);
```

We also need to be able to handle a WM_DESTROY message; the only thing this window owns is a timer. We also need to post a quit message:

```
if(wTimerLong)  KillTimer(hScrWnd,ID_TIMER);
PostQuitMessage(0);
```

That wraps up the C code for the screen saver. Now let's take a look at what is in some of the other files.

vidsaver.rc

The resource definition file for Video Saver includes several different categories of information, as shown in Table 19.5.

Table 19.5. Categories of information in vidsaver.rc.

Category	Description
Include files	These are some of the same include files that we used in vidsaver.c. Definitions of constants and structure come from windows.h.
File resources	There are two file resources that will be included in the executable: a bitmap and a Wave file.
Strings	These strings are used in various places, including configuration dialog. They also include the name of the file where configuration information is stored (control.ini).
Dialog includes	There are two dialog include files. vidsaver.dlg defines the high-level dialog for Video Saver configuration, and scrnsave.dlg contains more or less standard dialogs for handling passwords.

Afterthoughts

This screen saver was one of the most enjoyable C programming projects I can recall. There is something about seeing something move—really move, that is, like video does—on the screen that is fascinating to just about everyone. I always upload early versions of software projects to CompuServe, usually in the Multimedia forum (**GO MULTIMEDIA**). The screen saver got the biggest reaction of anything I have ever uploaded! I hope it brings you pleasure as well.

Integrating Video with Other Media

Although video in and of itself is interesting, and can often be compelling, you will often need to combine it with other media to achieve results. The most common combination is video and audio, and we'll look at that, but we'll also look at some interesting and powerful possibilities with other media.

One of the most interesting combinations involves video and animation. I have mentioned this combination elsewhere, but in this chapter, you will take a detailed look at the mechanics of making this combination work.

Video/Animation Possibilities

There are a number of different ways that you can use video and animation together; they range from the simple to the complex. On the simple end, you can export a video to an animation program, or add an animation to a video sequence. On the complex end, you can use a product such as 3D Studio from Autodesk to create sophisticated 3-D transformations to video images.

The ways in which video and animations can work together include:

➤ Adding an animated overlay to a video (see Figure 20.1).

➤ Animating elements of the video image (see Figure 20.2a-b).

➤ Adding an animated sequence to a video.

➤ Exporting a video in an animation format for use in an animation.

➤ Altering all (or portions) of a video sequence with an animation program for re-import.

➤ Creating transitions from one video clip to the next using an animation program.

Because video is so new, and because animation programs are now so powerful, I'm sure that no one has yet probed the full range of possibilities for video/animation.

Figure 20.1. An overlay added to a video.

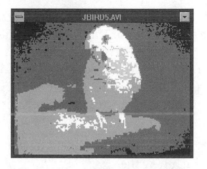

Figure 20.2a-b. Two frames from a video with an animated bird beak.

Converting Video for Animation

To use video images in an animation program, you must export the images in a format that the animation program can use. For this example, we'll export video for Animator Pro.

Exporting a DIB Sequence

It's easy to export a DIB sequence. First, select the portion of the video you want to export with the Mark In/Mark Out buttons. Then use the File/Extract menu selection to bring up the dialog box shown in Figure 20.3.

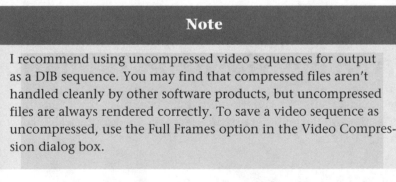

Figure 20.3. The Extract File dialog box in VidEdit.

Use the list box at the lower left of the dialog box to select DIB Sequence as the export option. The filename is the base filename for a numbered sequence of files. I usually reserve four characters for a name, and four characters for the numeric sequence. For example, I might use a filename such as **face0000.bmp** as a base filename. Note that I used the extension .BMP instead of .DIB. This makes the files easier to load into programs that recognize the .BMP but not the .DIB extension.

As the video sequence is saved to bitmap files, the filename is incremented for each new file.

Note

I recommend using uncompressed video sequences for output as a DIB sequence. You may find that compressed files aren't handled cleanly by other software products, but uncompressed files are always rendered correctly. To save a video sequence as uncompressed, use the Full Frames option in the Video Compression dialog box.

Converting the DIB Sequence

Some programs, including Animator Pro Version 1.2, won't be able to import a DIB sequence directly. You'll need to convert the files. It would be tedious to convert these files one at a time, so I recommend a program such as Image Pals from U-Lead that will convert a batch of files in one step. Animator Pro expects a .TIF file.

Importing the DIB Sequence into Animator Pro

Figure 20.4 shows a typical Animator Pro screen, with the POCO menu pulled down. The cursor is positioned on the Numpic menu selection. This opens the dialog box shown in Figure 20.5.

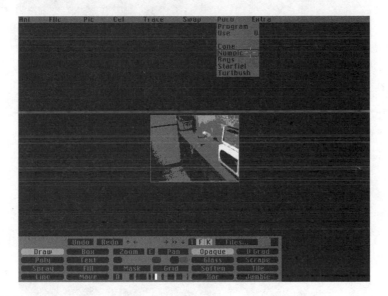

Figure 20.4. Animator Pro POCO menu.

Click option 2, Load Pics as Flic, which will display the dialog box shown in Figure 20.6. You can click on or type the name of the first file in the sequence of numbered files.

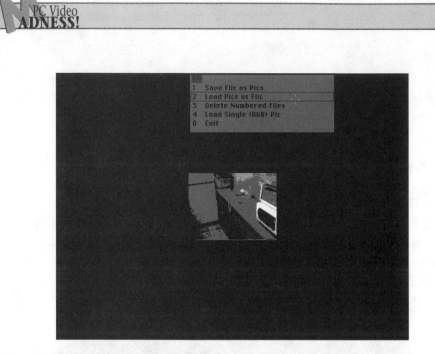

Figure 20.5. Dialog box for saving and loading numbered image files.

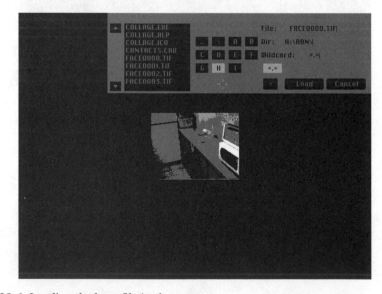

Figure 20.6. Loading the base file in the sequence.

When you click OK, Animator will seek files in the sequence, and then display the message shown in Figure 20.7. This message tells you how many images Animator found, and allows you to choose how to handle the conversion. You have four choices:

Append   Add the new images to the existing FLC file.

Insert   Insert the new images at the current position in the FLC file.

Replace   Replace the existing frames with the new images.

Cancel   Do not import the images.

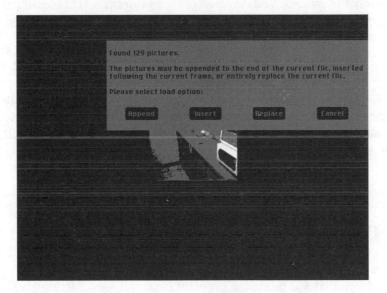

Figure 20.7. Choices for adding the new images in Animator Pro.

As you can see, this enables you to combine the video and animation frames in any way you need to. Most of the time, you'll want to choose Replace so that the video images are the only images in the file.

To save the file as an FLC animation, use the Flic/File... menu selection. From this point on, you can use any Animator Pro capabilities to alter or enhance the video images.

Converting Animations to Video

When you have finished enhancing the video images in your animation program, you will need to put them in a form that can be imported into VidEdit. In VidEdit, you can reunite the video and the audio, or add a completely new and different audio track.

VidEdit has an import option for Autodesk Animator files, but it is not a completely reliable process. In general, I like to use POCO Numpics to output a series of .TIF files, which I then convert to .BMP files for import as a DIB sequence. This is a very reliable process. You can always try to import a FLC file directly, but I often find problems (such as incomplete frames) when I do this. Using a DIB sequence is much more reliable.

To import the DIB sequence, use the File/Insert selection. This will bring up a dialog box just like the one we used to export the original DIB sequence (see Figure 20.3). Select DIB Sequence in the list box at the lower left of the dialog box, type "*.bmp" as the filename and press the enter key, and then select the base filename for the DIB sequence and click OK. You now have a video file, which you can save with full frames or compressed. If you want to add audio, now is the time to do it.

Special Effects with 3D Studio

By far the niftiest special effects possible with video files are created with 3D Studio, a sophisticated 3-D modeling program from Autodesk. Although 3D Studio is not cheap, it is extremely powerful as you will see shortly.

A brief introduction to 3D Studio will help you understand how it can be used with video files. 3D Studio allows you to create 3-D objects of just about any description and complexity, and then animate them. For example, you could create a simple box and then animate it so it tumbles. Or you could create an entire room, with windows, furniture, and even pictures on the walls, and then fly a "camera" through the room as the animation.

With 3D Studio you not only can create the 3-D object, but you can assign realistic-looking materials and surfaces to them for rendering. Figure 20.8 shows a typical single frame from a 3-D rendering. Note that both the apple and the plywood base look photo-realistic; both surfaces were generated by 3D Studio using texture mappings. That is, a bitmapped image was projected to cover the surface, with adjustments for viewing angle, lighting, and reflections.

Once you have converted a video into an FLC file, you can use it as a texture map in 3D Studio. This means that you can have moving videos on all kinds of surfaces; the possibilities are literally endless.

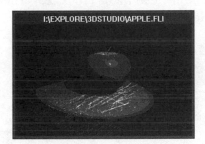

Figure 20.8. An example of texture mapping in 3D Studio.

For this example, we will create a flat, rectangular object the same size as the video image, apply the video image to it, and then animate the object.

Creating the Object

Figure 20.9 shows a typical 3D Studio screen. If you are familiar with architectural or mechanical drafting, you will recognize the view for each quadrant. The top left of the screen shows a top view, the top right shows a front view, the bottom left shows a left view, and the bottom right shows a "user" point of view that offers a 3-D view of the object.

To the right of these quadrants are the menus, with special-purpose buttons at the lower right. The menu changes as you make selections from it, and the buttons perform such tasks as re-aligning views, enlarging and shrinking views, changing the axes of a view, and so on.

In Figure 20.9, the active view is at the top right, labeled Front (X/Y). In this view, a grid is active, with 10 units separating grid points. The menu to the right shows two words highlighted—Create, at the top, and Box, at the top of the indented portion of the menu. 3D Studio uses this kind of vertical menu. Indented

selections are all possible choices for the highlighted item higher up on the menu. In this case, we can create any of the objects listed, including Boxes, Spheres, Hemispheres, Cylinders, Tubes, Cones, and so forth.

Cross hairs appear in the active view in Figure 20.9. The coordinates of the current point appear at the top of the screen. The X coordinate is -80, the Y coordinate is 60, and the Z coordinate is 0. Note that the X/Y coordinates are exactly one-half the size of a typical video frame (160x120). The selected point will be the upper-left coordinate for the box.

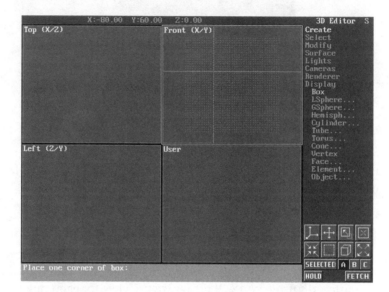

Figure 20.9. The 3D Studio screen.

If you are not familiar with 3-D coordinates, the Z coordinate represents the third dimension. To create a box in 3 dimensions, you must click four times:

➤ Once to establish the upper-left corner.

➤ Once to establish the lower-right corner.

➤ Once to establish a root for the Z direction.

➤ Once to establish a length for the Z direction.

These four clicks uniquely define the new object in three dimensions. After the fourth click, a dialog box opens asking for the name for the new object, as shown in Figure 20.10.

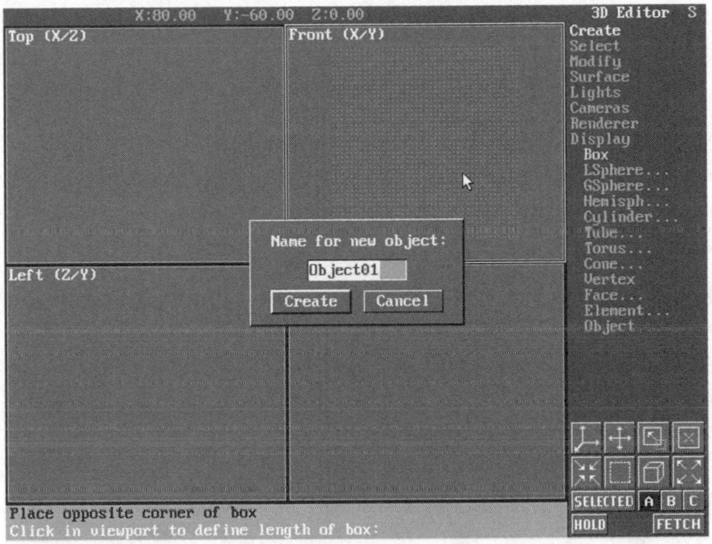

Figure 20.10. Naming an object in 3D Studio.

Once you name the object, it appears in all four views, as shown in Figure 20.11.

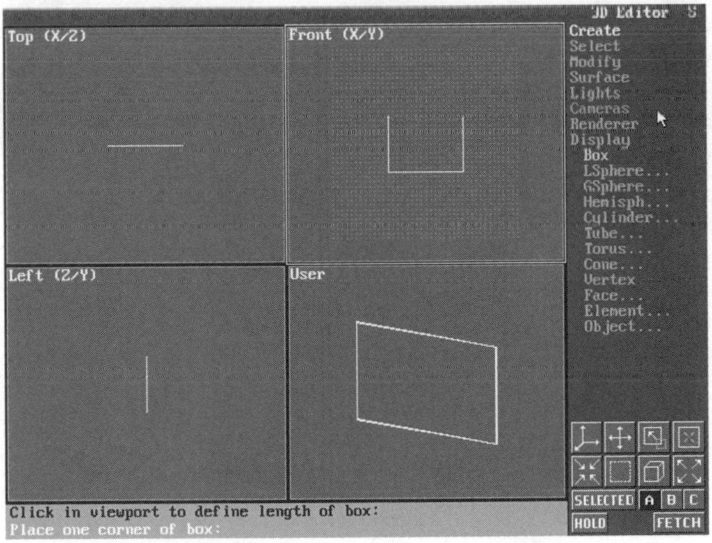

Figure 20.11. A 3-D object in all four views.

Note that I have given the object a very small dimension in the Z direction; it is a very thin, flat, rectangular box. We could just as easily have created a cube by using a large length in the Z direction.

The box is a very simple object. Using special tools built into 3D Studio you can create extremely complex and sophisticated objects, and you can also import complex objects from products like AutoCAD. You can have more than one object at a time as well.

Figure 20.12 shows the Program menu pulled down. Some of the programs listed can be used to create objects (2D Shaper, 3D Lofter, 3D Editor), but we are interested in two of the others: the Keyframer (for animations), and Materials Editor (for handling texture maps). The remaining menu choices—box, grids, waves, and ripple—apply special motion effects to surfaces.

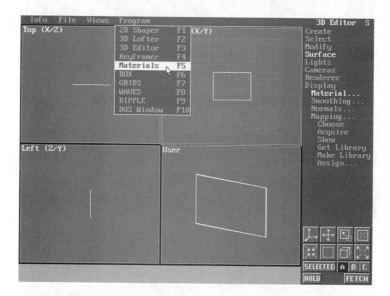

Figure 20.12. The Program menu.

Creating/Applying the Texture Map

Figure 20.13 shows the Materials Editor screen. I have already defined a material using Texture Map, and rendered a sample (the box at the upper left of the figure). This is all you need to do to create a new material with an FLC file. To assign the file, click the Texture Map button at the far right of the row of buttons.

Figure 20.13. Materials Editor screen.

To make the material a part of the current materials library, use the Material/Put menu selection (see Figure 20.14).

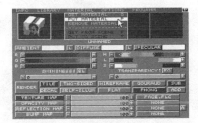

Figure 20.14. Putting a material into the materials library.

This will bring up a dialog box requesting the name of the new material (see Figure 20.15). Materials with the letter *T* after the name are materials that use a texture map. A texture map can be a single image file, or, as in this case, an FLC file.

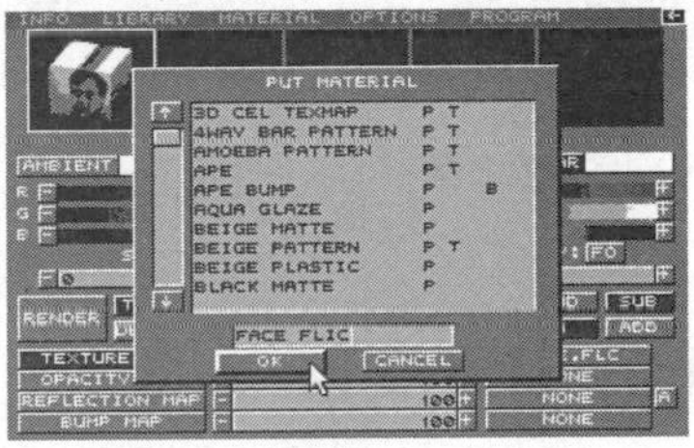

Figure 20.15. Assigning a name to a new material.

Once a material is in the library, we can return to the 3D Editor and apply the material to our object. This involves three steps:

1. Choosing the material.

2. Applying the material.

3. Assigning mapping coordinates (to control scaling, origin, and so forth).

Choosing the Surface Material

To choose a material, use 3D Studio's nested menu structure, Surface/Material.../ Choose. This displays the dialog box shown in Figure 20.16, where you can select the current material by clicking on it in the displayed list. Note that there are various letters and codes to the right of the names; these indicate various special features of the materials.

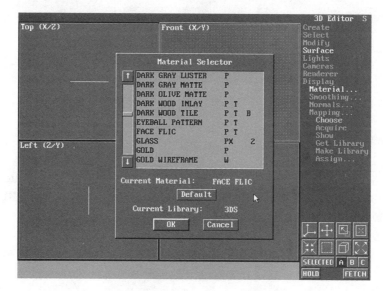

Figure 20.16. Selecting the current material.

Applying the Surface Material

When you have selected our new material as the current material, you can begin assigning it to objects. Figure 20.17 shows the menu selection needed to set up for assigning materials: Surface/Material.../Assign.../Object. You can then assign the current material to an object simply by clicking it.

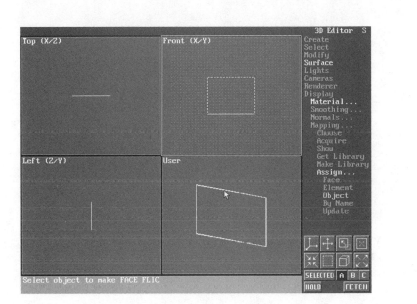

Figure 20.17. Assigning a name to a new material.

Applying the Mapping

However, if you were to try rendering the object now, you would see an error message stating that the object does not have mapping coordinates. Mapping coordinates control how the texture map is applied to the object. Figure 20.18 shows how 3D Studio displays mapping coordinates. The coordinates shown are for mapping to a plane; 3D Studio also allows you to apply maps to a cylinder or sphere, wrapping the image as required.

If you were to apply the mapping coordinates as shown, only the portion of the image covered by the object would appear on the object's surface, so you need to scale the coordinates to be the same size as the object (see Figure 20.19). This scaling is best done using the Front view, where you can fit the mapping to a region, using the size of the object as the region.

Finally, you can apply the mapping coordinates to the object with the Surface/Mapping.../Apply.../Object menu selection (see Figure 20.20).

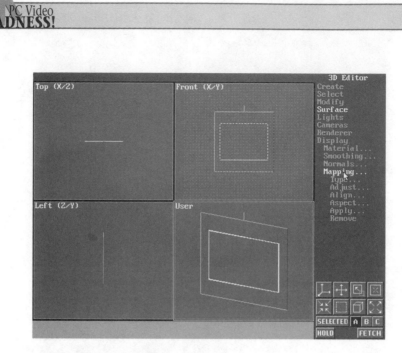

Figure 20.18. Mapping coordinates in 3D Studio.

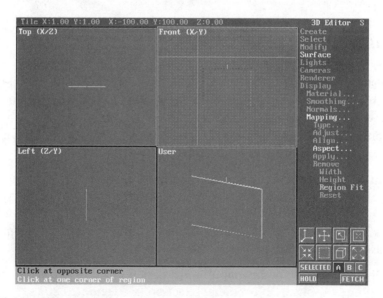

Figure 20.19. Fitting mapping coordinates to a region.

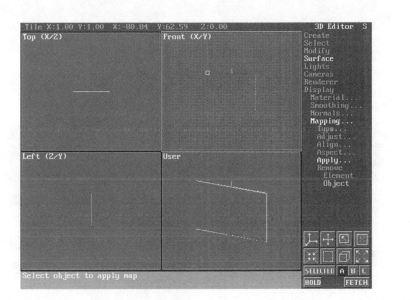

Figure 20.20. Applying mapping coordinates to an object.

Rendering a Still Image

You now have a complete object: it has surfaces, a shape, size, and you have applied a material to the object. The next step is to render the image. Until now, you have been working with the object as a *wire frame* object. That is, you have only seen the object as an outline, without any of the surface properties displayed.

You can render any of the views shown, as well as several views not currently shown. The most interesting view to render is the "user" view, because it shows the object in three dimensions. The menu selection Renderer/Render brings up the dialog box shown in Figure 20.21.

This dialog box offers a large variety of options for rendering; the most important ones are summarized in Table 20.1.

```
                    X:-12.42  Y:1.02    2:-3.89                    3D Editor
 Top (X/Z)                        Front (X/Y)                      Create
                                                                   Select
                                                                   Modify
                                                                   Surface
                          Render Still Image                          s
         Shading Limit:   Wire    Flat    Gouraud   Phong             as
          Anti-aliasing:  None    Low    Medium    High             rer
                          Anti-aliasing Parameters                   ay
                                                                    ler
                                                                    p...
              Shadows:  On   Off     Filetype:    GIF                :...
          Force 2-sided: On  Off      Driver:   VGA320X200
 Left (Z/Y)   Mapping:  On   Off    Resolution:    0X0
      Auto Reflect Maps: On  Off      Aspect:    0.0000
                                      Viewport:    User
      Hidden Geometry:  Show  Hide   Filter Maps:   On
          Background:  Rescale Tile    Turbo:      On

         Render Output:   Display   Hardcopy      Disk

                          Render   Cancel

 Select viewport to render                      SELECTED A B C
                                                HOLD       FETCH
```

Figure 20.21. Rendering a view.

Table 20.1. 3D Studio Rendering Options.

Option	Description
Shading Limit	The buttons to the right of this option each use different algorithms for determining how to shade surface materials. Wire means no shading at all— just render the wire frame. This is used for quick renderings. Flat is the simplest form of shading; it makes no attempt to smooth curves, rendering them as a series of small planes. Gourand shading is more complex and lifelike, but it takes several shortcuts in the interest of shorter rendering times. Phong shading is the most complex, and results in the most life-like lighting and shading.
Anti-aliasing	Anti-aliasing is used to smooth boundaries and transitions. The more you use, the better the image will appear. However, this also adds rendering time.
Shadows	This turns rendering of shadows on and off.

Option	Description
Force 2-sided	This turns 2-sided mapping on and off. If on, as in this case, the material will be applied to both sides of an object. In this case, you want the image to show on both sides of the object, so that you can still see the image if you flip the object.
Mapping	This turns mapping on and off. You want it on, so you can see how the image looks as a texture map.
Render Output	You can render to the display, to a printer, or to disk for later viewing.

When you render the view, it takes less than a minute to get the result shown in Figure 20.22.

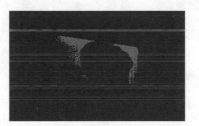

Figure 20.22. A rendered image.

The first thing to notice is that you do, indeed, see the first frame of the video sequence on the surface of the object. The second thing to notice is that the image is very dark.

Adding a Light

3D Studio isn't just for objects. You can create three different kinds of lights, and you can even create cameras. In this case, the ambient, or existing, light isn't bright enough to display the object properly. You can add a light with the Lights/Omni.../ Create menu selection. Omni lights shine in all directions equally. You can also add spot light, which has adjustable direction, intensity, fall-off, and so on.

To place a light, just click in a view. This displays the dialog box shown in Figure 20.23. This allows you to adjust both the color and overall intensity of the light. You can even turn the light on and off if you want to.

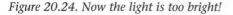

Figure 20.23. Adding a light to a view.

If you once again render the view, you get the results shown in Figure 20.24.

Figure 20.24. Now the light is too bright!

As you can see, the light is too bright now. You can go back to the dialog box shown in Figure 20.23, and enter values of 175 for the Red, Green, and Blue sliders. This cuts the light by 32%, and gives normal values for the object, as shown in Figure 20.25.

Figure 20.25. Now the light is just right.

Animating the Object

Now we have all of the ingredients for the object, and it's time to "move" to the next step: animating it. For this, you use the Keyframer, available via the Program/Keyframer menu.

The Keyframer looks a lot like the 3D Editor that we used to create the object (see Figure 20.26).

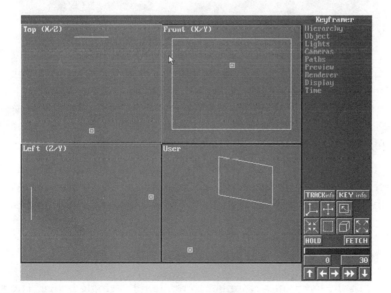

Figure 20.26. Keyframer screen, showing light and object.

By default, the Keyframer starts with 30 frames. We had 129 images, so we'll need 129 frames. To set the number of frames, use the Time/Total Frames menu selection. Then use Time/Go to Frame to go to the last frame (see Figure 20.27).

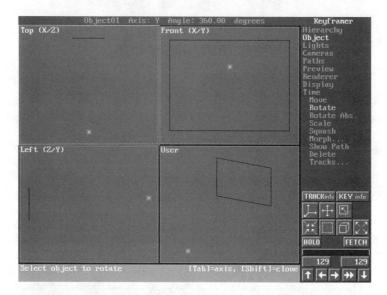

Figure 20.27. Moving to the last frame.

For this demonstration, we'll now rotate the object 360 degrees using the User view. Rotating through 360 degrees gives us one complete rotation, and using the User view means we'll get a complex, interesting rotation. If we were to rotate the Front view, we'd get a simple rotation because we are looking at the object straight on.

By putting the rotation at the last frame, frame 129, you are instructing the Keyframer to calculate the intervening 128 positions for the rotation. When you render the animation, you'll get a smooth rotation over all 129 frames.

Rendering the Animation

Rendering in the Keyframer is similar to rendering a single image. The primary difference is the ability to select the number of frames to render (see Figure 20.28).

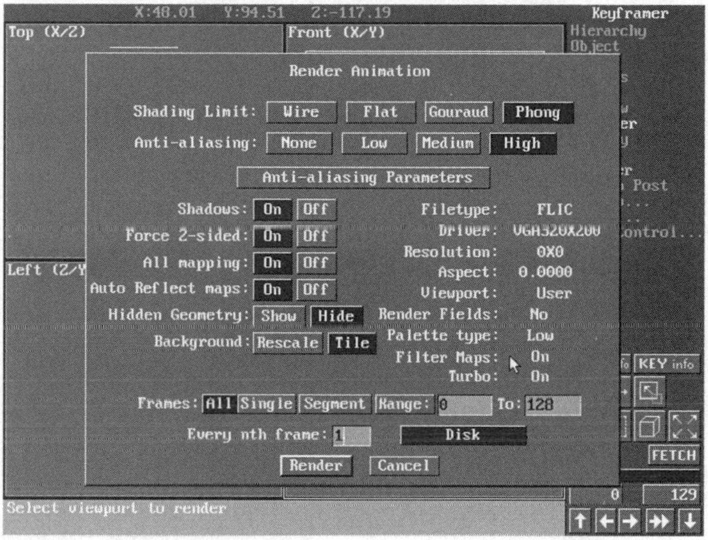

Figure 20.28. Rendering an animation.

Rendering takes a while; I used a 486/66 to do the rendering, and it took about 10 seconds per frame for a total of a little over two minutes for the complete animation. I used an image size of 160x120, which is quite small; at larger sizes and for more complex views, rendering can take a lot longer. (See Figure 20.32, which shows a 320x240 animation that took 6 hours to render!) To set the image size, use Renderer/Setup/Configure (see Figure 20.29).

During rendering, you'll see a dialog box like the one in Figure 20.30 that keeps you informed of the progress of the rendering operation.

Figure 20.31a-b shows two frames from the animation. Note that the lighting is different for these frames; as the object rotates, it catches more or less light from the single light source. This enhances the sense of rotation in three dimensions. Of course, if you wanted even lighting, you could easily add more lights.

You can also render more complex images. Figure 20.32 shows a frame from an animation that displays the same FLC file, but on four faces of a cube. It also uses a background image, and adds a spotlight as well as an Omni light. You can see the cone of the spotlight on the left face of the cube. You can't see it in the black and white image on the page, but I put a red light inside the cube, just for fun.

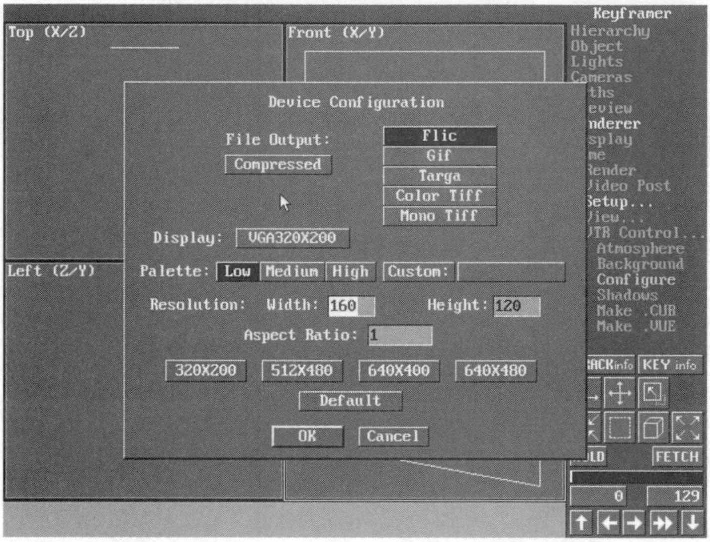

Figure 20.29. Setting rendering configuration.

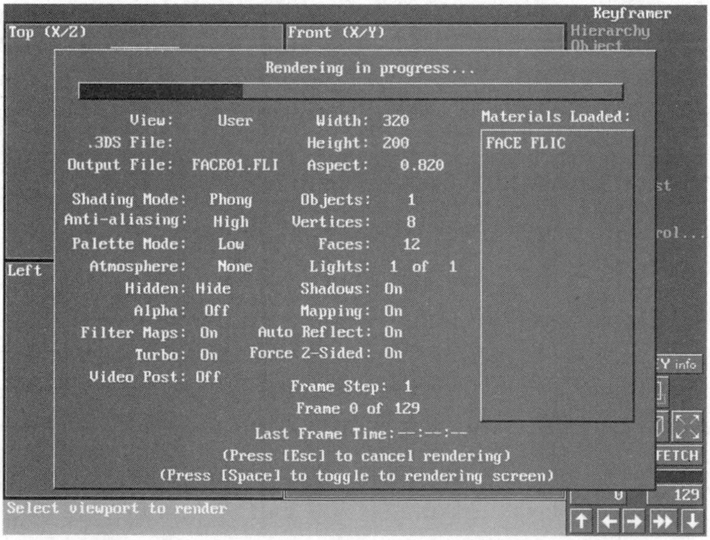

Figure 20.30. Rendering in progress...

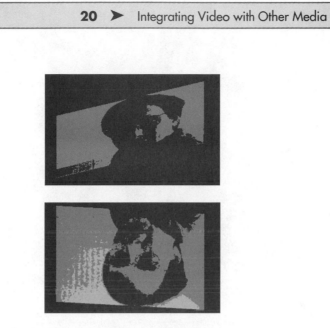

Figure 20.31a-b. Two frames from a 3D Studio animation.

Figure 20.32. A single frame from a more complex animation.

## PART VI

Reference

A

A Guide to the CD-ROM

The CD-ROM at the back of this book is more than just a collection of neat stuff. It's a special issue of a CD-ROM magazine called Nautilus. You'll find a wide variety of interesting material, most of it having something to do with Video. For example, there's a video karaoke program and a music video from Windham Hill, featuring John Gorka.

If you haven't seen an issue of Nautilus yet, you are in for a really nice surprise. I chose to put a special edition of Nautilus in the book because I think it's one of the neatest things going on in the CD-ROM universe. If you are interested in multimedia, Nautilus is where you'll find not just information but actual working samples of many of the latest hot multimedia software, as well as lots of useful raw materials for multimedia. Video files, bitmaps, sounds, and music are just a part of the resources you'll find on every Nautilus disc.

A CD-ROM can hold more than 600 megabytes of programs and data, so it can take a while to ferret out all of the goodies on the CD-ROM. The Nautilus issue has a useful table of contents that will make it easy to find what you need. Following the section on installing Nautilus, you'll find an outline of the contents of the special issue included with this disk.

Installing Nautilus

Installation of the Nautilus disk is easy. Put the disc in your CD-ROM drive, then open the file manager of your choice to display the files in the root directory of the CD. Find setup.exe, and double-click it to run it. After that, just follow the on-screen instructions.

Note

Even if you have already installed Video for Windows 1.0, you may want to install again from this disk. I've provided a more recent version of the Indeo driver which will give you much better playback than the version that shipped with Video for Windows 1.0. Most of the files on the CD-ROM use the Indeo codec and will benefit very noticeably from the improved driver. The new driver is provided free of charge by Intel.

The installation of Nautilus will copy some files to your hard disk. These are the executables and DLL (dynamic link library) files. They will load much more quickly from your hard disk than from the CD-ROM. I don't recommend running Nautilus directly from the CD-ROM; performance suffers heavily each time an executable or DLL has to be read from the CD.

Once you have installed Nautilus (and the new video drivers), you're ready to roll!

Using the Nautilus CD

As part of installation, Nautilus will create a program group. There are two icons you need to know about to access the CD. You can access a special video browser by clicking on the icon that is a miniature image of me (Figure A.1), and you can access the complete Nautilus issue by clicking the Nautilus icon (Figure A.2). This program group is created when you install Nautilus.

Figure A.1. The author icon.

Figure A.2. The Nautilus icon.

The first thing you will see is the Nautilus startup window, shown in Figure A.3.

You'll need to select either "256 color" or "16 color," depending on the graphics capabilities of your computer.

If Nautilus does not detect your CD-ROM drive, click the button marked "Set Drive" on the left side of the window. You will see a dialog box asking you what drive letter to use for the CD-ROM drive (Figure A.4). Nautilus remembers the drive letter and other settings for future sessions.

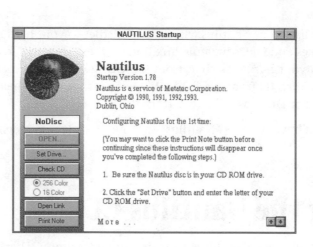

Figure A.3. The Nautilus Startup screen.

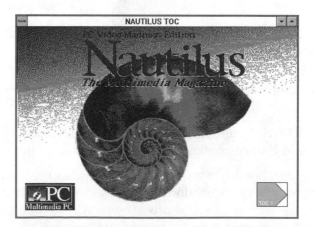

Figure A.4. Enter the letter of your CD-ROM drive.

When Nautilus knows the correct drive letter, you can open the magazine by clicking the OPEN button. This displays the "cover" of the *Nautilus* CD-ROM magazine (Figure A.5).

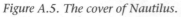

Figure A.5. The cover of Nautilus.

Click the large arrow in the bottom-right corner of the window to move to the first page of the table of contents (Figure A.6).

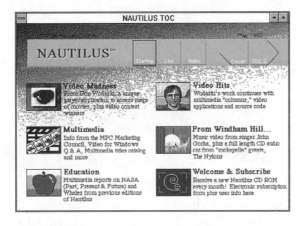

Figure A.6. The Nautilus table of contents.

Figure A.7. Video Madness information.

The first page displays six of the eight major sections of the magazine; the rest of the areas (and some special features) are shown on the second page of the table of contents. Use the large, blocky arrows at the top-right corner of the window to move between the two pages of the table of contents.

You can access any of the major sections or special features by clicking the icon for that section or feature. Each section or feature displays one or more choices

in a list; just click the one you want to explore and follow the instructions that appear on the screen. If you are in a hurry to explore the CD-ROM, that's all you need to get started.

An Overview of Nautilus

The following is a brief overview of the material you will find on the CD-ROM.

Video Madness

This is the same video browser than you can access from the program group, as well as the winning videos in a digital video contest sponsored by Nautilus. The video browser gives you access to hundreds of megabytes of video clips. You'll find everything from an angry giraffe to Bill Gates talking about Video for Windows. In between, there are some home videos, and fans of Sparky (the dog who made it to the moon in my earlier book, *Multimedia Madness)* will be able to see Sparky's latest video adventures.

The contest-winning videos include a toddler addressing the issues involved in digital video, a night-time emergency aboard an animated starship, and some humorous video from Scandinavia.

Multimedia

This section covers a range of multimedia topics and includes several multimedia examples. I've included the latest report from the MPC Marketing Council, and the Ask an Expert section (a regular Nautilus item) features Microsoft's Steve Linowes talking about digital video. The folks at Nautilus have also included an MPC titles catalog, and a hardware spotlight.

Education

This section includes two video-intensive columns from previous issues of Nautilus. There is a comprehensive report on NASA: Past, Present & Future and a great column about whales from the Cetacean Research Unit.

Video Hits

You'll find two different kinds of hits here: multimedia "columns" that I created for previous editions of Nautilus and various video applications and source code.

The columns cover a variety of aspects of digital video, including such things as what hardware works best and how to create 3D digital video effects using 3D Studio. The video applications include both the executable file and the source code. You'll find a video tester written in Visual Basic; a handy MCI command builder; and my favorite: a video screen saver. The video screen saver will not only play your AVI files; it will glide them around the screen while they play. A definite must-see item.

Windham Hill

This is a great section! The highlight is a music video of Windham Hill artist John Gorka; don't miss this one. This video makes the all-time best screen saver. Also featured: the Nylons wonderful cover of the hit, "The Lion Sleeps Tonight."

Welcome To Nautilus: Subscribe

How to subscribe to Nautilus, and the Nautilus Services section.

HighFive

Lots of shareware goodies here, including Whoop It Up, the Movie Time Screen Saver, a CD Audio player, Font Monster, and an image viewing utility.

Music and Sound

This section features both original music you can use in your own multimedia productions and some useful information and utilities. The featured items include: Bumpers, MIDI goes to the Movies, Classical Cwiz, and a Kim Keown music bed.

CD-ROM Directory

The following is a list of various CD-based resources.

Nemo Notes

This is where you will find technical information about multimedia, ranging from C/C++ programming tips to information about using True Type fonts. On this special issue, the focus is on fonts and video technical notes.

Industry News

A wide variety of reports on various industry topics.

Nautilus Letters

There are the usual reader letters, as well as Nautilus responses, but with a video slant.

Interactions

This section of Nautilus features Asymetrix' Media Blitz!, a program you can use to easily create complex multimedia sequences. Media Blitz! uses a simple time-line metaphor to allow you to simultaneously use bitmaps, video, MIDI files, WAV files, and more in your sequence. You can adjust the starting and stopping points, as well as the starting times and duration of all elements in the sequence.

Games and Entertainment

The games and entertainment section of Nautilus always contains surprises, and this one is not an exception. There are a couple of cute games—Planaria and Columns—as well as a collection of "featurettes" from Toggle Booleans. These include a bit recycler, an Elvis detector, and (my favorite) a mouse odometer. If you have a strong stomach, there's also a program that displays the current estimated amount of the national debt.

Commentary

Queen Noor of Jordan on "State of the World's Children."

Anti-Virus Solutions

Updated versions of several anti-virus utilities.

MCI Command
Strings Reference

MCI command strings have the general form:

```
<command> <device> <argument(s)>
```

The available commands for digital video are listed in Table B.1.

Table B.1. MCI Commands.

Command	Description
capability	Fills a specified buffer with a string containing information about the capabilties of the video driver.
close	Closes an instance of the video driver.
configure	Displays a dialog box used to configure the video driver.
cue	Prepares the driver for playback, and leaves it in a paused state.
info	Fills a specified buffer with a string containing information about the video driver.
open	Opens an instance of the video driver.
pause	Pauses playback.
play	Starts playing a video sequence.
put	Used to position various rectangular regions on the screen, such as playback window and the video image.
realize	Causes the palette to be realized into a display context.
resume	Resumes playback after a pause command has been issued.
seek	Positions and cues the video sequence to the specified frame. The video image at that frame is displayed.

Command	Description
set	Used to set the state of various parameters relating to the video file's display and operation.
setaudio	Sets values associated with playback. Not all video drivers support all options.
setvideo	Sets values associated with playback.
signal	Marks a position in the video sequence. When that position is reached, a signal message will be sent.
status	Fills a specified buffer with a string containing information about the status of the video driver.
step	Advances the current position.
stop	Stops playing. Does not close the file.
update	Repaints the current frame.
where	Fills a specified buffer with a string containing position and size coordinates.
window	Used to control various window properties.

To use a command string, you merely need to combine the command with a device and the appropriate parameters, if any. For example, to play a video file, you need only say:

   play c:\myfile.avi

The word play is a command, and c:\myfile.avi is the device. Optionally, you could include some arguments to specify what portion of the file to play:

   play c:\myfile.avi from 0 to 100

This would play the first 100 frames of the video file c:\myfile.avi.

If you will be using more than one command string for a given device—this is usually the case—you should get in the habit of using aliases. An alias is a shorthand reference to the device. You specify the alias when you open a file. For example, the following sequence of command strings will open a video file, position it on the screen, and then play it. All commands use the alias **aviFile** for the device.

open c:\myavidir\animals\myfile.avi alias **aviFile**
put **aviFile** window at 100 100 160 120
put **aviFile** destination at 0 0 160 120
realize **aviFile** normal
window **aviFile** state show
play **aviFile** wait
close **aviFile**

> ### Note
>
> MCI commands are not case-sensitive. You can use uppercase, lowercase, and mixed case for commands, devices, filenames, and parameters. By convention, MCI command strings are in lowercase.

The rest of this appendix explains each of the MCI commands available for video in detail.

Important: To save space, the device name is omitted from the command definitions. Remember that you must specify a device for these commands!

All commands accept the optional items `wait` and `notify`, although they are not explicitly listed in the command-string table. The `wait` flag will cause the video driver to not return control until the action requested has been completed. The `notify` flag has no meaning in Visual Basic because Visual Basic does not allow callbacks. There is no way to be notified when an action is completed.

The MCI video driver MCIAVI uses the `AVIVideo` keyword to identify the driver type.

Table B.2 lists each of the supported commands and parameters for the digital video MCIAVI driver. Not all versions of all drivers supplied by manufacturers support every command and parameter. MCI will tell you when the command or parameter is not supported: it will return an error if you call it with `mciSendString`.

Table B.2. MCI command strings for digital video.

Command	Description
capability item	Fills an application-supplied buffer with a string containing additional information about the capabilities of MCIAVI. The following optional items modify capability:
	can eject returns false.
	can freeze returns false.
	can lock returns false.
	can play returns true.
	can record returns false.
	can reverse returns false.
	can save returns false.
	can stretch returns true.
	can stretch input returns false.
	can test returns true.
	compound device returns true.
	device type returns digitalvideo.
	has audio returns true.
	has still returns false.
	has video returns true.
	uses files returns true.
	uses palettes returns true.
close	Closes this instance of the MCIAVI and releases all resources associated with it.
configure	Displays a dialog box used to configure MCIAVI.
cue items	Prepares MCIAVI for playback and leaves it in a paused state. This command is modified by the following optional items:
	output prepares MCIAVI for playing.
	to position positions the workspace to the specified position.

continues

Table B.2. continued

Command	Description
info items	Fills a user-supplied buffer with a string containing information about MCIAVI. The following optional items modify info: file returns the name of the file currently loaded.
	product returns Video for Windows.
	version returns the release level of MCIAVI.
	window text returns the text string in the title bar of the window associated with MCIAVI.
open items	Initializes MCIAVI. The following items modify open:
	alias specifies an alias used to reference this instance of MCIAVI.
	elementname specifies the name of the device element (file) loaded when MCIAVI opens.
	parent hwnd specifies the parent of the default window.
	style stylevalue specifies the style used for the default window. The following constants are defined for stylevalue:
	overlapped, popup, and child. type AVIVideo specify the device type of the device element.
pause	Pauses the playing of motion video or audio.

Command	Description
play items	Starts playing the video sequence. The following optional items modify play: from position specifies the position to seek to before beginning the play. to position specifies the position at which to stop playing. fullscreen specifies playing should use a full-screen display. window specifies that playing should use the window associated with a device instance (the default).
put items	Specifies a rectangular region that describes a cropping or scaling option. One of the following must be present to indicate the specific type of rectangle: destination specifies that the full client window associated with this instance of MCIAVI is used to show the image or video. destination at rectangle specifies which portion of the client window associated with this instance of MCIAVI is used to show the image or video. source specifies that the full frame buffer is scaled to fit in the destination rectangle. source at rectangle specifies which portion of the frame buffer (in frame-buffer coordinates) is scaled to fit in the destination rectangle.
realize items	Tells MCIAVI to select and realize its palette into a display context of the displayed window. One of the following items modifies realize:

continues

627

Table B.2. continued

Command	Description
	`background` realizes the palette as a background palette.
	`normal` realizes the palette normally used for a top-level window (the default).
	`window at rectangle` changes the size and location of the display window. The rectangle specified with the at flag is relative to the parent window of the display window (usually the desktop).
`resume`	Specifies that operation should continue from where it was interrupted by a `pause` command.
`seek` items	Positions and cues the workspace to the specified position showing the specified frame. One of the following items modifies `seek`:
	`to position` specifies the desired new position, measured in units of the current time format.
	`to end` moves the position after the last frame of the workspace.
	`to start` moves the position to the first frame of the workspace.
`set` items	Sets the state of various control items. One of the following items must be included:
	`seek exactly on seek exactly off` selects one of two seek modes. With `seek exactly on`, `seek` will always move to the frame specified. With `seek exactly off`, `seek` will move to the closest key frame prior to frame specified.

Command	Description
	speed factor sets the relative speed of video and audio playback from the workspace. Factor is the ratio between the nominal frame rate and the desired frame rate where the nominal frame rate is designated as 1000.
	time format format sets the time format to format. The default time format is frames.
	Milliseconds can be abbreviated as ms.
	MCIAVI supports frames and milliseconds.
	audio off disables audio.
	audio on enables audio.
	video off disables video.
	video on enables video.
setaudio items	Sets various values associated with audio playback and capture. Only one of the following items can be present in a single command, unless otherwise noted:
	off disables audio.
	on enables audio.
	volume to factor sets the average audio volume for both audio channels.
setvideo items	Sets various values associated with playback. The following items modify setvideo:
	off disables video display in the window.
	on enables video display in the window.
	palette handle to handle specifies the handle to a palette.

continues

629

Table B.2. continued

Command	Description
signal items	Marks a specified position in the workspace. MCIAVI supports only one active signal at a time. The following items modify signal:
	at position specifies the first frame to be marked.
	cancel an optional parameter that indicates that the signal indicated by the uservalue should be removed from the workspace.
	every interval specifies the period in the current time format after which the succeeding marks should be placed.
	return position an optional parameter that indicates the MCIAVI should send the position value instead of the uservalue value in the Window message.
	uservalue id specifies a value associated with this signal request that is reported back with the Windows message.
status item	Returns status information about this instance MCIAVI. One of the following items modifies status:
	audio returns on if either or both speakers are enabled, and off otherwise.
	forward returns true.
	length returns the length of the loaded video sequence in the current time format.
	media present returns true.
	mode returns one of the following: not ready, paused, playing, recording, or stopped.

Command	Description
	`monitor` returns file.
	`nominal frame rate` returns the nominal frame rate associated with the file in units of frames-per-second times 1000.
	`number of tracks` returns the number of tracks in a video sequence (normally 1).
	`palette handle` returns the palette handle.
	`position` returns the current position in the workspace in the current time format.
	`ready` returns truc if this instance of MCIAVI is ready accept another command.
	`reference frame` returns the nearest key-frame number that precedes frame.
	`seek exactly` returns `on` or `off` indicating whether or not seek exactly is set.
	`speed` returns the current playback speed.
	`start position` returns the start of the media.
	`time format` returns the current time format (frames or milliseconds).
	`unsaved` returns falsc.
	`video` returns `on` or `off` depending on the most recent `setvideo`.
	`window handle` returns the ASCII decimal value for the window handle associated with this instance of MCIAVI.
	`window visible` returns true if the window is not hidden.

continues

631

Table B.2. continued

Command	Description
	window minimized returns true if the window is minimized.
	window maximized returns true if the window is maximized.
step items	Advances the sequence to the specified image. This command is modified by the following options:
	by frames specifies the number of frames to advance before showing another image. You can specify negative values for frames.
	reverse requests that the step be taken in the reverse direction.
stop item	Stops playing.
update items	repaints the current frame into the specified display context. The following items modify update:
	at rect specifies the clipping rectangle relative to the client rectangle.
	hdc hdc specifies the handle of the display context to paint.
	paint an application uses the paint flag with update when it receives a WM_PAINT message intended for a display DC.
where items	Returns the rectangular region that has been previously specified, or defaulted, using the put command. The following items modify where:

Command	Description
	`destination` returns a description of the rectangular region used to display video and images in the client area of the current window.
	`destination max` returns the current size of the client rectangle.
	`source` returns a description of the rectangular region cropped from the frame buffer which is stretched to fit the destination rectangle on the display.
	`source max` returns the maximum size of the frame buffer.
	`window` returns the current size and position of the display-window frame.
	`window max` returns the size of the entire display.
`window` items	Provides an instance of MCIAVI with a window handle to the window that will be used to display images or motion video.
	The following items modify `window`:
	`handle hwnd` specifies a window to be used with this instance.
	`handle default` specifies that the window associated with this instance should be the default window created during the open.
	`state showvalue` this command issues a `ShowWindow` call for the current window.

continues

Table B.2. continued

Command	Description
	The following constants are defined for `showvalue`:

> `hide`
>
> `minimize`
>
> `restore`
>
> `show`
>
> `show maximized`
>
> `show minimized`
>
> `show min noactive`
>
> `show na`
>
> `show noactivate`
>
> `show normal`

`text caption` specifies the text placed in the title bar of the window.

Index

I

Symbols

(>) greater than symbol, 364
2-sided mapping, 601
3D Studio modeling program
  (Autodesk), 118, 204, 584, 590-607
    coordinates, 592
    objects, 590-594
    screens, quadrant views, 591-592
    special effects, 590-607
8-bit capture card (Video Spigot), 223
8-bit color mode (palettes), 221
40 quality setting (codecs), 235
50 quality setting (compression), 209
75 quality setting (compression),
  209, 236

A

accessing
  MCI with Visual Basic, 335
  Nautilus magazine (CD-ROM),
    613-616
Action Media II capture card, 194-195

action shots with camcorders, 87-88
activating screen saver, 7
active view (3D Studio), 591-592
active-interactive (digital video), 135
ADC, *see* Analog to Digital
  conversion
addresses, ports, 185
AdjustMagnification handler
  (Toolbook), 511-512
amplitude, 245
  gain adjustment, 248
analog images, overlays, 214
analog signals
  converting
    from digital, 246
    to bits/bytes, 134
    to digital, 244-245
    to digital signals, 17
  mono, 245
  sampling, 245
  stereo, 245
Analog to Digital conversion (ADC),
  178, 244

635

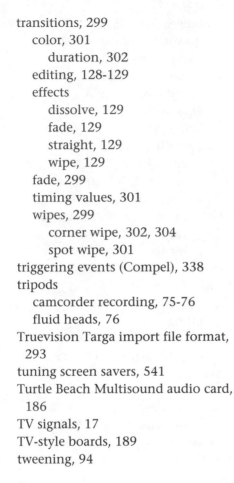